Peter Biddlecombe is a travel-hardened businessman. His much-acclaimed first book, *French Lessons in Africa*, described his travels through French-speaking Africa, and has been followed by seven more gloriously funny accounts of global business trips: *Travels With My Brief-case*; *Around the World – On Expenses*; *I Came, I Saw, I Lost My Luggage*; *Very Funny – Now Change Me Back Again*; *Faster, They're Gaining*; *A Nice Time Being Had By All*; and *Never Feel A Stranger*, all of which are available from Abacus Travel.

He is the first travel writer to have visited and written about over 170 different countries.

The United Burger States of America

Peter Biddlecombe

An *Abacus* Book

First published in Great Britain as a paperback original by
Abacus in 2002

Copyright © Peter Biddlecombe 2002

The moral right of the author has been asserted.

A CIP catalogue record for this book
is available from the British Library.

ISBN 0 349 11606 7

Typeset by Palimpsest Book Production Limited,
Polmont, Stirlingshire
Printed and bound in Great Britain
by Clays Ltd, St Ives plc

Abacus
An imprint of
Time Warner Books UK
Brettenham House
Lancaster Place
London WC2E 7EN

www.TimeWarnerBooks.co.uk

Contents

An Appetiser

The United States is, aw shucks, many things to many people. The biggest, most successful, consumer-oriented, gum-chewing – 'Hi, howyahdointoday? My name is Peggy Sue. I'm your server this evening. I'm here to make certain you have the best evening of your life. How may I be of assistance?' – back-to-front baseball cap-wearing, gun-slinging, Bible-bashing, neurotic, 100-percent knuckleball economy in the history of the world. The wasteland of the free. Home to the biggest bunch of self-centred, money-grabbing, hang tough, you-don't-get-what-you-don't-negotiate, testosterone-addled, planet-polluting, golf-obsessed, hamburger-heads of all time, who all hit Prozac for depression, Claritin for allergies, Rogaine for baldness, Celebrex for arthritis, Imitiex for migraine, Lipitor to keep their cholesterol down, Glucophage to keep their diabetes sweet and Viagra to, well, keep their radar up. Not to mention, the one place in the world where Jeez, they live in McMansions – it's true: I've seen them in Portland, Oregon – stay in McHotels, they accept people for what they're not; think it's sophisticated to use a knife and fork; intellectual to eat burgers, watch TV and drink beer at the same time; dress down to suit up; go to the office wearing a baseball cap, shorts, shoes (no socks) carrying a two-gallon can of Coke or a one-gallon Starbucks; think a double negative is a complete no-no and every year spend millions of dollars encouraging as many fathers as possible to go to Tampa with their children, and go on and on about George Washington being the father of the nation who, as I recall, was completely sterile.

But to me, the US is food. Huge, enormous, vitamin-fortified, artery-clogging, fat-laden, calorie-packed, prairie-sized, colonic-blocking, microwavable mountains of the stuff. Not just at breakfast, lunch and dinner: they hot dog all day. Every day. Everywhere. In cars. In taxis. Walking down the street. Crossing the road. Going to work. In the lift. In the office. Even, God help us, in the boardroom. Seeing an American without food in his hand is like seeing Rod without a blonde on his arm. And it's not just ordinary food, it's crazy food. Grain-fed marsh-mallow Fluff. Sea-fresh Hostess Twinkies. Home-fried extra superlite and lean pastries. Tenderised hot rolled cinnamon buns. Chive pancake spirals and tapenade crostini. Grilled, hickory-smoked, flame-golden bacon and peanut butter slice dripping in wild mountain blackberry syrup. Economy 52oz, Kentucky bourbon-marinated slabs of prime rib as thick as Brooke Shields's eyebrows. Quick-snax 40lb lobsters served with – what else? – pommes soufflé. All washed down with an Atlantic Ocean of microbrew with a cherry on top. With ice, ice and still more ice, until there's none left in McMurdo Sound.

Go into a restaurant. The menu is the length of the Old Testament. Not just what's on offer, but the million different types of everything that's on offer.

'Please, I wonder, could I have a roll? Is that possible?'

'You want sesame, sesame and onion, onion, onion and garlic, sesame, onion and garlic, garlic, cinnamon, cinnamon and sesame, cinnamon, sesame and onion cinnamon, sesame, onion and garlic, poppy seed, poppy seed, onion . . . ?'

Heaven help me. Can't these shroogs just give me a roll? An ordinary bread roll. Puh-leese. And if it's not too inconvenient, some cream cheese as well.

'Light, full fat, light with chives, full-fat with chives, herbs, light with herbs, full-fat with herbs, light with garlic, light with garlic, chives . . . ?'

My God. I shall be dead from starvation before I get the stuff.

And they don't serve only American crazy food. They serve every other type of crazy food you can imagine: Cajun, Cuban,

Mexican, French, German, Irish, Belgian, Spanish, Italian, Greek, Scottish, Polish, Hungarian, Russian, Ethiopian, Chinese, Japanese, Korean, Indian, Thai, Vietnamese, Lebanese, and, of course, Jewish. Everything, in fact, apart from English food.

But most of all burgers. Meat burgers, extra-meat burgers, triple-meat burgers, extra extra super giant out-of-this-galaxy, the size-of-the-Empire-State-Building burgers. Which is why, to me – excuse me, can you pass the ketchup? – the great United States of America, which spends over $120 billion a year on fast food, more than they spend on higher education, PCs, computer software, new cars, videos, books, recorded music combined, is nothing but a giant super, bumper burger. With fat fries on the side.

It has meaty bits you can get your teeth into, like Connecticut, where, in a car park in New Haven in 1900 – forget the Garden of Eden, forget the Big Bang, forget whatever it was Stephen Hawking was on about – the greatest thing that has ever happened in the history of the world happened. The discovery of the formula for the hamburger: $e = Mc^2$. e, that is, everything else equals as many McDonald's as you can think of. Squared. And the reason for the Scottish name? They deliberately calculated as part of their marketing strategy that if they could sell hamburgers to the Scots, who are notoriously generous with their money, they could sell hamburgers to anyone. And it's because of this undeniable Scottish influence that the whole hamburger business has been built on giving as much as possible as cheap as possible. Everything else that has happened before or since pales into insignificance or, as they say in Washington, into Al Gore, who is apparently still kicking himself that hamburgers are the one major modern American invention for which he was not responsible.

After Connecticut, there are smaller, less important meaty states like Montana, Wyoming, Pennsylvania, and who can forget all the hams in Virginia; chicken states like Kentucky, where a balanced diet is a hamburger in each hand, and, of course, Rhode Island where they are for ever boasting about having a fat old bird on the table, never mind a spruce young chick; and fishy states like Massachusetts, Maryland and Maine, where the local delicacy is, would you believe, lobsterburgers.

There are bun states like Nebraska, where Warren Buffett, the world's wealthiest investor, obviously kneads the dough more than most of us.

There are mushroom states, like New Mexico, where they developed the biggest mushroom cloud the world has ever seen; onion states like Washington DC, where for $39.95 you can buy scale-model replicas of the Polish cattle trucks used by the Nazis to transport Jews and others to the concentration camps, which is enough to make anyone weep, and tomato, chilli, cucumber and gherkin states – like North Dakota, where they're so innocent they still think O.J. Simpson didn't do it – which everybody leaves on the side of their plate.

There are french-fry states like Idaho, the potato capital of the world, where a local potato-head once asked me if I wanted my bottle of champagne decanted in order to remove the bubbles, and, of course, Texas, where politicians go around asking profound, searching questions, such as: 'Rarely is the question asked: is our children learning?' and are more than happy to fry anything so long as it's strapped to a chair.

Then there are the ketchup states like Michigan, where, in Detroit, it's reckoned a great day if you open your garage door in the morning and your jig rig, as they say, is still there. Mississippi and South Dakota, which are so far behind that if they're hit by a tornado, the worst it can do is cause them $100 worth of improvements. Ask for the house red in any of these states and they bring you the tomato ketchup. For salt, there's Utah where, one alcohol-free night, I stayed there a month. For relish, nothing can beat President Clinton's home state of Arkansas. And for every possible kind of fruit, what could possibly beat California, where the local zoos keep their animals behind bars for their own safety. They are also so PC that in the Chinese restaurants they have special white chopsticks for blind people.

Then there are the drink states: Georgia for Coke, Alaska for the ice, as in, 'Please, could I have some more ice in my Cheval Blanc?' and, of course, Washington State for coffee. Caff. Decaff. Latte. Super latte. Super super latte. Caramel macchiato. Ice-white chocolate mocha. With sugar white. Without sugar white. With sugar brown. Without sugar brown. With sugar delivered by a smoker. Without sugar not delivered by a non-smoker. But however you take it, take it hot, so hot that you deliberately scald yourself. Then you can sue them for every penny they've got so that you never have to drink their fancy coffee ever again for the rest of your caffeine-clogged life.

The whole of the States is like one huge, bumper burger chain, for ever changing and remodelling itself, adding and taking away ingredients, developing new flavours, and all the time restructuring, remarketing and relaunching itself. Whole towns, cities, practically states are torn down, reinvented, redesigned and rebuilt between sittings. Ten years ago Indianapolis was skid row. Today the entire city has been rebuilt with not one but two huge sports stadia. Twenty years ago, Florida was Alzheimer's little acre. There was more blue rinse on land than there was in the sea. Today it's the fast-moving, non-stop, viva la causa, hasta la vista, baby capital of Latin America. Five years ago, Branson, Missouri was zilch. Today it's got as many theatres as Cher has had facelifts. It's the twenty-four-hours a day, booming, if that's the right word, capital of country music, with shows not just at 8 pm weekdays, plus matinées on Wednesdays and Saturdays, but non-stop virtually round the clock, seven days a week, fifty-two weeks a year.

The US is also service. Speed of service. Everything must be now, *now*, *NOW*! Value for money. The most for the least. Buy 57 and you get 23 free. And whatever you do, don't look a day over twenty-seven and half.

But credit where credit's due, and in the US, there's an enormous amount of credit due, the Americans deserve it all. Whether it's the Protestant work ethic or the pile of credit-card bills stacking up behind the syringe on the PC work station that spurs them on, they're workers. If they want something, they don't baby out. They are prepared to work, work, work for it.

Most people I've come across in the States are either working day and night for themselves, their boss and their company, or they are working day and night for a string of other bosses and no end of other companies. And I don't just mean your blue-collar guys. I mean the big guys as well. I've come across computer-designers who double up as taxi-drivers in the evenings and at weekends, engineering managers who run golf clubs, even prison governors who work as bartenders and waiters. And there's no fuss about it, as there would be in the UK. 'Hell,' they say. 'I need the money, I'll get a job.' Any job. Some say it's because, being a nation of immigrants, it's in their blood. That's not true. The only thing that's in their blood is Coke, crack and huge dollops of fat. They do it because they need the money. Why do they need the money? Because they want to spend, spend, spend.

If, of course, they can't wait for the money to come rolling in, there's always credit. A Mexican only has to wade across the Rio Grande, shuffle into the first bank he sees and they'll lend him $1,000. With $500 he puts down a deposit on a car. Within twenty minutes he's up and running. He might not be rich, but there are not many poor people in the world who worry about where they park their car at night. And if that's how they treat the poor Mexican, you can imagine how they treat your average American.

There are, of course, bits that get in your teeth.

The noise. Or should I say muzak. It's everywhere. The US is the most muzakal society on earth. Even outdoor fountains have their own muzak.

The language, or rather, the verbals, as they say. Now copy me, baby, one more time. Sidewalks. Elevators. Howyadointoday. Those I can just about accept. Even lawn chairs instead of deckchairs. But are children really 'sub-adults', girls 'pre-women', gardeners 'petal-pushers', curtains 'window attachments', pens 'ink sticks', uniforms 'identity apparel', prayer books 'a worship resource', toothbrushes 'home plaque-removal instruments', barbers 'tonsorial parlours' or a swift short back and sides 'a hairstyle odyssey'? And what the hell is a warmedy, a phone-ducking resource or an ex-cleaning woman – as in a novel of Maeve Haran's, in which the phrase 'Get out of here, you old scrubber' became, in the American edition, 'Get out of here, you ex-cleaning woman.'

But before I get totally emmessyoud – MSUed, mentally screwed up – I'd like to bring closure to this discussion on linguistics by saying verbally that other things I don't understand are how they don't paint the kids' bedroom, they colour their world, or you can have 'Daylight Parking All Nite Long' and a World Series that has nothing to do with the world.

Over breakfast I once tried to ask some hop-head American hackedemic business professor from Harvard what made them foul up the language so much. 'Furrgettit,' he burbled as he made woop-de-do with his 12oz New York strip, three eggs and pile of hashbrowns the size of Mount Rushmore, all drowned in maple syrup with a cherry on top, 'It'snuttinit'sverbalarchitecture.'

Verbal architecture? I reckon it's because there's a law somewhere that says, 'Those who eat junk food speak junk speak.' Not that I would in any way want to go the whole nine yards.

Another thing I don't understand is how a country can be so namby-pamby and at the same time so violent. OK, I've got used to being turned away from bars because I look so young and to being told not to eat the toner you put in photocopier machines, nossir, not to put screwdrivers into my ear, and that hot coffee is likely to be hot but, God help me, do I have to be told when to go to the lavatory/men's room/rest room/comfort station/little boys' room? When you fly Midwest Express, they hand you a note, 'No rest rooms. To ensure a pleasant flight, may we suggest you prepare accordingly.'

As for the growing trend towards unprovoked and totally unwarranted violence, I won't say too much because I don't particularly want to get beaten up. All I will say is two things.

It's growing. More and more kids are following in their fathers' fingerprints. Second, it's becoming more acceptable. I forget the number of hotels I've stayed in where if you're not back by seven o'clock in the evening they dump your clothes and let your room out to somebody else.

Finally, books. Surely there's something wrong with a country where *The Origin of Species* is still banned but every family boasts at least one copy of the most famous and invaluable American book of all time, *Tissue-Cleaning Through Bowel Management*.

But much as we sneer, while desperately trying to master the art of eating with a fork and drinking out of a bottle, everybody wants to be in on the action. If immigration is the sincerest form of flattery, the US is the most flattered hamburger chain on earth.

Check out the menu. State by state by state. All fifty of them. Plus, of course, Washington DC.

See if, ya know, yar rilly, rilly like what I like.

Enjoy.

> Peter Biddlecombe
> Louis' Lunch
> New Haven
> Connecticut

The Burger States

Meat, chicken, fish, even veggies – there are as many different kinds of states as there are artery-clogging burgers. Some are red-raw and dripping with growth hormones such as clenbuterol and phenylbutazone, I mean blood. These are the meaty ones. In other words, cowboy country: Wyoming and Montana, the land of Wyatt Earp, wild Bill Hickok, mountain bears, grizzlies, and 4x4s in every handbag. Then there is Virginia and Pennsylvania, where history goes back further than last week and where they really got their teeth into something more solid than *Survivor*, *Friends* or even black-and-white repeats of the *Perry Como Show*. And, of course, Connecticut, where it all began.

Others are more white meat. Fight your way through the chicken feathers, and you can see why there is a lot to be said for them, but they'll never fly, let alone cross one of those twenty-two-lane side roads. Nossir.

The fishy ones range from upmarket 'lobster burger' Maine to Massachusetts which, even though it is home to my favourite Irish city in America, is so full of so many fishy things you practically have to walk around with a peg on your nose.

And, the veggie ones? Well, they're just tasteless. There's nothing there. Like veggieburgers.

The Meaty Ones

Well, yee-ha, as they say. The meaty states are as much the heart and soul of America as a genuine Texan longhorn is the heart and soul of a beefburger. This is where the cattle outnumber people, cowboy hats outnumber cowboy boots and it's best not to eat anything before flying in or out of Jackson Hole, Wyoming. Here the scenery is wild, the animals are wild and the prices are wild, especially during the holiday season, I mean vacation season. In the remaining three weeks of the year they're quite reasonable, provided, of course, that you don't want to eat or drink anything. The queues are so long they stretch all the way back to Fifth Avenue. Some people mistakenly refer to some of these states as the Rockies, because they believe their economy is rocky. No way. They are booming. Whatever bar, chuckwagon or dude ranch you manage to squeeze into, people are talking about bulls and bears and whether it's possible to bison or not. Especially as Ted Turner seems to be chasing every speck of dust in sight.

That said, it is true that Montana is more Robert Redford tough than Clint Eastwood or John Wayne tough. People tend to go there not for the mountains or the rivers, or even the grizzlies or mountain lions, but for the sky. To visit Montana and not go on and on about the Big Sky is like going to Little Rock, Arkansas and not going on about what'shername. The other thing that strikes me as odd about Montana is that once people get there they can't wait to get the hell out of there. There's no speed limit. It's the only place I've been in the States where people drive so fast you can't see all the little white crosses by the side of the road.

The meatiest states of all, however, have to be Virginia and Pennsylvania. Virginia was founded, according to an out-of-date, useless old book I discovered years ago at King's Cross Station, by one Sir Rycharde Bransonia, which turned out to be one of his ancestors' railway timetables.

The first white settlements were established at Rychardes-towne, now known as Jamestown, in 1607, although they were originally scheduled to have opened five years earlier. The first black settlements (Sir Rycharde always avoided the use of the word slavery – not good for the image) were established in 1619, ten years late. The first all-American independent government to exist in the whole of the US was formed in July of that year when a group of twenty-two Rychardestowne residents, accompanied by 220 lawyers and 2,200 lobbyists, got together and decided in their infinite American wisdom that once all the recounts had been completed, the second thing they should do was to levy the very first US tax: 10lb of tobacco on every man over the age of sixteen. The first, of course, was to have a couple of burgers and a Coke. Sir Rycharde, when he was not dressing up as Good Queen Bess, complete with beard, put even this session to good use. He had the whole discussion bottled to fuel his passion for being carried along by a constant stream of hot air.

Two of Sir Rycharde's Virginia men were also largely responsible for drawing up the two most important Lotterie documents of all time. The first, Rycharde Thomas Jefferson Bransonia, who, in spite of being fiercely pro-French and no doubt the owner of a holiday home on Mustique, was very much a man of principle and integrity and, above all, a master, if not the master, of that American genius for fine words and high-flown phrases that are completely divorced from reality. Witness his heartstopping statement at the beginning of the Declaration of Independence: 'We hold these truths to be self-evident that all men are created equal,' even though he happily bought and sold slaves all his life, kept over 250 of them on his own farm, flogged any who ran away, kept a slave as a wife as opposed to the more traditional wife as a slave and campaigned for what he called the 'backward' tribes to be driven 'with the beasts of the forests into the Stony Mountains'. He also, apparently, had a thing about ladies' gloves.

The second was Rycharde James Madison Bransonia, who came up with the first draft of the Constitution, 'We, the people . . .', which, again, completely overlooked the fact that 600,000 slaves happened to be living among them at the time, never mind the possibility that they might also be entitled to certain rights.

The fact that these two earth-shattering statements were not only delivered late but also not adhered to inevitably led to a civil war. The capital, Rycharde, now known as Richmond, was the capital of the Confederacy, where the likes of Jefferson Davis and Stonewall Jackson used to hang out at their local Virginia Megastore. But Sir Rycharde left his mark. Virginia provided many great leaders – Rycharde George Washington, Rycharde James Monroe, Rycharde Lea, Rycharde Woodrow Wilson – and the habit of completely disregarding documents you've drawn up and signed continues to this day. Look at the way the US one day fiercely upholds a country's sovereignty and independence and then the next completely ignores the sovereignty and independence of countries like Haiti, Grenada, Cuba, Panama, Libya and Sudan, not to mention the occasional Chinese embassy, and imposes completely ineffectual economic sanctions against seventy countries. How they sign test-ban treaties and then renege on them. How they did so much to create the United Nations and then refused to pay their dues. How they currently have no fewer than sixty treaties negotiated by one administration or other that still have not been ratified by the Senate.

The local transport system, also created by Sir Rycharde, is now known and recognised throughout the world as the Virginia Creeper, as every passenger knows to his cost.

As for Pennsylvania, what with William Penn, the Quakers, the Amish, the city of brotherly love and all those cheese steaks and hoagies and soft pretzels, I always used to think of it as a bit of a veggie state. But the more I go there, the more I discover about it, the more I'm convinced that it's not so much veggie as processed meat. After all, this is where they held meeting after meeting to process all the grand ideas coming out of that megastore of ideas next door.

Take the Declaration of Independence. Being born in a

stable is good enough for some people, but not for the Americans. The Declaration of Independence was born in a dingy room, full of horseflies, above a stable in Philadelphia. But instead of getting out in twelve days, clambering on to a donkey and heading for the sunshine, they stayed there and chewed it over for two whole years. The Articles of Confederation they are still counting, and recounting, and recounting again. The delegates from Rhode Island didn't even bother to turn up. Whether this had anything to do with Sir Rycharde was never established. Everybody else, of course, came by Stagecoach and was bang on time.

But hardly was the ink dry on their declaration before they were back for another seventeen weeks to chew over the Constitution yet again. At least, that's what they were supposed to be doing. Something must have gone wrong – maybe they were all concentrating on their hamburgers and Cokes – because it doesn't add up. I mean, how can they start off grandly saying, 'We, the people . . .' when they were quite obviously not the people? They were the élite, the big guys, or, as Jefferson called them, 'demigods'. They were businessmen, bankers, wheeler-dealers, doctors, professors and, of course, America being America, even in those days, lawyers. In fact, more than half of them were lawyers. So it should have begun: 'We, the élite, white, Anglo-Saxon Protestants . . .' If it had, I would have no argument with it. It would also, incidentally, have been a more accurate reflection of the America they were building as opposed to the America they claimed they were building. The very first article goes along with the whole idea of slavery. Why else is there the distinction between 'free persons' and 'all other persons'? Then there is no mention of democracy or political parties. Where was Jefferson when all this was going on? Probably off on some freebie to Boston or Miami. And how come they refused to tell the all-important people in whose name they were drawing up the damned thing what they were discussing, what they were voting on and why?

Then what did they do after days of agonised discussion

and debate and, no doubt, the occasional Virginia Coke, during which they decided they were going to have nothing to do with secret cabals and smoked-filled rooms electing one of their own as president and instead they were going to have a president who was directly elected by the people? They promptly appointed – appointed, mark you, not elected – one of their own, Washington. As if that wasn't bad enough, they even considered calling him 'His Mightiness, the President of the United States'. Mighty mistake, more like it.

The only explanation I can think of for all the glaring omissions, contradictions and saying one thing and doing another is that the documents are forgeries. After all, have you ever seen any American document more than two pages long with no drawings or cartoons or charts or photographs, not to mention one containing all those long words and dependent clauses? And the clincher is that they take more than one and a half minutes to digest. My own theory is that they were produced originally as a rap album and then as a music video. The only reason they've not been seen is that you-know-who was responsible for distributing them.

But even more important than Virginia and Pennsylvania is Connecticut, where it all began . . .

Connecticut

OK, stand up. You don't have to kneel down.

Just because I'm going to talk about the holiest of holies in the whole of the United States of America – yes, even holier than Graceland, even holier than Bubble Gum Alley in San Luís Obispo in central California – you don't have to throw yourself on the floor.

Take a bow, Louis' Lunch, where – take it away, Aaron – the first-ever hamburger in the whole history of the world was created in 1900. My God, I can hear those trumpets blasting away already. This miracle must, no question about it, make Connecticut not only the meatiest state of all but the number one state of all time, for all time.

Forget . . . what's the name of that university where Clinton didn't learn to do whatever he's never done in his life? Forget the so-called famous 17 acres of whatever it is that was the first something or other. Forget Wooster Street, with all its Italian restaurants. Forget Pepe's, where they invented the pizza as we know it today. Forget Sally's Pizza, which catered for Clinton's appetite while he was a law student. Well, part of his appetite. Instead make for Louis' Lunch, a tiny brick shack on the edge of a car park near the centre of New Haven.

The hamburgers are still there, still being gas-grilled, still being served only with onions and tomatoes on bread. The crowds are still there. The only thing that's missing is a plaque proclaiming the place a national historic landmark. For Louis' Lunch has obviously had a far greater influence on America, on American society and on America's standing in the world than any number of presidential libraries, Nobel Prize-winners and editions of *I Love Lucy*.

Just think about it. In 1900 the United States had only one type of running shoe. Now they have 257. In 1900, nobody had ever heard of stem cells. Now everyone knows they're the central core of a prison block. In 1900 everybody wondered where imports came from. Now we all know they come from overseas countries.

Portland up the road, for example, has not one but three national historic landmark awards – and they're just for quarries. Admittedly, Portland did supply the famous brownstone blocks for most of the famous public buildings in the whole of New England, including an estimated 80 per cent of the brownstone blocks in New York City. Even so, it's crazy. Especially when, after they received their plaques, they discovered that the last material you should use for building imposing public buildings is brownstone blocks, because they're vulnerable to bad weather and crumble easily over time. Edith Wharton, the old-world New York aristo who wrote about, well, the clashes between old and new New York aristos, loathed its 'chocolate-coloured coating' and called it 'the most hideous stone ever quarried'. She should worry. It won't be long before there's none left.

In fact, so important is Louis' Lunch in the history of the United States that Yale – that's the name I was trying to remember – desperate for prestige, decided, with the entire country to choose from, to establish itself just round the corner. Not only that, it also deliberately set up shop right opposite the famous green – famous because it was the first patch of green to be deliberately incorporated in any city in the United States to provide people with the space, the freedom and the natural open-air environment in which to enjoy their hamburgers.

Yale opened its Centre for British Art, the biggest collection of British art outside the UK, in New Haven because they knew that if Louis' Lunch wasn't round the corner, nobody would bother to come to see these important exhibits, so important no British gallery wanted them. The same goes for the Beinecke Rare Book and Manuscript Library. Even though their prized possession is, mein Gott, one of the few remaining original Gutenberg Bibles, they knew nobody would be interested if they weren't assured of getting a decent hamburger before inspecting the great book. Come on, you don't think they'd wait till afterwards, do you? Say what you like about them, the Americans at least have a genuine sense of priorities.

It doesn't stop there. Samuel Clemens – Mark Twain to you – who wrote all his great books in a rambling Mississippi steamboat-like mansion in Hartford's snobby West End, decided never to return to Connecticut when he got back from Europe in 1903 because he knew he couldn't compete with Louis' Lunch and its unique standing among his fellow Americans.

And so it continues, right up to the present time. Why were *Oklahoma!*, *My Fair Lady* and *The King and I* all premiered in New Haven? Why did Arthur Miller's *The Crucible* and *Broken Glass* both have their first nights in New Haven? Because they all needed the glory by association.

Today, of course, it's different. Unless young people can push something up their nose, they're not interested. The first

16

time I went to New Haven I asked a student – who was stretched out on the green looking as if he was half Connecticut – if he could tell me where I could find Louis' Lunch.

'Sorry.' He rolled his eyes in the air. 'I'm not doing geography. Havaniceday.'

The rest of the state, like the whole of the rest of the United States, is, by comparison, pretty boring. Orange, named after William of Orange, is about as exciting as a night out with a bunch of Dutch Rotarians all jealously buying their own drinks. Trumbull was the site of the first Methodist church established in New England. And it looks like it. Hartford, the state capital, is not just boring, but bland and faceless as well. The feeling is probably mutual. But then, it is full of nothing but insurance companies. I remember I once waited there hours on end for a train to New York. Which didn't come. So I had to take a bus which took me nearly four hours. It felt like four years.

As for Greenwich, the so-called fashionable hotspot for hotshot New Yorkers, it's out of this world. Houses there are not houses, they're mansions. Mansions are not mansions, they're starter castles. Nobody organises their own lunch or dinner any more. They all hire personal assistants to do it for them. But even after all these years, they're still so sore that Louis went to New Haven and not to their centre of the trendy world that they've banned all outsiders from using their parks and beaches. It's so exclusive even the tide can't get in. The only way you are allowed to use them is to go there accompanied by a Greenwich resident and pay $6 for the privilege. I was stopped in a park once as I was about to take my early morning constitutional (OK, I was on my way back to my hotel). I told them what they could do with their $6.

I went back to New Haven and spent it on another one of Louis' hamburgers instead. I felt sorry for him, because even though he invented them, he never made the money. Neither did the McDonald brothers. The guy who made the money was Ray 'If you've got time to lean, you've got time to clean' Kroc, who franchised their whole concept: quick, simple meals; no knives, forks, plates; unskilled labour; low overheads; fast turnover.

Youcanbetchalife it's the middlemen who always get on the beach at Greenwich. And I bet they don't pay, either.

Montana

All-righty, then, I'll tell you my big beef about Montana, hailed by many people as the most beautiful state in the whole of the US, and owned by Ted Turner, the founder of CNN. In fact, with over 25 million acres of forest, 500 different kinds of animals, more antelope than people, not to mention the occasional mountain, I reckon it should be renamed Monturner. My beef is mobile telephones. They don't work there, or at least, mine doesn't. And if you think that's not important, and that I should be going on about the joys of getting on my horse and getting out there and herding cattle through Big Belt Mountains with a bunch of city slickers, chasing after runaway cows in Bozeman and singing songs around the campfire in Missoula, forget it. There are more cattle in Florida today than there are in big, beautiful, beefy, mustangy Montana, once the world's biggest open-air cattle factory. Mobile phones are far more important.

Worldwide, they say. Coast-to-coast coverage, they say. Dependable communications, they say. Across town. Across country. Not in Big Sky country, it isn't.

In the old days, going to the States was always a problem as far as phones were concerned. First, you had to carry around so much money for the callboxes you ended up walking with a limp. Then came telephone cards. The trouble was, I always had the wrong card for the wrong phone, or if I had the right card, by the time I had dialled all the security codes and PIN numbers and the date of my mother's birth, I'd forgotten who the hell I was supposed to be ringing anyway. Mobile phones, when they arrived on the scene, weren't much use either, because they didn't work in the US. That is, our mobile phones didn't work in the US. Obviously, yet again, US technology was still in the Stone Age. Then came the answer to all our prayers

– well, most of them – the worldwide, coast-to-coast, depend-able communications, across town, across country, three-band, all-singing and dancing, most-modern-in-the-world mobile phone.

'It'll work worldwide?' I asked the busy little woman in the Vodafone shop in Oxford Street in London.

'Work. It will. Worldwide,' she said.

'And in the States?' I said.

'And in the States.'

'All over? Coast-to-coast?'

'All over. Coast-to-coast.'

I traded in my old phone, which was about the size of a telephone box. I walked, or rather staggered out of the Vodafone shop with my Motorola Timeport, the answer to my prayers. Well, most of them. It worked in Portland, Oregon. It worked in Boisie, Idaho. It worked in Salt Lake City, Utah. But Montana? No way. A million times I tried the select-your-network button, the change band, the find new network, the network search, the available networks. Nothing. I went to the local mobile telephone operators. They didn't know what the hell I was talking about. They also said they'd never seen one like mine before. Which is not the first time I've been told that, I must admit.

In desperation I rang Airphone, Vodafone's US victim – oops, I mean strategic acquisition. For hours on end I listened to a recorded message telling me that they were now called Horizon Wireless, but that they believed with their heart and soul in coast-to-coast coverage, dependable communications, across town, across . . . Then suddenly I was talking to a real, live human being. Well, I say a real, live human being: it actually sounded more like a Barbie doll on vodka and Red Bull.

I explained my problem. The one to do with the mobile phone. I was a lifelong customer of Vodafone. I had bought this phone in London, er, England. I had been told it was . . .

Did she understand what I was saying? Not a bit of it. She'd never heard of Vodafone. She'd never heard of the Motorola

Timeport. She'd never heard of . . . And all the time, breaking into our so-called conversation, was this recorded message, 'Coast-to-coast coverage . . . dependable communications . . . across town . . . across country.'

The Barbie doll told me to ring their global customer service number. They would solve all my problems. The number she gave me turned out to be the number of some factory in the middle of nowhere.

I rang Airphone again. 'I wonder if you could help me? I was speaking earlier to . . .'

I waited ages and ages and ages. Then I found myself talking to another Barbie doll. She didn't understand a word I was saying, either, but she offered to ring Vodafone for me to sort it out. Unfortunately she didn't know their number. Could I give it to her?

I gave her the numbers I had, and waited. And waited and waited and waited. 'Coast-to-coast . . . dependable communications . . . across town . . . across country. Wireless communication accessible to everyone.' After three or four days I had to hang up. I had some pathetic kind of a life to lead. I also had to earn some kind of a living.

Meeting over, lunch over, back at the hotel, I called Airphone again. Again I waited and waited and waited. Eventually: 'I wonder if . . . ? Earlier I spoke to . . .'

I ended up talking to some guy who was obviously a top man. He had heard of Vodafone. But could he tell me why I'd been told in London that my phone would operate coast-to-coast, but in Montana it didn't? No, he couldn't. 'Dependable communications . . . coast-to-coast . . . across town—' 'Tell you what,' he said in that rich, earnest accent all Americans adopt when they're out of their depth. 'I have the customer service number for Vodafone. Why don't you . . . ?'

He then gave me the very number I'd given the Barbie doll about three days earlier. So, in the land of customer-is-king, I have to make yet another call to Vodafone UK to wonder why my worldwide, coast-to-coast etc. etc. telephone isn't working in Montana. I wait hours for them to answer. I wait three more hours in a queue to talk to a real, live human being. When I finally get what sounds like one, he tells me I've rung the wrong number. I must ring another number. I go bananas. He says – surprise, surprise – that he can put me through, but I'll have to wait in a queue for the next available . . .

'But should my phone work in Montana?' I am at last allowed to ask the next available operator as calmly as I can.

He disappears. Two hours later he comes back. 'Yes,' he says. 'Yes.'

'Yes.'

He puts me through to the next available . . .

Two hours later, 'I'm in Montana,' I begin. 'I've got your Motorola Timeport. I was told it was coast-to-coast. All the advertising says coast-to-coast. Your own recorded message, which I've now heard two and a half million times, says, "Coast-to-coast coverage, dependable communications, across town, across country. Wireless communication accessible to everyone." So why doesn't it work?'

He goes away. He comes back.

'It's not coast-to-coast,' he says. 'It doesn't work in Montana.'

'But you say' – I'm beginning to lose it – 'in all your advertising . . . why I got the damned . . . in which case . . . how am I going to pay for all my . . .'

I write to Vodafone UK. They completely ignore everything I tell them. But they give me a goodwill credit of £50. Inclusive of VAT. Thank you, Celia Crane, senior business liaison officer.

As a result I hardly saw anything of the land of Sitting Bull, Little Big Horn, General Custer's jockstrap and Robert Redford's favourite bar, even though it's about the same size as Britain with less than one sixtieth of the population. When I wasn't looking for telephone boxes – and telephone boxes, I can tell you, are not easy to find in Montana – I was stuck on the phone trying to catch up with what was happening in the outside world.

Helena, the capital, I had to cancel. Billings I was in for a couple of days, mostly on the phone. What little I did see of it was pretty forgettable. It's certainly not cowboy country like, well, Wyoming. The town itself is small, quiet, bland, downbeat. Go and visit your local senator and it's more formica tables and chairs, Labour Party committee rooms, than grand oak-panelled offices and hugely under-used thick, solid-oak desks. Entertainment is minimal. Apart, that is, from the casinos. There are, I promise you, more casinos than mobile telephones. Big ones, medium-sized ones, little ones. Especially little ones. They're everywhere. Go into a grocery store, and I bet you, there will be a string of slot machines and a whole pile of rough, tough guys playing a little keno (bingo to you and me). For live action, all that was on offer was either a Bureau of Land Management briefing on noxious weeds given by the state weed and pest co-ordinator, Yank M. Out, or what was billed as a sharing experience on women's reproductive health, also given by— no, that can't be right. There must have been a mix-up somewhere.

I made for the restaurant on the twentieth floor of the Sheraton, which was anything but forgettable. It had its very own telescope. The staff said it was there so that people could look at the mountains in the distance, but they're so big you can see them anyway. Which can only mean that the real reason it is there is so that the cowboys can keep an eye on the old squaw while they are whooping it up on mountain oysters and ribeye steaks. The other thing I remember about the Sheraton is the red chardonnay. Red chardonnay? What the hell is red chardonnay? I couldn't resist it. I ordered a bottle. It turned out to be merlot.

'Why do you call it red chardonnay?' I asked Montana's number one master of wine, who looked like Annie Oakley's grandmother.

'Because it's so popular,' she drawled.

Outside Billings, as I say, it's more Robert Redford whispering in horse's ears than your hard-drinkin', chain-smokin', meat-chompin', spittin'-in-your-face and who-the-hell-are-you-lookin'-at kind of place. There are huge, endless tracts of smooth, gentle, rolling countryside where the occasional buffalo roams. Not much ranching, which surprised me, but a lot of wheat and sugarbeet, which also surprised me. Everyone told me that one in three of all cattle in the US are destined for McDonald's, and that most of them come from Montana. It didn't look like it to me.

As for the small towns, you never see them. They're either hidden away on the top of some mountain or other or completely engulfed by some glacier or other. Not that they are exactly what you would call small towns. Some have as many as five or six people. The rest obviously left because they couldn't get their damned Vodafones to work either. I ended up in one such town, Sidney. All I can remember is a map with a sticker on it saying, 'Here'. Which was completely useless, because I still didn't know where I was. What I did know, however, was that my phone didn't work there.

About the only excitement I came across was the miles and miles of empty roads linking the empty towns. It was just as well they were empty, because not only is Montana the only state in the US which doesn't have a speed limit, but kids of twelve and thirteen are allowed to drive. 'Isn't that dangerous?' I asked one trophy ranch dude who told me he was something big in the state's annual Testacle Festival, which takes place every September near Missoula. 'How else can they get to school?' he shrugged.

Testacle is, of course, Montanan for Rocky Mountain oysters. Be that as it may, it doesn't stop them having a ball.

The other thing that's scary is, because there's no speed limit, people drive like crazy. Back straights at 200mph. A right followed immediately by a left at 150mph. And what I was told after I opened my eyes was a decreasing-radius turn at 110mph. Some say they drive like that to get the hell out of the place as quickly as possible. Others say it's to avoid accidents – the less time they spend in Montana, the less chance they have of being involved in one. As a result, they kill everything in sight. Now, I'm not saying they're not safety-conscious – most cars and trucks have a safety seatbelt system for pets which you attach to your existing seatbelts to protect your cat or dog or whatever (available in three sizes, ten different colour choices) – but I did spot one or two roadside restaurants with signs up outside saying, 'From your grille to ours.' The more discerning barbecue their roadkill there and then. 'Barbecued racoon, anyone?'

In Tennessee they've gone a stage further. So many animals get hit on the roads there that they passed a law allowing drivers to take home with them any beasts they knock down and kill, which, of course, the States being the States, has given rise to a whole boom in roadkill cookbooks.

In the deep south the problem is not speed but booze. Because the speed limit is so low they have what they call 'tail-gate parties', where a load of drivers head out into the middle of nowhere doing a steady 55mph, bumper-to-bumper, drinking as they go. The theory is that because they're all together, because they're all doing 55mph, and because they're driving bumper-to-bumper, they'll all be safe. I wouldn't drink to that.

Meetings over. In Billings I decide to avoid the dude ranches, the authentic western guest ranches with swimming pools and bandanna-ed cowboys strolling around casually strumming guitars, spitting at anything that moves and telling everyone how much they like horses. Medium rare. Neither did I fancy trekking thick timber, as they say, because western Montana, according to an eco-cowboy I met, is contaminated by more than a hundred years' worth of arsenic, cadmium, copper and other toxic substances left behind by the mining boom. One quick look at the Big Sky, a deep breath and that could have been it.

Instead I tried to get to the Custer Battlefield Monument, about 60 miles south-east of town, which has now been renamed the Little Big Horn National Monument. This marks the spot where a bunch of Sioux and Cheyenne, led by Crazy Horse and Sitting Bull, wiped out five companies of the US 7th Cavalry. I wondered why it had been recast as a national monument to the Indians when it was they who massacred the cavalry and won the battle. But because my phone didn't work, I couldn't find out all the important things: when it opened and closed, how long it would take to see everything, whether there was a bar there.

I also wanted to get some ideas for a plan of mine: the Vodafone, Coast-to-Coast Coverage, Dependable Communications, Across Town, Across Country, Wireless Communication Accessible to Everyone National Memorial. Well, why not? I'm sure lots of coast-to-coast, dependable, accessible people would subscribe to it.

Take my advice. Next time you go to Montana, stick to the smoke signals. When you get back, however, write to Vodafone and complain, and they'll give you £50 credit. They gave it to me, so they should also give it to you. It might be boring, but it's a better deal than Steinbeck got when he went to Montana. He bought himself a hat that he didn't want in Billings; a jacket that he didn't want in Livingston and a rifle that he didn't want in Bute. And he called the dog Charley.

Wyoming

At first I thought, attaboy, Wyoming is my kinda country. Huge, wide, open spaces. Dinosaur tracks all over the place. Spectacular mountain ranges. More livestock than people. Real-live, dirt-encrusted, unshaven cowboys to the manure born.

But the more I got to know the countryside, the less enthusiastic I became. Sure, it has huge, wide, open spaces (ladies, be warned: the last thing you do is ask any cowboy the size of his spread – it might bring tears to your eyes) but most of them, like Yellowstone, the world's first national park, come with reins attached. You can't do this, you can't do that, switch off your engine to preserve the environment, don't park on the edge of the grass or you'll frighten the bison, you have yourself a good one. Gee whizz, if you spot an antler lying in the grass by the side of the road and as much as think about picking it up, I promise you, you'll be lucky to escape with four months in prison and six months' house arrest. Touch it and it'll be the electric chair. The national parks are also full to bursting point. With cars, with trucks, with those enormous RVs the size of battleships. But most of all with tourists desperately trying to find something to look at before they race back to watch repeats of *Laramie* on television.

As for the moose, bighorn, sheep, mule, deer, coyotes, badgers, squirrels, muskrats, beaver, porcupines, long-tail weasels, voles, over 175 species of birds, including eagles, and, did I mention, mountain lions and bears who live in the parks, they're not animals any more. They are a resource. Some of them, especially the gray wolf, which the US Fish and Wildlife Service has been breeding and releasing into the wild to kill the poor farmer's livestock, as if he didn't have enough to worry about, are even known as an electronic resource, because of the amount of hi-tech hardware wrapped around their necks. If you so much as think of looking at a young calf, their shock collars, which are bound to be made in Texas, will zap them until they stop or their heads drop off. A soft-spoken stick of dynamite in the US Forest Service once gave me chapter and verse on quotas, definitive population counts, hard data, self-regulation, depredation and the ethical problems of killing the resource you are studying. All I did was ask him where I could go to stomp a few snakes.

There are compensations, however. There is nothing more hilarious, for example, than hearing one of those earnest American tour guides explain why the Grand Tetons are called the Grand Tetons. Now, as anyone who managed to stay awake for even half of their French lessons knows, there is only one thing worse than calling a range of mountains the Grand Tetons, and that's explaining, in these days of political correctness, why they were called the Grand Tetons.

My own theory is that, even in those days, the French were fighting off what they saw as les creeping Anglo-Saxonisms. Calling the Grand Tetons the Grand Tetons was their way of getting their own back on le perfide Albion. But I'm sure even they can't have imagined American education would be so bad that the name would survive until today. However, some of the locals who originally turned down the idea of calling the whole state Cheyenne – because, they said, it sounded too much like *chienne*, the French for, well, a female dog – have just realised what Grand Tetons means and want to change it. The last proposal I heard, and the one apparently favoured by most locals, is Pilot's Knobs. I'm not saying a word, honest.

And why-oh-Wyoming would anybody want to call anywhere Jackson Hole? Locals say this was all the idea of the local postmistress, Maggie Simpson. Way back in 1895, David E. Jackson was one of the famous local fur-traders and early-day pokers with a reputation for tracking down any beaver that crossed his path. She was obviously familiar with him and thought the best way to commemorate him and his particular skills was to name the place after him. Whether the hole part is a reference to Jackson or to the town, nobody could tell me.

Either way, I'd have to think twice about spending any time whatsoever in Jackson Hole. I know hole is meant to be cowboy for valley, but didn't any of them even think about it? It's almost as bad as the idea of renaming Heathrow Airport Princess Diana Airport. I mean, do we really want to talk about the number of people queuing up to land on Princess Diana, the hold-ups in Princess Diana? Come on.

Names aside, Wyoming, the Cowboy State, is more designer cowboy than real cowboy. Goddarn it, even the horniest old critter who not only looks like a tired old cowpat but smells like one as well now calls winter the 'cocktail hour'. That's the time not to come to Wyoming.

First, it will be full of skiers. Even the Swiss come here, because, apparently, snow is not just snow. There are a million different types of snow, and Wyoming has the very best, powdery snow in the whole world for breaking every bone in your body.

Secondly, they don't just have snow, they have snow, snow, snow. Some years they get about 5ft of the stuff which, on an average person, would just about come up to— Hey, maybe that's why they call them the Grand Tetons. Maybe it was just the French being French, and nothing to do with getting their own back on les Anglo-Saxons.

Thirdly, there's nothing but skiing, ski-racing, cowboys on bucking-bronco skis being pulled by cowboys on horses and soaring 60ft into the air off a 4ft-high jump, dog-sled racing and all those boring conversations about which ski slope is better than which, and do you know I met Charles at Klösters only the other day.

The land of the legendary Shoshone, Crow, Blackfeet, Bannocks and, my favourite, the Flatheads – now, why don't we hear more about them? – has given way to soft Oklahoma sandstone, Douglas fir, cedar, Pacific redwood, hotels with stuffed bears climbing all over the place and RV hook-ups with 20amp electricity. The towns are Gucci creations: the sidewalks handcrafted, as they say, from designer planks. The genuine wild-west saloons are still covered with wet paint and the last time a shot was fired in anger was when President Clinton was elected.

You want to cowboy up and go out hunting? For real? American real? What about a trek 10,500ft up Rendezvous Mountain, which is so wild and bleak you wonder where the forest rangers go to get away from it all? Sure. There's a 2.4-mile aerial tram at your convenience. It'll take you right there. You won't even have to get snow on your nice, new, genuine, handcrafted cowboy boots. You want to go look at the elk? No problem. You take a sleigh ride from outside the Wildlife Art Museum. What else would you do? Get those boots wet? Or how about bears? I'll get you a couple of snowmobiles and a guide. He'll even rope them for you so that, city slicker that you are, you can get a better shot. Too tame? You want some real excitement? Fancy hunting, or rather treeing, a lion with dogs? I'll get you a snowmobile, a driver, an instructor, a first-aid attendant and an insurance quote. Well, you never know, do you?

In Florida they've gone a stage further. To ensure that nobody ever goes home disappointed, various wildlife parks buy in decrepit, moth-eaten old lions and whatever from zoos and safari parks all over the world eager to clear out their stock and bring in young blood to boost the attendance figures. The super American hunter is then allowed to practically push the barrel of his rifle down the poor dumb animal's throat to prove what a crack shot he is. And if that's not bad enough, they video the whole sad show so that the world's greatest hunter can stagger back to his condo with not only the head, the paws, the tail and the chewed-up teeth, but also his very own film of the momentous occasion.

Wyoming hasn't gone quite that far, but you can bet your genuine British Bates Isabell dressage saddle that it's coming. In the meantime, they are sticking with the stills. Just off the town square in Jackson Hole there's a photographic studio where you can dress up in all the old gear, duke it up, and have a sepia-tinted photograph of yourself taken hunting whatever it is you want to hunt. But don't leave it too late in the day. At six o'clock every evening, as regular as innocent people being mown down by crazed lone gunmen all over the States, there's a genuine, realistic and historic gunfight in the town square. Genuine because they use genuine blanks. Realistic because it's as realistic as Billy the Kid escaping from Will Cody. And historic because everybody taking part looks as though they were there the day Billy the Kid escaped.

If you just want to escape the crowds, rest your head on the Grand Tetons and dream dreams, that can also be arranged. Included in the price is your very own fluffy down comforter. Whatever a fluffy down comforter is.

Wyoming is out of this world, too, when it comes to wildlife-watching. Out of this real world. There is no trudging miles and miles through packed snow and ice, no freezing to death on lonely mountaintops. No fleeting, faraway glimpses of what you think might have been whatever it was you were looking for. Instead you can sit in the local art museum sipping a latte and there, right in front of you, watch a pack of wolves take out an elk.

A tad too strenuous? What about seeing the glorious sunset over the Grand Tetons? They have special 'Watch the sunset over the Grand Tetons from your very own soaking tub' programmes. You don't even have to leave your own bathroom, or even somebody else's. What could be more convenient? And some traditional Wyoming fare while you're watching the sunset? No problem, sir. I'll send out for some sushi right away. The Masa Sushi make some of the best sushi east of the Pacific. We'll have none of your chuckwagon cooks or vulture pie and thick black coffee here, nossir.

You think this is soft? Let me tell you, even the animals don't have to rely on finding their own food. It's done for them. The elks, for example, eat alfalfa pellets supplied courtesy of the US Fish and Wildlife Service. What else?

Follow in the footsteps of the likes of Kit Carson and bed down for a night under the stars? Are you outtayoomind?

In Jackson Hole the emphasis is on upscale lodging – that means there are saddles fixed to all the hotel banisters so you can practise your riding skills – complete with health spas built in. Instead of dragging yourself all the way to Wyoming and using up your hard-earned, expensively bought, new-found energy in the great wide open, all you have to do is go and work out for a couple of hours in some super deluxe fitness centre. What could be better? You can watch your bank balance go through the floor, your blood pressure soar through the roof, while all the time, on the other side of the temperature-controlled double-glazing, is some of the most spectacular scenery on earth, and you don't have to go anywhere near it. Well, I say some of the most spectacular scenery on earth, but I've stayed at plenty of hotels where I couldn't even see the double-glazing for the bears. Everything, even the branding-iron towel rails, the horse-collar mirrors, the cowboy and Indian sheets, was covered in black bears. There were baby black bears on the reception desk, on the tables, on the window ledges. Medium-sized black bears on special display stands and shelves. Dirty great black bears blocking the corridors, the doors and, of course, the windows. Still, at least they were dead. Which is more than can be said of the trappings of one hotel I came across in Wabasha, Minnesota where, when you checked in, they gave you a real, live cat, complete with litter tray, for company. Or they tried to, anyway.

Much as I would like to bed down for the night under the stars, any star, actually, I liked the sound of the Rusty Parrot. It sounded my kinda style. A saloon downstairs. Sawdust. All-night poker sessions. A battered old staircase, heavy red flock wallpaper. A corrugated-iron roof outside the bedroom window. A string of horses tied up across the street. I should be so lucky. It turned out to be another one of your super-comfy, luxury-linen, and no doubt fluffy-down-comforter, four-star, four-diamond hotels. As well as all the usual tours, it ran a special 'spring safari' into Yellowstone Park. All the year round.

In the end I risked my life on the most dangerous thing in town. I flew in and out of Jackson Hole Airport. If you don't want to scare the hell out of yourself, look away now. Even though it's the busiest airport in the state, it doesn't have a control tower. The pilots simply land and take off whenever they fancy. No asking air-traffic controllers for permission, no waiting for their approval, no checking weather conditions, no nothing. It's foot down, yee-ha, let's get this kite off the deck, and they're away.

You think I'm exaggerating? A few days before I was there planes had been landing while the runway was still being cleared of snow and ice. What's more, two planes actually took off using the same runway. At the same time. So don't tell me I didn't risk my life in Wyoming. Rodeo-riding? That's nothing.

Virginia

Forget Thomas Jefferson, Generals Lee and Jackson; forget Williamsburg, for over eighty years the capital of the biggest, most important British colony in America, and forget even Rocky Mount, the moonshine capital of the world.

My first contact with the state, I mean the commonwealth of

Virginia – they insist on calling it the commonwealth because it wasn't when it was founded and it isn't today – was a carpet-fibre factory in the middle of the night, breeze-block offices and a chief executive who was an ex-Vietnam colonel with an obsession for rubber gloves.

I landed at Tri-Cities which, at the time, was a tiny, two-bit airstrip on the borders of Virginia and Tennessee. I got a cab to Abingdon, which was a nice, well-behaved little town that could have come out of a Louisa May Alcott novel. Not that I've read any, but you know what I mean. All chintzy curtains, wooden floors and millions of little women swooning over apple-pie recipes. I checked into one of America's most famous heritage hotels, the Martha Washington, which was all chintz curtains, wooden floors and millions of little women swooning over apple-pie recipes. The would-be upper-class old bat on Reception told me it was a converted ladies' college. When I asked her what a converted lady was, she went all Orphan Annie on me. Then it was off to Bristol which, as far as I could tell, was a factory estate in the middle of what used to be a Civil War battlefield. Except that in Virginia, it's not known as the Civil War. It's the War of Northern Aggression.

The Declaration of Independence, the Constitution, the election, or rather appointment, of the first president, they all passed me by. Instead I found myself wandering around Bristol in the middle of the night visiting aircraft hangars crammed full of textile machines spinning at a million revs a second. Up into the roof we climbed, to see the start of the process. Down through the building we went to watch the thousands of different strands dropping floor after floor until, at ground level, they somehow all came together to form a single thread. Twenty-four hours a day, seven days a week, fifty-two weeks of the year they spun, producing millions of miles of the stuff every second.

The reason I remember the company so well is the chief executive. He was unlike any other chief executive I've ever met anywhere in the world.

First, he didn't have an office. Offices meant people sat in them. His job, he said, was to walk around. The factory. The warehouse. The storeroom. The car park. Other people's offices. That way he could not only be on buddy-buddy terms with everyone, he could actually see what was going on, what was not going on, what jobs were on time, what jobs were late, where there were problems.

Second, he never took any decisions. His job, he said, was to make certain everybody else took the decisions. If they were the right decisions, so much the better. If they were the wrong decisions, they could be corrected later. But at least decisions were taken when they should be.

The rubber gloves? He was obsessed with cleanliness. A clean factory meant a clean balance sheet. When he had first arrived the factory, he told me, was filthy. There was rubbish everywhere. In the car park. In the reception area. In the offices. All over the plant. He didn't say a word about it. All he did whenever he saw any rubbish was pick it up and put it in the nearest bin. For a week, nothing happened. After two weeks, other people, he noticed, began picking up the odd bit of rubbish. In three weeks, everybody had joined in. In four weeks, people had stopped throwing rubbish all over the place. Instead it went straight into the bins, which was why the place was now always so clean and spotless. Except for the rubber gloves. Whenever any visitors came to the factory the place was always spotless. Except for the car park. When he took them back to their car, somehow or other, in the centre of the car park, there was always a pair of rubber gloves.

By the time I got back to the converted ladies at the converted hotel it was time for a traditional Virginia breakfast: grits. There's not much I can't stand about American food, especially if it's about 26oz, dripping with blood and needs washing down with a couple of bottles of Cab. But grits, they're the pits. For years they were the reason I never went anywhere near Virginia – the real, old-money, horsey, pink-jacketed, historic

Virginia, not the artificial, built-up, office-block, shopping-mall, hi-tech, land of freedom Virginia you hit about fifteen or twenty minutes outside Washington, DC, where the State Senate has actually passed laws forbidding people to sleep anywhere but in their own bedrooms. Fall asleep in the kitchen, the living room or even, after a heavy lunch, in the dining room, and under Bill 925, county code enforcers will be through the door and carting you off to jail in seconds.

Now that I've learned to stay awake and to conquer my fear of grits – I have a 12oz New York strip instead – I go there whenever I get the chance. After all, where would they be without us? Although Jamestown, the site of the first English settlement, might give you the impression that they would prefer to forget that it was here, in 1607, lured by some giant American television network, that over a hundred destitute, would-be English castaways sailed into Chesapeake Bay to set up the new Jerusalem, to stop, according to a pamphlet of the time, idle persons from doing nothing but engage in 'lewd and naughty practices'. Whether it was because, deep down, they knew it was a stupid thing to do that they decided to name the place after the wisest fool in Christendom, King James I, I have no idea. All I can say is, it's a bit of a coincidence. But while they were at it, at least according to the authorised version, they thought they might as well convert the odd native 'from falsehood to truth, from darkness to light, from the highway of death to the path of life'. But, typical of the English, the whole thing fell apart. Within a year, half the would-be do-gooders were dead, and the rest were too old, weak and emaciated even to write a letter to the *Daily Telegraph*.

In the end the whole thing was saved by the illustriously named Captain John Smith. He reorganised the show, put it on a firm basis and saved virtually everybody's life. The survivors showed their appreciation in the traditional British manner, first by making him president of the Council of Virginia and admiral of New England, and then, because they were jealous that he had married Princess Pocahontas, by not only throwing him out on his ear but also sending him a solicitor's letter saying he had no right to do what he had done in the first place. They'd changed the rules of the game, and he was no longer an item, as they say. Back he went to London, alone and penniless, or rather, dollarless. He died in a house near Holborn Viaduct and was buried in St Sepulchre-without-Newgate, where even today his tomb is deliberately overlooked by American tourists.

Williamsburg, the old colonial capital, might not have been as ruthless with its leaders, but it is nevertheless a bit scary. Maybe it's me. I'm not at ease in American theme parks with real-live human beings walking around in them. Mice, cats, dogs, I can handle, but real-live human beings, even if they're dressed in seventeenth-century designer clothes, take some getting used to. But if you can stand it, it's worth it, because this is where it all happened – in typical British style.

All the poor old colonial farmers would get together at the Old South Meeting House, some, like Lord Fairfax, struggling to make ends meet on a measly 5 million-acre smallholding, and over glass after glass of the local moonshine – known variously as White Lightning, Skullcracker, Happy Sally, Gutrot or Rotgut – moan about the weather, the price of wine and the taxes they had to pay to the government in London.

In the Raleigh Tavern, named after the founder of the state, Ralegh, who, as a glorious example of the Ammerican edukashunal system, spelled his name in ninety-six different ways, they not only moaned about the weather, the price of wine and the taxes they had to pay, but also, no doubt, towards the end of the evening, agreed not to import any more slaves and more importantly not any more slaves from Britain.

Then on another riotous evening in the Slug and Cactus Leaf, they heard that the British had blockaded the port of Boston. Boston had banned all trade with Britain. So, slugging back a couple of gallons of port and slapping each other on the back, they toasted the health of the Bostonians and all who sailed in her. The following morning they woke up, luckily or unluckily as the case may be, in their own bedrooms and discovered that they had severed all links with their homeland, declared themselves independent, were in rebellion against the Crown and had one hell of a bar bill to settle.

You don't believe me? Let me tell you, I've just looked at a plastic jug of the local moonshine, which is still produced even today around Rocky Mount in the Appalachians, and I guarantee it would make anybody do anything. Even go against their age-old prejudices.

The rest, as President Bush would say, is histrionics.

What the Americans have done is to take everything at face value in commemorating these highly serious and carefully considered historic decisions. With the aid of the Rockefeller millions, they have created in the centre of town Williamsburg as it used to be, in all its colonial glory. Under the British, naturally. There, at one end of the main thoroughfare, which is about a mile long, is the College of William and Mary, which is supposed to be the second-oldest college in the US. At the other is the Capitol. In between are all ye olde-worlde shoppes run by ye olde-worlde Americans trying to speak ye olde-worlde Englishe. A word of advice. Don't bother with the Governor's Palace, home to all the British governors of Virginia. When I went there, some old Colonial harpy in a ginger wig was going on about why the Americans should apologise to the Indians for all the injustice they had heaped on them. I asked her when the Americans were going to apologise to the British for killing their soldiers. All I got was a stream of eighteenth-century abuse that would have made Moll Flanders blush.

If that wasn't bad enough, when I got back to my hotel I found in the middle of my room a baby's cot. Which, I can tell you, sobered me up. Immediately I thought they knew something I didn't know, which just shows you how guilty the Americans still make us feel about the Civil War and all that kind of thing. Then I realised they were just up to their old tricks, blaming the innocent for the sins of the guilty. All the same, it was the biggest turn-off I've ever come across to inviting anyone back to your room.

York, the nation's first capital, as opposed to the nation's first colonial capital, is, on the other hand, typically American. It's a sprawling mish-mash of highways, factories and scruffy, derelict houses. It was here, in the courtroom, that the Continental Congress signed the Articles of the Confederation in 1777. You could have fooled me.

Richmond, the present-day capital, is neither one thing nor the other. It looks and feels as if it is in some kind of timewarp because I swear they think they won the Civil War and that Richmond is the capital of a great conquering nation. Everyone talks about the Confederacy, the White House of the Confederacy, home to the Confederate president, Jefferson Davis; the Virginia campaigns; Robert E. Lee and his horse, Traveler, the grey gelding he bought for $200 in gold, and Stonewall Jackson, as if, for all the Confederate world, they're all alive and well and standing with their boots on the throat of the northerners. Then, of course, there's Monument Avenue which, without the slightest embarrassment, they say is the greatest street in America. If they had really won the war, if Richmond was now the capital of the world, they couldn't have built anything more grand and imposing and impressive than Monument Avenue. It's so grand and imposing and impressive it's almost worthy of the French. Running the entire length of the street, which is about as long as the Champs Elysées and lined with as many trees, is one giant monument after another. To the heroes of the Confederacy who, of course, weren't heroes. They were, whisper it not, especially in Virginia, losers. They lost the war.

First, there's Jeb Stuart, the Confederacy's most famous cavalryman, killed during the Battle of Yellow Tavern on 11 May 1864. He is more famous for his fancy plumed hat than for winning any battles. Then comes a giant statue of Robert E. Lee. OK, he was a nice enough guy. He loved animals. He worshipped Traveler. He even built a special stable for him

37

right next-door to his house after the war was over and he retired and went back home. But you'd have to say that he was a disaster. He couldn't give orders, he could only make suggestions. And every one of them was wrong. He not only lost all the major battles – Beaver Dam Creek, Glendale/Fraysers Farm, Malvern Hills and, of course, Gettysburg and Petersburg – he lost the war as well.

Then there is another one, of Jefferson Davis, the one and only Confederate president, who must have been crazy. He was not only slave-mad – blacks, he maintained, were better off as slaves in America than tribesmen in Africa – he also believed that to own a slave was a natural right of man, and that wherever a slave-owner went his slaves should follow. Not only did he want slavery to be exported to the north, he also dreamed of seeing Mexico and the whole of South America become slave-owning nations. On the other hand, he was a great fan of Robbie Burns and Sir Walter Scott, so maybe that affected his judgement.

Southerners maintain that he was a consummate politician, but I can't see it. If he was such a good politician that he could become the first president of the Confederacy, how come he couldn't negotiate his way out of the Civil War in the first place? It's not as if one side was threatening to invade and destroy the other. They were arguing about principles: the right to own or not to own slaves, the balance of power between the state and federal powers. Surely, as soon as Abe was elected president in 1860, the two of them could have sat down and schmoozed out a compromise: an agreement in principle, an agreement to disagree on implementation, a committee of inquiry, a joint working party – the kind of thing politicians do every day of their sordid non-working lives. Or, if that was too much for them, they could have organised a baseball game or something and gone into a sudden-death play-off. Even when he saw that his side was losing, good old Jefferson Davis couldn't negotiate so much as a peaceful settlement, let alone a compromise with the Yankees. He left everything to rough, tough, warmongering Robert E. – 'It's well that war is so terrible, else we should grow too fond of it' – Lee.

Next comes the lemon-sucking, long sermon-loving Stonewall Jackson. Unlike all the others, his monument faces north. The Virginians say that this is to show that even in death he has the strength and determination to face down those damn Yankees. To me it proves how stubborn and stupid he was. After all, it was because he wasn't looking in the right direction that he was shot by his own troops at Chancellorsville in 1863.

After Stonewall there is Matthew Fontaine Moury, pathfinder of the sea, commander of the Confederate navy, who is so famous that the Museum of the Confederacy couldn't tell me what he did wrong or how many battles he'd lost. They also couldn't tell me why there is no statue of Stephen Mallory, the Trinidadian who was navy secretary during the Civil War and one of the few successful Confederate leaders. My guess is he didn't have a spin doctor.

Then, for some reason, there is a rather twee monument to the Wimbledon tennis champion Arthur Ashe. Which I think is a big mistake. Arthur Ashe was a man of peace, not a man of war. He united people in having a good time, not in causing death and division. He was black, not white. And, most important of all, he was a winner, not a loser. By all means have a statue of Arthur Ashe, but not in Monument Avenue. It should be in New York or Washington. What Arthur Ashe did was of national, not regional importance. If Richmond really wants to honour him, they should rename boring old Richmond International Airport the Arthur Ashe International Airport. As it is, his statue proves my point that Americans don't really understand what they're doing or saying. Instead of Monument Avenue, it should have been called Monumental Mistake Avenue.

Pennsylvania
I think I've been everywhere and experienced everything Pennsylvania has to offer. A hangover in Temperanceville. The

delights of Intercourse. I once even spent an unforgettable weekend on the shores of Lake Erie with the body of a dead woman.

But much as I will rise to Pennsylvania's defence whatever the criticism, I'm afraid I don't buy this stuff about William Penn, the saintly Quaker, a man of peace, eager to start a community based on Christianity, justice and equality. As far as I can see he was shipped out as a result of a sordid deal between his father, an admiral and one of the Parker Penns, and King Charles II. The King owed his father £16,000. He couldn't pay. OK, said the King, instead of £16,000, how about a couple of million acres in the New World? Done, said father, and his nibs was on the next boat.

Now I know all about this Philadelphia and city of brotherly love business – it means that if the police beat you up in front of a video camera they will immediately take you to hospital afterwards – but I can't for the life of me understand why they didn't call the place Franklin, or even Franklinville or, I suppose, given the American genius for yukky names, HappyBenjyFrankyVille. Rather than the Cradle of American Liberty, it's more like the Cradle of Benjamin Franklin, the short-sighted, harmonica-playing son of a man who changed shades and colours every day of his life (he was a dyer).

Carpenters Hall should be the Benjamin Franklin First Continental Congress Hall, because this is where the First Continental Congress took place. Presumably they only called it Carpenters Hall because they wanted to see if the congress would work. Independence Hall should be the Benjamin Franklin Independence Hall, because this is where, in 1776, along with his colonialist cronies, he ditched the motherland, the Crown, Parliament and everything they held dear and signed the Declaration of Independence and, eleven years later, having attended every single negotiating session, the Constitution as well.

The Congress Hall should be the Benjamin Franklin Congress Hall, because this is where Ben attended the very first meeting of the US Congress. The Liberty Bell Pavilion, where

40

the cracked remains of the great ringer lie in more pompous state than George III, should be the Benjamin Franklin Liberty Bell Pavilion.

Look at the streetlighting. He set up the first whale-oil street-lighting. The paving stones. He invented paving stones. The clean streets. He came up with the idea of cleaning the streets. The clean air. He thought up smokeless chimneys. Fireplaces. He invented what's known as the Pennsylvania fireplace. The fire brigade. He came up with the idea of volunteer fire brigades, no doubt because of the success of his Pennsylvania fireplaces. Post offices. He created the modern post office, not to mention the revolutionary idea that letters should be delivered to the people they are addressed to. Public libraries. Old clever clogs established them as well. Hospitals. Them, too. He also set up the Academy for the Education of Youth which, as it became more and more prestigious, was reduced to calling itself the University of Pennsylvania.

If you buy a burger, it will be called a Benjamin Franklin burger. An ice cream? All the money in the world says it will be a Ben & Jerry's ice cream.

Two days in the place and, I tell you, everybody looks like Benjamin Franklin. In fact I went there once when everybody *was* Benjamin Franklin, which gave me quite a turn. At first I thought I'd been hitting too many Benjamin Franklin cocktails in the Benjamin Franklin Bar in the Benjamin Franklin Hotel, but it turned out they were all genuine Benjamin Franklin look-alikes out to attract more people to Benjamin Franklin's home town. All it will attract as far as I'm concerned is demands to amend the Benjamin Franklin Constitution to give people the inalienable Benjamin Franklin right not to be accosted by Benjamin Franklin look-alikes, especially after a heavy Benjamin Franklin night out on the Benjamin Franklin tiles.

But in spite of all this Benjamin Franklin hero-worship, this over-preening respect for his enormous range of achievements, his undying belief in life, liberty and freedom of speech, what did they do when they slapped him on the back of their new

$100 bills? They removed the trademark beaver fur – the very basis upon which the American economy and the never-ending supply of greenbacks was built – from around his neck in case it upset people who did not believe in life, liberty and freedom of speech.

The brotherly love business is a bit heavy as well. Get caught feeding the pigeons in Washington Square and you're in for a $300 fine, which doesn't sound very brotherly to me, even if you don't get beaten up by the police. On the other hand, Philadelphia is pleasant. It's as if it was designed by George Eastman to get people to use more of his films. It's civilised. Almost wimpish. The heartland of the WASPs, the White Anglo-Saxon Protestants. Shops display signs saying they're closed for 'Sabbath observance'. People don't seem to raise their voices. It's as if it's full of shellshocked victims who can't take any more of New York. It's cultured. They use knives and forks. They play classical muzak in the lifts. When you check out, the hotel staff wish you 'a safe stay in the destiny of your final destination'. They go fox-hunting. They even play cricket. In many ways, it's one of the few places in the States where you feel you could sit, read Jane Austen, sip dry sherry and not feel too out of place. Well, maybe apart from South Street.

Nobody, of course, mentions sisterly love. That's because there wasn't any. Up until fairly recently, for example, sisters were barred from the most important and influential places in town: the oyster bars and cellars. To protect men from their crude, debased conversation, they were also banished to special sister-only rooms in hotels and restaurants.

Pittsburgh, Pensivania, ahz fahnd the exact opposite. At one time it was all gommed up with stillmills. It was so bright, pilots could steer their planes by them. Because of the huge smoking chimneys, however, the atmosphere was as black as soot. Streetlights had to be kept on twenty-four hours a day. Salesmen had to take half-a-dozen white shirts with them to the office every morning in case a client cawd and they had to go aht and slippy through the smog to meet them dahntahn for some chitchat and a crewsant. No longer. Today Pittsburgh is as clean and bright and well swept as, well, Philadelphia. Some say they had no alternative. It was the pits. The death rate was exceeding the steel-production rate. The first time children born in Pittsburgh saw the light of day was when they went to Philadelphia. Something had to be done, if only somebody could find the plans they had written and put on the desk just a few minutes ago. Others say the steel industry just rolled on. Industries live and die, towns live and die with them. A few even maintain that it was nothing to do with the steel industry at all but more to do with Pittsburgh also being home to Henry J. Heinz, who started by selling bottled horseradish and, among his 57 varieties, ended up converting the world to the joys of eating plate after plate of baked beans for breakfast.

But it was Andrew Carnegie, the Scotsman who probably did more than anybody else to turn Pittsburgh into the most profitable steel town in history, who pulled the plug on the place. As a Scotsman down to his borrowed sporran – he even plastered the walls of his home with tartan wallpaper – he got sick to death of the way, after everything he had done for them, they still insisted on calling it Pittsburg, and not Pittsburgh, as in Edinburgh. In disgust he then changed his name from Andrew to Dale and devoted the rest of his life to haranguing others about his phenomenal powers to influence people.

Inevitably, Pittsburgh suffered. Today, now that the smog has cleared, you can actually see what it's really like: a teenage Chicago. A huddle of fancy art-deco skyscrapers squeezed between three rivers where fishermen actually catch fish; a million iron bridges, which no doubt kept the steel mills going a couple of weeks; a wonderfully politically correct statue of the famous local songwriter Stephen Foster, who gave us such delights as 'Camptown Races', with a slave sitting at his feet strumming a guitar; a tiny hillock on the south side of town grandly named, in the Jeffersonian tradition, Mount

Washington, which somehow doesn't seem right; a railway line which I'm sure was built originally to deliver US government grants, cheap loans and tax loopholes to steelmakers worth over $150 billion, but which now seems to carry nothing but 20-mile-long goods trains; hi-tech industrial parks – Pittsburgh is the fifth biggest hi-tech producer in the US – and an Ikea on practically every corner. Even more importantly, Pittsburgh invented the Big Mac.

Penn Station I like, with its sparkling rotunda. The Mellon Hall of Science is fun. So is the Allegheney Country Courthouse and jail. And, of course, it gets as cold as Chicago, although somehow or other it's not the same kind of cold as in Chicago.

At the other end of the block are fun towns like Downington and Altoona, which has the only airport I've ever been to in the US with no cabs. Late one evening I staggered out of there ready to crash into a cab. No cabs. Not one in sight. Not one expected. And nobody around to ask I got into town by literally thumbing a lift from a guy who had this thing about English coats-of-arms. In between are towns like Gettysburg, York and, of course, Lancaster, the centre of Amish Country, although Intercourse is where all the action takes place.

Gettysburg is heartbreaking. The town itself is pretty much touched-up small-town America. A pretty-looking hotel, some straightforward main streets, some seedy back streets. The battlefield area is even more depressing. Sure, it's well cared for: the grass is cut, the odd patches of maize are well cultivated. The statues and the memorials all over the place to entire cavalry units and regiments of soldiers are impressive. But somehow, perhaps more than at most old battlefields, you get the feeling that all that agony, all that suffering was crazy. Just a few years after all that fuss and bother in Philly, it beggars belief that a state that did so much to make sure everything worked was fighting to the death over what they thought they had all agreed upon. If that's not bad enough, it's incredible that Pennsylvania, home to the great Benjamin Franklin, could then go to war purely on the say-so of the governor. The State

Assembly had voted 88 to 55 to submit the decision to the people, the fair, decent, democratic, Benjamin Franklin thing to do. But the governor stepped in. We go with the Confederates, he said. So much for all Franklin's fine words and high-flown phrases. Even then there was no need to prolong the war as they did. And for what? The Confederates were a lost cause. They deserved to get creamed. They were doomed from the beginning.

The other thing that surprised me was how disinterested, almost, the blacks were about the whole thing. If I were black, surely I would have rejoiced that the whole of the north actually took up arms to uphold the fact that all men are equal, that slavery is an abomination, that the entire concept of slavery should be abolished. In England we only held parliamentary debates about it; in the US they went to war about it.

Visit Gettysburg today and there's no way you get the impression that this war was about slavery: the right to own slaves or the right not to own slaves, let alone to consider the entire concept of slavery. I couldn't find any reference, either, to the number of black soldiers who took part in the fighting, let alone any memorial to the black soldiers who died in the conflict. What's more, there is no indication that this was a defeat. It was 'the greatest battle ever fought on the continent and one of the most decisive battles of world history'. Gettysburg is 'the most visited, most written about and most intensely studied battle ever recorded'. Pennsylvania is where 'a nation was born'. Gettysburg is where 'a nation was saved'.

Far from winding up my visit with the Gettysburg Address, I ended it with another kind of speech which was considerably longer than Lincoln's 271 words. A young guy, tall, slim, gangling, clean-shaven, with a barcode hairstyle, latched on to me, the way Americans do, as I was heading back into town. He told me he had just been busted. The police had found him with a block of low-grade marijuana which he'd bought for $800 from a dealer in Philadelphia. Usually he broke it up and sold it to all and sundry, including some pretty high-up sundries in and around Gettysburg, for anything between $1,500 and $2,000 a shot. With the money he was making, he was hoping to travel, first the States and then the world.

Somebody, however, had split on him. Who it was he had no idea. The police didn't have to say. He'd been to court. His lawyer, he said, was old and drunk and always turned up late, which annoyed the judge. As a result he'd been sentenced to what he called juvie time, six months in a state penitentiary with a bunch of other nico-teenagers. He reckoned he had got off pretty lightly. Others have been jailed for six years for stealing a pizza. One poor guy had been banged up for seventy-five years for making a threatening phone call. Now this guy was waiting for a vacancy so that he could begin serving his sentence: with over 500,000 Americans in prison on drugs charges, compared with 50,000 in 1980, there was no room for him. When there was a vacancy, he was told, they would call him. He would have to turn up at the jail with his own toothbrush and toothpaste, his own plastic mug and at least six different changes of clothing. He would then be banged up for six months. It was an interesting insight into the American way of doing things.

'I've already reconciled myself,' he kept telling me. 'I know I've done wrong. I know I've got to go to prison. My only objective now is to get through it.'

To get through it he'd decided to do as he was told, work hard, try to build himself up, do some studying – he'd never passed any examinations at school – and come out a better man.

Good luck to him. I hope he does it. It's about time Gettysburg had a winner.

My battlefield tour over, I was faced with a decision. Visit what was described in the official Gettysburg Visitors' Guide as Eisenhower's 'home and barn featuring Eisenhower's farm machinery' or go and have a drink. I went and had a drink. Although afterwards I wished I had decided differently. A guy in the bar who, funnily enough, also looked like Benjamin

Franklin, told me that Eisenhower had never wanted to be a politician. He always wanted to be a professional baseball player. Even at West Point he played baseball, under an assumed name.

'Eisenhower,' he said, 'used to tell the story of how, as a small boy in Kansas, he went fishing with a friend, and how, as they sat on the side of the river, they talked about what they wanted to be. Eisenhower said he wanted to be a major league player. His friend said he wanted to be president of the United States. Neither of them achieved their ambition.'

York turned out to be the original York, the first capital of the United States, as opposed to New York. This is where the Continental Congress signed the Articles of Confederation in 1777. As with the Articles of Confederation, it was difficult to find the interesting bits, but when I did it was worth it.

As for Amish Country – Americans tell you they're Dutch only because they can't say Deutsch, but in fact the Amish originally came from Zurich in Switzerland – it's not what I expected. I thought it was going to be miles and miles of wide open space with a tiny cluster of houses forming the Amish town, and all around it solitary, electricity-free houses and stables silhouetted against the horizon. No way. It's more AmEx country. It is two jam-packed, fast-moving highways crammed with Amish Country markets and Amish craft fairs and Amish tearooms and Amish guest houses. Squeezed between the two highways is the perfectly manicured, immaculately looked-after Amish countryside, with perfectly manicured and immaculately looked-after Amish houses, barns and stables.

Inside the houses are the perfectly manicured and immaculate-looking Amish, the men in their dark, buttonless suits, long beards and black felt hats, the women in their buttonless black dresses, their black capes and bonnets, and their perfectly manicured and immaculate-looking oil lamps, gas-fuelled refrigerators, flat irons, treadle sewing machines and high-powered battery-operated laptop computers.

'Shhh,' one of the Amish elders, Moses, who looked as

though he could have been there when the waters parted, whispered through his straggly grey beard. 'The bishop said we could have one so long as we didn't tell him.'

Inside the barns and stables are perfectly manicured and immaculate-looking Amish horse-drawn ploughs, stalk-cutters, muckspreaders, carts and wagons. Outside, briskly trotting along the sides of the roads, are perfectly manicured and immaculately looked-after Amish horses pulling tiny, boxed carriages. Swooping all around them are Amish kids on rollerblades, which are acceptable to the Amish because they're non-mechanised, engine-free technology.

But alone, isolated, self-sufficient it is not. In fact, judging by the mass of electricity cables and fast cars all over the place, it looks as though there are more non-Amish living in Amish Country than there are Amish.

Lancaster, the oldest inland city in the US – this is where George Washington or Old Muttonhead, as his ever-loyal vice-president, John Adams, used to call him, was declared father of his country – could virtually be any county town anywhere. It has bars and pubs and nightclubs. It even has a jazz festival. But the centre of Amish Country? Never. It hasn't even got a hitching post for the horses, though it does have what they call a petting farm. About ten miles from Lancaster I did, however, manage to enjoy the non-stop thrills and delights of Intercourse, a tiny collection of shops and houses, as well as the Intercourse Motel where, over a coffee, an old man who looked like a renegade Amish prophet told me that he and his cheese Danish were enjoying a hymenical experience. Within seconds, I cannot deny, I was in Paradise, which was further down the road.

But not everything Amish is Amish. I've come across plenty of Amish shops and stores that are no more Amish than a Salvation Army car-boot sale. In Manhattan there's an Amish farmers' market which even I noticed was full of non-Amish things such as balsamic vinegar and Perrier, and which is run and owned by Turks. Amish farming is not necessarily any more organic, free-range, hormone-free, animal- or environmentally friendly than any other kind of farming, although, of course, some individual Amish farms are. As for Amish recipes in Amish restaurants, Amish chicken is no more likely to be genuine Amish chicken, pan-roasted with herbs in a wood-burning oven, than Yukon Gold whipped potatoes are likely to come from the Yukon, to be gold, or even necessarily whipped.

Which brings me to the weekend I spent with the body of the dead woman. She was over 7,500 years old but as she was from Florida it was, I admit, difficult to tell. At first I thought she was just all shrivelled up, leathery and as black as soot because of an overdose of the sun. In fact she had been discovered in a bog near Cape Canaveral and was being hailed, together with a mass of other bodies and bits and pieces, as one of the earliest traces of civilisation in North America. Which came as a hell of a shock. Most people didn't think civilisation in North America could be traced back 7,500 days, let alone 7,500 years.

For some reason or other I can't remember now I was at the Mercyhurst Archeological Institute in Erie, where they were putting this poor woman and a number of other bodies into a specially constructed environmental chamber, to be desalinated and freezedried. After that the scientists would get to work. All I can remember is this black, wizened lump in a wooden box about the size of the ones in which they ship vintage port; a lot of talk about whether she should be called she or it; when, where and how she or it should be buried, or reburied, and who the hell would be responsible for settling any multi-multi-million-dollar lawsuits for damages brought by any of her descendants.

All in all, I'd rather have been in Philadelphia. I mean HappyBenjyFrankyVille.

The Chicken Ones

Kentucky Fried Chicken. Colonel Sanders. Kentucky is, of course, a chicken burger state or, as it is correctly spelled in schools and colleges throughout the US, a chikin burger state. So, too, is Rhode Island. There's no way that can ruffle any feathers.

In one way, Kentucky is the biggest chicken state of all. Come the Civil War, with the south arming and recruiting like mad, Lincoln called for support. He wanted 75,000 men. At first Kentucky were chicken. They turned him down. But by the end of 1861, they had changed their minds, crossed the road and became part of the Union war effort.

Today nobody can accuse them of being chicken, let alone chicken-hearted. They run the most expensive horse race in the world, the Kentucky Derby. On race day, the whole racing world is packed into Churchill Downs like battery hens, the fat old Attila the Hens in the stands, the young spring chicks out in the middle of the track. First prize is US$1 million, which, you have to admit, is not chicken feed.

Rhode Island may be the smallest state in the US – you can drive through it quicker than it takes to boil an egg, unless, of course, you're chicken and stick to the speed limit – but in no way is it henpecked. It was founded by the last person who could be called 'chicken', a Londoner and a fierce non-conformist libertarian, dissident and friend of the Indians – he is said to have spoken many different Indian languages, although, of course, to American ears, it could just as easily have been Welsh – with the unlikely name of Roger Williams. He should have had a grand Old Testament name like Ebenezer or Josiah, or even Tom Jones. But, Roger Williams? It makes him sound like the secretary of a Home Counties tennis club.

Anyhow, our Roger was so much of a fierce non-conformist, libertarian, dissident and friend of the Indians that he was threatened with deportation from, of all places, Massachusetts, that home of staid, tea-loving, taxpaying royalists and arch supporters of Britain and everything British. They hatched a plot to send him back to England in an empty tea crate. But he came under the wing of the Anglicans, who warned him one night that it was impossible to make an omelette of establishing a new civic community without breaking the eggs of free speech and free thinking. Early the following morning, before the cock crowed once, let alone thrice, he was up, with his wife, Ann, clucking around like a mother hen, and, together with children and servants, they flew the coop and made for this island which, obviously, since he was the descendant not of chicken-farmers but of a long line of fierce Non-conformists, libertarians, dissidents and friends of Indians, he promptly called Rhode Island.

Originally derided by the Bostonians, or rather, Bawhstonians, as the Sewer of New England, Rhode Island was in many ways a model little state. It dealt with the Indians with courtesy and respect. Similarly the slaves. Not that it had many. By the late 1700s, out of 7,000 inhabitants, only 200 were registered slaves, fewer than the great libertarian Thomas Jefferson had tucked away on his own farm. While everybody else was strutting up and down trying to rule the roost they were also the first to abolish slavery altogether.

Not content with founding Rhode Island, our improbably named Welsh firebrand then went on to hatch the First Baptist Church of America. As for the Rhode Islanders, the only time they got egg on their faces was quite recently, when the mayor of the capital, Providence, was up before the beak, had his wings clipped and was sent to jail for some felony or other, although it didn't seem to worry him or his supporters too much. He was no sooner released than he was back on his perch again: his second term of office he served while still on probation.

Both states, in their own way, are finger-lickin' good, but if you're after real chicks, you should go to Key West, Florida. They're all over the place. At any one time there are literally thousands of them strutting their stuff, stretching out all over restaurant tables, huddling into corners in bars, wandering down the middle of the road, stopping traffic, doing everything they can to find somewhere to bed down for the night. Many of them are so desperate that they somehow manage to get through cat and dog flaps and are found in the morning asleep on the kitchen floor. Anywhere else they would be a menace, but in Key West, they're part of the scenery. Or, if you prefer, poultry in motion.

Kentucky

Kentucky was the last of the fifty-one States I visited. It should have been the first. It has everything. Horses, bourbon, style, fun people, although how they're supposed to be descended from the Bourbons, I have no idea. Oh yes, and the Abbey of Gethsemani which, if not exactly horse heaven, is pretty much as close to the real thing as I reckon I'm likely to get.

First, horses. Churchill Downs, in Louisville, is America's most historic and famous thoroughbred racetrack, the oldest continuously operated track in the country, and home to the legendary 1¼-mile mint julep-soaked Kentucky Derby. Lexington is Newmarket, Ascot and the stables next door all rolled into a single haybag. Keeneland is one of the most discreet and beautiful racecourses in the world. It's so discreet they don't even have any loudspeaker announcements. It's also been the home for the last thirty years of the world's most important yearling sales. But, unbelievably for Americans, they would never dream of mentioning it. Then there's everything else. Horse parks, stud farms, museums, some of the most fabulous horses in the world. After my own, of course. And, finally, bluegrass. Kentucky bluegrass is famous among your real, money-no-object horse-lovers the world over. It's foie gras, caviare and, of course, Big Mac, or rather, Kentucky Fried Chicken, or Poulet Frit Kentucky, as they say in New Orleans, all combined. Many people have it flown in specially for their loved ones: racehorses, eventers, showjumpers, even the occasional overpampered hack.

Which of them is best? I can never make up my mind. Sometimes I think it's fast horses and slow women. Or was it slow horses and fast women? Oh no, that was something else. There's only one way to find out: the Kentucky way. Line them up for the Peter Biddlecombe Handicap which, I can assure you from experience, is some handicap, and – mint Goddamn ju-leps all round – let them fight it out between them.

OK, so now, loading into the stalls, starting with the nearest to the rail, is Louisville, pronounced LooVol, on the banks of the Ohio, one of the nicest little towns in the south. Churchill Downs comes next. A mecca for all horse-lovers. Not that I'm a fanatic. I was in Louisville all of twenty-three minutes before I went out there to take a look at the place. Next to Churchill Downs is Lexington. If Louisville is racing, Lexington is all plastic gloves and surprised expressions, in other words, stud farms and fast breeding. Judging by the things I saw, they do an awful lot of breeding in Lexington, the lucky breeders. It's also twinned with that other famous horse-breeding centre, Kildare, home not only to the Irish National Stud but also to one of my favourite bars, the Vatican, 'neat dress essential', discos Friday and Saturday nights only. Next is Keeneland. The greatest horse sales in the world. Started in a tent in 1943. Now total annual sales are way up in the billions.

Now comes Horse Parks, Stud Farms and Museums. They're everywhere. All beautifully presented, all beautifully managed. Next to Horse Parks, Stud Farms and Museums is Kentucky Bluegrass. Some say it's not just the grass that does it, it's the secret ingredient. Either way, there's a special aura about him. Then Style. You might not like it, but Kentucky has got style. Not only does it have the best horses, it has the best bars and the best parties as well.

Playing up and resisting the handlers is Bourbon. The best bars and the best parties can only mean they've got bourbon as well, at least in Kentucky. They're impossible to separate. Tennessee whiskey is something else. So is the local moon-shine. I've been in bars I can't remember where it's been on sale for as much as $10 a gallon. But be warned, you not only have to bring your own plastic jug, you have to finish your drink before the jug melts.

Alongside Bourbon is Fun People. It's only natural: horses plus booze equals fun people. Another round of mint Goddamn juu-leps for everybody. I'll stick with the straight bourbon.

Finally, the Abbey of Gethsemani. Way out in the middle of nowhere, all on its own, surrounded by shhh . . . nothing but silence. It looks like a one-trick pony.

For news on the betting, over to Seamus in the bar, I mean, in the betting ring.

> Churchill Downs, the favourite, is riding high at 9–4 followed by Style at 5–1, Bourbon at 7–1, Louisville at 8–1, all the others, Lexington, Keeneland, Horse Parks, Kentucky Bluegrass and Fun People at 10s. The Abbey of Gethsemani is quoted at 16–1. God bless him.
>
> OK, they're loaded. They're under starters orders. They're just about ready. They're ready, they're set, they're racing. First out is the favourite, Churchill Downs, closely followed by Louisville, and on the far side, Lexington, who are both running along nicely, although Louisville's got a long stride and is a very good mover. He's a couple of lengths ahead. He's giving them all a fair start.

Churchill Downs, with its famous twin towers, was, I thought, going to be out in the middle of nowhere, set in beautiful, rolling downs, a bit like, say, Epsom or Goodwood. But it's practically in the middle of downtown Louisville, completely surrounded by houses. How they get all those horses and all those people in and out for the big races, I have no idea. But they do – and far, far quicker than it sometimes takes me to get out of the car park at Plumpton or Lingfield.

Apart from being the only place in the world where a retired soldier's thoughts turned not to glory and honour and the triumphs of past battles, but to ways of smearing a scab over a dead chicken, Louisville also boasts the world's biggest base-ball bat, all 120ft of it, outside the offices and workshops of Hillerich and Bradsby, the world's leading manufacturers of baseball bats, although apparently it's touch and go now whether more are used on the pitch or by police forces in the likes of Los Angeles, Philadelphia and Cincinnati, with or without 6in nails through the middle of them. It's also touch and go whether they're used more for trying to keep law and order or for provoking the breakdown of law and order, judging by the video film one sees nowadays of various police forces in action in the States.

Lexington is horses, horses and still more horses. In addition to the racetrack, the sales, the plastic gloves and surprised expressions and everything else, they have over seventy horse statues all over town, all painted in different colours, different styles, different liveries. On top of that, everywhere you go is called either the Thoroughbred Room, the Stable Door, the Favourite or the Winner. When I checked into my hotel I was convinced I was going to be shown to the Stud Room. Instead I got landed with the Old Nag. Nothing changes.

> The three of them are just about settled now as they race through the first half-mile. They've got a nice lead on the rest of the pack. A nice steady rhythm, a nice spring. Not far behind and going well is Keeneland, a good winner last time out. With a pedigree like his, he should have no problem staying the distance.

Hoop Jr, one of the first horses to be sold in Keeneland in 1943, went on to win the Kentucky Derby. It cost US$10,200. Fourteen others also sold at Keeneland have also gone on to win the Kentucky Derby.

> Home Parks, Stud Farms and Museums was Best Turned-Out in the paddock. He was slow out of the stalls. He's got a lot to find.

Kentucky Horse Park: over 1,000 acres dedicated to the wonderful world of the horse. Fabulous.

Crossing over now from the far side, coming alongside the others, is Kentucky Bluegrass, who's extremely well backed. He's cooking.

Some say that, like all the good things in America, Kentucky bluegrass originally came from England, shipped out as straw packing for all the expensive Wedgwood destined for the poor colonialists' houses. Once here, it adapted, took off and became a big hit. Which, of course, is typical America. They ignore the Wedgwood and go for the packing.

Strung out behind, going along at a good gallop, are Style, Bourbon and Fun People, who's a lovely-fronted filly, unbeaten so far, although it won't be long before she meets her match. But they don't seem worried. Style and Bourbon are enjoying themselves. They've got the edge on Fun People who, like all fillies, is being niggled along.

Style is southern style. Fancy hats, fancy waistcoats, lots of dressing up. Well, until the drink starts flowing, and everyone is swacked on those Goddamned mint juleps. Then anything goes.

Bourbon, I always used to think, was not quite the right thing, until I went to Kentucky and saw how they moved the booze. Especially all those ginned-up old haybags. But after extensive research in the bars of Louisville, Lexington and everywhere in between – especially the one in Bardstown, Kentucky's second oldest city and the 'Bourbon capital of the world', where I saw an old soldier count out all his money on the bar before he began so that he knew how many drinks he could afford – I have to agree that it's pretty good stuff. At least 51 per cent of the grain from which it is distilled must be corn. It cannot be more than 160 proof. It must be aged at least two years in new, charred, white-oak barrels. It cannot be drunk unless you're wearing a cowboy hat, a cowboy shirt, Levi's and cowboy boots and are step-dancin' on the top of the bar of your local. Well, maybe you can forget the cowboy hat. And the funny thing was, the second glass was better than the first, the third better than the second, and the fourth— Wait a minute. Is somebody moving the floor?

The trouble with bourbon is that they try to produce it with all the mystique and tradition of the old Scotch and Irish whiskies but market it like Americans. Today, for example, there are ten distilleries in Kentucky and between them they produce over 200 different kinds of bourbon. I ask you, how can anyone form an honest opinion of that many different kinds of bourbon? The answer is with difficulty.

Many people swear by Makers Mark, which is distilled just outside Loretto. To hear people talk about it, you would think it was hundreds of years old, but it was founded in 1953 by a certain William Samuels. His ambition was to produce a smooth, slightly sweet, upmarket bourbon, not the gutrot that everybody else was churning out at the time. He did it by reducing the amount of rye in the mix. He also decided to rotate all his barrels, not keep some of them tucked away in the hottest part of the warehouse which could then be sold later with a fancy name at a fancy price, like everybody else was doing. Unfortunately, there is not much of it around: only 350,000 cases a year are made. Still, you stand more chance of getting a bottle of Makers Mark than you do of winning the Kentucky Derby. Just.

My favourite bourbon is Blanton's, which is practically made by hand. Every label tells you when it was dumped. Honest. That's what it says. Where it was stored, on which rick and practically the name of the person's grandma who individually selected, filtered and bottled it by hand. Or maybe I remember it because the girl behind the grand old bar in de Sha's, Lexington, 'established 1985', would not belive that I was not Australian. Me? Australian? Flaming Apples, do I sound like a dingbat?

Fun People is fun people. Maybe it was the bourbon, or maybe it wasn't, but I seem to remember everybody in

Kentucky being cheerful, friendly, relaxed. Not the automatic have-a-nice-day cheerfulness you get in some parts of the States, but the normal, genuine cheerfulness you get when you fling open the door of a bar and promise to buy everybody inside all the bourbon they want until they drop.

Last, scraping paint at the back of the field, on the rear side, all alone is, I suppose not surprisingly, the Abbey of Gethsemani. He's the kind of horse John Francome would call a good Christian. If he goes any slower, they should throw a blanket over him.

The Abbey of Gethsemani is way out in the middle of those rolling hills, built about the time of the Civil War, a few miles from where Lincoln was born. His first teacher is buried in the cemetery outside the monastery gates. Gee whizz. It was amazing: I've never known so many Americans keep so quiet for so long. From three o'clock in the morning when we got up – well, when some of us got up – for Vigils, to last thing at night, when even more of us turned up for Compline. And there was no talking along the corridors, no talking in the library, no talking in the dining room during meals. No talking outside in the monastery grounds. It was heaven. As I say, not exactly horse heaven, but heaven just the same.

Along the straight there seems to be some jockeying for position as they kick away and race out to the country, Louisville, Churchill Downs and Lexington still way out front, four lengths, maybe five ahead. Keeneland, sticking like glue to the tail, is coming up strongly. The pace is fast and furious.

The first million-dollar horse sold at Keeneland was a son of Secretariat called Canadian Bound. It happened in 1976. The price: US$1.5 million.

Now look at this. Kentucky Bluegrass is showing plenty of dash. He is coming up strongly. He's now in contention, racing down the centre of the track.

Some say that it's not the bluegrass that makes the bluegrass, it's the marijuana mixed in with it. Way out in the outback, Kentuckians have switched from producing moonshine to cultivating the odd patch of marijuana, hidden away in the middle of their tobacco crops. It's easier, they say. More profitable. It doesn't give you a headache, you can't overdose on it, and what the hell, it makes those horses run faster.

Style, Bourbon and Fun People also look as though they've put down their drinks and are beginning to make up some ground, but they've got it all to do. Come next grass, they could well be up with the leaders.

Style. Well, I say style. They certainly know how to drink. I've been in some sessions in my time but, believe me, never anything like a Kentucky session. Everything starts slow, cool and oh-so-southern polite, but before the first round of mint juu-leps has even left the top of the bar – wowee.

Bourbon. I wanted to visit the distillers of Wild Turkey out at Lawrenceburg, but the town was still recovering from a freak fire which had burned down one of their seven-storey warehouses containing over a million gallons of booze, sending flames leaping 50ft into the sky and most of their precious bourbon into the Kentucky River and from there into the town's water supply. I was told it might still not be safe. Apparently it was the first fire in Kentucky where everybody not only rushed to help but took a bucket with them as well. An empty bucket.

Jim Beam I liked, because it's the only distillery I've been to anywhere in the world which has not only a church but also a cemetery on the company premises. Are they trying to tell me something or are they trying to tell me something? Not even the tobacco companies are that considerate.

I also liked, or at least I think I liked, Labrot and Graham, which I remember at the time sounded like something else. As for Buffalo Trace, Hancock's Reserve and all the others I tried they were, er, fantastic.

Fun people. I met the leader of a greybeard rock group, who drank Black and Tans; a chef who wanted to go to Maine and open a restaurant; a policeman who told me how to recognise the best quality crack; a pillar of the community who was drinking bourbon two glasses at a time and a real kinko who could only have been his wife who was eating the buffet two plates at a time. That was all within five minutes of the first bar I went into.

Still in a world of its own, right out at the back of the field, is the Abbey of Gethsemani.

Unless you're a Thomas Merton fan you won't understand what the Abbey of Gethsemani means. It's a bit like Churchill Downs and racing fans: once it's in your blood it's difficult to shake it off, if that's the right phrase.

A million years ago Thomas Merton was all the rage. Well, around the 1950s, to be precise. A minor lad about town, the son of a not particularly outstanding New Zealand painter, he travelled extensively when he was young. He was on the fringes of the New York scene, a struggling minor poet, and then he gave it all up and entered the Abbey of Gethsemani as a Trappist monk, one of the strictest orders in the Catholic Church. On top of all the usual, they take a vow of silence, sleep in their habits on straw beds and never go anywhere. Merton wrote a book about the whole thing. How he grew up. His travels. How he became a Catholic. How he joined the Trappists. It became an international bestseller, hailed as the twentieth century's answer to *The Confessions of St Augustine*. It still sells widely even today.

Around the final turn into the home straight, with five
furlongs left to travel, Louisville seems to be trying to kick
clear and spear into the lead.

Louisville is the United Parcel Service air hub. Send anything UPS
and they automatically push the envelope through Louisville.
They didn't have to tell me. Somehow I always knew that.

Lexington is still upside and trying to follow him.

In Lexington the name Lewinsky is held in awe, especially
among those looking for strong, sturdy and what are known
locally as upright masculine structures. Major Thomas Lewinski,
a British architect, is credited as the driving force behind their
Greek revival architecture, all clean lines and massive columns:
Doric, plain, Ionic, scroll and Corinthian, highly ornate. Another
architectural name recognised in Lexington with slightly less awe
is Frank Lloyd Wright. Here he experimented with his open-plan,
less-is-more, functional prairie-style homes, making use of what
were then new materials such as steel and reinforced concrete.
   I was told that for some reason women spend their lives
looking for the Wright man while men will go for Lewinsky any
day.

Keeneland is hardening all the time and battling to stay
with the leaders.

Keeneland's record year was 1984, when sales totalled over
US$175,000, over eighty times more than in their first year. The
average sale is nearly US$600,000, over 110 times the opening
average. The highest-priced filly ever sold at auction was a
Seattle Slew called Alchaasibiyeh, which fetched US$3,750,000
in 1984.

Horse Parks, Stud Farms and Museums is being hunted
hard.

The American Saddle Horse Museum is my favourite. It pays tribute to Kentucky's native breed of horse, the Saddlebred.

Fun People is also there, and beginning to take up a prominent position.

The first crowd of fun people I fell into in Lexington told me they were all from the UK, the University of Kentucky. Every time I checked into an hotel after that I put down that I was from the UK, and I got a discount. It's the first time being from the UK has come in handy.

Where there is Fun People there is also Bourbon. They're both coming down the middle side, both galloping hard.

Surprisingly, not all Kentucky is hooked on bourbon. For years it was a dry state. Because of the Bible, say the Godfearing, upright non-drinkers. Because of the moonshiners, say the rest. Many's the top Kentuckian today who's had his education paid for not by IBM or even Berkshire Hathaway stock, but by moonshine.

Even today large parts of Kentucky – seventy-five out of 120 counties – are still dry. Barren is dry. So are Letcher, Clinton and, perhaps surprisingly, Bath. There are even, would you believe, whole golf courses that are dry, though of course, the guys who play golf there go out onto the course with two trolleys. Christian, on the other hand, is wet. So are Marion, Carmel, Perry, Nicholas and Meade. Washington, however, is half dry, half wet. What they call moist.

The Abbey of Gethsemani looks as though it has decided it's had enough. It obviously doesn't want to be considered part of the race. It's standing there, eyes closed.

Merton I first discovered in, of all places, Merton Public Library. I was working at the time on the *Merton and Morden News*, a local newspaper in south London, and doing some research for a local history feature. Instead of Merton, London district, home of Emma, Lady Hamilton, mistress of Lord Nelson, I turned up Merton, Thomas, poet, Trappist, in the United States – biography. I got the book, which in the UK was edited by Evelyn Waugh and called *Elected Silence*, from a line by Gerard Manley Hopkins. I was hooked. From then on I read practically everything Merton ever wrote, and he wrote over fifty books. I also decided that one day I would go to the Abbey of Gethsemani. Years later, I made it.

Four furlongs to home. Churchill Downs is out there by a nose. Three furlongs to go. No, he's not. Keeneland is tucked away behind him.

The Kentucky Derby winner in 1998, Fusaichi Pegasus, was bought at the Keeneland sales earlier the same year for US$4 million.

Two furlongs to go. So are Louisville, Lexington, Horse Parks, Studs and Farms, and, showing no signs of greenness, Kentucky Bluegrass and our three mint ju-leps, Style, Bourbon and Fun People, which are now getting a clear run.

The final furlong. The final furlong. All heads are turned for home. They're racing to the line. About three lengths covers the whole field. They're all throwing their hearts at the winning post. I don't believe it. *I don't believe it!* It's a photo. It's a photo! All of them! On the nose! They're all winners. Except, of course, the Abbey of Gethsemani. He's just standing there, staring up at the sky. But since the last shall be first, he's obviously not worried.

Rhode Island

It was the snowstorm of the century, they said. More than 12,000 homes were damaged or destroyed all the way from

New Jersey, through New York and Connecticut, up to Boston, Massachusetts. Rhode Island was buried under at least 2ft of snow. In some places it was 4ft deep. State highways were blocked. Virtually all of the smaller roads were impassable. Power lines were down. Eighteen people were killed. And more was on the way.

I was in the middle of it, just outside Warwick, in an hotel at a state intersection. The power had been cut, and we were on emergency supplies. Trucks couldn't get through with deliveries. I was surrounded by Americans.

'Trust the Japanese!' an elderly CEO kept screaming at me across reception. 'Just-in-time deliveries? They can keep it.'

The only thing in the kitchen was hamburgers. Which, since I am married to a non-smoking, non-drinking, vegetarian worried about E-numbers, did not necessarily upset me.

'OK, everybody. OK.' The manager, an eager young Moonie in a button-down shirt and regulation suit kept marching up and down the corridors like an old-fashioned town crier. Colonial, of course. 'No need to panic. Everything's under control. Everything's under control.'

A reject from the Chippendales jogged up the corridor after him. 'Hey, man. The Cokes. We're out of Cokes.'

'Christ!' the manager screamed. 'The Cokes! I forgot the Cokes!'

You can always tell when Americans have a crisis. There are no Cokes. Then they immediately all go off into a big hissy fit that gives you confidence that they are the most heavily armed nation in history.

I wasn't worried about the Cokes. I went back to my bourbon. I wasn't worried about the snow, either. I've been to Rhode Island so many times I reckon I can find my way around whatever it's buried under. And for a long time it was buried.

Providence, the capital, is coming along nicely nowadays. It has a smart new railway station, and the town centre has been spruced up. There is a big new convention centre, some new hotels and some very stylish new restaurants. The Capital Grille is one of the best I've been in anywhere in the US. The food, especially the dry-aged steaks, is fabulous. The wine list is fantastic. The service is out of this world. I'd go there any time. In fact, many's the time I've been there at three or four o'clock in the morning – my three or four o'clock in the morning, that is. I've flown into Boston from London, arrived early evening, got a train, a bus or even a limo to Providence and made straight for the Capital Grille. I tell you, whatever the experts say, a couple of large bourbons and a huge plate of potato skins and you soon forget the jetlag.

Why a relatively out-of-the-way town like Providence should have so many terrific restaurants is a mystery. Some say it's because the Mafia spend the week in New York and their weekends in Rhode Island. Whether that's true or not, all I can say is *grazie mille*. Probably the best Italian restaurant I've been to in the US is in Providence.

As for the town itself, they've begun to tackle some of the back streets and no-go areas. They even discovered a river. For generations it had been hidden under masses of road decking. Off came the decking. They lined it up with two other rivers they hadn't lost, the Moshassuck and Woonasquatucket, which are either Welsh or Indian names, or maybe both, brought the whole thing into the centre of town, landscaped it, built bridges across it, put a series of granite platforms down the middle of it and then, presumably as a tribute to sophisticated Welsh or even Indian central-heating technology, stuck wood-burning stoves on top of them.

Now, on summer evenings, the whole of Providence and its third or fourth wife strolls along the new banks of the rivers trying to pronounce their names and enjoying what they call the delights of European sophistication: choking on the smoke from the wood-burning stoves and listening to loudspeakers the size of Welsh harps belting out Maria Callas singing Catalani's famous aria, 'La Wally'. The only thing missing are miners' helmets. The canaries have been used for other purposes.

In the old days, however, it was a mess. The station, which

has now been pulled back about half a mile, used to be almost in the centre of town. Many's the time I caught a train from South Station, Boston, Mass., and by the time it came within hailing distance of Providence, people were scared to get out of their seats, let alone walk along the corridor, open the door and step down on to the platform. The town centre was practically out of bounds day and night. I remember once taking a two-minute walk from the corner of one street to a bookshop on the corner of another. People couldn't believe I didn't get a cab. And the hotels! They were New York back street, 1920. In one I used to stay in there were so many locks and bars and bolts and shutters on the door that by the time I'd finished locking myself in at night it was time to start opening up to get out again the following morning.

Not that, the Capital Grille apart, there's much going on in Providence, which apparently sits on top of seven hills, although for the life of me I can never find any of them.

The First Baptist Church of America, founded by Rhode Island's own founder, Roger Williams, is the very first First Baptist Church of America, if you see what I mean, whereas the Rhode Island State Capitol is only the fourth largest free-standing marble dome in the world. With all that fierce Welsh, non-conformist, dissident hot air around, you'd have thought they would have generated enough support to make it the largest. It looks a bit like Leeds Town Hall with a lick of paint, but for some reason everybody seems to think it's one of the oldest buildings in the world. 'Yes, sir. One of the oldest buildings in the world,' I was assured by a big Rhode Island Democratic honcho who sounded as if his prostate was on the blink, his eyes filling with glycerine left over from the last election.

Benefit Street on College Hill is supposed to be one of the most historic streets in the US because this is where, for the first time, the US government handed out vouchers for cash to the poor and needy. It also boasts four centuries' worth of buildings: clapboard colonial, federal, Greek revival and

Victorian. This covers the length of time it takes to cash the vouchers and for the people in need to receive the benefits.

Just outside Providence is Saunderstown, where I once attended a three-day non-stop Tina Turner concert in a mock Alpine village. Or it could have been an American management conference. It was difficult to tell the difference. Company songs or, as the Americans say, corporate audio identities, are not unusual in the States. Even the big firms of accountants and management consultants have their own company songs. The only ones that don't seem to have them are the dot-coms. But then, they weren't around long enough for anyone to write the chorus, let alone the first verse.

The conference, I remember, started late. There was some big top-management debate about the amount of maple syrup that should be poured all over the Virginia ham, three sunny-side-ups and French waffle for breakfast. When we finally got going the chief executive, who looked as though he had been hitting the magic mushrooms a bit too hard, told us he was scrapping the entire programme for the meeting. Instead he wanted to talk about motivation. Motivation meant a company song. What were our suggestions?

He asked me what I thought. I suggested the one about going up the Swannee. Well, how was I supposed to know he was being serious? It was my first American management conference. I thought it was just the usual let's-have-a-joke warm-up routine, but he was being serious. Serious. SERIOUS. Everybody else, of course, then took it serious, serious, SERIOUS. After hours of agonised discussion it was finally decided that – surprise, surprise – the song should be Tina Turner's 'Simply the Best'. From then on it was nothing but 'Simply the Best' blasted all day and every day through every loudspeaker not only in the Alpine village but within a 200-mile radius of it. Before meetings started, half a dozen times during meetings, after every meeting was over, we all had to stand up, wave our bottles of mineral water in the air and join in 'Simply the Best'.

After my big mistake at the beginning, I was hoping it was going to be my last American management conference. But on the final evening I got a big hug from the CEO and an invitation to the following year's event because, he said, of the wholehearted way I accepted their choice of song, the enthusiastic way I participated in the singing and, even more important, because I encouraged everybody else to join in. What he didn't know was that we'd all been singing 'Simply Divest'.

Newport, of course, used to be simply the best. Thames Street, which was once known as Bloody Alley, was the place to be. It was full of bars, brothels, everything anyone could ever need. Benjamin Franklin, George Washington, Lafayette and the rest of the revolutionary Rep pack used to hang out here; crooks, pirates, every type of adventurer you can imagine made it their home from home. Then came the African slave trade which, probably more than anything else, was responsible for its decline and fall. The city fathers decided in their wisdom to levy a dollar a head on each slave landed and to use the money not for vital social services like more boozing and whoring, but to begin cleaning up and renovating and rebuilding the city. First, just like today's town-planners, they put in fancy cobblestones, and then luxuries like drains and walkways and shopping malls.

Before anyone knew what was happening its reputation had plummeted so far that the likes of the Astors, the Rockefellers, the Vanderbilts and, of course, the Bouviers and Kennedys moved in. The Astors, the Rockefellers and the Vanderbilts, they say, were your ordinary, run-of-the-mill multibillionaires. The Bouviers and the Kennedys were not. They were snobbish. They refused to ride in the same car as their chauffeurs. The effect this had was to drive out the navy, so today Newport is full of nothing but wannabe châteaux and wannabe sailors in their reject Ralph Laurens, bought at factory outlets up and down the country. It's the kind of place where kids give their mothers a mammogram for their birthday.

As for the châteaux, that's what they call them, but they're not so much châteaux as large country houses. True, they're big and impressive, and most of them are set in some fancy gardens, but Château Latour they are not, never mind Château Margaux. Beechwood, the Astors' pad, is, I suppose, OK. The Breakers, the Vanderbilts' Italian Renaissance-style shack, is a bit upmarket. A Great Hall two storeys high, Caen stone columns all over the place. Stained-glass skylights, bronze candelabra. It was here that Grace Vanderbilt insisted on inviting the German ambassador to dinner just as the First World War was about to break out. The staff protested, but she insisted. When the dinner was over and the ambassador was on his way home, all the staff not only quit, they also told her they had all spat in the soup. But a château? Mais non. Similarly, the Elms, which is said to be modelled on the Château d'Asnières near Paris and the Rosecliff on the Grand Trianon near Versailles. The Château-sur-Mer? Now that's pure Victorian.

I went to look at the Bouviers' house, where Jacqueline Bouvier Kennedy was brought up. I thought it would be another mansion, but it looked more like a farmhouse. Across the fields was Eisenhower's old shack. For a while, therefore, the president and his successor were next-door neighbours, officially or unofficially.

My favourite is the Chepstow, a big Italian-style villa of the type you see nestling in the hills deep in the middle of Sicily. The one with all the heavies in sharp suits and dark glasses hanging around outside studying the menus. Well, Italian-Americans have strong connections with Rhode Island. Tiny John O. Pastore, the first-ever Italian American to be elected a state governor, was elected in Rhode Island. 'Rhode Island is the smallest state in the union,' he used to say, 'and I am the smallest governor in the United States.' Mamma mia, how all the guys in dark suits and dark glasses laughed. Newport is also, of course, just a few hours' drive from New York. Not that that's important.

What is important is the role it played in American history. This is where, for the first time in the United States, they played polo.

The Fishy Ones

Some of these states are not just fishy, they stink to high heaven. I don't just mean US senators driving home late with a girl in their car, the car plunging off a bridge on Chappaquiddick Island near Martha's Vineyard, the girl being killed and the driver not bothering to report the accident or the girl's death for nearly ten hours. Nobody is arrested. Nobody is charged. Nobody goes to court. Nobody is responsible. Maybe one day the scales will fall from my eyes and I'll understand why they say the American sense of justice is as tight as a crab's pincer.

Take Massachusetts. It was fishy from the start.

How come the *Mayflower*, under the command of an old whaling captain with forty-seven officers and crew on board, didn't land at Virginia, as it should have done, and ended up at Cape Cod instead?

How come, wherever they talk about the *Mayflower*, the Pilgrim Fathers, the brave, indomitable spirit of the poor, simple, Godfearing Englishmen who left hearth and home and set out packed like sardines for cod's own country, etc. etc., nobody ever mentions all the small fry who were also on board, such as the Dutch, who also happen to know a bit about fish as well? Or the fact that the pilgrims' leader was not your simple, Godfearing, horny-handed son of the soil, but a big fish, a lawyer and judge, a parliamentary draftsman, a big landowner and a textile tycoon? Or that they depended for their livelihood first on selling fish to their enemies, the despised, fish-eating Roman Catholics and, when the English Civil War broke out, meat and veg to the almost equally despised meat-and-two-veg-eating slave-owners and their families?

Neither have I ever been able to understand how, in March

1770, an English soldier on guard duty outside the Customs House, slipping on the snow and ice making his musket go off accidentally, could start the Boston Massacre. Massacre? Only three people were killed in the fighting that erupted afterwards. Which, sorry as I am about the three people, doesn't sound much like a massacre to me.

Then there's the whole Boston Tea Party, Paul Revere business. I can't for the life of me believe that in order to protest against British taxes fifty men, all dressed up as Indians, sashayed down to the harbour and threw over 300 chests of tea into the water. Come on, they're Americans. They must have also thrown in half a million packs of dried milk, 2½ tons of lemons and about 10 million little pink sachets of Sweet 'n' Low. If you ask me, they weren't protesting about the increase of British taxes at all. More likely, Americans being the arch-advocates of free trade, the Earl Greys were protesting about the *abolition* of British taxes. As for the whole 'no taxation without representation' business, Massachusetts and all the others broke away from the UK because they believed so fervently in no taxation without representation. Right? OK, try asking a Boston barman or cab-driver to deduct the Massachusetts sales tax from your bill because you're not entitled to vote in the US, and you'll soon see how much they believe in no taxation without representation. If, that is, you get out alive.

As for Paul Revere, he was a teabag if ever there was one. How could he have galvanised opposition to the British by riding through the night screaming 'The British are coming! The British are coming!' when they were already there? In any case, it wasn't just the British. The Germans were there as well, with their smooth-bore muskets which, at a range of 100yds, had a margin of error of no less than 3ft in any direction. And riding through the night? He only rode a measly 20 miles. I do that before breakfast and I don't make a fuss about it. In any case, on 4 June 1781, Captain Jack Jouett rode 40 miles non-stop from Cuckoo Tavern to Charlottesville to warn Thomas

Jefferson, Patrick Henry and the rest of the Rep pack that the British were coming. Israel Bissell rode nearly 350 miles in five days. As soon as shots rang out on Lexington Green, he was on his horse and going like the clappers to Worcester, to Connecticut, to New York and finally to Philadelphia, yelling 'To arms! To arms! The war has begun!' Where's all the publicity for them?

Some say Jouett got the shoulder because Longfellow couldn't think of a rhyme for Jouett, which can't be true. I mean, what about blue it, do it, suet, to it, woo it? Well, maybe they're right. As for Israel Bissell, whatever he did, he wasn't considered a kosher American hero. These were, of course, pre-Lieberman times. Now he would probably have been nominated as vice-president and got a big convention smacker from Tipper, God help him.

And then what about Bunker Hill? The Americans celebrate it as a victory, but to me, whichever way you look at it, it was a defeat. The battle didn't take place on Bunker Hill anyway, but on Breed's Hill nearby. Funny, that.

And how could Massachusetts go on and on about the evils of slavery, condemn the south, risk in 1820 the break-up of the States itself and in 1850 provoke the Civil War when all the time it was itself practising almost equal discrimination against black people? Blacks were forced to cough up anything up to $500 as a guarantee of good behaviour, they were virtually banned from voting and there were colour bars in trade unions.

It didn't stop there, of course. Don't you think it's fishy the way the Americans are still rewriting history? I don't want to labour the point because I know any fairminded person will agree with me, so I won't mention, for example, the film *U.571*, which recreates an important and historic event in the history of the Royal Navy as an all-singing-and-dancing American triumph. Neither will I mention *The Colditz Story*, which shows what British prisoners of war can achieve under American leadership. Or *The Longest Day* or *Saving Private Ryan*, which both make out that D-Day was pretty well an American-only affair.

It wasn't. There were more British and Canadian troops on the beaches of Normandy than American soldiers.

Instead I'll mention, just in passing, *The Patriot*, which showed how the beautiful, innocent, family-loving Americans fought in 1776 for the side that abolished slavery. They couldn't have. Slavery wasn't abolished until 1865. How pitched against them was the cruel, ruthless might of the great British empire. It wasn't. It was only a handful of English gentlemen. How British soldiers set fire to whole villages. They didn't. How they burned the inhabitants alive. They didn't. How the kids they didn't burn alive they killed separately one by one, shrieking mindlessly as they did so that famous, blood-curdling English scream that has echoed down through the centuries: 'Stupid boy.'

The other thing that strikes me as fishy, Nantucket apart, is how a state with such a casual regard for honesty and integrity could end up as the intellectual centre of the whole USA. A bunch of slippery eels, the lot of them.

Maine, though, is pure fish, so it can't help being fishy. It was discovered and founded by one shipload of fishermen after another. First, Leif Ericsson and his merry band of Viking fishermen, who stumbled across the jagged coastline and landed there several thousand years before you-know-who. The problem was that no sooner had he landed than he realised he'd left his mobile phone behind, and promptly headed home, never to return again. Then, they say, came the Irish, the Eskimos, the occasional Russian submarine and finally, of course, a shipload of dissenting English fishermen who made it all official. Although how they thought they could live a life dedicated to poverty, austerity and simplicity surrounded by nothing but lobsters I have no idea. All that is fishy enough, but tell me, if you lived in a state founded by fishermen, whose biggest industry is fish and where tourists pour in for fishing, what would you choose as your state symbol? That's right: the pine tree.

Maryland, too, is as fishy as hell. They say it is named after

Charles I's French wife. Her name was Henrietta. So how come the chowderheads didn't call it Henriettaland, or even Henland? It could then have taken its rightful place on the perch alongside Kentucky and Rhode Island. And how come Cecil, Baron Baltimore could found the original settlement when he didn't have title to the land, whereas William Claiborne, a Kentish-born fur-trader, did? How come he was allowed to claim that all colonists would enjoy 'the full rights of Englishmen' when they quite clearly didn't? How come, during the English Civil War, a pirate, Richard Ungle, could plunder the entire state claiming he had been authorised by the English Parliament to do so when he hadn't? How come they could pass a Toleration Act that made it a crime to call anyone a 'Heretic, schismatic, idolator, Puritan, independent, Presbyterian, Popish priest, Jesuit, Jesuited papist, Roundhead, Separatist and the like', and then, in the next breath, turn against the Quakers so fiercely that they declared they were better treated by the Indians? As for the blacks, they weren't considered worthy of any kind of tolerance at all, especially the 10,000 criminals dumped there between 1717 and 1767. They were treated a million times worse than even the poor Quakers.

I'll tell you another fishy thing about Henriettaland. It's strange that Baltimore is not more German. After all, they virtually built it.

Fishy, that.

Massachusetts

Massachusetts has everything. I should know, I've criss-crossed it a million times, although the one place I've never been to is Springfield, home of the Basketball Hall of Fame, where I have a couple of aunts and a cousin. But that's families for you. Or at least, that's the Biddlecombe family for you.

Bawhston, or rather Boston, as I think I've said many times before, is one of my favourite American cities, if not my habsholoote favourite. If I had to be bawn Amerikern, it would be a reahl pleashaw to be bawn in Bawhston and speak propuh English. Although why they call it Beantown I don't know unless, American education being what it is, it's to recall the source of the tea that went into those famous teachests.

I adoah Beacon Hill on the north side of Boston Common, with its narrow eighteenth-century streets where they keep the gaslights on day and night, presumably because they've heard they're not dependent on the Arabs for the fuel. Charles Street, at the bottom of the hill, has the only bookshops I've ever found that have a special category for anonymous authors. Newbury Street looks to me like an upmarket residential street that has fallen on bad times and has opened up the ground floors of the houses as shops. Bostonians, however, insist that it is one of the three most expensive retail sharping areas in the States. It's so expensive that the dress shops are called wearhouses. None of them is allowed to sell secondhand clothes. Instead they call them 'closet clothes', because they've just come out of the closet. They don't have anything as common as litter bins. They have wine barrels instead.

There is a pet shop called A Fish on a Leash and, one of my favourites, Emak and Bolios, sells fabulous frozen yoghurts. Eat their whole range of thirty-five in one go and they give you a prize: another range of thirty-five.

'But why Emak and Bolios?' I once asked them.

'Everybody calls their shop after the owners. We thought the customers were more important, so we named it after our first two customers,' they told me. Only in Boston.

Washington Street, the old theatre district between Boyston and Kneeland, the so-called Combat Zone, is a bit run down and seedy, but I've never had any problems there. In any case, it's a good short-cut to South Station.

I also, whenever I get the chance, take a stroll across Boston Common, which is slap-bang in the middle of town. Not because it's pleasant and relaxing, or because of the sights you see, but because it's got what I think is the most miserable statue I've seen anywhere in the world: four broken-down knights on even more broken-down horses which, the

Bostonians always say, is Ted Kennedy's campaign committee preparing for a shot at the presidency after that incident with the car.

Chinatown is great fun; North End, the Italian, or rather Sicilian, end of town, is even more fun. Here you realise that Boston is not 100 per cent Irish after all, although if you even think such a thing in Boston, you'll be out with your balaclava helmet down around your knees in no time at all, because everyone you meet, whether they're Chinese, Italian or even American, makes out they're feckin' Oirish, as they say, or if not 100 per cent, then pretty damn 99.9 per cent Oirish.

Late one evening I went into a Chinese restaurant down near the back of South Station. It was in the middle of the Big Dig. Practically the whole of the centre of the city was being torn apart so they could push an enormous underground tunnel from one side to the other. The result was total chaos. Instead of sitting for hours in a jam, I thought it would be better to eat then try to get a cab when things calmed down. A waiter who looked like Mao Tse Tung on steroids ambled across to me.

'Sohowyedointoday?' I drawled, as they all do.

'Oh, mighty,' he sighed. 'No complaints at all now, Tankbitogod, though me feet, me feet were killin' me earlier.'

'You're . . . you're . . .' I stumbled.

'Oh God, I am, tankgod,' he handed me a grease-stained menu. 'Sure, isn't it the same wherever you go in this feckin' town?'

I took the menu. 'So where are you from?'

'Dublin. Me mother, the Lord have mercy on her, a blondie gerril, not a bolter on her, fell in with this sailor. Quare, mighty quare. But here I am. Tubercular. Tongue eight times normal size. Beer gut a sumo wrestler would die for.'

'So how long you been here?'

''Tis a million years next Tuesday, God bless ye. Now, if ye think I've got time to stand here all day listening to an old knacker like yeself, I haven't. It's flyin' here. Now, will ye cast your eye on the watchamacallit? I haven't the time to be talking to ye. This is not feckin' Oireland, I'll be telling ye.'

I didn't want to upset him so I ordered a 7, a 12, a 23 and a small 31. I thought if I ordered the 26 he might throw a tantrum.

Across the river is Cambridge and, of course, Harvard and MIT, the Massachusetts Institute of Technology, which everybody says is the intellectual centre of the US. All I can say is, it doesn't look like it. It looks more like a training centre for salesmen who want to administrate their way to becoming personnel managers. Neither do the staff look particularly smart. What always amazes me is why any top businessman would want to go there to be lectured at by a bunch of high-class string-pullers who have little or no real, hands-on, get-the-business-or-we-die business experience. School is school, business is business. I don't see many Harvard business brains sitting on the boards of major companies, or even the subsidiary boards of major companies. A lot of them, though, got caught up in the dot-com boom, which only goes to prove my point.

What they are good at is writing long, long, detailed, technical books on all aspects of management which always make me think 'What the hell am I doing wasting my time on this junk when I could be reading something far more worthwhile like the latest James Ellroy?' They are also good at thinking up theories and concepts like T-Groups, Learning Organisations, Quality Circles, Corporate Culture, Total Quality Management, Vision, Re-engineering and Empowerment before they all come crashing down to earth. But ask them to run a hot-dog stand and they haven't got the testicular fortitude – unless it's in Russia. Go into any coffee bar in Harvard and you hear stories about how, after the Berlin Wall came down, any Harvard business professor with even half an algorithm to his name was hotfooting it to Russia on a US government grant not only to help them set up their own Western-style businesses but to ensure that they tucked away a personal share of the action as well. If that's true, it's another theory to add to the list: Corruption.

Women, of course, have nothing to do with any of this. To them lecturing and writing books and attending courses and travelling and advising the world are of no account. The only important thing as far as they are concerned is their hair, which we have on the highest possible intellectual authority in the land, former first lady and senator for New York, Hillary Clinton. Your hair and how you wear it are the most important factors in your life, she told a group of graduating students at Yale. 'Pay attention to your hair,' she intoned. 'Because everybody else will.' Eleanor Roosevelt, thou shouldst be living at this hour.

Outside Boston, on weekdays I'm usually dragging myself up and down Interstate 90, Massachusetts' own Electronics Valley, second only to Silicon Valley in attracting investment and venture capital. Most of the big electronics companies are there; so, too, are most of the major electronics subcontractors, which build the machines that enable the electronics companies to build the products they build. I'm not technical – I'm still amazed every time I turn on the electricity switch by the door and the gaslight comes on – but from what I've seen up and down Interstate 90, the companies behind the companies that give us all the latest electronic whizz-bangs deserve some share of the glory. Take microchips. A microchip is a microchip. Right? Wrong. It's a million different components researched, developed and agonised over day and night by thousands of different companies working in the tiniest, tiniest dimensions. Then, once they've decided what they want to make, another 1,000 companies agonise day and night over the best, quickest, cheapest, safest, way of doing it. From what I've seen up and down Interstate 90 – the technology, the people, the time, the dedication – each microchip should cost $10,000, if not $100,000. Instead they are being produced for pennies. It's crazy.

But Massachusetts is not just electronics, it's also big in jewellery and precious metals. Attleboro, Millis, Mansfield and a thousand other towns are full of businesses, large and small, making all the bits and pieces that go into earrings, necklaces, bracelets or whatever for everybody from Wal-Mart to Tiffany's. One company I once visited told me that their fastest-growing line was what they called breastee jewellery, for the woman who is not, as they say, as well endowed physically as she might be financially. Attleboro especially they call the jewellery capital of the world, or rather, the jewellery component capital of the world, although to look at it you wouldn't think it had two papier-mâché rings to rub together. See what they do with a kilo of gold, what they mix in with it, and you'll never think of buying jewellery again. At least, not as an investment. It's too big a risk. You might buy it for other reasons, but that, I suppose, is another risk.

Weekends, if I get the chance, I'm either out exploring the bars of Boston – ''Tis a pint I'll be having, tanksbetogod. And one for yourself while you're at it' – or traipsing round the likes of Concord, where, thanks to the fortune his family made out of manufacturing pencils, Henry David 'Simplify, Simplify' Thoreau lived in a 10x5ft cabin by the pond for two years and two months in complete solitude, apart from the time he spent going into town twice a week to do his shopping. Or Plymouth. Or shuffling around some old colonial towns with, if you can imagine such a thing, the odd village store built as far back as 1880. Of course, they probably applied for an environmental impact study way back in 1757 but as they couldn't afford to make any campaign donations they had to take their place in the queue like everybody else.

The trouble is, the people are more Olde England than New England. I once went into a bookshop in Lexington where, they say, the American revolution began. The old bag running the place, who looked as though she had just survived a fatal accident, kept following me around. Whenever I picked up a book she'd bark, 'What are you looking at that for?'

'Well, it's a book,' I would reply nervously. 'Isn't that what you're supposed to do with—'

'Be careful. Don't drop it.'

'No. I can assure you, I have in my time looked at one or two—'

'Are you going to buy it?'

Well, I suppose it made a change from the usual have-a-nice-day routine.

Salem I steer clear of. I've had enough of old witches to last me a lifetime. So I don't particularly fancy visiting their Witch Museum, their local school, Witchcraft Heights, or the manufacturers of Ye Witchcraft Game, Park Bros, who also, incidentally, invented that equally absurd and preposterous game Monopoly. I've also managed to steer clear of Gloucester, which calls itself the whale-watching capital of the world. Not that I've got anything against whales. It's just that the local hero is Clarence Birdseye, who invented fishfingers here in 1925. And I don't want anything to do with them, either.

I did, however, once force myself to go to Cape Cod. I wasn't going to. I wasn't keen on the idea of wandering around in a Black Dog Café T-shirt watching WASPs hyper-ventilate on the thrills of knee-pitting, but in the end I gave in. I'm tempted to say it was all a cod, but it wasn't. Or at least, the fourteen or was it fifteen different towns along the codpiece of land that juts out into the Atlantic from the main-land were not. But it might have been the number of bottles of chardonnay I needed to wash down all that seafood. Anyhow, I vaguely remember that for some reason I ended up in a town called Sandwich. My goodness, for a moment I thought I saw Jonathan Aitken bathed in a shaft of light telling someone or other on high how he could re-equip the heavenly battalions.

I've never been to Provincetown, way out on the furthest point of the Cod, where the pilgrims originally landed in 1620. You can just imagine the excitement they must have felt at being able to get there without the help of Richard Branson and a bunch of stroppy, deadend, overmanicured hairballs making a fuss about your hand luggage. But as it's buried under

30,000 tourists every summer, I don't particularly want to go there. I must also admit that I can't get used to everyone referring to it as P-town. Maybe I'll have another bottle of chardonnay. That might change my mind. I might even go and visit my relatives as well.

Maine

Maine is supposed to be nothing but lobsters, lobsters and still more lobsters. Lobsters for breakfast. Lobsters for brunch. Lobsters for dinner. They even, God help us, do a yukky lobster ice cream. The reason lobster is so popular? There is hardly any cod left.

For me, however, Maine means the most expensive cab ride I've ever had anywhere in the world. One Friday evening I was in their biggest city, Portland, meandering from bar to bar, trying, for the life of me, to get a drink. Every one was packed with people, more like sardines than lobsters.

'You'll have to wait an hour. At least. I can't serve you now. Now, if you'll just move . . .'

'Thirty minutes. Forty-five. No, it'll be an hour before . . .'

'A beer? Are you kidding? Can't you see all these people?'

Was the president in town? Was Madonna giving a free concert? Was Elvis returning to earth? No, it was something far more important, the highlight of their social calendar. An ice show was in town. Nobody, no bars, no restaurants, had time or space for anybody or anything.

That was when I decided to quit Portland which, for all its so-called Victorian touristy charm, is not exactly one of the world's great cities. Especially if you can't get a drink, let alone a meal, on a Friday night.

The following morning, early, very early, I tried some of the towns scattered along the famous 'craggy' coast – 255 miles as the crow flies, 3,500 by land. They all seemed to be full of boats and yachts, more Hull than Monte Carlo, for catching lobsters. I say catching lobsters: it looked to me as though there were so many lobsters out there that they were practically climbing into the boats voluntarily just to get some breathing space. Some of them were so desperate for air they were scrambling in still chewing the bait. As a result the poor, hardworking fishermen are forced to drive the latest pick-ups and SUVs in order to survive.

In spite of that, everyone, I reckon, was not only a Republican but had enormous respect for George Bush Snr. Ask any of them about their business, and all they would say was, 'Watch my ships.'

The other thing I discovered was that the poor, hardworking fishermen don't just catch any old lobsters, they catch their very own lobsters. They divide up stretches of the sea among themselves and fish their own areas. Like oilfields, they are bought, sold or passed down from one generation to the next.

At first I thought of going to Bethel. A real gonzo I'd met in Portland around midnight, when I finally managed to get a beer, told me that at Bethel they were planning to hold the first-ever North American Wife-Carrying Championships. I thought it might be fun to see red-blooded Americans carrying off their own wives. After all, I've been to plenty of places where I've seen them carrying off other people's. But when I discovered that the plan was to encourage the poor, downtrodden husbands, who've already got more than enough to contend with, to carry their own wives back to their own homes, I decided against it. I didn't want to be seen doing anything to insult the oh-so-sensible, equality-minded sensitivities of the wives – and there is, of course, no such thing as a North American Husband-Carrying Championships. I also thought that watching guys struggling through life with their wives on their backs might be too much for me.

I wondered about New Gloucester where, I was told, there was the last remaining Shaker community in the States. But much as I would have liked to have visited them, I didn't quite fancy the idea of standing there on the outside, pressing my nose up against the glass and gawping at people who have the courage to live their lives the way they want to live them.

In desperation, I decided instead to head for Kennebunkport, ex-President George Bush's home town. Money, luxury hotels, bars, maybe a whole string of enormous homes or châteaux. A bit like Newport, Rhode Island, or the Hamptons, Long Island. That's what I thought it was going to be like, but I couldn't have been more wrong. It's a collection of some rather smart blue-rinse buildings, huddled together on either side of a circular turntable bridge over what can only be described as a muddy creek. Like something out of a Hitchcock movie. Or, if you can do joined-up reading, like something out of a W.G. Sebald novel.

I checked into the first hotel I came to, the Kennebunkport Inn, which was very Laura Ashley and had an Iranian chef called Mo, short for Mohammed, and a tall, stooping barman. He reminded me of a retired philosophy professor who'd put Descartes before the horse and wondered why, when it wouldn't drink, nobody heard the noise it wasn't making, either. It was out of season and the place was empty. In fact, I was the only one there.

I took a stroll through the town. Within three minutes I was back at the hotel. The barman, who obviously believed in the principle of differential treatment, was nowhere to be found. I took another stroll. Within two minutes I was back at the bar. Coming in as I was going out was a man who looked as though he believed in the twenty-five-hour clock. He told me that the local council wanted to erect a statue of George Bush Snr in the middle of town, but the only site they could find was opposite a Chinese restaurant. They decided against it in case the statue threw up.

My next attempt was more successful. Well, slightly more successful. I saw signs outside banks boasting proudly that they had 'community roots since 1871' and signs outside shops proclaiming to the world that they were run by a family and not by a parent company, and that they were closed so they could go on 'hiatus'. I stumbled into the Literary Bean Café, which turned out to have three small bookcases of secondhand paperbacks and mugs of watery coffee.

I found a tiny restaurant which was still serving what they called 'Breakfast Specials from the North Pole'. I asked some overheated Eskimo Nell what a Breakfast Special from the North Pole was.

'Corned-beef hash,' she smarmed. 'It's Santa's favourite.'

I fled.

Instead I had lunch in a shack on the other side of the bridge where the lobster came in a pie and the blueberry pie came as a soup.

I also discovered a roaring trade in secondhand wine bottles. Apparently, when George and wife, Barbara, go anywhere in Kennebunkport for a meal, visitors and tourists want to grab their empty wine bottles as a souvenir. The descendants of the Pilgrim Fathers give them the bottles and then the descendants of the Dutch immigrants charge up to $20 each for them. The descendants of Italian immigrants charge for every empty bottle they can lay their hands on, whether or not George Bush has been in the same room as it, let alone drunk from it, making Kennebunkport the only place in the world where the wine bottles are worth more empty than they are full.

Back at the hotel I found the barman, who turned out to have been an editor on *Time* magazine, a friend of the founder, Henry Luce, and a drinking buddy of more or less everyone in the United States. But he couldn't find the booze. Or, rather, he couldn't get to the booze because he couldn't undo all the locks protecting it. So I spent the evening in what was virtually a dry bar, surrounded by empty wine bottles, drinking the local homemade brew. But it was worth it. We spent the evening reminiscing and gossiping and pretending to get bombed out of our minds on beer that was about 0.001 per cent proof.

One story I remember. The philosopher barman, who was a dedicated conspiracy theorist, told me he had just had the shock of his life. His mother had recently died. She had been a pillar of the local establishment, well regarded, well respected, practically an icon. People would go to her for advice. She always preached the strictest of strict codes and behaviour. While he was sorting through her house, deciding what to keep, what not to keep, he opened her jewellery box. Inside was a very well-used cocaine spoon. I had another watery beer to help him get over the shock.

The following morning came the big problem: snow. Tons of it. It was the heaviest snowfall of the year. That evening I had to be across country in Manchester, New Hampshire. I discovered that a shuttle bus ran from Portland to Manchester. I could pick it up in the Parking Rite Lot only ten minutes away, near Exit 3 of the Maine Turnpike, heading south, just outside Kennebunk. Mo gave me the name of the local taxi company. Easy, I thought. I'll call them early, book a car and I'll be there waiting when the shuttle bus arrives.

I rang the taxi number.

'I'm sorry,' said the usual snappy woman's voice the other end of the line. 'John's not working today. He's got a cold.'

'John's not working today. He's got a cold?' I repeated.

Good God almighty. What kind of country is this? This is America. Twenty-four hours a day, round-the-clock, non-stop service, service, service. But she was adamant. John had a cold. He wasn't working.

'OK, can you give me the number of some of the other taxi companies in town, and I'll call them.'

'No,' she snarled. 'John is the only taxi company in town.'

The only taxi company in town? Heavens above, this is Kennebunkport. This is where an ex-president lives. This is America.

What should have been simple now became a nightmare. I phoned taxi firms up the road in Kennebunk, in Kittery, in Biddeford, in nearly every town in Maine. Nobody answered the phone, or the drivers were off sick, or there was no way they could get through the snow to reach me, let alone make the Maine Turnpike. I was on my own. The great American dream does not exist in Maine.

The only taxi I could find to take me on the ten-minute journey from Kennebunkport to meet the shuttle bus at Exit 3 of the Maine Turnpike had to come through the snow and ice all the way from Portland, a million miles away. The fare was $100. But slipping, sliding and once almost careering off the road in the thick snow and ice, we made it to the parking lot for the shuttle bus. The cab-driver, another Maine service-to-the-customer freak, wanted to drop me there in the snow and head back to Portland in case he got stuck. No thought for me. Ten minutes out in that snow, and I'd have been doing my Captain Oates impersonation. I made him stay until the bus came. Then I gave him the equivalent of about five slap-up lobster dinners.

But don't worry. If you want to go to Maine, there's a much easier and a much cheaper way. Go bananas aboard the flight to wherever else you're going in the States. The airlines have this secret agreement that if anybody should as much as raise an eyebrow at the completely impossible service to which they are subjected flying across the Atlantic they will, in the most friendly manner possible, make an unscheduled stop at Bangor, Maine and hand them over to the full majesty of Maine law, under which just even hinting that you might be considering asking for a second microbottle of the airline's lousy wine could land you in jail for up to six months. Actually ask for one and it could be the electric chair.

Maryland

At first I thought Bawlmer, I mean Baltimore, was simply the other end of the Washington–Baltimore Parkway. But as the traffic got worse and worse, I began to realise that Baltimore is more than just a never-ending line of trucks. It actually exists in its own right. Well, just about. Most of the time it gives the impression it is just about hanging on by its fingertips, but at least it's still there. At one time, though, it was the fastest-growing city in America and probably the fastest-growing anywhere. Barnham's City Hotel which, with 200 rooms, was twice as big as anything in Europe, was the world's first luxury hotel.

The Inner Harbour is, of course, the big thing. They go on and on and on about it all the time. The first inner-city regeneration programme in the US, a new concept in tourist/visitor dynamics, a revolution in rehab. The waterfront is completely unlike any other part of the US I've come across, I'll give them that. It's all shops and bars and restaurants, oh yes, and a bit of an open-air theatre where you can get bored out of your mind by a bunch of wastepaper baskets you wouldn't pay to go and watch in a million years. Especially as most of them seem to be covered in gold paint and stand stock still for hours on end. And they wonder why even the Indians called the place Patapsco, which means boring. Moored in the harbour is the 145-year-old USS *Constellation*, the last ship built by the US Navy whose secrets were not stolen by the Chinese.

Lexington Market across the way is far more fun. It's more natural and cheaper as well. There's a lot more excitement in Little Italy. But then, Little Italies all over the States tend to be exciting. There's also a lot to be said for Roland Park, which prides itself on the fact that all its houses still have a front porch, although how long that's going to last is debatable.

But the most amazing place of all is the Baltimore Civil War Museum, near to where the first people were killed in the Civil War. If the first shots were fired in Massachusetts, all I can say is that either they were the unluckiest people in the world, or these guys had some pretty fantastic weaponry. I must ring up the Chinese and ask them about it. The other thing that's odd about the Civil War Museum is that it is in the old train station, while the train museum is in an old roundhouse.

Not that I'm giving Baltimore the bird. The man who did that was Edgar Allan Poe, hailed by the Americans as a second-grade before-midnight Stephen King. In fact, he did more than give them the bird. He gave them the Raven, which he named after the local football team. I'm not a great Poe fan, but to give you an idea of how exciting the nightlife is in Baltimore – not for nothing is it the national funeral directors' favourite convention city – I've spent many a happy hour at his graveside at Westminster Churchyard, where ghouls rush in, especially on 19 January, his birthday, when somebody leaves him three roses and a bottle of cognac. Some say one of the roses is for him, one for his wife and one for his mother-in-law, who is buried with him. Which tells you what his chances are of getting any peace in the hereafter. As for the cognac, I know I would need more than a bottle a year to put up with my wife and mother-in-law in such close proximity twenty-four hours a day, 365 days a year. In any case, I always thought his favourite drink was a hundred-year-old Emilio Lustau Amontillado.

There's no way the anonymous donor can be a friend of Poe. He's more likely to be a reject from the House of Usher. A real friend would have dug him up years ago and shipped him back to Boston, where he came from. There he would have the time of his life, especially with his wife and mother-in-law still in Baltimore. Even if he was dead.

What I did discover while wandering round his graveside in the middle of the night was where he got the idea for his House of Usher: Suitland and Fort Meade. Both towns are terribly ush-ush. Suitland, which is more open-necked shirt and pair of slacks land than suitland, is home to the US National Maritime Intelligence Center, which analyses everything US nuclear-powered subs hear all around the world, whenever they're not entertaining visiting dignitaries or smashing into innocent Japanese fishing boats. If a Russian nuclear sub sinks mysteriously during naval exercises in the Barents Sea, they know about it in Suitland, Maryland before Brassbuttonland knows about it in Moscow.

As for Fort Meade, it's the world centre for land-based intelligence. Make a telephone call, send a fax or e-mail anyone anywhere in the world, and it will end up on the supercomputers tucked away deep in the heart of Fort Meade. For this is the home of Echelon, the round-the-world spy-on-everything computer operation which the French, because they were excluded from it, say exists and the US, Britain, Canada,

Australia and New Zealand, because they are all in on it, say doesn't exist. I'm no sage in Baltimore, all I know is that when I've been there I haven't seen an awful lot of hi-tech equipment all over the place bearing any resemblance to all the hi-tech equipment I didn't see around GCHQ in Cheltenham either. As for that e-mail you sent this morning, be careful. They're on to you already.

Not that I know anything about Suitland or Fort Meade, honest. I only stumbled across them because I was staying once at the Holiday Inn on the wrong side of the Inner Harbour. Across the road was a string of scruffy bars. In one of them one evening I met two overworked, underpaid, middle-aged, dedicated, patriotic flatheads. You know the type. A pulse, a sparkling urine sample, the ability to eat hamburgers while watching Oprah at least twenty-five times a week. Top-rank secret-service officers. One of them, who looked as though he'd had three-o'clock-in-the-morning dumps for the whole week, kept jumping all over the bar and giving me graphic descriptions of the best way to kill a man. 'Put your fingers here.' He jammed his fingers behind his ears. 'Put your fingers there.' Now he jammed them by the side of his neck. 'Smash his head between your fists.' He smashed his hands on the bar.

The other man, who looked as though he'd reached thirty-nine some years earlier and decided to stay there, was obviously very attached to his young niece, who was with him for the evening. He gave me not only the lowdown on Suitland but on Fort Meade as well. How long they had been operating, how far they could stretch, how they could find out what anybody was saying or even thinking anywhere in the world. I wish I'd taken down everything he told me, especially the top-secret plan he said he was working on to zap millions of volts of electricity into big military computers all over Russia, not only to take them out but to make it look as though something inside them had gone wrong and they had destroyed themselves. On the other hand, from what I remember, his niece did take down everything she could.

Having got the lowdown on Suitland and Fort Meade, I made my way to the state capital, Annapolis, where they signed the treaty which saw the end of the American revolution. The trouble is, the news doesn't seem to have trickled down yet, which is probably what comes of having the French in on the act.

I got dragged around the town by some demented eighty-year-old Welsh throwback dressed up as Merthyr Tydfil's answer to Scarlett O'Hara. As she flounced towards me in her full *Gone With the Wind* regalia, the pillars of the State House quivering behind her, suddenly I could see the attractions of spending the rest of my life down a coalmine.

Cadets at the Naval Academy she called middies, presumably Welsh for midshipmen. Students at St John's she called Johnnies, and with a flourish declared that in summer the lawn in front of the college was littered with Johnnies. Standing at the back of the Naval Academy, looking as though her shingles had broken loose, her ginger wig slightly off-centre, the awe in her voice worthy of Catherine Zeta Jones studying the size of her prenuptial agreement, she proclaimed that we were privileged to be looking at 'the largest roof of any US Navy canteen anywhere in the world'.

Well, I'm sorry, but I couldn't help it. I just collapsed.

'What about the dustbins?' I can remember gasping. 'Are they also . . . ?'

I got the stare.

'Someone,' she pronounced crisply, 'has got a toothache this afternoon.'

The Veggie Ones

The veggie states are like veggieburgers. Pathetic. Tasteless. Nondescript. And liable to make anyone with at least one red corpuscle left in their body throw up. On this basis, both Delaware and Kansas are eminently qualified. Delaware because even though it has evolved into a major commercial centre, everybody I came across seemed to want to deny its very existence, and Kansas because everyone I met there appeared to be not only a complete vegetable but eager to deny any kind of evolution at all.

Look at American history – quick, in case you miss it – and you can't deny that they're vegetables. Take Delaware, which was more or less saved by Lord de la Ware. The original settlers were ready to give up and go home when suddenly, like the 5th Cavalry, Lord de la Ware arrives on the scene with a relief convoy of three ships and persuades them to stay, stick it out, stiff upper lip and all that. They do as the good lord tells them and, of course, win through. In humble gratitude, they decide to name the state after him – but get his name wrong. How much of a vegetable do you have to be not to be able to spell De la Ware?

Come the Civil War they were as solid for the Union as a wet cabbage. They were for Abe, for everything he stood for and everything he wanted to do, but they quibbled about it all. They didn't see why they should be told this, forced to do that, coerced into not doing the other. They were worse than a bunch of Florida state officials trying to organise an election. Finally, the clincher: they were colonised largely by Swedes.

Kansas, you probably instinctively feel, should be red meat. No way. Ranching ain't no longer what it used to be. The days of enormous herds of cattle on open ranges are long gone. Today it's all young beasts kept in pens, vegetables, grain, hormones and get them to market as quickly as possible before the goddamn price collapses.

The Chisholm Trail, huge stockyards, Abilene, Dodge City, the cowboy capital of the world. None of them believed in evolution, in keeping up with the times. They thought, like the dinosaur, they were going to live for ever. Today the most exciting thing in Dodge City is the Kansas Teachers' Hall of Fame. Instead of huge 52oz steaks, what were they eating in the Riverside Park? Quiche.

The laugh is, however, that vegetarians all over the world

who make a big fuss about even having a meeting are happily eating meat products supplied by the veggie states. What do cottage cheese, sour cream, yoghurt, margarine, marshmallows, milkshakes, gumdrops, chewing gum and a thousand other products have in common? The hides and bones of cattle or, if you're not worried about quality, pigs. Then there is the whole question of flavours and colours. French fries contain flavours derived from animal products. Additives providing a pink colour come from crushing the bodies of the female Dactylopius Coccus Costa, a tiny Dactylopius Coccus that gorges itself on red cactus berries which turn its eggs pink and Costa a fortune to breed and harvest in Peru and the Canary Islands. Over 50,000 of them and you've got enough to colour all the strawberry and fruit yoghurts you'd need to last you a good few animal rights demonstrations. It's the same with beer and wine. They are made with the aid of finings. Finings contain casein, egg white or isinglass – in other words, gelatine.

About the only genuine, guaranteed, 100-per-cent vegetarian product you can trust in the States is pizza. There I've seen a range specially made for vegetarians, with added pepperoni for extra flavour.

Delaware

Going to Delaware, I thought, would be easy. The second-smallest state – or, as they say, the forty-ninth largest – in the Union. The first to ratify the US Constitution, presumably because they could twist everybody's arm in a single morning. A nice quiet little hideaway, I was told, only a couple of miles from New York and a couple more from Washington.

A nice, quiet little hideaway? It is such a nice, quiet, little hideaway that it is impossible to get to. The great American 'expert assistance – whenever you need it' Express even told me it didn't exist. And, my God, were they expert about it.

I called the Visitor Information Centre in the state capital, Dover. 'Hi,' I said, dropping into America-speak. 'I've heard all about you. How do I get to you from Newark, New Jersey? I've got a meeting in Newark on Wednesday. I've got to be in Miami on Friday. I thought I'd . . .'

'I've no idea,' replied the automatically programmed have-a-good-day chirpy hinky on the other end of the line.

'But you must have. What's the nearest airport?'

'I've no idea. Call the Delaware Helpline.'

I rang the Delaware Helpline.

'No idea,' said the Delaware Helpline automatically programmed have-a-nice-day not-so-chirpy goofball.

'OK, so if you can't tell me what the nearest airport is, what about the train?'

'You'll have to call Amtrak.'

'You mean you're the Delaware Helpline and you don't even know if there's a train to Dover?'

Silence.

I called Amtrak. They didn't know, either.

'Wait a minute. You're Amtrak, right?'

'Right.'

'And you're telling me you don't know if Amtrak goes to Dover. Right?'

'Right.'

I called Greyhound Buses.

'You'll have to go to Penn Central. They'll tell you.'

'But can't you tell me now?'

'No.'

In desperation, I decided to ring the American Express platinum cardholders' special service which, for all their huff and puff about 'expert assistance – whenever you need it', I've always found completely useless. I'm in deepest Poland and I need money, I call them. Can they help me? No way. I'm in L'vov in deepest Ukraine and I need money. Can they help me? No way. And so it goes on all over the world.

From Gatwick Airport, just as I'm about to board my flight to Newark, I call their secret Platinum Card Helpline.

'I'm going to Newark, New Jersey,' I say. 'How can I get from there to Dover, Delaware?'

'Where?'

'Dover, Delaware.'

The girl goes away. I feed more money into the phone box.

'There's no such place.'

'Of course there is. It's—'

'It's not coming up on my system.'

'But I tell you, there is. It's the capital of Delaware.'

Eventually, after another fifteen-minute wait, she comes back. She admits Dover exists.

'OK, so what's the nearest airport to Dover?'

Again she goes away, this time for two days.

'Baltimore,' she comes back to me.

'Baltimore?' I practically shriek. 'Baltimore is a million miles away!'

By now everybody in the airport is gathering around me eager to experience at first hand the quality of advice and help American 'expert assistance – whenever you need it' Express gives its valuable fee-paying platinum cardholders. 'The nearest airport is New Castle,' one very informed, very helpful, very courteous non-American 'expert assistance – whenever you need it' Express guy tells me.

I pass this information on to American Express.

'It's Baltimore,' insists the expert. 'New Castle is not in my system.'

'OK, call American Express in Newark and ask them,' I suggest. 'They'll know.'

'I can't,' she says. 'They're not open. They don't open until—'

'But you say "expert assistance whenever you need it". I'm paying big fees for my platinum card. I need expert assistance, and I need it now.'

'I'll call you back.'

'But I'm just about to get on a plane.'

'I'll call you on your mobile.'

'But you can't use—'

'In that case,' I'm told very primly, 'you'll have to ask someone when you get to Newark.'

Down goes the phone.

At Newark, New Jersey, I try the information desk.

'We can only help with ground transportation,' says the very nice, very friendly but completely useless information desk lady. 'You'll have to talk to the airline.'

'Which airline?'

'No idea. We're just ground transportation. Have a nice day.'

Do you know, I couldn't find anyone in the whole of Newark Airport who could tell me anything – *anything* – about getting to Dover, Delaware, the first city of the first state of America. I was forced to return to the American 'expert assistance – whenever you need it' Express platinum cardholders' special service all the way back in the UK.

After twenty minutes of 'We're trying to help you. Do you want to talk to Global Assistance?' I was still no further down the line. I asked the girl to give me the number of American Express in the US. She gave the wrong one. In the end I found it for myself.

'I'm at Newark Airport, New Jersey,' I began.

This time I was told that the nearest airport to Dover was Philadelphia. After some debate about this, the girl barked: 'There are no flights there tonight. They're all fully booked.'

'What's the name of the airline whose flights are all fully booked?' I asked quite reasonably.

Silence.

'If you don't know the name of the airline, how do you know all their flights are fully booked?'

The superefficient American Express platinum card service for which I'm paying an enormous price then put the phone down on me.

I rang back and asked for the supervisor.

She just giggled.

Once again a small crowd was gathering around me marvelling at this terrific service. One guy told me that Shuttle America flew to New Castle. I repeated this to the supervisor, who denied that such an airline even existed. It wasn't on her system.

'But it does,' I said. 'There's a guy standing next to me who says . . .' I give up. 'What about Amtrak?'

'There's a train,' she eventually finds out. 'It leaves Newark Station at 4.06. It'll take you to Wilmington. After that you're on your own.'

'Where's the station?'

'There,' she snaps. 'Right at the airport.'

I had spent over an hour on the phone. By now it was almost 3.45 pm. 'Right at the airport,' turned out to be another thousand questions, inquiries, pleas for help and an $11 ride away by cab to the middle of Newark.

Did I ever get to Dover?

No. I got as far as Wilmington, the nearest town.

Was it worth it? After all the energy I expended trying to find out where the damn place was, no. There's nothing there. Well, hardly anything apart from the super five-star Hotel Dupont built by the family to entertain their customers. Which, I reckon, was the beginning of their downfall, because just to look at the size of it, let alone the luxury inside, you just know they've got to overcharge you like mad in order to pay for the damn thing. The Hotel Dupont apart, there were also a million office blocks all belonging to – guess who? – American Express. Their Merchant Operations are in Wilmington, Delaware. Their Centurion Services operations are there. Their Treasury Operations are there. Their Financial Advisers' Operations are there. Their Accounting Operations are there. Their giant Credit Corporation is there. And – surprise, surprise – their Travel Operations are there too.

After all the heart attacks finding the place, leaving it was simple. I called a local travel agent – no, not American Express – and asked them to book me on the flight from Wilmington to Boston, Massachusetts, on the airline that didn't exist, Shuttle America. Yes, they said. No problem. What's more, the airline that didn't exist took American Express. I called ahead and fixed for a limo to meet me at Boston. I turned up at the airport that didn't exist, New Castle. I checked in. 'Boston,' I said. 'Boston,' agreed the girl. They called the flight. 'Boston?' I asked. 'Boston,' everybody replied. I clambered on. They slammed the doors. 'Welcome aboard,' the rather precious, sissy flight attendant trilled, 'this Shuttle America flight to Boston Hanscom Fields.'

Boston Hanscom Fields? Where the hell was Boston Hanscom Fields? I'd never heard of it. Naturally, when everybody said Boston, I'd assumed it was Logan. Now I was trapped on a plane that didn't exist, flying from an airport that didn't exist to an airport I'd never heard of.

Do I want to go to Delaware again? What do you think?

Incidentally, if anybody from American 'expert assistance – whenever you need it' Express would like to know, to get to Dover, Delaware you get the train to Wilmington and a bus, just $4, and you're there. Alternatively, fly to New Castle. Out of the airport, turn right, and you can't miss it. But I expect they'll just continue to deny it ever existed.

Kansas

The trouble with Kansas is that it has not only not evolved, it still doesn't believe in evolution, either. Take the famous John Scopes 'monkey trial' which took place in 1925. You'd have thought they would want to forget the whole sorry affair. Not the good people of Kansas. While I was there, swinging happily from tree to tree, they were holding a week-long celebration to mark the seventy-fifth anniversary of the event and busy counting the number of whiskers on the Almighty's beard.

Any mention of Charles Darwin still sends them into orbit. If man evolved from monkeys, they say, why do we still have monkeys? Drawings depicting several species of animals in various embryonic stages by Ernst Haeckel, Darwin's contemporary and supporter, they still reject.

The age of the earth, the big-bang theory and the whole concept of evolutionary theory they not only still reject, but the

Kansas Board of Education has removed all reference to them from the state's schoolbooks. Mind you, I've seen other American schoolbooks that maintain that President Truman dropped the atomic bomb on Korea to end the Korean War; that General MacArthur led the anti-communist witch-hunts in the 1950s; that Kennedy was assassinated while Nixon was president; that the Sputnik was a Soviet nuclear missile poised to strike at the heart of America; that the equator runs through Texas; that the world is flat and that George W. Bush is a serious politician. As for Stephen Hawking, I bet you two coconuts to three bananas that Kansas would reject him as well if only they knew what the hell he was talking about.

The even more amazing thing is that they are not alone. Other states including, of course, California, are planning to follow suit. Even the majority whip in the House of Representatives sees evolution as an intellectual poison that will eventually warp the mind and rot away the soul.

'But shouldn't people have the chance to study both sides of the question and make up their own minds?' I asked one elderly matron, who definitely looked as though she was descended from an orang-utan, complete with long, curly orange whiskers, who practically ran me over outside the Center for the Improvement of Human Functioning in the state capital, Wichita.

'No,' she barked. 'Ignorance is a better alternative. Just because you dump one theory it doesn't mean you have to have an alternative.'

'OK,' I said, desperately trying to make a stand for civilisation. 'You believe in dinosaurs?'

'Yes, of course. What'sthisgottadowithwhatwewere talkin-about?'

'You believe they roamed the earth for 150 million years?'

'Suretheyroam'dthearthfor150millionyears.'

'So,' I raised myself to my full Abraham hand-on-waistcoat Lincoln height, 'if God created everything in seven days, as you say, how come dinosaurs roamed—'

At which she promptly turned and stomped off into the center to hurl a couple of hundred clay pigeons at a wall, in order to, as she yelled back at me, 'destress her mind'.

The result is, just as they have opened a 98,500-square foot, $60 million, futuristic learning, creative and community centre known as Exploration Place, school buses have been diverted to protect children from seeing a 5m high replica of Michelangelo's *David*, even though parents are happy to let them spend no end of time watching film after film about a sweet young, innocent girl living with seven dwarfs; flesh-coloured crayons have been renamed peach and Indian red pencils chestnut and Adam and Eve have once more been thrown out of religious studies and put firmly back on the scientific curriculum. Not that I should imagine they're worried. After all, they've been thrown out of better places than that in their time. As a result, basic to the studies of Kansas school-children now is a book called *Of Pandas and People: The Central Questions of Biological Origins*, written by a Pratt school board president, Willa Beth Mills. Sorry, I'll rephrase that: written by Willa Beth Mills, a school board president in Pratt. In it she preaches what they call Creationism. Variety in nature is a result of 'intelligent design' by an 'intelligent agent'. All I can say is if that's true, it's about the only intelligence you'll find in Kansas.

Classes no doubt now debate such serious issues as: if Adam and Eve were created by God, how come they have belly buttons? If God made Adam then He rested, how come after He made Eve, nobody's had any rest ever since? If Adam is supposed to have ruined everything for the rest of us, how come God's boast to for ever 'put enmity between men and women' has turned out over the generations to be such an idle threat?

In other parts of the States it's the complete opposite. In Arizona, for example, all references to God and religion are completely banned. Christmas has been abolished; even the slightest prayer has been outlawed. In Alabama, they put their own spin on things. I shall never forget, one hot, sweltering

Sunday morning, a black preacher in a tiny town down near Mobile explaining his version of the creation story.

'The Lord creates Adam,' he began, mopping the sweat off his brow with a vast white handkerchief. 'Was Adam grateful?' he shrieked. 'Was he hell! All he kept on about was wanting a bit of rib.' Which is not the way it is normally described in the theological books I've seen.

Undaunted, mopping his brow even more, the good preacher continued: 'And when the good Lord gave Adam his bit of rib was he grateful, did he kneel down and bless the Lord with all his heart and soul and mind and strength? No, he did not. Knowing how sinful man is, his first words on seeing his bit of rib were probably "Stand back, baby, I don't know how big this thing is gonna get."'

Now, I'm not saying that Wichita, at the heart of the US, where the Big Arkansas river meets the Little Arkansas river, just happened to evolve – sorry, mustn't use that word, I mean develop – into the boring old, Bible-thumping, good, clean joke town it is today. It was probably created that way. Visit four of their seven Western Heritage Sights and you'll win yourself a special limited edition collector's belt buckle FREE! While stocks last, of course.

My first morning there I was talking to one of the locals over a quick breakfast of three eggs, six rashers of bacon, four sausages, three slices of French toast and half a gallon of maple syrup. Thank God I didn't have the bumper all-American breakfast.

He told me he was a Godfearing ex-cowboy whose friends called him Isaiah 'because one of my eyes is 'igher than the other.' I reckon one half of his brain was higher than the other, too. Call it instinct. He also kept on about the New York Stock Exchange being where a bunch of élite easterners swapped cattle with each other.

When he finally shuffled off I couldn't help but repeat what he had said to the restaurant manager, a Cambodian from Oklahoma.

'Don't worry,' he said cheerfully in a beautiful, no-holds-barred all-American accent, 'these people, they are so stupid the mind-readers only charge them half-price.'

To restore my sense of balance I decided to forgo my journey to the wide, open land south of Emporia and its Teacher Hall of Fame where the prairie stretches to the flat horizon. Not to mention a trip I'd been planning to make to Manhattan, Kansas, which calls itself the Little Apple. For a town to do that, especially in Kansas, I thought was worth a visit. Down towards the Texas border, I was told, things were getting desperate. The water table has dropped 5ft in recent years. What little rain they had had been immediately soaked up by the soil. Some hotels in the area were so badly affected they had to close up to three or four lanes in their swimming pools.

Instead I decided to take a turn of the local bookshops which I always find is a good move, especially if there are no bars open. I say bookshops. What with evolution being out of line, and practically everything else as well, they were more Bible shops than bookshops. There were big Bibles, small Bibles, everyday Bibles, thought-for-the-day Bibles, huge presentation Bibles, massive, massive-presentation Bibles the size of two tablets of stone.

There was the Teen Devotional Bible, which proclaimed that it was written by teenagers. That must have come as a shock to you-know-who up there who has always proclaimed that he wrote the Bible. And if that wasn't enough to make you take the name of the Lord in vain during a Thanksgiving supper, inside, each book was introduced by a two-page spread featuring a 'cast of characters' with 'snapshots' of the action. Genesis: 'God creates a really cool world. The humans mess it up bad.' The Tower of Babel: 'The result of a bunch of folks way back when who thought they were way too cool.'

Even more amazing was the Women's Devotional Bible, which contained a startling chapter: 'Men: They're Human Too.'

A not-too-devotional woman who looked as though she had

suffered from diarrhoea for at least twenty years caught me smiling weakly. She went bananas. 'Everything is true!' she hollered at me.

True? I was tempted to come out with all the old arguments. If you wear glasses you shouldn't approach the altar of God (Leviticus 21: 20). Owning slaves, however, is OK (Leviticus 25: 44). Burning bulls is OK (Leviticus 1: 9). Selling your daughter into slavery is OK (Exodus 21: 7). Working on the Sabbath is not only wrong, it deserves death (Exodus 35: 2). Swearing deserves stoning (Leviticus 24: 10–16). And do you believe everybody in the Bible actually existed? What about the good Samaritan? But I couldn't be bothered. My attention was distracted by another woman who had obviously just seen some biblical epic on television. She was going up and down the bookcases selecting Bibles by weight, picking up different ones and complaining, 'This doesn't seem like three hours long.'

To be fair they did have other books as well: *Reformation History*, *Giants of the Faith*, *Worship, Discipleship and Evangelism*. No D. H. Lawrence, no Henry Miller, no Angela Carter. And definitely no *Inherit the Wind*. But they had humorous books – *500 Clean Jokes* and *The Ultimate Guide to Good Clean Humour* – lots of local scenic postcards of people sitting at home reading the Bible and a whole series which seemed to recast famous books in the Kansas style.

Take Dickens's *A Christmas Carol*. In the Kansas version, on Christmas Eve Bob Cratchit and Scrooge are hurling Romans 3: 10–19 at each other. Scrooge is down on his hands and knees quoting Romans, 5: 8. And on Christmas Day, Cratchit, his family, Scrooge and even Tiny Tim are sitting down to an enormous Philippians 4: 6–7.

Their story of the *Titanic* was even more remarkable. In case you don't know the ending, I'll tell you. The ship sank not because it hit an iceberg, but because wicked old Chester was far more interested in money than anything else, and Luke 12: 20 had to be taught a lesson. So there. What happens to people who make fun of the books? Probably Matthew 25: 41, knowing my luck.

While I was going along the racks of Bibles checking out some of my favourite passages – Ephesians 5: 22, Colossians 3: 18, I Timothy 2: 11 – I overheard a young guy who looked as though he only read paperbacks if they had a plastic cover ask one of the all-American-as-Kansas-apple-pie assistants if she had anything on jobs. She directed him to the Old Testament section. I was going to ask her where the self-help books were but I thought she might just tell me to find them myself. Not, I suppose, that they're worried about whether they do any business or not. If they go bust they've only got to open any one of their Bibles at Chapter 11 and they're safe.

As well as a gospel outreach muzak section they had singalong Messiahs, swinging Messiahs and even too-hot-to-Handel Messiahs. But in spite of all this, 96 per cent of all American schoolchildren recognise Ronald McDonald better than they do the Christian crucifix. It makes you think.

Don't get the idea Wichita is all Bibles and nothing else. Once a year the wackos break out, go really wild and have what they call a Tomato Day. From 7 am to noon, the whole world can turn up at the Sedgwick County Extension Education Center and enjoy a non-stop round of lectures, tastings, contests, food and children's crafts, all on the theme of tomatoes. I was going to go, but in the end I thought it would be too much for me. The old ticker and all that. I asked the hotel porter if there was anything else on offer for the slightly more discerning visitor. He suggested a thirty-minute walking tour of the trees of Wichita.

OK, Wichita may be boring – it's so old-fashioned that they've even banned premarital dancing – but, no doubt thanks to Wyatt Earp, who established his reputation here as a lawman, it's well behaved, well mannered, safe, almost trouble-free. People leave their homes unlocked. They park their cars outside in the street at night and know they'll be there in the morning. They can wander around at night and not be hustled or mugged or beaten up. Not that there's anything to do in Wichita at night: there isn't even a cinema. The only strip club in town is not in town, it's way out in the middle of nowhere and is bound by so many city rules and ordinances that, I was told, the girls keep their clothes on. If they break the rules they face stiff penalties.

And there's plenty of money around, no doubt thanks to another cowboy, Jesse Chisholm, who blazed his famous trail across those brown, rolling, Wichita dry-as-dust prairies along which the cowboys drove their longhorn cattle all the way from Texas to the railway in Kansas. A lush new Hyatt has just opened, and more and more big, expensive homes are being built, most of them for the big guys working either at Boeing, which has a small plant on the edge of town employing around 20,000 people, or Cessna or Learjet or Raytheon, which between them turn out 60 to 70 per cent of the world's general aviation aircraft.

By the way, I haven't forgotten Kansas City. It's not in Kansas. It's in Missouri. Why I don't know. Probably because it just evolved that way. But don't tell them that in Wichita.

The Bun States

Most Americans call these states the Great Plains. Because they are great – they cover literally millions of acres – and because they are plain boring. Literally mile after mile of nothing and cans of Cook-Aid. You think I'm kidding? Not even the Mormons stopped here on their mad rush to the promised land and non-stop fatherhood. And that's just the towns I'm talking about. The open country is even worse. There have been occasions when a passing tumbleweed has been the highlight of my day.

But these states are important because they are the states that produce the materials that produce the buns.

Iowa, which contains over 25 per cent of all US Grade A farmland, is nothing but corn. Nebraska, the great American desert, is known as the Cornhusker State. St Louis can be fun in an arch kind of way, but Missouri is grain, grain, grain with a bit of cotton and tobacco thrown in. Illinois, with all that fertile soil, is the Prairie State, while the cornfields of Indiana go on and on and on for ever and ever and ever.

The other reason why these are the bun states is that there's not much there to get your teeth into, apart from the occasional sesame seed – exactly 198 to each Big McBun – unlike, say, those fantastic, sticky, sweet, soft cinnamon buns made by the austere old German Baptist doughboys at the Knaus Berry Farm at Homestead in the heart of rural Florida. Now, that's what I call a bun. I gottahaveone. I gottahaveone. I gottahaveone. Now. Now. Now.

Iowa

Iowa is not as boring as they say. It's worse. It's corn, corn and still more corn. It's not just the occasional field of corn, but corn that goes on mile after mile after mile. Over 20 per cent of the corn produced in the US comes from Iowa, although on a bad day, it seems like 200 per cent. If that's not exciting enough, it also produces around 15 per cent of their soya beans as well. With over 85 per cent of the state taken up by farmland, wherever you go, wherever you drive, whoever you talk to, you're surrounded by huge fields of gently swaying debts. For in spite of the huge areas involved – some fields stretch halfway round the world and back – the intensive farming and the sky-high yields, most farmers are not making hay. They are struggling, like all farmers struggle. They are also suffering, as in, if it carries on like this we'll have to start voting Democrat.

The reason is their success. The higher and higher they push up their production levels, the less money they make, even though, whisper it not in this land of red, raw, unbridled capitalism that is for ever screaming about European Union subsidies, the federal government is paying them in subsidies far more than they earn from commodity sales.

In the bad old days, when they were planting by moonlight, fertilising with buffalo manure and making money, most farmers were producing around 150 bushels an acre. Today, with good conditions, some powerful lobbying and a Republican administration, they can make 200 bushels an acre. Some are even hitting 300. One farmer out near Manchester, by ploughing deep, planting genetic and voting Republican in federal state and local elections, is getting as much as 400 bushels. His crop is so thick that by the time he's finished harvesting he has to turn around and start all over again. There's no time to plant a fresh crop.

'But why are you going for 400 bushels an acre?' I yelled up at one poor millionaire in a tractor the size of the Empire State Building.

'We have to. We have no alternative,' he yelled down at me. 'The price is so low.'

'But isn't it so low because there's so much around?'

'Sure. You get better prices when there's a shortage. Supply and demand. Everyone knows that.'

'So why don't you produce less instead of more?'

'Duh.'

The signs of their success are everywhere. I don't mean brand new SUVs somersaulting all over the highways, I mean broken fences, empty houses, collapsing barns, derelict silos and huge slugs of bourbon. Because the more successful they become, the less money they make, the more farmers drop out, the fewer people go hunting duck or pheasant or geese or even deer, the more houses stand empty, the more schools close down, the more towns shut up shop, the more young people leave, the more trouble they have finding people to take part in important events such as the State Hot Dog Eating Championships, the harder life becomes for the people who are left behind.

The result: Iowa is going to have big problems trying to become the fun spot of the US. Miami apart, it already has more old people than anywhere else in the States. As the people who are left grow old, so the state becomes poorer and poorer. In fact it's the very poverty that's given it its name: wherever you go, all you hear is 'I owe a beer', 'I owe a bottle of bourbon', 'I owe a million to that goddamn bank'.

Altoona is the exception. There you never hear people talking about money. Because Altoona is home to Prairie Meadows, the first combined racetrack and casino in the whole of the US. At first they faced big problems. Most of the racing community were against them: slot machines, they said, were gambling, and they didn't think anything as sordid as gambling should be associated with racing. But as it has developed, and as the operators have ploughed more and more of the poor punters' hard-earned losings back into racing, so Prairie Meadows has become more and more accepted as a unique venue where people can lose on the slots what they've just lost on the horses.

As for Des Moines, the capital, I can honestly say that all the time I was there I didn't see a soul on the streets. There were precious few people in the hotels, either. What's more, I didn't come across anything of interest. Of course, the fact that everything was covered in snow, the whole city was huddled behind closed doors preparing for the caucuses for the 2000 presidential elections and I was only there between planes may have had something to do with it. But in spite of all the jokes, it did take me a bit more than three and a half minutes to get around Des Moines. It took five and a half minutes, because the car stalled, and as the driver was from Concord, Massachusetts, he was reluctant to restart the engine immediately because he wanted to get a feel for the place.

Now don't get me wrong. I like Des Moines. On the odd one or two occasions I've been back over and above the call of duty, I've discovered that the locals do have a life apart from corn. Sport, for example. They play mailbox baseball. They drive like mad at mailboxes, swinging their baseball bats out of the windows of their tractors, then, just at the right moment, smash them to smithereens. For relaxation, they read *The John Deere Tractor Date Book* and for a day in the country, they all jump in the tractor and head out to Ames, where there is a 10-mile stretch of countryside covered by huge metal hangars. These are home to 5,000 sows which between them are responsible for over 10 per cent of America's huge annual pork production.

So if you ever start going soft and getting damn-fool ideas about wanting to spend quality time with your family, take them to Iowa. It'll soon put you off the whole crazy idea.

Nebraska

You're the fourth-richest man in the world. You're worth an estimated US$50 billion. In 1965 you started Berkshire Hathaway, and over the last thirty-five years you have delivered staggering compound annual returns of just under 25 per cent. A single share bought when you first began is now worth over US$70,000. Today it's the most famous investment vehicle in the US, if not in the whole galaxy.

You might look slightly crumpled and have a thing about Cherry Coke and crackers, but to millions you're revered as the Oracle of Omaha, the sage, the investor of the century. To other less enthusiastic players, you're the greatest investor of all time. Through your efforts, in other words, through the dividends that flow non-stop out of your company, you've created goodness knows how many minimillionaires and sent hundreds of thousands of kids to college, families on holiday, people to hospital and old people to rest homes and whatever lies beyond.

So tell me, why on earth do you want to live in boring, staid, strait-laced Omaha, Nebraska, that glorious town on the west bank of the Missouri which, apart from the Reuben sandwich, gave the world such glorious delights as the first rodeo organised by Buffalo Bill Cody in North Platte in July 1882, the invention of spree killing in 1958 by a certain Charles Starkweather and his girlfriend, Caril An Fugate, who went out and murdered eleven people (when asked why he did it, he said, 'I never ate in a high-class restaurant, I never seen the New York Yankees play, I never been to Los Angeles . . .') and an even worse atrocity, if such a thing is possible, TV dinners? And with the whole world to choose from, why on earth would you want an emerald-green office on the main street opposite a church?

What's more, Warren Buffett (pronounced the American way, Super Super Rich), takes home his regular $100,000-a-year salary to an ordinary, not very large house in an ordinary street. No fence, as far as I could see; no vicious guard dogs, either. For getting around town, or backwards and forwards to and from the airport, he uses local taxis, or he did until very recently, when he started receiving death threats. Presumably for not buying expensive houses and foreign cars.

The answer is because that's how they do things in

Nebraska. Low-key. Understated. Laid-back. Old-fashioned. Conservative with a big K. Not the American way at all.

Unless, of course, Warren Buffett doesn't actually live in that ordinary, boring house in that ordinary, boring street in ordinary, boring Omaha. Maybe he's got a huge penthouse apartment in New York, an enormous château in California and goodness knows what hidden away in the jungle in Brazil. Maybe he's whooping it up all over the place. If he is – and for his sake, I hope he is: he deserves it – that is also the Omaha way of doing things. Serious at home, fun when you're away.

But whether he does or not, the only time you know Warren Buffett is in town is when he takes over the local Civic Auditorium for what he calls the 'Woodstock for Capitalists', the annual meeting of the ever-grateful shareholders of his enormous, never-ending money-making machine, where, every year, before he begins his speech, he taps the microphone and says, 'Testing, testing. One million, two million, three million.' Then practically the whole investment world, and Charlie Munger, his right-hand man, a lawyer and, would you believe, a friend for over forty years, sits at his feet and scrambles to pick up the pearls of wisdom.

Others go on about earnings and price – earning ratios, bell curves, fat tails, conventional bond-to-earnings yield valuations, six-sigma events, the Black–Scholes options pricing formula, who they saw the company president having lunch with the day before yesterday and the whole alphabet soup of investment in which 'L' is the pessimists' delight, 'U' means a prolonged, long-drawn-out agony, 'V' a sharp shock followed by a sharp recovery, 'W' a false dawn, 'X' means 'jump, jump, jump!' and 'Z' that it's too late, it's all over. You had your chance. It's the end.

Buffett, however, in between sips of Cherry Coke, tosses out his very own investment clichés: 'Share options are lottery tickets', 'The macro just doesn't mean anything', 'Short-term quarterly targets lead to poor long term decisions', 'When a manager with a great reputation takes on a company with a poor reputation, the company survives, not the manager', 'Nothing sedates rationality like large doses of effortless money', 'Overstaying the festivities will eventually bring on pumpkins and mice, but they nevertheless hate to miss a single minute of what is one helluva party', 'There is nothing wrong with putting all your eggs in one basket as long as you watch the basket', 'Unless you know what a business is going to look like in ten years' time, it's not worth looking at it'. And, of course, his most famous investment advice of all: 'A girl in a convertible is worth five in the phone book.'

On the other hand, maybe Buffet, a skilled bridge player, only looks the enormous success he is because Omaha looks as though it has had a charisma bypass. They even call their airport an airfield. Take the city centre. Ask someone to take you to the most exciting place in town and they'll drive you through ConAgra's corporate office complex – they call it a campus – all low-key office blocks, parkland setting, manicured lawns. No way would you think it was the second-largest food group in the US.

'Pretty, isn't it?' one of Mr Buffett's local shareholders remarked to me.

'Zzz,' I enthused.

Then comes the Market Square, which has been revamped, like a million market squares all over the zzz of zzz. There are a couple of bars, a handful of restaurants and two or three clubs where, so heavy are the city restrictions on anything you can think of, apparently the girls drive audiences wild by loosening the top buttons of their raincoats. Not that anyone's interested. The only figures they're interested in are on the back pages of the *Wall Street Journal*.

In one bar on Jackson Street I found everyone talking stocks.

'My kid, he's sixteen. He works all the time. He's got $20,000,' another local Warren Buffett shareholder told me. 'He wants to put all his money in stocks. I tell him he's crazy. He should be spending it all on girls and booze. That's what I did when I was his age. Then I think to myself, I'm stupid. Here am I arguing with my kid because he wants to invest his money for the future. I'm stupid. Whatyahave?'

'A block of Berkshire Hathaway,' I said.

Another Berkshire Hathaway shareholder schmoozed up to us.

'Let the kid alone. Let him lose his money,' he yucked. 'In the long run only three things count as far as the stockmarket is concerned: earnings and the price–earning ratio; that the relationship between the two is geometric, not linear, and whether you can get out before the other knuckleheads suck up to some smart analyst on Wall Street.'

In the next bar along Market Square, I actually came across someone who wasn't one of Mr Buffett's shareholders. What was the highlight of his year, I asked him.

'My dental appointment,' he said.

In fact, Omaha is so boring it's about the only town I've been to in the USA that doesn't have any convention business. Maybe people don't want to be seen coming to Omaha. Maybe they think people will think they're Berkshire Hathaway millionaires and the family will start talking to them again. Maybe they're scared people will think they believe in more important things in life than a double cheeseburger and a triple chocolate milkshake.

Not that Omaha doesn't have, Warren Buffett apart, its successes. It is home to the world's largest private health insurance company. It's the biggest telemarketing, telephone call centre and credit card authorisation centre in the US because, they say being at the centre of the USA, and home to a vast mish-mash of Czechs, Croats, Poles, Germans, Italians, Irish and Israelis, everybody can understand their American accent. Fred Astaire and Henry Fonda both came from Nebraska. 'Everybody understood what they said,' another of Mr Buffett's local shareholders, whose name I couldn't quite catch, told me. On the other hand, Crazy Horse also came from Nebraska, and nobody took any notice of what he had to say.

112

Omaha is also home to Strategic Air Command's underground nuclear nerve centre, so I hope to goodness it's being run by the Fred Astaires and Henry Fondas rather than the Crazy Horses, otherwise we're all in trouble.

Talking of Fred Astaire and Henry Fonda, for those who remember the days of Bing Crosby and Mickey Rooney and black-and-white flickering pictures, Omaha has another big success: Boys' Town which, I have to say, is nowhere near as yukky as I imagined.

Remember the story? Father Flanagan meets this scruffy lad carrying a young kid on his back.

'Put him down, son,' says the kindly old priest. 'He's too heavy for you.'

'He's not heavy for me,' says the kid looking up at the sky, 'Ave Maria' as rearranged by Aaron Copeland beginning to sound softly in the background, a youthful hernia beginning to throb gently in his groin. 'He's my brother.'

From that, Boys' Town was created. Father Flanagan collected down-and-out kids from all over, divided them into small groups and put them into ordinary family houses under the supervision of adult helpers in a separate town of their own, complete with its own police station, its own fire station and its own farm to provide the food. Except that he got the boys to run everything themselves.

I thought the enterprise had died out years ago, but there it was, alive and booming in Omaha, Nebraska. Except that Boys' Town is no longer Boys' Town, it's Boystown, which seems to suggest that they now take in girls as well. On the last estimate, over 8,500 mistreated and disabled boys and girls every year. It's also no longer really a town, more a mini city, with schools, colleges, sports facilities, a training centre, churches and, of course, statues of the boy, his kid brother on his back, who started it all. The farm is also enormous. It seems to stretch for ever. It's also no longer on its own. Both Boystown and Omaha have expanded so much, they're now side by side.

Boystown is also booming because more and more of its old

boys are making good, going on to run giant corporations and coming back every year to help the old town, which is, after all, their home, to give present-day kids the benefit of their experience, to select recruits for their ever-expanding empires and, of course, to sign the odd cheque or three. The whole thing seems such a good idea I'm surprised it hasn't taken off more worldwide. Maybe the fact that it's based in Omaha has something to do with it.

Outside of Omaha, however, things change dramatically. Everything is boring on a more dramatic scale. Nebraska's corn harvest is the third-largest in the world. They also have sorghum, soya beans and the largest planted forest in the US, all 22,000 acres of it, not to mention America's largest collection of sand dunes. To stop you from nodding off, the place is regularly lashed by heavy rains, hailstorms, blizzards and tornados.

But against all the odds, I had more than my fair share of excitement in Nebraska – and it was nothing to do with going to the theatre in Lincoln.

One morning, on the way to some meeting or other, we pulled into a petrol station round the back of the revamped Market Square in Omaha. We filled up with gas. Not being a typical American, the driver went into the shop to pay. I went to the toilet – I mean the little boys' room, although why the Americans are so obsessed with little boys I have no idea. It was locked. I guess they were scared somebody might go in there and try and clean it up. Instead I went to join the driver inside the shop. I wanted to check out the magazines in case they had the *Economist*. We both went up to the cash desk together. But instead of taking our money, the schmuck behind the cash desk just looked at us. Straight in the eye.

'OK,' he said quietly. 'Don't say a word. Just turn round and walk down the aisle to the back of the shop. Just stay there. Don't say a thing. *Don't turn round.*'

My God, I thought. This is it. In a gas station. In of all places, Omaha, Nebraska.

We both turned round. Slowly. We walked down the aisle, past the stacks of food, past more stacks of more food, past even more stacks of even more food. When we reached the back of the shop, we both stopped and just stood there.

'Just stand there,' the schmuck behind the cash desk barked. *'Don't move!'*

We stood there.

My life flashed past me. Then, because I couldn't believe it was so boring, it flashed past me again.

'OK, turn round,' the guy barked at us once more. 'S-l-o-o-o-w-l-y. *But don't say a word!'*

We turned round s-l-o-o-o . . ., I mean slowly.

'OK, I've called the police,' the guy continued. 'Just stay there until they arrive. *Don't move!'*

Oh no, I thought. I'm going to be beaten up, kicked all over the place, every bone in my body broken. Then they're going to take me back to the station. Please, please, somebody have a video. Then at least they'll take me to hospital afterwards.

Within seconds the police were there. All round the perimeter of the petrol station. All round the shop. We were completely surrounded.

'OK,' the shopkeeper suddenly snapped. 'You can relax.'

Gee whizz. Did I relax? Well, not as much as that. But I took a couple of deep breaths, I can tell you.

Then he told us what it was all about.

'When you came up to the cash desk, I saw this kid crawl into the back of your car. I couldn't tell you, otherwise you'd have raised the alarm, gone running out there, grabbed the kid. There's no knowing what might have happened. That's why I told you to go to the back of the shop and keep quiet while I called the police. It's OK, they've got him now.'

The kid, it turned out, was taking part in some kind of initiation ceremony. In order to graduate from his junior gang to the big boys' gang, he had to jump a car at a petrol station and force the driver to take him to some prearranged venue where the rest of the gang would be waiting to welcome him into their ranks. What they were going to do with the driver and any passengers he had with him, he didn't say.

Nebraska might be boring. But not for me it wasn't. No thanks to Mr Buffett.

Missouri

Adventure. Danger. Excitement. Mark Twain. Charles Lindbergh. Solo flights across the Atlantic. Trolley cars that go clang-clang-clang. Tennessee Williams. Scott Joplin. Tina Turner. Vincent Price. Old poets who wear the bottom of their trousers rolled. The Spirit of St Louis? No way.

When they talk about the Spirit of St Louis, pronounced, inevitably, St Lewis, they mean nothing less than three of the most stunning inventions of all time: the hot dog, the ice-cream cone and the do-it-yourself suicide kit much favoured by the mob, with or without the canary.

When Lewis – pronounced, inevitably, Louis – and Clark set out from Missouri to journey across the Louisiana Purchase with forty-five men, all 'good hunters, stout, healthy, unmarried men, accustomed to the woods and capable of bearing bodily fatigue in a pretty, considerable degree', it was to find the most profitable franchise outlets for their new products. President Jefferson, in that brutal, punchy way all Americans have, said it was to explore, 'the Missouri River and such principal streams of it, as by its course and communication within the waters of the Pacific Ocean, offers the most direct and practicable water communication across the continent, for the purpose of commerce'. But as he also said that all men were equal, yet bought and sold slaves all his life, kept over 250 on his farm and one as his wife, there is no point in paying much attention to whatever he says.

It's also obvious that Lewis and Clark were more of a couple of fawning salesmen sucking up to the chief executive than explorers. Just look at how they behaved. If you were a serious explorer and you came to the Three Forks of the Missouri, would you immediately rename the three rivers Jefferson after the president, Madison after the secretary of state and Gallatin after the secretary of the treasury? And if that's not bad enough, they then followed the Jefferson until it divided into three tributaries which they called Wisdom, Philosophy and Philanthropy, even though none of the locals had the slightest idea what on earth those words meant, let alone how to pronounce them. So much so that today they've been renamed Big Hole, Beaverhead and Ruby.

Like all salesmen, Lewis and Clark promised everyone the earth which, as far as they were concerned, continued up the Missouri, across the Rockies, down the Columbia River, all the way to the Pacific and back again. Meanwhile, the poor people back home in St Louis, who were desperately trying to cope with a sudden influx of hunters, traders and half the east coast looking for Judy Garland, decided to commemorate for all time the invention of the hot dog, and what they thought was going to bring them untold riches, by building an enormous single-span stainless steel arch, at 630ft twice as high as the Statue of Liberty, on the banks of the Mississippi in downtown St Louis. Securing such a massive structure into the riverbank was not a problem. They just sent out to Grand Boulevard for a couple of plates of Ted Drewe's famous frozen custard – another St Louis speciality – which is so thick that it not only looks like freshly mixed concrete, it has exactly the same consistency. Turn a plate of the stuff upside-down – if you can lift it – and it just sticks there. Hence the role it played in securing the famous arch. The people behind the scheme were known as arch-advocates.

Had they not then blown all the rest of their money on testing their new ice-cream cones, they could have built a second arch alongside it. But it was not to be. Instead clever old McDonald's came along with their double arch and stole all the glory, not to mention the market as well.

The do-it-yourself suicide kit was a much more straightforward proposition. Without any big promotions, advertising campaigns or even franchise operations, it is as popular today as ever. First, find yourself a sack. Next, a victim. Finally, a length of cord. The rest is easy. Knock the victim out, double him up like a pocket knife, tie the cord around his neck and then loop and tie it around his knees. Insert victim in sack and run like hell. The victim, when he comes to, tries to straighten his knees. When he straightens his knees, he pulls the cord and immediately chokes himself. Just imagine what Jefferson might have done if it had been invented when he was around. I shudder to think.

The Spirit of St Louis is still kicking itself to this day. But it's not St Louis's fault, it's Missouri's fault. St Louis is simply in the wrong state. If it were in New York, Massachusetts, New Jersey, even tiny, insignificant Delaware, it would be a world-class city. It would be buzzing with life. People would be flocking to it from all over the world. Instead it's in Missouri. Not that there's anything wrong with Missouri, just that it's not somewhere else.

A lot of people criticise Missouri. They say its slovenly, dirty, scruffy, hard-bitten, mean. Boondocky, even. I wouldn't go that far. Partly because I don't know what boondocky means.

The north, I find, is a bit like Iowa, Illinois, Wisconsin, Minnesota. All long, long never-ending prairies. The east is like Virginia, all green, rolling hills. The south is where the southern states begin: the Ozarks, hickory-smoked ham and country music. In the Civil War, it split every which way. Some backed the Confederates against the Union but refused to take sides. Some backed the Union against the Confederates but refused to take sides. Others backed the Confederates or the Union, enlisted, fought and died for one side or the other.

It was from here, from Independence, Missouri to be precise, that the settlers – men, women and children led by President Harry 'S. for Settlers' Truman – set out from his tiny haberdashery shop in the summer of 1846 to walk with their ox-drawn carts and tented wagons the 640 miles to Fort Laramie, Wyoming. In the days they heaved and sweated like bulls, well, oxen. In the evenings they gathered round their campfires singing hymns. In the distance wolves howling and Teton Sioux whooping it up. Not because they were planning anything nasty, but because they couldn't stand the singing. I'd probably do the same if I heard 'Abide With Me' every night for over 400 nights. Ahead of them, according to the advertising at the time, were 'oats ½in thick through the stalk and 8ft high . . . clover grows to 5ft, covering the hills with natural hay'. And all genetically unmodified as well.

Thomas Jefferson thought it would take 500 years to tame it, civilise it and break it in. Yet again he was completely wrong. From what I've seen of it, it will take at least twice that time.

Today, however it seems, Missouri wants to be friends with everyone, partly because it is virtually at the centre of the USA. Two miles outside Lebanon is a stone monument marking the exact spot. Get within spittin' distance of it – and I've been unfortunate enough to witness that, in some cases, this can be as much as 100 miles – and everyone will tell you that in the old days, wherever you were heading, north to south, east to west or wherever, you had to go through Lebanon. Which, even in the land of natural exaggeration, strikes me as unlikely. But am I going to argue with some gook who can spit 100 miles? In any case, Lebanon is volatile enough as it is without me causing any more trouble.

That said, yes, I can see St Louis being the natural cross-over point for people going from north to south or from east to west or wherever. In fact, in many ways, I reckon it should be the capital of the US, except, of course, that it lacks the natural characteristics of a capital city. It's organised, it's safe, it's pleasant, the mayor hasn't been to jail, they're low on kink-chasers and there are not enough fat, giggly interns in town wearing fancy berets, although presumably they could soon change that.

It's the one half of the McDonald's arch that dominates everything. Officially, it's supposed to mark the very spot where the west begins: the opening up to the wide, wide yonder, the land of opportunity, where men are men and women wear the trousers.

I don't believe that. First, because nobody can agree on where the west begins. In Texas they say it's the Brazos River. In Philadelphia they say it's the Alleghenies. In Brooklyn they say it's the Hudson. Unless somebody's stolen it. In Concorde, New Hampshire they say, 'Duh.' The truth, of course, is that, America being the world's greatest democracy, it begins wherever the biggest, toughest, reddest redneck in town says it begins, although between you and me, nothing, except perhaps a broken arm, will persuade me that it doesn't begin on the western state lines of Minnesota, Iowa, Missouri, Arkansas and Louisiana. In other words, as near as damn it, on the 100th meridian.

Secondly, are you seriously telling me that the gateway to the west is on the banks of the Mississippi tucked away behind an old cathedral and a courthouse? Admittedly, not any old courthouse, but the courthouse that saw the Dred Scott trials which, many claim, marked the start of the Civil War. Dred Scott was a negro slave born in Missouri which, at the time, was a slave state. As a young man he lived and worked in Illinois, a non-slave state, where he was treated as a freeman. He came back to Missouri and found himself considered once again a slave. He went to the court insisting that he was a freeman. The case went all the way to the Supreme Court, which ruled there was nothing they could do about it. Dred Scott might have been a freeman in Illinois, but in Missouri he was a slave. Case dismissed.

In fact the arch is so tucked away that the first time I went to St Louis I had to ask someone where it was and I was practically standing underneath it. If it's where it's supposed to be, where the west begins, it should be in the middle of an enormous open plaza. Cars, trains, trucks, even the occasional ox-drawn cart should be able to drive under it. Through it you should be able to see the wide, open spaces of the Great Plains.

If you're going to build a monument as spectacular as the one half of the McDonald's arch, so spectacular that it deserves to be one of the Seven Wonders of the modern world, you don't hide it on the banks of a river round the back of a cathedral and a courthouse. The Eiffel Tower is not standing in the middle of nowhere. The Arc de Triomphe is not up some side street. The Statue of Liberty is not stuck behind the TWA terminal at JFK Airport. If you're going to build these crazy monuments, you've got to display them in all their glory. Now, the fact that the arch is buried away can only mean one of two things: that the people of St Louis are stupid, which I cannot accept, or that the arch has got nothing to do with the opening up of the west and all those boondocks (I still don't know what that means, but it sounds right). No, what it is is the first part of a massive project of golden arches to promote hot dogs that got overtaken by events. To put it politely. Go and have a look for yourself, and you'll see that I'm right. It's downtown, where the action is, in the side streets, where all the best franchises are, and on the riverbank, which guarantees a steady market. What could be better?

As for the city itself, I've got no arguments about that. Outside the big boys – Boston, New York, Chicago, Miami, San Fran – it's one of my favourites. It's no wonder it's the place where everybody wants to meet.

Old buildings have been turned into hotels and apartment blocks. The International Fur Exchange building, the Thomas Jefferson building and the American Zinc building are now one grand hotel, the Drury Plaza. The Manhattan Coffee Co. is now the Westin Hotel. The old twenty-storey Gateway and Lennox Hotels are now part of the Convention Hotel project which, when it's finished, will incorporate another thirty-storey, 900-room hotel. The famous Union Sation is still there. But it's more enormous shopping mall than station. The showboats ploughing up and down the Mississippi to Memphis and New Orleans are still there. But they're more casinos than showboats. All the blues and jazz clubs are still there but, I was told, they're more likely to be full of undercover police, so determined is St Louis to keep its squeaky clean image, than the real thing. Poor Scott

Joplin would turn in his grave if he knew what was going on. Or rather, not going on.

The rest of the city is clean, modern, concrete-block functional. Apart, that is, from the famous cathedral basilica of St Louis. Outside, it looks stern, solid, Roman. Inside, it's Byzantine gone mad. There are mosaics and tiles everywhere. Not a square inch is left uncovered. If the Pope ever pulls off his deal of a lifetime and unites the Eastern and Western churches, I tell you, this place will be in the running for the new East–West Vatican. It would probably mean dumping a great chunk of the skull of St Louis himself, which is kept in the cathedral, but as it is French and, therefore, no doubt completely empty, it shouldn't cause too many problems. There would probably be more complaints if they had to rename the Cardinals, their local football team, as the Patriarchs, knowing the typical American's sense of priorities.

Outside the city centre, like most big American cities, St Louis splits half and half. The south is white, German, Italian, Irish. The north is black. Somewhere in the middle is Central West End, which is upmarket, all neat lawns, smart houses, three or more cars per family. Throw a champagne bottle from there and it will land in Union Boulevard, which is as poor, desolate, rundown, dangerous, and crime-ridden as you can get. Once grand homes are now dumps. Clumps of grass grow through the pavements. What shops there are are boarded up. Monday nights, however, everything is forgotten. Everyone goes to watch the football match.

As for the rest of the state, Kansas City, once the wild, rough, stockyard, rail and grain centre of the lower midwest, is only half as good as it could be. The other half is in Kansas State, which is maybe why it doesn't quite come off.

In theory, it's got everything. Jazz? Apparently Kansas City was a big player in the development of jazz. There are still jazz clubs all over town. For what it's worth it's a mecca for big-band blues, whatever that is. Booze? Somehow or other KC was untouched by Prohibition. The 1920s, as a result, were party

122

time. While the rest of the US was dying of thirst, these guys were drowning in the stuff. Food? The city is recognised as the barbecue capital of the world, partly, I would guess, because all the decent restaurants, especially on the plaza, get full up so quickly that it's just easier to stay at home and cook your own than to queue up waiting for a table.

If none of that adds up to a sophisticated lifestyle, it has also got human bowling. Fully grown, intelligent people strap themselves on to a fully grown, intelligent person's-sized skateboard so that other fully grown, intelligent people can hurl them towards six 5ft-high, giant, heavy bowling pins. No wonder Lindbergh did everything he could to get away from the place.

KC I also remember for one of the smoothest landings I've had anywhere. I'm not saying we came crashing down on the runway. It's just that for a moment I thought the wheels were going to go through the roof of the plane.

Finally, it's got what is to Americans the most important place in the whole of the US, if not in the world (after, of course, Graceland): Carroll Building. In midtown, KC, on the second floor, thanks to a tiny mouse called Mortimer, Carroll Building saw the birth of the world's biggest and most successful entertainment empire. This is where Walt Disney began his cartooning career.

Born in Marceline, northern Missouri, Walt moved as a child to Kansas City, where hi-ho he delivered newspapers, hi-ho hi-ho went to high school and hi-ho hi-ho hi-ho spent a spell in the Red Cross Ambulance Corps in the First World War. Back home he couldn't get a job as a newspaper cartoonist, so off to work he went, in 1920, zip-a-dee-do-dah, as a commercial artist for Laugh-O-Gram Studios. Where Mortimer Mouse came from I have no idea. Probably from Walt's lunch bag. Three years later, Laugh-O-Gram stopped laughing. They went broke. But, inspired by the friendly little rodent, Walt headed for Hollywood. The rest, as they say, is hard cheese.

Today, as a tribute to Walt's creative genius, not to mention Mortimer's, the building not only looks as if it has been taken over by Mortimer's millions of descendants, obviously still living off the royalty cheques, but by rats as well. It looks as though it is about to collapse into the dirt unless something is done about it soon. Even if nothing can be done, and it just collapses, it'll still be better than Graceland.

A modern-day Kansas City legend, Charles, I also met in a downtown bar near the plaza. He was old, pushing eighty. He was as thin as a rake. His clothes were threadbare. He lived in a one-room flat with – can you imagine in modern-day America – no television, no heating and no air-conditioning. But he was worth exactly $958,777. I know because the barman told me. He looked after the old man's accounts, paid his bills for him and kept his finances in order, all for the price of an occasional bottle of beer. I was so impressed I bought him a drink. The barman, I mean, not Charles. I only hope when I get to Charles's age I'll find a friendly barman to look after me. It sounds a better idea than some stroppy matron gagging on a mix of oestrogen, progesterone, tryptophan and triple Bloody Maries.

But in spite of having such a good deck of cards, KC doesn't seem to know how to play them.

Which, come to think of it,
Is probably not surprising
Because it is also the world headquarters of the cards
   you don't play:
Birthday cards, yucky anniversary cards, insincere
   get-well-soon cards
Even happy divorce cards
And all the usual schmutter.

A special thank you for being in KC
To Hallmark Cards
Who, I'm convinced,
Will one day
Produce a card
With a verse

124

That doesn't make you throw up.

Which I suppose is only to be expected
When the company was founded by a man
Called Joyce Hall
Named after a famous local Methodist bishop.

Not that anyone ever sends me any cards.
The only cards I ever get
Are quickly followed by a P45.

I've never managed to get to Fulton, Missouri, where
Churchill gave his 'Iron curtain descending across Europe'
speech, which we now think of as a major turning-point in the
history of the world but which, at the time, was completely
ignored by President Truman and a whole load of other
American bigwigs in the audience. But for some reason or
other, I've spent years of my life in Springfield, down in Ozark
Mountain country. When I first went there Springfield wasn't
just a one-horse town, it was about one third of a one-horse
town. The airport was practically a shack. The town itself was
a village. Today, it's booming. The airport is big and impressive. It has a population of about 300,000. It's also paradise for
anyone with even the slightest interest in anything outdoors.
I've seen shopping malls. I've seen aircraft hangars. Let me tell
you, their local Bass Pro Shops Outdoor World is both. It has
over 300,000 square feet devoted to nothing but sports gear
and sports gear and more sports gear, everything from a fishing
net to almost any kind of gun you can imagine.

Just outside town on the empty Ozark Plateau is another
crazy American idea. 'Why spend all that time and money
building theatres for just one show a night?' some smart guy
obviously said. So what did they do? They built what they call
'the live entertainment capital of the world': a whole string of
over thirty theatres open for the full range of music America has
to offer, providing it's pop or country music, shows starring all

the big names, such as the Baldknobbers, Jim Stafford, Mel and Pam Tillis, practically all day and all night as well. They have more theatre seats than Broadway, more theatregoers than Broadway and a far, far greater turnover than Broadway. The second most popular 'auto destination', as they say, in the US after Orlando, Florida, it's also crammed with casinos, casinos and still more casinos. In fact, many people don't go there just to see a single show, they go there for their holidays. Saturday afternoon they start at one end of town, doing all the shows in turn, and then drive off or fly out the following Saturday morning.

The whole thing is so tacky, so commercial and, unfortunately, so successful, that there is only one name the town could possibly have: Branson. He'll probably deny it. But who else has an ego big enough to name an entire town after himself?

Illinois

I'm worried about Chicago, the Windy City, or, as I suppose the Americans would say, 'Chicago-baby-what's-happ'nin-to-yah-yah-not-the-good-time-town-yah-used-to-be.' Or words to that effect.

Don't get me wrong, it's a great city, one of my favourites. It has the twenty-four-hour-a-day buzz and excitement of New York, the style of Boston and, in the middle of winter, the warm, sunny embrace of central Siberia. As for the wind, it's not that bad as long as you walk around with a couple of ton of rocks in your pockets. It also boasts, would you believe, a sewage system that was once voted by readers of an American engineering magazine the first of the seven modern wonders of the world. Now you tell me Americans don't get out and about much.

North Michigan Avenue, the Magnificent Mile, really is magnificent. The stores are huge temples to fashion: the biggest Ralph Lauren in the world, the biggest Gap in the world, the biggest collection of designer clothes in the world. Even the biggest popcorn store in the world, guaranteed to make certain that, having spent the entire US defence budget on all those Armanis and Versaces, you'll never be able to get into them.

The hotels are out of this world. They're about the size of St Peter's in Rome and as lush and extravagant as an Elton John birthday party. One of them, the Hotel Monaco, not content with offering all the usual facilities, even provides you with a companion in your room as well, no charge. Admittedly, it's only a goldfish, but the thought is there. The tank, of course, is extra, and the water . . . unless, of course, you're looking for an alternative to a late-night sushi.

The Drake, up on the banks of Lake Michigan, is my favourite. For some reason, whenever I stay there I always get the same room. I won't tell you which one in case you grab it and ruin my run of luck.

The bars and restaurants are amazing. Every time I'm in Chicago I try to get into Tru on St Clair Street. Their 'caviare staircase' of eight glass steps holding four different kinds of caviare and four garnishes sounds so typically American I've just got to sample it to find out why I think it's so disgusting. But they're always fully booked. I've tried all the tricks. 'Left my wallet there last night. Wonder if I could drop by and collect it? Say, while I'm there, how about dinner?' 'Hey, is Rick there tonight?' Rick is, of course, the owner and chef. 'I don't know if anyone's told you, but Michael Winner's coming to see you this evening.' That usually empties any restaurant anywhere in the world at a moment's notice. But I still haven't cracked it. Maybe one day I will. If I do, knowing my luck, it'll be the day Michael Winner is there as well.

The office blocks . . . well, I know it's not the thing to rave about office blocks, but Chicago does have three of the world's top ten. The Chicago office blocks, or rather, skyscrapers, are something else. They have a style all of their own. After the Great Fire of 1871, which might, of course, just have been another ploy to head off Michael Winner, they started putting up the first-generation skyscrapers: the art-deco Chicago Board of Trade Building where, would you believe it, they are still looking at the possibilities of electronic trading, the Auditorium Building and a whole string of others that look not so much like mere solid blocks as solid blocks somebody has tried to disguise. Then came the international, modern, postmodern and, of course, completely wacky, completely impractical Frank Lloyd Wright buildings. The international, modern and post-modern are easy to spot. They're nothing like the art-deco office blocks.

The Frank Lloyd Wright buildings are even easier to spot. They're completely unlike any other buildings on the planet. I once went out to Oak Park and River Forest, which is like a Frank Lloyd Wright modernist memorial park containing more Lloyd Wright buildings than anywhere else in the world. They were all completely different, all completely impractical. As for his 'little jewel', Unity Temple, all I can say is it makes anything Lord Rogers has designed look eminently sensible and prac-tical. What surprises me about the Americans, among the million other things that surprise me about Americans, is why they still think Lloyd Wright is such a big success. Maybe one or two of his ideas have been taken up, such as open-plan living, but I cannot see anywhere in the States wave after wave of hip-roofed prairie houses with tortuous front doors, rooms with ceilings so low even the Japanese would have trouble standing up in them, huge fireplaces that would wipe out the earth's few remaining forests on a cold Sunday afternoon, masses of intricate woodwork that nobody is able to do any more and fancy, arty windowpanes worthy of the Notre Dame in Paris. I mean, how come, if the mad, caped old man obsessed with the 'beautiful material that spins like a spider and produces a tension so perfect that you can balance a monolith on a pinpoint' was such a towering influential figure in the world of architecture, nobody has been influenced by him?

The real highball, who was far more important and far more influential than Frank Lloyd Wright, was, I reckon, Louis

Sullivan, who virtually invented the skyscraper. But nobody seems to talk about him. It's almost as if they are embarrassed by his common sense and the sensible, functional buildings he designed.

But even more important than either Frank Lloyd Wright or Louis Sullivan, even more imposing than anything created by that other Chicago architectural genius, the great minimalist Mies van der Rohe, is their little historic water tower. My God, they make so much fuss about it you'd think it was designed by Leonardo da Vinci, made by Michelangelo and paid for by Al Capone. It's a water tower, for heaven's sake. What's so amazing about a water tower? We've got water towers in Britain that are a hundred times the size. But, I suppose, if it makes them happy . . .

Up towards the Lake Michigan end of the Magnificent Mile, jutting out into the lake itself, is the Gold Coast, which is just that. Except that it is old gold. This is where the old mooks live who got rich on the stockyards when Chicago was the beef capital of the world, and on the Chicago Board of Trade in the good old days when, so the story goes, trading was so fast and furious and the pits so jam-packed with people clamouring to buy that if you waved your hand in the air to buy stock in the morning you couldn't get it down again till the exchange closed in the evening. By which time, of course, the stock you'd bought in the morning had been bought and sold a dozen times over and you were now worth another $1 million.

At the other end of the Magnificent Mile, the southern end, is the great Art Institute of Chicago, where I once spent a rainy Sunday afternoon desperately trying to avoid ringing up Tru's to see if they had a table free. 'Hi, my name is John Dillinger. I wonder if . . .' And that other Chicago institution, the Loop, their famous, twenty-four-hour-a-day overhead railway system. Stand the Loop up in the air and you get Sears Tower, America's tallest building at 1,454ft and with almost as many storeys as you hear travelling the Loop, especially early in the morning when you're desperately trying to remember which hotel you're staying in, not to mention the name you checked in under.

I've even been to the Chicago opera. The last time was to see a particularly frisky *Così Fan Tutte* complete with subtitles flashed up tickertape-style in huge letters above the stage. Luckily, everyone was so busy proving they were Nobel Prize-winners by reading them out loud that I couldn't hear the sound of them munching their popcorn. Of course, I couldn't hear the singing either, but then, who goes to the opera in Chicago for the singing? The Americans don't. They go there to play with their laptops and holler down their mobile phones.

But the trouble is, every time I go to Chicago I swear it's getting worse. Slowly, almost imperceptibly, but it's happening.

First there was that Great Fire of 1871, which destroyed nearly 200,000 buildings, about one third of the total, and prompted the introduction of structures that could survive Mrs O'Leary's cow kicking over a candle: steel frames, brick floors, ceramic cladding.

Then there was the dash for growth: skyscrapers. Everywhere else in the world this meant putting up new, taller buildings. Not in Chicago. In Chicago they took existing buildings and just jacked them up higher and higher, often with people still working in them. Having jacked them up higher and higher, they then faced the problem of getting the people back down to earth again, so they invented the lift, or as they called it, the elevator, because it solved the problem of the elevation of the building. Trouble was, they needed to fill all the buildings with people, but nobody could get into town because access to Lake Michigan was blocked by a huge sandbank. Their solution: get rid of the sandbank and dump all the sand in the middle of town underneath all the buildings they had jacked up for the people to work in.

Then came Prohibition, so called because it prohibited the police from arresting famous local businessmen, the likes of Al Capone or Bugs Moran or anyone remotely connected with breaking the law, on the basis that as most of them were either

Italian or Irish, or even half-Jewish, nobody could understand a word they were saying.

And so it has continued up to today. The Magnificent Mile is still jam-packed with people. But lots of people I know who used to live in the centre of town are moving out. Not good. There are more promotional organisations than ever before. Even the great Magnificent Mile has its own range of come-and-visit-us promotional material. Always a bad sign.

Then there are jobs. Companies I used to visit in and around the Futures Exchange, the Options Exchange and the Mercantile Exchange, not to mention those nice elderly gentlemen with eyeglasses in Little Italy, have closed down and moved on. An even worse sign.

Finally, the clincher: renovation. Wherever you look something is being renovated. Stores, hotels, back-street shops all seem to be being rebuilt, restyled, redecorated. The streets on either side of the mile used to be virtually jungle, postmodern or not, I couldn't tell. The first time I went there I was warned not even to glance out of the window on to Rush Street behind the Marriott Hotel in case I got shot at. Now it's all been improved and gentrified. Even the swish, old-gold Gold Coast is getting a facelift, although there, I was told, they are doing it the Gold Coast way. Rebuild, restyle and redecorate as much as you like, but no second kitchen, because a second kitchen means you could sublet and the last thing we want in here is not only the wrong people but too many of the wrong kind of people. OK? OK.

A couple of blocks further north, in Lincoln Park, which is more new gold, it's the same story. Walk along one of the streets just north of Old Town and you can see any number of three- or four-storey houses, all limestone columns, balustrades and fancy fruit-and-flower friezework, going up. To the Americans, of course, they're not houses but mansions. And the columns and balustrades make them Georgian, beaux arts or even classical. But for all that they still have to have baseball courts or even a roller-skating or hockey rink in the basement or they won't sell. Now, that's real bad news.

The traffic also seems to be getting worse. Much worse. Which is odd, because you would have thought that if people were leaving, if companies were leaving, the traffic would get better. Not so. In the old days it used to take me at least two hours to try to cross the Magnificent Mile from east to west just to avoid their damned water tower. Now it takes three. A big, big watery minus.

Drive out of Chicago and you can see where all the people and the jobs are going: to the suburbs, or the burbs, as they say. They are booming. Keep on driving and you hit open country. You begin to realise why Illinois was privileged to witness the invention of one of the greatest contributions to world peace: barbed wire. A certain Joseph Glidden saw the problems created by cattle wandering around all over the place, the fuss and bother between cowboys and farmers and the acute shortage of wood for fencing posts, so he did what anyone would do in the circumstances. He sat down and had himself a big mug of coffee when, Eureka!, the idea for barbed wire hit him, so much so that the first strands he made were produced with the help of his old coffee-grinder. The result: it changed the face of the West probably more than anything else. Suddenly, everybody knew exactly where they were and what was theirs and what wasn't. Farmers could fence their land and grow their crops unhindered by roving cattle. Ranchers could fence their land, keep their cattle on the best pastures and begin cutting down on the number of cowboys they needed. Towns and cities could decide whose was whose. The Internal Revenue could decide who didn't have to pay what and for what reason and still sue them for every penny they had. As for electric wire, that was too complicated for Illinois. That could only have been invented in Texas.

In fact, chasing people who've quit Chicago, I reckon I've seen most of what there is to see in Illinois that's not covered in barbed wire.

In Charleston I once met a group of Japanese businessmen

who were frantically running around wondering not only why everybody raved about the place but where all the antebellum houses had gone.

In Champagne, which had definitely lost its fizz if it ever had any, I met an old lady who looked and smelled like Annie Oakley's grandmother, who told me, law or no law, she always carried a gun in her handbag.

'But if someone attacks you,' I protested, 'there's no way you can say, "Excuse me for a moment, but can I try and find my gun in my handbag?"'

'No.' She grinned a row of yellow teeth the size and colour of tombstones. 'I agree. But when he's running away I can shoot him in the back. Pwah. He's dead.'

Wherever I went in Illinois, everyone agreed with me – a rare occurrence – that Chicago was losing people and jobs. As they lost people, tax revenues began to dry up. As they lost jobs, the people who were left had to travel further and further for work, blocking up the roads more and more. As people and jobs moved out of town, deliveries increased. There was more pressure on the roads but less money to deal with it. Things were also becoming more dangerous.

In Champagne I wanted to travel back to Chicago by train. They practically went down on their hands and knees and begged me not to. Chicago was now so dangerous, they said, that it was not only dangerous to get off at Union Station, it was probably even more dangerous to travel on the train. I'd probably get mugged sitting in my seat. With the situation as bad as that, and people getting the wind up about even the thought of travelling there by train it's no wonder they call it the Windy City.

But not to worry, Chicago. Whatever happens, I'll still love you. You're my kind of village.

Indiana

They say that Indiana is the crossroads of America, because if you can see through the fumes belching out of the back of 500

133

racing cars peeling rubber round and round the streets, not to mention the muck and grime pumping out of the smokestacks of Gary on the shores of Lake Michigan, you can see all the trucks shooting backwards and forwards across the country.

Not true. It's the dead end of America. Not just because it was home to James Whitcomb Riley, author of that famous American classic *Little Orphan Annie* and such classic poetry as

Such a dear little street, it is nestled away
From the noise of the city and the heat of the day,

but because it's where the bulk of the American funeral business, or the Big Au Revoir, as they call it, is based. Not the holes in the ground, but the fancy coffins, shucks, I mean caskets, that go in them. Not just fancy caskets, either, but super-super-fancy caskets. Not wood, because wood, even the most expensive carved, mahogany coffin topped with hardwood, is dull, boring and – can you imagine, in spite of all the money you spend? – can rot away in a matter of years. In any case, the US has practically run out of wood for coffins. Instead, for the world's greatest-ever disposable society, we're talking about the ultimate non-disposables: 18-gauge steel, 32oz solid copper, even bronze. My God, come the Day of Judgement they'll still be intact. In fact, so solid are the caskets that, come the Day of Judgement, if there's nobody around to crank them open, the poor guys inside won't even be able to rise from the dead to be at the Day of Judgement at all.

But the super-super luxury doesn't stop there. Inside you can have your coffin lined with crêpe, satin, velvet, hand-fluffed doeskin or common or garden silk, in which case, if the earthworms don't get you, the silkworms will. If that's too ordinary for you, and you feel you are really heading off on life's great adios, you can have it lined in denim. Denim smooth, denim rough, denim with holes in and stains all down the front. Still too conventional? How about that awful stuff people splay out all over the dashboards and rear windows of their cars? Or

134

maybe you wouldn't want to be seen dead in that, either.

If you are, or rather if you were, a golfer, you can have your casket lined with crêpe, satin, velvet, hand-fluffed doeskin or silk with pretty little patterns all over it of people who will for all eternity be trying to get the ball on to the green, let alone a hole in one. For some people, of course, this might be an advantage. It means they will never have to buy a round in the clubhouse after the game is over. If you're a tennis-player, you can have pretty pictures of little men in big baggy shorts trying to knock a ball over a net. If you're a sailor you can have pretty pictures of little men messing about in boats. When I told them what my special interests were, they doubted whether I would ever find a special lining to match my requirements, but they said they would try.

If that's not bad enough, you can also commission to travel with you to the next world your very own multimedia biography: a yukky mish-mash of photographs, videos, recorded reminiscences from family and friends and even embarrassing answering-machine messages. The cheap version, which nobody would ever dream of ordering for one of their loved ones: $595. The super-deluxe platinum package, written by a professional historian complete with professional narrator: $4,195. Extra if you want it on the internet.

Given that the cost of dying in America is considerably higher than the cost of living, it's probably just as well that the death rate is still one per person. At those prices, it's obvious why nobody wants to die twice.

Not that I started out with the slightest intention of digging up any information on the American way of death. I was in Indianapolis, one of your original rust-belt cities, home of the Indy and spiritual pitstop of Steve McQueen.

Everybody warned me not to go there. Napolis, they called it. Some said it put the nap into Indianapolis. Long on name, short on attractions, they said. It had no scenery, no mountains, no beaches, no nothing except a thick cloud of choking fumes which took a year to clear, by which time they were enveloped in another thick cloud of choking fumes. In winter it was cold and in summer it was still winter. About all it had in abundance was nothing. India-no-place.

But it's changed. It's not like that any more. It's climbed out of the grave and come back to life again. Or, if you like, the midwest has had a heart transplant.

Originally designed by Alexander Ralston, the man who helped Pierre l'Enfant design Washington – so the chances are, whoever is coming to get him, the president will still be able to escape – it was admittedly a one-time smokestack city. They were major motor manufacturers. At one time they manufactured more than sixty different makes of cars, including all the famous names like Stutz, Duesenberg, Marmon, Premier, National, Cole and Herff-Brooks. Then, as manufacturing dried up, the city became a major supplier. When the supplies business dried up, it was on the skids.

Today, however, it is roaring ahead, for all the world as if Steve McQueen was still at the wheel. It's a big, bustling – more interstate highways run through Indianapolis than through any other US city – racing for the winning post and the chequered flag. The reason for this phenomenal turnaround is not baseball, their first, last and greatest love of all time. Every brick wall has a basketball hoop. Whole towns shut down even for a school basketball match. Not basketball. Not college football. But your ordinary, bottom-of-the-heap football.

The Colts, one of America's top football teams, were based in Baltimore, Maryland. They wanted a new, all-singing, all-dancing, purpose-built, domed sports stadium all of their own. Baltimore turned them down. Indianapolis stepped in and promised them everything they were asking for, plus that other essential ingredient vital to any US sport you can imagine: money. Lots and lots of it. They also offered to pay the players millions. Not surprisingly the Colts up and quit Baltimore and moved to Indianapolis.

'We didn't steal the Colts,' said the Indianapolis mayor at the time. 'Baltimore lost them.'

Oh yes, Mr Mayor, pull the other one.

All the same, since then, even though from what I can gather the Colts are not exactly America's leading football team, they generate over $25 million a year for the city.

After the football stadium, Indianapolis built one world-class sports facility after another, starting with a huge swimming complex, shucks, I mean natatorium, complete with three swimming and diving pools and a bicycle-racing track. Any more and they could have been in the running for the Olympic Games and really lost a bundle. But while sport is naturally everything in the US, they didn't neglect – what do you call it? – oh yes, culture. They found new homes for the Indianapolis Symphony Orchestra and the Indianapolis Repertory Theatre. Not brand-new multimillion-dollar new homes, like they did for the footballers and swimmers and cyclists and all the other sportsmen, more renovated facilities. But who's complaining? They could have been completely overlooked.

Then they took a long, hard look at the city itself and restored what they could restore, rebuilt what they could rebuild and built afresh as much as they could. The whole downtown area was renovated and partly enclosed. A huge, fancy-looking 12,500 square-foot Artsgarden now straddles one of the city's busiest intersections. The old Union Station was part renovated and part rebuilt and turned into another one of those theme markets. Museums, stores, restaurants and night-clubs have been opened, garden pavilions have been planted and over forty major office blocks and hotels have appeared. The place is booming.

India-nap-olis has become the cornbelt sports city with the sunbelt sports sizzle. One sports event after another now takes place in Indie. They even hosted the Pan-American Games, only the second US city ever to do so. On top of that, of course, it is also home to the four largest one-day sporting events in the world: the Indy 500, the Brickyard 400, Pole Day for the Indy 500 and queuing up for a late-night drink in Broad Ripple Avenue.

The other thing I remember Indianapolis for: the time. So determined are they to remain in the forefront that they don't bother to put their clocks back and forwards like the rest of the US because, they say, it confuses the farmers. So much for all those old Hossier jokes about the Indies being backward. The only problem is that some parts of the state disagree and, America being the land of the free, they just put their clocks backwards and forwards along with the rest of the US. As a result, driving across Indianapolis is like travelling across six or seven different time zones. It plays havoc with the old watch. It also means once you escape, however wide awake you've been, you're likely to be two or three hours out. Which is OK if you're just heading for the bar, but not if you're heading for a meeting. Which is how I ended up in the middle of the casket business in Aurora.

I was driving back and forth across the state visiting companies. In Huntingdon, up towards Fort Wayne, I couldn't help but notice a Dan – 'Republicans under the bondage between parent and child' – Quayle Centre and Museum full of such historic exhibits as bonny bouncing baby photos, leather jackets and campaign posters. Of that famous blackboard with that famous worde one ite, there wase noe signe. I arrived at my last meeting bang on time. That is, bang on time according to my watch, but somehow or other I'd missed a time change. The guy I was going to see couldn't wait. He had to go across and visit a firm in Aurora, but he'd left a message that if I arrived I was to follow him.

When I found him he was in the centre of this big casket-production area. I've been in plenty of factories in my time, but here the attention, the dedication to detail and the sheer esprit de corpse was unbelievable. There's no way these guys would build half a casket in inches and the other half in millimetres. They would simply bury their differences.

At one end of the line three big, beefy gregarious Southern frat brats in scruffy, filthy jeans, T-shirts and baseball caps were on their hands and knees counting oh-so-slowly the number of stitches either side of a pile of pretty little pink pillows. One stitch too many on one side or the other and it was out. In the background a CD-player was pumping out 'Tea for One'.

As for the caskets themselves, not only did they have to be made to absolute but absolute perfection, they also had to be polished to the very highest polish that man can polish. Even when they close the lid of the casket to shift it – sorry, I mean even when they seal the casket reverently to transport it with the utmost decorum from one end of the plant to the other – they do so with the maximum possible respect and dignity. In other words, back to the real world, they also shove a sheet of greaseproof paper between the gum rubber gasket that runs around the lid and the casket itself to ensure that not the slightest trace of a mark is left on either side.

'But why?' I began. 'It's only going to end up . . .'

'Because,' said the most solemn American production manager I've ever met in my life, 'if we don't, the bereaved family, more especially the loved one's wife, will say it's marked, it's shop-soiled, and demand their money back. Years ago we even had one case where, because of the slightest mark on the rim, the grieving widow accused us of trying to sell her a secondhand casket.'

He also had, even for an American, a very odd turn of phrase. Other casket-manufacturers in town he referred to as 'Team Nasty'. Their chief executive officers were 'captains of the Team Nasty'. And an old, old friendly competitor was a 'friendasaurus'.

From Aurora the caskets are shipped out regularly to funeral directors all over the States. Special disasters – plane crashes, train crashes – all warrant special deliveries. Then it's over to the funeral directors, who conduct their business with the grieving wife and family as soon as it is convenient and appropriate to do so. Usually this means after they have called the insurance company, been to the lawyer and booked their tickets to Acapulco. In some dire cases, of course, it might be as soon as the grieving widow's new Mexican toyboy telephones to say they've got an hour-and-a-half window coming up in a few days and could everything be fixed for then?

American funeral directors, apparently, are like funeral directors the world over. I thought they'd be like your usual American businessmen: T-shirts, jeans and back-to-front baseball caps, but perhaps with a black ribbon sewn neatly around the bottom of their caps in deference to their profession. Their offices, I thought, would have neon signs outside flashing 'Funerals to Go'. But no. Although the big corporations are moving in, most funeral businesses are still, by and large, Mom-and-Pop affairs. Most are based in towns and villages which they and their parents before them have served for generations. Most are middle-aged or older. Most shun as many of the modern ways of this world as possible. Less than 40 per cent have e-mail. Which is surprising when you consider that funerals are big business, some say as big as $100 billion a year, maybe more when you throw in certified death midwives, obituaries-and-ashes mailing companies, live online funeral services, cremation-cams of your loved one's cremation, and, for the stuck-up, cremation paintings (paint a picture with glue, then throw the ashes of the dearly departed all over it), not to mention companies offering to scatter your ashes in space, body hoists, embalming fluids and the like.

Back in Indianapolis that night, I switched on the television to see how much further technology stocks had fallen on the NASDAQ. There was a report on severe flooding in North Carolina. There on the screen, floating down the high street of some small town, was a row of caskets. Apparently, the storms had loosened the ground and, because these were basically nothing but huge, highly engineered, lovingly and beautifully made, highly polished, airtight boxes, they had bubbled up to the surface and were floating off into the sunset. What the now-impoverished loving relatives thought, I can't imagine. What their lawyers thought, I can imagine.

The Cheese States

I always think Wisconsin should be butter. But it isn't, it's cheese. Actually, the truth is it's beer, but as beer is alcohol, and alcohol is practically banned in the States, along with t*b*cc*, mortadella, shouting 'Fire!' in a crowded theatre and calling a woman a chick with major-league hooters instead of a breasted American who is pectorially superior, it's best to avoid all mention of the subject. Not that American beer is much good anyway. In fact, to give you the cheese on it, as they say, I reckon that, deep down, the breweries agree. Look at bottles of American beer. In eight cases out of nine, they don't even bother to put the alcoholic content on the label. Not that that's a great help one way or another. If the beer is so weak, what's the point of putting the alcoholic content on the label? You're hardly likely to have a stand-up fight with somebody because his beer is 2.1 per cent alcohol and yours is a whopping 2.23 per cent. But go into a US store on a Sunday morning, when many of them refuse to sell what they call alcoholic beverages, and try telling them beer's not an alcoholic beverage because there's no alcoholic content mentioned on the label, and you'll soon see how understanding, tolerant and consumer-oriented they are.

So it doesn't grate on my nerves too much to think of Wisconsin, and its next-door neighbour Minnesota, as cheese states. Thanks largely to the Scandinavians and the Germans, it's dairy country. The Scandinavians cleared the forests. The Germans planted the barley. They both then started breeding contented cows. The Scandinavians because they're always drinking gallons of milk and being healthy. The Germans because they know better than anyone that if you're going out for a night on the b***, the best thing to do is to line your stomach with milk first. And if you drink as much b*** as the Germans do, that's one hell of a dairy industry.

Butter and cheese, however, they discovered only by accident when they started reading some of Garrison Keillor's Lake Woebetideyou stories to the cattle. The milk curdled before they even got to the bit about all the women being strong, all the men good-looking and all the children above average, let alone all the references to old frame houses, lawn sprinklers swishing across the grass, flower bushes by the porch, dogs, lights behind the curtains and the charcoal smoke in the air. Suddenly they were in the butter and cheese business. Today, wherever you go, there are cheese stands, cheese delis, cheese boutiques, cheese centres and cheese co-operatives. You can even stay in cheese houses or, if you're a big cheese, cheese hotels, where, whatever the rind or reason, they serve traditional three-course cheese meals: cheese candy, then cheese, followed by cheese ice-cream.

To me they're also cheese states because I can't help but give a weak, cheesy grin whenever I hear them going on about freedom of the individual, freedom of expression, the right to life, liberty and a home free from fear. Freedom of the individual? Freedom of expression? The right to life, liberty and a home free from fear? There's none of that in either state. You're not allowed to drive without seatbelts. You're not allowed to climb on to a bike without a safety helmet. If you're lost in the frozen wastes, suffering from exposure and on the point of death, you're not even allowed to crawl inside a moose in order to survive. Even if it's dead. No doubt because of all the Scandinavians around, Minnesota was also the first state to infringe their citizens' freedom to destroy themselves by insisting on the lot of them not smoking. By the hairs of Strindberg's beard, if that wasn't bad enough, they banned everybody from smoking practically before they even gave them permission to start planting tobacco so that other, less mollycoddled, people could have the freedom to kill themselves. Not only that, they were the first to ban smoking in airports, even in the bars, so that the cheese states became the first place in the whole of the United States where you could go into a bar and not have a smoke with the alcohol they didn't serve while waiting for your plane not to arrive.

As if that's not bad enough, they were also the first to go bananas on recycling. Not only does everything have to be recycled, including the non-alcoholic beer, which some say tastes better than the real thing, but everything has to have its own separate containers: cans, bottles, plastic, radioactive materials, state rules and regulations forbidding you from doing whatever you might think of doing.

Then, of course, there's the whole question of the Sioux and the Chippewa. What happened to their rights? Weren't they entitled to any kind of freedom from having Garrison Keillor rammed down their throats? And what about the rest of us? Surely we deserve the right to be protected from the total, non-stop, twenty-four-hour-a-day promotional saturation of their production? Wherever you go in the States, whoever you see, whatever you're talking about, they all just look as though they're doing nothing but saying, 'Cheese, cheese, cheese.'

Not that their cheese is any better than their beer, thanks to the Food and Drugs Administration. According to the experts in the FDA who want to spamoflage everything in sight, cheese is the second most dangerous foodstuff in the whole of the US after all the other most dangerous foodstuffs. All cheese, they say, must be made with pasteurised milk. In other words, they want to kill off all the dangerous bacteria such as salmonella, listeria and e.coli which gives cheese, especially French cheese, its taste. They're even talking about introducing the same regulations for imported cheese as well.

If they do, a fabulous, soft Roquefort, a Tetilla Gallega, a

Stilton, even a Gruyère, will all be banned. Instead, after a delicious meal of hamburgers, you'll be savouring the delights of a weak, thin, slice of wet cardboard that tastes like buzzard puke. Personally, I reckon there'd be more flavour to the FDA order banning foreign cheeses in the first place.

To make matters even worse, being Scandinavians and Germans, not only are they obsessed with sticking to the FDA regulations down to the final umlaut, they also insist on putting their tasteless cheeses in all kinds of fancy packaging which is impossible to open. Let me tell you, Harry Houdini escaped from Appleton, Wisconsin, where he was born, far easier than you could spring a lump of wishy-washy Monterey Jack American cheddar out of its bacteria-free, pollution-free, biodegradable, environmentally friendly, genetically modified, sweaty plastic pansy pouch.

Now, doesn't that make you want to say Parmigiano-Reggiano?

Wisconsin

For all the hype about Wisconsin being the beer state of America, the capital, Milwaukee, is pretty dull, flat and insipid. A bit like most of their beers. In fact, given the size of their dairy industry, it should be called Milkwaukee instead.

Before I went there I thought it was going to be all bierkellers the size of baseball pitches, beer flowing in the streets and hearty, thigh-slapping, strapping, 20-stone Americans in their designer lederhosen getting schlossed out of their tiny minds. The men, of course, would be putting on the Fritz. They'd be wearing those long green raincoats, tiny Tyrolean hats, dipping the schnitzel (which has a completely differing meaning altogether in Milwaukee than it has back in Baden-Baden) and sporting not huge beer guts, because you're not allowed to say that in politically correct America, but huge liquid-grain storage facilities, while the women would not be drunk but chemically inconvenienced. Instead it's like a small town; a very small-town Chicago.

It's got some fancy buildings, like reject designs for Chicago, nothing grand or spectacular. Except maybe the vast new sports stadium, Miller Park. When it's completed. It also has some bars. The hype says hundreds. Well, if that's true, I certainly didn't see them. In a good few days of trying to get beered up, I reckon I did more damage to my feet than to my liver. I didn't even notch up a dozen. So if they're there, they're pretty well hidden, which is not the case with much in America. As for the ones I did find, they weren't a patch on the bars in, say, Boston or New York, or even swinging high spots like Champaign, Illinois, let alone the real grown-up bars you find in Ireland, the Czech Republic, Poland, even downtown Moscow, which are in a glass of their own. Not that I'm complaining.

Some hopheads go on and on about bars. They must have this. They must have that. Not me. I'm easy. I only go into bars at my wife's suggestion. Whenever I even think of having a drink she threatens to pack the dogs into the car and go out for the rest of the day. Well, with an incentive like that, what would you do? My requirements, therefore, are minimal. So long as a bar has got good beer, good people and good laughs, I'm happy. I'm not even fussy about women in bars, so long as they're other people's.

It's just that American bars are different. They're not the obvious place to go for a firkin good time. They take getting used to. First, there's all the inn-appropriate fuss the guys behind the bar make about serving the stuff in the first place. In the UK you amble into a bar, fight your way through the piles of vomit, push aside the piles of stale bar snacks containing samples of fourteen different types of urine and then wait two hours to be recognised by a passing barman. In Ireland, you drop a glass on the floor, the place empties, you stroll up to the bar and your Guinness is already there waiting for you. Within ten minutes you can be fitshaced out of your mind.

Not so in the US. You walk straight in, straight up to the bar then it takes two hours for the barman to decide whether you're old enough to have a drink in the first place. In many states you can vote, marry, divorce, remarry, divorce, remarry, divorce and die for your country before you're twenty-one but you can't drink a glass of weak beer in a public place. Then, if there's the slightest doubt, there's all this brew-ha-ha about whether you are who you say you are. They want IDs, birth certificates, your mother's birth certificate, your auntie's inside leg measurement, the lot. Now, I know I don't look my age but, God help me, in one bar just outside Gettysburg, Pennsylvania, they even asked me for my passport before they would serve me. It took me all my strength to get up off the floor and give it to them.

It wouldn't be so bad if the beers were worth all the aggro. They're not. In fact, after a couple of drinks, any bar is fine by me. But in America it takes more than a couple of drinks because American beer is not like other beer in the world. I'm not saying it's tasteless, it's just that it's better if you drink it out of a dirty glass. It somehow gives it more flavour. German, Czech, Belgian beer, especially the ones made by the monks – three glasses and you're trappiste – are solid, chewy beers; masses of body, bags of taste, a meal in themselves. They not only make you intoxicated, they leave you unable to say in . . ., intoxed, intoxygated, or whatever. Not that anything is better in the world than that first nine pints of Guinness at the airport bar just after your plane has landed in Ireland. It's like dying and waking up in heaven. No, it's even better.

American beers, in comparison, always seem a bit weak and watery. In other words, a pour show. That goes for the mass beers – even the Samuel Adams, one of my favourites – as well as most of the micro brews. As for Budweiser, it's flatteringly known as beer used twice.

Maybe it's because they're not strong enough. Maybe because there's not enough in them. Take, for example, Rocking Roll, made in Pennsylvania. Hops, would you believe, are the fifth ingredient they list on the bottle. Drink it all day and all night and your bladder would give out before you even slipped slowly to the floor. I mean became accidentally horizontalised.

Maybe it's because they chill them so much. One black Bavarian-style beer I tried in Milwaukee was so chilled that I'm still suffering from frostbite. And as for putting ice cubes in it, I'm sorry, but whether they're made of mineral water or not, I don't care. It's crazy.

Or maybe it's just that I need more practice.

Then there's the atmosphere. None of the bars I went into in Milwaukee had what you would call that English/Irish pubby feel about them. One evening I ended up in some ratty sports bar downtown drinking something called Pete's Wicked Ale, which had a strange chocolatey, winey taste, more Pete's Wacky Ale than Wicked Ale, if you ask me. The whole bar looked and felt as if it was covered in a thick layer of their famous Wisconsin cheese. Maybe it was because there wasn't an American in sight. Instead it was full of Indians and Bangladeshis and Turks and Kurds and Iranians. Sure, they were cheering on the teams on the string of televisions all over the place, but somehow it didn't seem real. It lacked conviction, as if their passports depended on them acting and behaving like Americans. Especially when I realised that the Indians and the Bangladeshis weren't even drinking.

The only time it showed any hint of an atmosphere was towards the end of the evening, when the door opened and in walked a guy wearing a collar and tie. The place suddenly went quiet. He turned out to be an Irish priest who was visiting the States for the first time and staying with relatives who lived nearby. He told me he didn't wear his clerical collar because he didn't want to attract attention to himself.

One of the Iraqis offered me a lift back to the hotel. I could tell he was an Iraqi because every time we stopped at traffic lights, he wound down the window of the car and screamed out at the top of his voice, 'Hussein! Murderer! Dictator! I kill you with my own hands!' On second thoughts, I suppose he could have been an undercover CIA agent. You never know nowadays.

Just two minutes out of Milwaukee you can see why the beer

is so watery. They've got nothing but lakes: 15,000 of them. They say there are 15,000 of them, although the real figure is 15,119. I should know, I've seen every one of them. Again and again and again.

On one trip I had to get to Clear Lake, which is so far from Milwaukee even I was beginning to look forward to an American beer when I finally arrived. Not that there was much there when I did. Apart from even more lakes.

Meeting out of the way, I made for the nearest bar. I wanted to sample the local brew, to talk to the locals about American beers and maybe collect a few more Bill Clinton jokes. The only thing anybody was interested in was mineral water: Perrier mineral water. Because the water in Wisconsin was so pure – yawn – that Perrier wanted to sink a high-capacity well – yawn, yawn – to tap the spring water flowing into – zzzzz – Schmudlach Creek and the south branch of Wedde Creek, which flow into the Mecan, pronounced McCann, River, famous for its brown trout, mayfly hatches and the Karner blue butterfly, an endangered species whose numbers have been reduced by 99 per cent over the last fifteen years. Yaargh. That's when I fell off the chair.

Everybody was up in arms about it, even though Perrier were promising they would draw off as little as 350 gallons a minute from the Mecan Springs capacity of 6,000 gallons a minute. The money they were going to spend, the number of people they were going to employ were all irrelevant. It was the principle that counted. They were so worked up about it I didn't even get a chance to ask anyone why the crisps tasted better than the beer.

My last evening in Milwaukee I'm dreaming of some of the best beers I've had in my life. Those last six pints of Guinness at Shannon Airport before heading back home. Liefman's Old Brown, a fabulous, dark, creamy Belgian beer. The 12-degree Staropramen I discovered in Prague before I did whatever it was I did, which I deny. Legend Stout in Lagos. Mandalay Lager Beer. Or maybe it wasn't. Maybe it was just because I'd spent

148

all day in the sun traipsing around one pagoda after another with no shoes on and it just tasted like the best beer in the world.

Then there are all the hangover cures. In Germany, they give you bananas, red meat and milk. In Haiti, I was presented with thirteen black-headed pins to push into the cork of the bottle responsible for my condition. Best of all was a lethal mix of equal parts port, brandy and white crème de menthe that was so powerful that even now I can't remember who gave it to me or where I was when I drank it.

Instead of heading back straight to my lonely hotel room for another evening spent looking through the window at the traffic lights changing in the rain, as I usually do whenever I'm on a trip, I dodged into a bar round the back of the big, gleaming Performing Arts Center. The place was practically empty. Standing behind the bar was this drop-out who looked as though he was three firkins short of a barrel. On his head was a baseball cap proclaiming 'Wanker'. On his T-shirt was the slogan 'I feel like a Wanker'. They were serving a beer made in New York called Wanker.

'Fancy a Wanker?' he yelled at me as soon as I set foot inside the door. 'You can have a Wanker Lite or a Big Wanker. Most guys around here go for the Big Wanker.'

American beer? It makes you say 'Cheese.'

Minnesota

Poor Minnesota. As if the winters are not bad enough, never mind having the Mall of America in their midst, they also have Garrison Keillor to contend with. Not that I'm saying he's boring. It's just that there must be some reason why hardly anybody lives there. And worse. He goes on and on and on – 173 years to date, 200 million books, 700 hours of broadcasting, all about his goddamned Lake Wobegon. I tell you, if I could get enough pasteurised, plastic cheese from Wisconsin I'd smother the place. It's not that he's Norman Rockwell with a typewriter. He's Norman Rockwell with a typewriter covered in

Vermont treacle. Yuck. And no wonder he's called Garrison. He uses an army of words when a platoon would do.

I first came across Garrison Keillor in, appropriately enough, Duluth, which more than lived up to its name. I was dragging myself around the place visiting Minnesota mining and manufacturing companies. I even hit Austin, which gave us Mrs Thatcher's childhood Christmas treat, Spam, where I met two woebegones who behaved as if they ran the United Nations Security Council. They spent their lives organising – wait for it – Spam sculpture competitions all over the world. Then for some reason I ended up in Duluth, at one time, it is claimed, the largest freshwater port in the world. Things, however, had changed. I found it so exciting that I spent the whole of my time there reading about Lake Wobegon. It almost made Duluth seem like Las Vegas.

Yet to Minnesotans, Keillor is God. No, that's not true: he's more important than God. He captures their shallow personalities, their inadequacies, their unimportance and the wide range of two subjects they don't talk about: winter and winter. Everything is in his shadow. The Twin Cities, Minneapolis–St Paul, or the thirty-five bifurcates, as some people mysteriously insist on calling them. The Mall of America, the largest shopping mall in the whole of the known universe, and quite possibly the unknown universe as well. The snow. The ice. Those 10,000 frozen lakes.

In theory, of course, Minnesota should be a Swede dream. The land is rich and fertile. The air is clean and crisp. The place is full of hardworking, tough-living Scandinavians who think nothing of rolling around in the snow in temperatures of −20 degrees Centigrade. Stark naked. It could have been one of the richest, most go-ahead, dynamic states in the Union. Minneapolis–St Paul could have been another Boston, Chicago, even New York. It has everything going for it. A big trading centre, commodities, good communications, Lake Superior. Then it was struck by the curse of Garrison 'Flower bushes by the porch, old frame houses, dogs, lights coming from behind curtains' Keillor. Today it's so bad the Swedes don't even talk about the saunas and jacuzzis they had last night and again this morning, although why they didn't solve the problem and go for his throat I can't imagine. Why else they are called the Gopher State I have no idea.

Minneapolis–St Paul, as a result, is a smörgåsbord of seatbelts, crash helmets and no cigarettes. In theory, it should be a wild mixture of everything rough and craggy and way out and everything smooth and sophisticated. Some even claim it's young and swinging and, would you believe, theatrical. But they must have died in the 1920s or maybe the 1930s.

To me, Minneapolis, at one time the flour-milling capital of the world, still looks as though it kneads the dough. For all its so-called swinging theatricality, it is still dominated on one side of the Mississippi by General Mills and on the other by Pillsbury's Best. At one time they were deadly rivals, bombarding each other with such delights as Cheerios, Wheaties, Jolly Green Giant vegetables and, of course, Hamburger Helpers. Now, together, they are bombarding the rest of us with such delights as Cheerios, Wheaties, Jolly Green Giant vegetables and those damn Hamburger Helpers. The rest of the place looks as though they've spent all their money on nothing but Cheerios, Wheaties and the rest of the stuff. The riverfront is practically derelict; the town itself looks as though it could do with a decent meal.

St Paul, though, is completely different. It's old, responsible, a touch Victorian and, with a name like that, very Irish, as opposed to Damascene, Catholic. Mark Twain always referred to it as 'he' as in, 'He is a manufacturing city, of course – all the cities of the region are – but he is peculiarly strong in the matter of commerce.' After all, you could hardly say, 'St Paul, she is a manufacturing city,' although I suppose in some parts of the States that would be more than acceptable.

In the old days it was the launch pad, or rather the wicker basket, for immigrants descending into the vast, never-ending farmlands of the west. Today, it's – sorry, he's – still in the immigrant business, except that the immigrants he's after are better dressed, well-heeled and prepared to blindly sit out five-day seminars and conferences in his brand-new convention centre.

For entertainment facilities they've also built a new science museum, a hockey stadium and, the ultimate in convention relaxation, a healing garden, on Harriett Island in the middle of the Mississippi, with steps, Ganges-like, going down into the river. Which sounds more John the Baptist to me than St Paul, but then, I know nothing. But the difference doesn't end there. In Minneapolis, I find, people are more airy-fairy, New Age without quite knowing why they are New Age. They talk about skills-orientation, validating the feedback, rebounds, my darkest hour and, no doubt as a tribute to the all-pervading influence of General Mills, agonise over what was the best thing before sliced bread. In St Paul they're more down-to-earth, practical, and, thanks to their rich Irish ancestry, they call a spade a shovel. They talk about getting on with the job, fixing it, wrapping it up and not sweating the petty things or petting the sweaty things. Even the down-and-outs work for their money. Most play some kind of instrument. Some dance. One morning after breakfast (three General Mills Milk 'n' Cereal bars, Cheerios on the side and a large bloody mary), as I came out of the hotel a local tramp, or street crazy, as they call them, proceeded to take his jacket off, roll it up neatly, place it carefully on the edge of the flowerbed and wrap a dirty blanket round his shoulders before giving us all a hearty round of 'The Star of the County Down'. When it comes to giving to beggars, I stop at nothing. So I gave him nothing.

He grabbed me by the arm. 'Tell me, do you know the difference between Minneapolis and St Paul? In Minneapolis they eat the frosted shreddies and throw the plastic toys away. In St Paul, they eat the toys and throw the frosted shreddies away.' I gave him $5 to go away.

At markets all over town you also see Laotians hard at work, most of them Hmong who fought with the Americans in the Vietnam War. Which is terrible. It must have been bad enough fighting with the Americans in the first place, but then to end up in Minnesota? It hardly bears thinking about. They are now hmong the biggest sellers of herbs and spices in the States. The local Hmong newspaper, however, is still waging war against 'communist collaborators'.

But wherever I am in Minnesota – whether it is in Sven and Ole's Pizza on Lake Superior, covered in leeches and mosquitos, the saw-tooth mountains in the background, discussing the merits of throwing back an 8lb lake trout, or trying to avoid the sight of the Mall of America, which is so big that the car park is in North Dakota and the check-out line in Wisconsin – I keep wondering what the place would be like if, instead of worshipping Garrison Keillor, they'd hung on the words of that other famous Minnesotan writer, F. Scott Fitzgerald. There would be no dog on the porch then, I can tell you. There'd be crates of booze. And, as for what was coming from behind the curtain, it wouldn't have been a light.

The Bacon States

Why do I think of New York, New Jersey and North Carolina as the bacon states? It's a pig to explain. It's probably got something to do with them being pigheaded, male chauvinist pigs, making a pig's ear of everything, saving their bacon and ending up pigs in clover. And if that doesn't offend huge sections of the population, certainly of New York and New Jersey, not to mention some of their more fundamental brethren in North Carolina, I don't know what will.

When I first went to New York everybody was pigheaded as hell. Everybody knew better than everybody else in the world. Everybody was ready to land you one in the middle of your face if you didn't agree with them. Everybody had their snout in the trough. Everybody was going hog wild. Everybody was a rageaholic. It was fantastic. It was like living in the middle of a non-stop family row. It was all shouting, hollering, doors slamming and phones being crashed down. People were so wound up about everything that they used to go to the fortune-teller twice a week to have their fists read. In fact, the first time in my life I heard gunfire was in the middle of New York. But I managed to escape.

Then, over the years pork-barrel politics took over. It was a case of all hams on deck. They started to clean it up. Norman Dinkins, the first black mayor, was probably the first to try. But without much success. I remember meeting him a couple of times in Gracie Mansions, the official mayoral concrete bunker. He was a nice guy, but he didn't have any real muscle. He was an innocent who had strayed into the world of politics. Ed Koch started to really grapple with the place. His big mistake, however, seemed to be that he preferred publicity to policy. Rudy Giuliani was the guy who did it. The result is that today New York is a Big Apple without the core. Gone is all the rubbish. Gone is the violence of the 1960s and 1970s. Gone is that feeling of menace, that undercurrent of violence. Gone is good, cheap, housing, good public hospitals, almost-free universities and Rudy's wife. But that's another book.

All they're interested in now is bringing home the bacon. In other words, money, money, money. Everywhere you go it's NASDAQ, the Dow Jones Industrial Average and my God, we're heading for a triple-top. Quick, get Alan Greenspan on the phone.

In the old days McDonald's on Wall Street used to be an ordinary hamburger bar. Now there's a doorman in a tuxedo, a pianist and a tickertape machine pumping out all the prices. They've even closed the downtown honky-tonk bar, Hogs and Heifers – what else? – not because the likes of Julia Roberts, Drew Barrymore and Daryl Hannah used to drape the walls with their bras, making it the swingingest place in town, but because of the occasional late-night outbursts of dancing.

So can you please tell me how, amid all this hectic frenzy, this concentration of massive financial brainpower, *The New York Times* managed to publish the wrong figures for New York municipal bond yields for weeks on end without anybody noticing? It wouldn't have happened in the old days. The first day the guy at Salomon Brothers responsible for supplying porkies to the *NYT* would have been taken out, shot and turned into pork-skin chicharrones before breakfast. Cooked with huge dollops of melted pig fat.

Much the same has happened in New Jersey. It used to be the dustbin of the dustbin of New York. Or, if you like, the rind on the fat of the bacon of New York. Now it not only calls itself the Garden State, but it really is a garden state although, as in all gardens, if you look hard enough you'll find the odd pile of rubbish happily rotting away in a corner somewhere. Jersey City used to be a dress rehearsal for the Balkans. It was mile after mile of filthy, dilapidated factories, derelict offices and car parks that looked like something planned by Slobodan Milosevic. Just to think of going there was to take your life into your hands. Going there now is no longer a rash thing to do, let alone one of the more rasher things you could do. Pork-barrel politics scores again.

As for North Carolina – oink, oink, oink – it's no longer a pig in a poke but the pig state to end all pig states. It's the centre of America's multibillion-dollar-a-year pig industry, and it's home to some of the largest pork-production plants in the world, each capable of slaughtering around 20 million pigs a year. Not that you would notice. The air is a glorious mix of methane, ammonia and chlorine. The talk in the bars along Interstate 95 is whether there is more job satisfaction in spending all day hauling tons of pork parts around by forklift truck or scraping worms out of a pig's intestines. What's more, the population is outnumbered 2–1 by pigs. Let's hope they never come across *Animal Farm*.

My real beef – if that's the right word – about North Carolina, however, is that it's so pigheaded. Now, I know in addition to the pigs it's big on research. It's got plenty of way-out companies. It's got a big textile industry. But it's also big on religion. Not just religion. But their kind of religion, interpreted their way, to their standards. Which means – excuse me. May I finish what I'm saying? That it's very difficult to . . . Well. No. Hang on. Let me finish . . . Try to . . .

Oh hell. Give me another slice of that fat-back pork.

New York

OK, I'm a klutz. They want some schmaltzy meeting. Like a noodge, I schlepp to the office. This nudnik keeps me waiting. He keeps on kibitzing and kibitzing. It's enough to make anyone want to kvetch. This schmuck then decides, OK, no meeting. I tell you, I was meshuga, I almost threw a broigus.

New York is a million things. A million fast-moving, non-stop, no-time-to-even-breathe things. But it's also Jewish. Heavily Jewish. Not because there are many of them. They make up only around 10 per cent of the whole New York State population. But because they make themselves felt. They yell, they shout, they argue about everything. They won't even eat or drink anything that agrees with them. They march, they scream, they take out full-page ads in *The New York Times*. They raise money. They donate. And they vote. They're probably the most active voters in the world. Why? Because, they say, James Madison, who came up with the first draft of the US Constitution, was a Jewish scholar, so he obviously passed the word around and they've been busily voting ever since. In fact, although they make up only 10 per cent of the population, they regularly account for over 30 per cent of the votes cast in any New York election. And – surprise, surprise – they have no problems with the chads.

Now, while I am more than prepared to go Gentile into the good night as I came Gentile into the good day, I don't think it does any harm once in a while to don the old black fedora, black suit, black shoes, twirl the dreidels, grab the nearest black umbrella, forget to shave for a couple of days and check out what the opposition is up to. To show a bit of chutzpah, in other words. And I can finally get the hang of the old mama-loshen, try pastrami without mayonnaise, go around using words like 'schmo' or worse, call my tailor dreek or even bubkes, and tell my wine merchant he's an alter kocker and he should go shtup himself. If you get my drift.

After all, we're all fed up with the rest of the place. Wall Street, with its vast canyons of money-laundering banks, completely cut off to mobile phones. Manhattan, bought by the Dutch in 1626 for £15, where nowadays you can hardly get along the pavement for kids stuck in pushchairs outside fashionable restaurants while their mothers are inside lunching. Why haven't they done something about it? They have. They sued one of the mothers, who turned out to be Danish. 'But this is what we do in Copenhagen,' she pleaded. The case was thrown out, she sued the city for $20 million and the pavements are still full of kids stuck outside restaurants.

Brooklyn, which used to be, in no unsoyten toyms, a dump, especially around Williamsburg. Now it's bright and clean, with hi-tech companies all over the place. There is even electric light.

The Bronx. My God, I remember the Bronx. But it's all disappeared. Instead they're playing cricket. On a proper cricket pitch, at Van Cortlandt Park, and for a proper league (though admittedly it's called the Calypso Night Cricket League). Would you ever have imagined such a thing were possible? I wouldn't. Not in a million years.

Harlem. I first went to Harlem when it was still owned by the Dutch. Now it's Hamilton Heights, Hudson Heights and some other fancy name. South Harlem they tried to rename Sotla, but for some reason or other it didn't catch on. Chinatown. Little Italy, that yuppie, low fat, yogic, chardonnay-sipper's heaven. SoHo? Gornisht. Nothing but gornisht.

As for the sights, we've all seen them all. The Guggenheim, the Flatiron, Broadway. Times Square, Fifth Avenue, the Empire State Building. The Oyster Bar in Grand Central Station. Reuben's, the down-to-earth deli on Madison Avenue, which reckons it invented the corned-beef, sauerkraut and Swiss-cheese sandwich. We've all done them a million times, including the occasional visit to one of those cool Upper East Side apartments, not to mention the Statue of Liberty, with its never-ending queues of lonely old klutzes who only go there so that they can brag that they have spent all day inside a woman and it only cost them $10.

Now that wandering the streets is no longer fraught with danger, the excitement has gone. There are people around at all hours of the day and night, taking cabs, riding the subways – where you can watch the weirdos, spot passengers on the fiddle as well as on the violin and shrink with fear as way-out rappers leap into the carriage at the last minute, boom box in hand, to serenade the world – or risking their lives on the Staten Island ferry.

We've also all learned to tawk New York tawk. No prollem. Tsamatta? Icegotannafyah? Hootoadjadat? Whattaya-dink-I-am-a-schochtet? Yanutz. Fuggedaboudit. Gedaddaheeuh. In other words, I think, old chap, this matter warrants further consideration, don't you? Super. Toodle pip. A select few have even grasped the subtleties of New York stockmarket speak. 'Bonds retreated on bearish comments from the fed.' What the hell is Alan Greenspan doing now? Can't he tell us what he's thinking? It would save us all a great deal of time and money.

The market has been affected by technical factors.

We've got no idea what's going on.

The market is beginning to look a little extended.

Jump.

We've learned not only to eat New York eats – hamburgers, duckhash browns, hamburgers, whadeveryaheatwidafawk, hamburgers – but also, much more complicated, to drink addabah and read dapaypuh at the same time.

It was New York where we learned the sophisticated art of tipping, American-style. In any other city in the States it's an indollarable situation. We all know the theory: restaurants, 15 per cent; barmen, what's left on the plate plus some; providers of other special services, whatever they ask for, plus your wallet, plus the cab fare, and hope to God that's the last you'll ever see of them. But it never works that way. There's always something you miss. You know when you have from the frozen smile, the cab door that happens to slam shut just as you're helping your niece into the back seat. I used to worry about it. Why tip the barman and not the doctor who saves your life? Why tip the housemaid and not the entire McDonald's? Why tip at all? Surely it's downgrading, insulting, humiliating? Apparently not. In New York there's no problem. You just throw money at everyone and everything and run for cover.

And we've all learned to live twenty-four-hours a day because New York is not anything if it's not a twenty-four-hour-a-day city: twenty-four-hour hotels, twenty-four-hour bars, twenty-four-hour restaurants, twenty-four-hour news channels, twenty-four-hour wedding chapels, twenty-four-hour whatever you can think of. Although I once discovered quite by chance that there are limits to even the New Yorkers' concept of twenty-four-hour service. I once walked into a twenty-four-hour drive-in bank somewhere between Fifth Avenue and the United Nations headquarters. They refused to serve me. Not because it was the middle of the night, but because I wasn't in a car. I was going to complain but then I noticed the instructions were all in English, Spanish and braille. Braille? Do blind people drive cars in New York? Do twenty-four-hour drive-in banks in New York serve blind people driving cars? It was all too much for me. I fled to the nearest twenty-four-hour bar.

We've dragged ourselves all over New York State as well. Years ago I used to go to Albany, the capital, for meetings with a Mafia look-alike. He wore an overcoat and gloves whatever the weather. He was also the only man I've ever met who could eat a hot dog sideways.

Binghampton I used to visit with an electronics whizz. Wherever we went, he would say he was with IBM. We got discounts in all the bars, all the restaurants. We even got the IBM corporate rate at the only decent hotel in town. I've even been to Alfred. I remember arriving there late at night, in the middle of winter, covered in snow. There weren't any restaurants open, and neither were there any cakes, burned or otherwise.

As for Buffalo, famous as the jumping-off point for Niagara Falls as well as for the invention of Buffalo wings, or chickens' spare parts, as they call them in Africa, I was there the winter the falls froze over. It was uncanny. You couldn't imagine how all those millions of gallons of water that crash down the falls every second could possibly freeze, but they did.

I've even done Gatsby country, Long Island, the Hamptons and anywhere that serves champagne, although I reckon he got out at the right time, even if being shot dead on a floating sunbed was not quite how he would have planned it. In his day, 'when he first picked out the green light at the end of Daisy's dock', whatever that means, it was obviously fun. Cheerful red and white Georgian colonial mansions overlooking the bay, with the lawn starting at the front door and running a quarter of a mile to your very own beach. Not any more, it doesn't. Everywhere there is the whiff of barbecued vanity. It's like an upmarket Coney Island full of dot snots, dotcom millionaires who appear twice on covers of top management and business magazines. Once on the way up, once on the way down.

I heard one chevrah in regulation khaki shorts, T-shirt and baseball cap, braying, 'I paid $25,000 for this trip, and I'm goddamn going to enjoy every penny of it.' I'm not saying he was bombed out of his head, but everybody was calling him Tini, which, I gathered, was short for Martini. And I ask you, who in their right mind wants to eat scrambled tofu with Kim Basinger at Babette's, shop with Cindy Crawford at the Barefoot Contessa or, God help me, have an iced cappuccino with Calvin Klein at the Golden Pear café? On top of all that, of course, the Clintons have moved in, which means that the Hudson River is now known as the Whitewater.

There are in fact four Hamptons: Southampton, Bridghampton and East Hampton, plus Westhampton which, for some reason, doesn't count. East Hampton is the one that matters. The houses there are the size of prisons. Luxury prisons, I'll admit, surrounded by more armoury than it takes to guard Fort Knox. A typical pad would run to 29 bedrooms, 42 bathrooms, a 20-car garage, a 3,000-square-foot garden pavilion, a 250-square-foot beach pavilion, a gatehouse, his-and-hers squash courts, his-and-hers tennis courts, a basketball stadium, an Olympic-size indoor swimming pool and a landing strip for a 747.

The beach is full of Hispanics who only seem to go in the water fully clothed while the ordinary locals don't dare venture anywhere near it unless they are surrounded by servants, hampers packed to bursting point and a million napkins.

161

To get to the Hamptons from downtown Manhattan took me as long by train as it took me to queue up for a cup of coffee at the farmers' market in Amagansett. The first time I tried it I got lost. How did I know when Wass-eye came up on the loudspeaker that they were talking about Woodside? As a result I ended up in Port Jefferson in the middle of some Dickens festival. The place was full of strange types badly lookalike Dickens characters, walking around in top hats and shawls, talking in loud Dick Van Dyke English accents about cleaning chimneys and wishing everybody, 'Good tidings'.

Everybody else, of course, flies in by helicopter. But whatever you do, don't try to go there any time between Memorial Day and Labor Day. It's so packed you won't even find airspace for your helicopter, let alone anywhere to land it.

In between trips to the Hamptons, I suddenly, don't ask me why, found myself being invited by various New York dentists to those fancy light lunches and dinners where, over soup that wasn't worth a noodle dying for, let alone a chicken, sautéed haddock, salt beef, lockshen, vegetables, not to mention salad, relish, fruit juice, rye-bread rolls and, for dessert, apple crisp, I kept being given what was called Jewdex, a questionnaire about as long as the Book of Lamentations quizzing me about whether I preferred to take my steak with chips or red cabbage. In other words, an oh-so-subtle investigation into my Jewishness.

I'm not easily influenced, but after having red cabbage spilt all over me for about the third or fourth time, even though I'd asked for chips, I thought I'd better check out the areas where everyone's son is a doctor, the daughter-in-law doesn't know how to make even a good chicken soup and Momma only ever gets off the phone when the car comes to collect her on Sundays to take her to her favourite son's house for lunch with him and that klutz of a wife of his. I thought I had better do it in the traditional way, so I borrowed some money for the bus and started taking a look at Jewish New York. It was a revelation. Although I fear I'll be going round and round it for at least forty years before I make any sense of it all.

First I trudged the Lower East Side. It's all Italian now, but at the turn of the last century it was the most crowded place on earth. A single room here, they used to say, cost $10,000, and the occupants paid a dollar each. Then I made for the clothing district. At one time 234 out of 241 clothing firms here were Jewish but, again, they've moved on.

Then I stumbled across places like Brighton Beach, known locally as Little Odessa. There are now so many Russian Jews in the area that the shops have signs in the windows saying 'English spoke heir'. This was once the smart end of Coney Island. Then it fell on hard times. Now it has replaced the Lower East Side as home to, some claim, over 50,000 Russian and Ukrainian dentists, all living with their mommas.

In Crown Heights, Brooklyn I called in on the Lubavitchevs. The whole family, whether old or not so old, looked as though they were founder members of the tribe of Abraham. The men wore the usual long, black coats, beards, sidecurls and big, black hats; the women, ancient and not so ancient, were in long, old-fashioned dresses apparently left over from the 1950s, and moth-eaten old wigs. They are so strict you get the impression that Moses actually staggered down Mount Sinai not with just two tablets of stone but with ten. Not only that, but they believe the Messiah has landed, and that he is Rabbi Menachem Mendel Schneerson. Or rather was, the rabbi having now gone ahead to make all the arrangements for his followers all over the world. Even so, Judaica World round the corner was still awash with postcards, photographs, and full-scale portraits of him. There was even a banner across the street still proclaiming, 'Messiah is on the way'. It made you wonder what would have happened if twentieth-century marketing techniques had been going strong 2,000 years ago.

I'd no sooner gone inside the shop/shrine/spiritual supermarket than a wizened old Lubavitchev, who may have been Abraham's father and kept looking over the top of his tiny, wiry glasses, presumably to save the lenses from wearing out, started following me around and threatening me with the end of the world.

'The end of world.'

I feigned end-of-the-world shock.

'The end of the world,' he repeated.

'How do you know?' I asked.

'Six signs,' he whispered. 'There are six signs.'

I stooped down to catch the six signs heralding the end of the world.

'The big board,' he said. 'I lost millions in the seventies, and it's happening again. NASDAQ. The economy. Greenspan. Unemployment. People are not saving . . .'

For all his 631 commandments, the only world he was interested in was the financial one.

A dentist, who told me later that he was not a Jew but of Hebraic genealogy, came to my aid. He invited me to lunch. As I had enough cash on me, I accepted. We went round the corner to an authentic Jewish restaurant. I could tell it was authentic because I'd no sooner got through the door than the waiter was telling me that his mother made better chicken soup than they did.

The dentist and the waiter then somehow got into a big row about the Yiddisher Jesus, whether Columbus was Jewish or not and whether, if you're ever arrested, you should always automatically plead innocent until your momma persuades you you're guilty. Which, of course, is never. By the time the chicken soup came I was desperate for a David and Goliath cocktail – a small one and you're stoned.

Afterwards, as we hadn't been able to discuss the problems of the world in the restaurant, the dentist suggested we moved on to a Jewish nightclub called, he said, Let My People A-Go-Go. Much as I was tempted, I didn't have any money left so I made my excuses and left, although to this day I wish I'd gone, if only to see if it was true or not. Although from what I can remember of Tel Aviv, Jewish nightclubs are not the most exciting places in the world. The Jews tend not to go to them if they get too crowded. But clip joints, now they're a different matter altogether.

Instead I decided to head for Monticello, where I'd been told by another dentist that there was an all-Jewish, as opposed to 10 per cent Jewish, resort and country club. I wanted to see if they would let me in. When I got there it looked more like a souped-up 1950s *tschotchke* motel, but everyone looked as though they had prostate problems. Even the thousands of kids running around all over the place. I headed back to the chardonnay-chic bars of SoHo.

It convinced me. If I was a Jew in New York, Jewdex or no Jewdex, I think I'd rather be a Gentile. You don't like it? Kish mire im toches.

New Jersey

New York is like Michael Jackson's nose. It's for ever changing, updating and reinventing itself. New Hampshire, ditto. Except there it tends to be the seasons that are constantly changing. Winter is snow. Spring is when the snow turns green. Summer is when it melts. Autumn is when it looks like it's going to snow again. In New Mexico it's the people. First, they were Indians, then they were Americans, then Americans and Mexicans, then Americans, and now they are Mexicans again.

But New Jersey? No way. It hasn't been new for a million years. And what Jersey has to do with it I couldn't tell you.

Some say that, having solved the theory of relativity, the only reason Einstein, the thinking woman's Richard Gere, chose to live in Princeton, New Jersey when, for the last twenty-one years of his life, he had the whole of the cosmos to choose from was to try to unravel this problem. But it beat even him. In fact, about the only thing he ever managed to do while he was at Princeton, apart perhaps from lending a certain degree of prestige and status to their football team, which it desperately needed, was to write letters. He wrote in 1939 to warn President Roosevelt that the Nazis would try to develop the atomic bomb; in 1945 saying that the use of the bomb on

Hiroshima now made war unthinkable; in 1953 attacking Senator Joe McCarthy and his anti-communist witch-hunts; in 1954 to Bertrand Russell, begging him to try to raise enough money to help him escape or he would be dead in a year. But the post in New Jersey was so bad that apparently none of the letters ever arrived. If they did they might as well not have done for all the notice anyone took of them. Other people say that the only reason he lived in Princeton was that it was all he could afford living on the patent royalties from his first important discovery, the photo-electric effect.

If New Jersey was no good for Einstein, it wasn't any good for the rest of us, either, because it was here, in a barn in Menlo Park, that some hotshot electronics hink, Thomas Edison, ruined everything by inventing the telephone, which at one stroke took away any excuse for arriving home in the middle of the night without first ringing up to explain why you had to work late at the office. On the other hand, to be fair to him, if he hadn't also invented electricity, we'd all be sitting around watching television by candlelight.

Then there is the New Jersey state slogan. I'm sorry, but however much they insist on calling themselves the Garden State, as far as I'm concerned they're more Backyard State. Worse, the Backyard State of New York. I know they have vast, wide, open green areas where stressed-out old scientists can go hunting deer for all of six days a year. Many's the time I've driven through them backwards and forwards between New York and Philadelphia via a couple of dozen factories, chemical plants and, heaven help us, insurance companies. At one time I thought New Jersey consisted entirely of insurance companies.

Now, of course, I know that New Jersey is in fact the capital of the white-coat world of hush-hush additive companies. Colour additives, aroma additives, taste additives. Every kind of additive that makes fries taste like fries, pizzas taste like pizzas, crisps taste like crisps and . . . my God, that tasted like something the dog brought in.

Visit one of the additive companies along the New Jersey Turnpike and you'll never believe your eyes, let alone your nose or tastebuds, ever again. Talk about the cosmological constant – which Einstein also discovered in Princeton but rejected because he couldn't believe it – everything, but everything, is smothered in additives. You want a rich, shiny, rosy-red apple? Additives. You want that lump of steak to smell like a real steak? Additives. You want that lettuce to look fresh and crisp? Additives. Natural, organic food is smothered in additives. So is vegetarian food, some of which – whisper it not – are made from non-vegetarian bits and pieces of dead bodies.

I have, for my sins, been invited to the occasional New Jersey homestead which, rightly or wrongly, immediately feels somehow sub-New York. No non-stop flowing champagne. No vodka martinis. No hot-and-cold running chardonnay. Instead everything is very practical, very sensible, very boring. In New Jersey they even build homes with kitchens. In New York, no self-respecting member of the drinking classes would dream of having such a thing as a kitchen when they can spend all their life eating out at places like John's of 12th Street, the Knickerbocker Bar and Grill or the Carnegie Deli, not to mention the Oyster Bar at Grand Central Station.

Then there's the people. First, the accent. In spite of all dose jokes, New Jersey is still very much Neuwe Joisey, Thoity-turd Street and joistunmoreanIblawyerbrainsaut. That's when you can understand what dese guys are saying.

As for understanding what I say, about the only people in New Jersey who can do that come from Macedonia, Lithuania or Outer Mongolia. For years most of the porters and baggage-handlers at Newark Airport seemed to be Togolese. Seeing as I've spent a million years of my life in Togo and, perhaps surprisingly, can string one or two Togolese, or rather Evé, words together, I was in my element. Either because of that or because I've got a Togolese diplomatic passport, which I reserve for special occasions, they would whisk me through the check-in, passport control, immigration. It was fantastic. It made it worthwhile coming and going from Newark as opposed to JFK or La Guardia.

Now, of course, I go to the States so often that the US Customs and Immigration authorities have given me my very own passport credit card and it doesn't matter any more.

Sawreeboutatfellas.

Second, the buddy-buddy factor. I honestly believe that Americans are the friendliest people in the whole of the United States, and that America is the easiest place for any Englishman to relocate outside the civilised world. But you would not credit the number of English businessmen I've come across who've found it impossible to settle in New Jersey with their families and have upped and moved back to such thrilling towns as Walsall, Milton Keynes or even New Malden, which tells you how desperate it must have been for them living there with their computer-controlled rotating beds, robotic lawn-mowers, instant barking dog alarms, not to mention automatic kitchens complete with sinks that automatically wash the vegetables, refrigerators that automatically order fresh supplies when stocks run low, taps labelled H and C, Hot and Coke, and bottles of wine that automatically shriek at you when they are ready to be drunk.

American businessmen, however, tend to leave New Jersey because they can't get used to their kids going to birthday parties and being given poisoned sweets or finding sharp objects stuck in the cake. One told me that when he realised he was spending more time at his local hospital having his kids' cakes and candies X-rayed for metal objects than he spent playing golf, it was time to leave. The hospitals, by all accounts, haven't changed much since Damon Runyon's day, when he claimed things were so bad that the doctors didn't even bother to try to get you better. All they did was place odds on you not lasting the week, or recovering and, if you recovered, never being quite the same again. As for parents with young daughters, as soon as they're old enough to say rohypnol, let alone temazepam loprazolam, they're off.

Jersey City is not just old, it's so old, it's prehistoric. Dinosaurs roam the streets late at night. I reckon there are so many dark, satanic mills there that one day I'll bump into William Blake. To tell you how behind the times they are, I once visited some hotshot electronics company with an ultra-smart marketing vice-president who knew everything. He'd just been taken for a ride in a website scam. Some slick New Jersey operators had sold him an all-singing, all-dancing website for millions. He then spent more millions putting everything on the site, including the automatic vegetable-washing kitchen sink. He launched it expecting worldwide acclaim, but nobody could get on to it. He then discovered that the same guys had sold the same site for the same exorbitant fee to forty other companies. No wonder nobody could ever get on to it – it was permanently overloaded. Did he complain? Did he demand his money back? Did he go to the Sopranos? No way. He had his reputation as an ultra-smart marketing vice-president who knew everything to protect. So he didn't say a word. He just coughed up even more money for a second site.

Not that such a thing would ever happen in the hi-tech stretch of waterfront along the Hudson River facing Lower Manhattan, the so-called New Jersey Gold Coast. It is, I am told, the only new part of the state. I tried to get there once to check it out, but the place was blocked off with fire engines. Apparently, two new high-rise buildings caught fire at the same time. Very reassuring. Worse still, even though clouds of thick black smoke were pouring out of the buildings, the fire alarms didn't go off.

The same goes for Newark. OK, the airport is new, but have you ever been to Newark itself? Some people rave about its Jewish neighbourhood, Weequahic, the restaurants, Perry's, Sinclair's, Brothers and the Tavern, where on a Saturday night Frank Sinatra, Woody Herman or the Three Stooges used to entertain the locals. But that's about 300 years old. Newark today is passé and miserable. It's like New York pre-Giuliani, all down-and-outs and rubbish and people rushing to get to somewhere else. About the only fun spot I've ever come across there is Hobby's Deli on Branford Place, which serves the best triple-decker you can imagine: tongue, turkey and pastrami. Although I must admit that a deli full of goofballs baying for more tongue is a touch disconcerting.

As for Trentham, the state capital, all I can say is that if Jersey is the Garden State, Trentham is the compost heap. It's the only town I've been to in the States where if you risk all and go into a restaurant the waiters warn you not to drink the water. The whole town was so rich and smelly and in such an advanced state of decay that the federal authorities moved in, sacked everybody in sight and took over the running of the place themselves.

Princeton, thanks to Einstein's energy multiplied by the square of the speed at which they serve drinks, is different, but it's still not exactly switched on. Not in a million years can I imagine Einstein moving there for the social life. It's full of smarts who look as though they've been up all night patenting another DNA sequence rather than multiplying, as they do everywhere else. In other towns in the States most people's brains are pickled before they die. Einstein's brain was pickled afterwards, thanks to Thomas Harvey, the chief pathologist at Princeton Hospital, who said he removed it by cracking the skull 'like a coconut'. If that wasn't bad enough, he then proceeded to chop it up into pieces ranging in size from 'a turkey neck to a dime', put it in a Tupperware box and drove it in a rented Skylark across the States to San Francisco, where he presented it to Einstein's granddaughter, Evelyn, who then, like all women, popped it in the fridge and promptly forgot all about it until one day, doubtless in a mad rush to get to the hairdresser, she went to the fridge, grabbed the box and . . . No, no, it doesn't bear thinking about. All I can say is, I hope the dog gets more replies to his letters than poor Einstein did.

Then there's Fort Dix, which was an army camp. Now it's a state penitentiary. Don't ask me how I know all about Fort Dix. All I will say is that I know the chaplain. We first met on a flight from Denver, Colorado to Newark. He was reading Etienne Gilson, the French philosopher and theologian, which amazed me. I didn't think anyone in America had heard of Etienne Gilson, let alone still bothered to read him. Fort Dix, he assured me, was a centre of learning. In order to stimulate the inmates' creative abilities, he said, whenever the guards handed out any library books they first deliberately tore out the last twenty pages.

Atlantic City I've never been to. But that's deliberate. I reckon if I don't particularly rate the New Jersey I know, the New Jersey I've spent years of my life in, going belly-up at any crap table, as they say, in Donald Trump's gambling seaside paradise is hardly going to change my views. But I did check out the only city in the US without a name: 287/78, so called because it stands on the crossroads of the big two interstate highways, 287, which runs from 286 to 288, and the 78 which runs from 77 to 79. Clever guys, these Americans. In England the city would probably have been called something glamorous like Northampton.

287/78 is, however, the future. It's what Americans call an edge city, as in on the edge of the real world. It's totally artificial, constructed solely because the site happens to be where two interstates intersect, because there's a demand for office space in the area, because it's green, pleasant, open countryside and, most important of all, because it was cheap to build and quick to deliver a return. It already boasts more office space than many old city centres, a bigger shopping mall than many towns and a busier airport than some states have. But no deer. I took a stroll down road 64/57 and looked at the book shops in 62/97. Finally, around the corner in 23/102, I went into bar 53/9. There, huddled in a corner, was a group talking of simultaneous binomial equations, stable equilibrium analysis, non-linear complex adaptive systems, co-ordinating functions and what happens if the string breaks. This was a bunch of Pakistanis talking about flying kites.

That's how new New Jersey is.

North Carolina

If New York is the Big Apple, North Carolina should be the Big Sock. It is responsible for producing over 60 per cent of all hosiery, a hi-tech American word for socks, sold throughout the US. The trouble is, it's much too serious and straitlaced for that kind of thing. Not like South Carolina, which is all frilly, flouncy petticoats, big hats and that southern drawl.

North Carolina is South Carolina's elderly, spinsterish, non-smoking, non-drinking, put-a-sock-in-it elderly aunt, or even great-aunt. It's strict. Goes to church twice on Sundays. Not just Jane Austen in a severe black crinoline but Jane Austen in a severe black crinoline and a strict US Baptist bonnet as well. Maybe because it sees itself as God's own or, perhaps more importantly, Billy Graham's own country. For this is where the only prophet ever to be honoured in his own land was born in 1918, as he says in his autobiography with the honesty, modesty and truthfulness for which he is well known throughout the world, on 'the hard, red clay where my father eked out a bare existence'. In fact, his father was a prosperous dairy farmer, something which, for some reason, the Reverend Billy doesn't mention too often. Probably because word got out shortly after he was born that only two kings arrived from afar bearing gifts because he already had more than enough gold of his own.

The whole state is Billy Graham. There are churches, church conventions and theological colleges, the size of Nazareth, Bethlehem and Jerusalem combined, all over the place. The churches boast of being 'prayer-conditioned'; billboards beseech: 'Don't let worry kill you – let the Church help'. Inside worshippers sing stirring old traditional hymns like 'Drop-Kick Me, Jesus, Through the Goalposts of Life' and sit rapt as preachers such as the Reverend Joe Chambers, who runs the Paw Creek Ministries, call down the wrath of God not only on Power Rangers and Barney the Dinosaur but also on Cabbage Patch Dolls for being the work of the devil incarnate. I'll never forget one happy-clappy church I stumbled into one Sunday morning in the back streets of Charlotte. Talk about embarrassing: the preacher was begging everyone practically on pain of death to hold up their cross. I was the only one who didn't do so. My wife wasn't with me. You think that's going to extremes? They even have a Dial-a-Prayer service for atheists. You dial the number and nothing happens.

The biggest church convention they ever had was the National Baptist Convention USA, organised by the largest black Church in the whole of the US. It attracted over 40,000 people. Unfortunately, they had to spend it trying to forgive their leader and forget the fact that he had just been convicted of swindling them out of $4 million of their own money and jailed for five and a half years.

As for the theological colleges scattered everywhere, they're not like any other theological colleges I've seen. One lecturer, who spoke a string of different African languages, told me they devoted half their lives to studying the Good Book, by which, of course, I thought he meant *Look Homeward Angel*, the great American novel about small-town life in North Carolina that Maxwell Perkins, a humble literary editor, if such a person exists, wrote in the 1920s for the great author Thomas Wolfe while lesser literary names, such as F. Scott Fitzgerald, Sinclair Lewis, Theodore Dreiser, Upton Sinclair, John Dos Passos, William Faulkner and, of course, Hemingway were busy writing their own masterpieces. I read it sitting in one of their famous white rocking chairs while waiting for a plane at the airport at Charlotte. It all rang true. The arguing, the fighting, the non-stop drinking. People striding up and down shouting to themselves at the tops of their voices. Or maybe they were just hollering into their mobile phones. It's difficult to tell nowadays.

What I don't understand is why it is still so popular – it's never been out of print since it was published in 1929 – never mind why it is rated a great American classic. For all the arguing and fighting and non-stop drinking, it's a bit clichéd. If I wanted arguing and fighting and non-stop drinking I could have stayed at home and not bothered with the book in the first place. Neither is the writing exactly crisp or to the point. It's also much too long and too unwieldy, I would have thought, for American tastes. The only possible reason I can think of for its success is the title. The Americans, with their famously long attention span of 3.7 seconds, their picture-oriented culture and their complete inability to read, let alone understand, the simplest sentence, must think it is *Look Homeward, Angels* – in other words, Anglo-Saxons – and buy it because they think it's about throwing us kind, warm-hearted, peace-loving, former colonial oppressors out of their hamburger-infested paradise. Once they've bought it, of course, they never read it. If they did they would be in for a double shock. First, it's got nothing to do with us nasty, hateful, baby-eating Brits, and second, it's nothing like North Carolina.

But, of course, *Look Homeward Angel* wasn't the Good Book the theological lecturer was referring to. His Good Book was the one full of such theologically baffling phrases as 'mincing as they go and making a tinkling with their feet', 'a lodge in a garden of cucumbers' and, one of my favourites, 'when they arose in the morning, behold, they were all dead'.

On the other hand, I suppose it's more theological than some of the theology you come across in other parts of the States, such as alimentary 'God loves a chocolate brownie with extra nuts and whipped cream' theology, which is enough to make even the confirmed chocoholic throw up.

The other half of their lives they spend debating what they call their Constantine captivity to apocalyptic eschatology and drawing up massive plans to convert not just the ungodly throughout the world but also the Jews, Muslims and Hindus who, they claim, have 'darkness in their heart that no lamp can dispel'. Until, presumably, a North Carolina preacher arrives on the scene with a portable lighthouse, a couple of dozen 1,000-watt bulbs and a Cabbage Patch doll to scare the hell out of them.

If that's not enough to be going on with this side of the Last

Day, these modest, everyday Christians have also laid plans to convert the whole US, city by city, starting with Chicago. Over 100,000 of them at a time, one of North Carolina's religious stormtroopers told me, are going to descend on each city, hand out millions of leaflets, whizz frisbees all over the place and organise puppet shows until all unbelievers are buried in fire and brimstone.

One hamhead I've known for a long time – a top executive in one of the big electronics companies in North Carolina's famous Research Triangle between Raleigh, the state capital, Durham, an old tobacco centre, and Chapel Hill, a college town – used to be the hard-drinking, hard-living, hard everything else type. Then, suddenly, after joining the famous Million Man march in Washington, he more or less did a St Paul on the spot. Now you can hardly talk to him without getting a non-stop lecture on why evolution is wrong, why abortion is wrong, why pop culture, rap music, violent and pornographic films and videos are wrong, why recreational drugs are wrong, why rampant feminism is wrong, why political correctness is wrong, why multiculturalism is wrong, why the O. J. Simpson trial was wrong, why it's wrong to stop kids saying prayers before foot-ball games – in short, why everything is wrong. His solution is to do as the monks did in the Middle Ages. Go and live in a secure, gated community, educate your children at home and pray the whole thing will not blow up in your lifetime or that of your children.

At first, I thought he was a pain. Once I almost jammed his Bible down his throat to shut him up. But eventually his constant lecturing on the importance of religion in one's life – 'Christianity is the moral foundation we all need. Christian politics is the way to achieve our goals' – completely changed my way of life and made me a more religious person. I am now religiously against whatever he says.

As usual, though, I'm in a minority of one. More and more people in the US are becoming more and more religious. It might not be my kind of religion, or yours, but it's happening.

Even on the subway, it's not unusual to see people reading their Bibles or prayer books, and not just because they hope it will stop them from being mugged. Go into people's offices, or ovacles, as they call those prissy open-plan office cubicles, and you might see a Bible on the desk. Or a Christian Yellow Pages, which enables Christians to buy from fellow Christians. Suggest a drink after work. Most poor, downtrodden British businessmen insist on rushing home. In North Carolina they will be racing off to meetings, attending deep meditation sessions or organising another Million Man march.

Whole towns and villages all over North Carolina are also now renouncing drinking, smoking, talking, breathing. Snoop Doggy Dog? Even think of mentioning his name, and you'll be driven out into the wilderness. Instead, everyone is up before dawn and works through the day. Earnest, dedicated, safe. 'It's better than Germany,' one old textile mill-owner, an Indian from India, told me. 'These people know how to work. I've never made so much money so quickly anywhere in the world.' The fact that a majority of the workers in North Carolina hail from all points south of the Rio Grande – poor, desperate Vietnamese, Cambodians, Indians, Sri Lankans and Mexicans, for the most part – is, of course, a detail.

The managers tend to be equally dedicated. If you're at the bottom of the heap and you don't measure up, and you're not from North Carolina, they will dedicate themselves to getting you fired as quickly as possible. If you're just above the bottom of the heap and you're from North Carolina, they will dedicate themselves to creating even more problems for you. They will send you off on no end of courses, seminars and intensive, week-long brain-washing sessions in Christian management virtues such as how to be ruthless but lovable, ways to improve your management style by pretending to listen to your colleagues and do whatever you have to do to get through the course and then go back to being your same old bullying self.

It's probably largely because of this serious work-work-work ethic that the biggest city in the state is about as exciting as a stack of surgical stockings, although with a name like Charlotte, you'd have thought it would be up there with the likes of New Orleans, Boston and San Fran, maybe even New York. The New York of today that is, not the New York of ten or twenty years ago.

It has a handful of skyscrapers – well, I say skyscrapers: actually they're only around forty storeys high – a bit of retail and an oh-so-important parking deck that everybody raves about. Uptown and South End are about as exciting as half a stack of surgical stockings. The most swinging place in town is the airport, where anybody looking for any fun is heading off to Atlanta, New York or even Washington. Which tells you a lot about North Carolina. Not that you can blame them. Wilbur and Orville Wright only invented the aeroplane to get away from North Carolina. They may have managed that, but they are probably still waiting for their luggage to arrive.

As for the rest of the state, apart from the occasional swing along the Blue Ridge Parkway which, especially in autumn, gives a reasonable impression of New England, they don't seem to have much more than the hard, red clay of Billy Graham fame and apples. Their strong Christian fundamentalist beliefs, which are so strong and so fundamental that for a long time they barred Jews and Roman Catholics from holding state office, probably have a lot to do with it.

Come to think of it, given that combination of Christian charity and understanding and pork-barrel politics, maybe North Carolina should be called the Little Apple after all.

The Salad States

If there is one thing that obsesses the Americans more than salad, it is all the other food they shovel down day after day after heart attack. And, like all the other food they somehow manage to put away, we're not talking small potatoes. We're talking huge bucketfuls of the stuff. Whole forests of mushrooms, onion rings the size of Yosemite National Park. Enough tomatoes, chillies, cucumbers and gherkins to fill the Grand Canyon from tourist-infested end to tourist-infested end.

Normally, on the basis that if anything is good for me, I don't like it, you'll never catch me in the same restaurant, let alone hotel, as a bowl of salad. Except, that is, for a good Caesar salad, as in seizer the anchovies and chuck 'em in. How anyone can even think of having a Caesar salad without anchovies is beyond me. Yet in this land of enormous food obsessives, it is amazing how difficult it is to find a really good Caesar salad. In the best restaurants in New York, sure. In Boston, San Fran and LA, OK. Now and then in Miami, once they realise that the original Caesar was Spanish. But anywhere else it's risky, and I don't mean just in downmarket places but in the top-of-the-pile eateries as well.

I once ordered a Caesar salad in one of the best restaurants in Palm Beach, Florida, probably the richest 14 miles of coast-line anywhere in the world. It arrived without the anchovies. I called Elmer, who had promised to do everything he could to ensure that I had the best evening of the whole of my miserable life, and explained as politely as I could that Caesar salad was made with anchovies. Could I please have some anchovies?

'Momentarily,' he smarmed.

Within two minutes, he was back. In one hand was my original Caesar salad. In the other was a plate piled high with anchovies.

Now, for the last time, a good Caesar salad does not contain soggy lettuce, bits of bread crust, dead caterpillars, mouse droppings or even left-over lumps of chicken. It does contain crisp cos lettuce, croutons fried in oil with a hint of garlic, freshly grated Parmesan, and anchovies. The dressing is not a dollop of mayo or a drizzle, as they say, of vinegar. It is olive oil, as virgin as you can get, which is not as virgin as it used to be; lemon juice; salt and pepper. Finally, a coddled or even a half-pampered egg. Mix it all up together. Sprinkle some more Parmesan on top. It's almost as good as a half glass of champagne. Non-vintage, of course.

But not to worry, I got my own back on Elmer. I went up to the buffet bar and made a stack of vinegar and prune sandwiches and left them in his car, which was parked out the back. With a bit of luck, if he's ever stopped by the police, they'll slam him away for pushing heroin. Vinegar and prunes smell like heroin. That'll teach him to give me a lousy Caesar salad.

The Mushroom Ones

New Mexico and Arizona are obviously mushroom states. New Mexico once had a mushroom 1,000,000ft high and over 2,000,000ft wide hovering virtually all over it. Arizona, especially the vast desert area around the Grand Canyon, seems to be the result of a giant mushroom explosion. I'm not talking about the almost complete lack of any intelligent life. If that was the case, practically the whole of the US would be one giant mushroom state, with the exception, perhaps, of Louis Lunch, Connecticut and what's the name of that bar in Boston I can never remember? No, I mean in appearance. Local puffballs, not to mention inkcaps, blewits and shaggy parasols, go on and on about giant meteors crashing into the area 50,000 years ago and creating huge craters measuring over 4,000ft wide. Don't believe a word of it. New Mexico looks like that because some long-serving, dedicated local employee was in such a hurry to escape and get back to China that he dropped the whole bag of tricks and before you could count from one to Strontium 90, the entire place looked as though it had been inundated by a bunch of tourists.

Then there's the fact that both states have been kept in the dark for so long. Apart, of course, from those few seconds shortly after 5.30 am on 16 July 1945, when the good, honest, hardworking, trusting people of New Mexico realised for the first time what was going on at PO Box 163, Santa Fe, NM. As opposed to the whole of the US Postal Service, their families, their friends and their friends' friends, who had known all along. Which, in my book, makes New Mexico one hell of a killer state, if not the greatest killer state of all times.

Similarly, for years the native Americans of Arizona – Arizona has the biggest native population in the US – not only knew nothing about anything, but they didn't have any reservations, either. Well, apart from the nineteen the US government so generously gave their fourteen tribes after stealing all their land from them in the first place.

Both states look as though they've been overrun by strange mutations. New Mexico has had more UFO sightings than anywhere else. Most of them by bored housewives, most of them after lunch, and most of them of men, in one form or another. Arizona claims invasions of masses of strange, shrivelled-up, nut-brown aliens, usually around the end of the year, generally on or close to golf courses and more often than not dressed in a strange combination of white shorts, white shirt and white shoes.

But in both states you're guaranteed a warm welcome. The welcome in New Mexico is the more genuine, it's just that it will take longer to wear off. If it wears off at all.

New Mexico

I couldn't get to PO Box 163. Maybe if I'd been Chinese, it would have been possible. I did try. I had a hard drive across the desert. Actually, there were hard drives all over the desert, as well as no end of empty briefcases. I risked my life at the hands of the Santa Domingo Pueblo Indians. The main danger was going into their homes, which are 600 years old but could easily be ten times older. I was battered by the dust devils or mini-tornados. I even wore a bola tie.

But just as I was getting close – I could tell I was getting close because of all the floppy disks and 3M brand DC6150 cartridges marked 'Top Secret – For Chinese Eyes Only' scattered around everywhere – I suddenly hit a highly radioactive uranium 235 security barrier and everything went belly up.

I tried explaining to the military nosebleeds that Sergio had sent me to look for locations for a series of new-style tagliatelli westerns. But they pitched a fit, as they always do whenever you ask them a perfectly simple question, and it was either head back to Santa Fe or risk the nuclear option. Given the choice I decided to head back to Santa Fe using the latest W88 technology, although I'm sure for a few dollars more I could have built it myself. After all, if I want to see a live nuclear bomb, there's always the one on show at the China Air Dynamics Research and Development Centre in Mianyang, Sichuan, though it's funny that they never tell you where it came from.

What I did learn was that the US Air Force's new slogan, 'No One Comes Close', had nothing to do with their bombing record in the Gulf War, never mind Kosovo, innocent Chinese embassies being the exception. Instead, a very friendly military policeman dripping with nuclear bombs told me that it was 'an atomic sentence', which amazed me. First, because not in a million years had I ever imagined that an American military policeman would know what a sentence was (apart from being posted to Los Alamos and having to deal with visitors claiming they were looking for sites for tagliatelli westerns). Second, I had never realised there was such a thing as American grammar. But he was serious. Atomic sentences, apparently, are sentences with just one verb. Such as, 'The cat . . .' What am I talking about? Such as, 'America accidentally bombed the Chinese embassy in Belgrade.'

There are also, he informed me, molecular sentences, which are made up of a lot of atomic ones. For example: 'The Americans accidentally bombed the Chinese embassy in Belgrade because they deserved it and were just sitting there asking for it.' Or: 'The US cruiser the *Vincennes* accidentally shot down Iran Air Flight 655 killing all 290 people on board.' Or: 'The USS *Saratoga* accidentally fired at a Turkish destroyer, killing five men and injuring eighteen others.' 'Two US marine jets accidentally dropped bombs on a look-out post at the Vieques training ground in Puerto Rico, killing one civilian and injuring four others, three of them civilians.' 'A US Navy submarine accidentally sank a Japanese fishing boat killing everybody on board.' 'Four Canadian soldiers were killed and eight wounded when they were mistakenly bombed by a patrolling US F16 jet during night training near Kandahar in southern Afghanistan.' 'Four wedding guests were severely wounded after their wedding convoy was attacked outside Khost by US forces.'

Who says the Americans don't care about the English language as well as the accuracy of their bombing?

Santa Fe was a real fandango. It must be the biggest pseudo-capital of all the pseudo-capitals in the world. There it is, 7,000ft up in the desert at the foot of the Sangre de Cristo mountains, and it's all kiva holistic fireplaces, punched tin, New Age lumps of wood, Hopi flower-arranging ceremonies, dusty old kilims and strips of dried chilli hanging all over the place. And, God help me, if I bang my head on another native pot, I'll be out of my mind. But all this New Age, weirdo, design-oriented, environmentally obsessed nonsense I could put up with if it wasn't for one thing: Santa Fe has more spas than bars. More spas than bars? I ask you. How the hell can that be a real town? No wonder Billy the Kid was so desperate to get out so quickly.

The first evening I stayed there I got the shock of my life. I'd been out all day, dragging myself from one meeting to another, choking on incense and mesquite, hounded to death by wind chimes and strange, so-called spiritual conversations that made the *Reader's Digest* sound like the Summa Theologica. On top of all that I was still trying to digest my lunch: a mung bean and a stalk of guava. I pushed past all the goosedown duvets and goosedown pillows covered in cheeky little coyotes and those Godawful jaw-dropping little rhymes to get into my poor, lonely, desolate hotel room and drown my sorrows with a super, super, sugar-free, fruit-free, taste-free, natural, unpasteurised orange juice, no doubt choc-a-bloc with e.coli 0157:H7, which was all they had on offer. I looked out of the window. There was a huge, deep red glow on the horizon. It was a few seconds, I can tell you, before I realised it was the sun setting over the surrounding desert. It's no wonder Conrad Hilton, who grew up around here, decided there was a future in the hotel business. It's also no surprise that once he left he never came back again.

My meetings over – I'd been the only one at any of them wearing shoes: everybody else had been in sandals – there was nothing else to do but hit the Santa Fe Trail. Most people think this has something to do with some superhighway built in the 1800s stretching 1,200 miles, all the way here from Independence, Missouri. But think about it. If that were true, it would be called the Independence, Missouri–Santa Fe, New Mexico Trail, just as flights are always London, Gatwick–Boston, Mass. I mean, how would you know where you're going if you didn't know where you were coming from?

No, the real Santa Fe Trail, or rather, the real pseudo-Santa Fe Trail, is round all the pseudo-sights of pseudo-Santa Fe itself: the ancient Spanish architecture they only started putting up in 1957; the literally hundreds of museums full of what they call valuable historic artefacts, which are about half the age of stuff I've got piled up in barns back home waiting to be burned; I don't know how many art galleries bursting with unsold works by world-famous American artists I've never heard of; a million fat old mamas huddled Mexican-style on the pavements selling what looked to me like junk jewellery made in Taiwan.

Just how much of a fake the place is, and how important it was to the Mexicans, can be judged from the fact that they gave it up without a fight. All US Brigadier-General Stephen W. Kearny had to do was offer them free tickets for a week in North Dakota (the guys who were slightly hesitant got tickets for two weeks in North Dakota) and they were off. They didn't even hang around long enough to attend the Victory Ball at La Fonda, the local bar, probably because they knew that, instead of hitting what little booze there was likely to be on offer and waving their maracas at all and sundry, they'd be subjected to a lecture on Vietnam, the environment and the dangers of smoking. But Doña Tules Barcelo, the owner of the biggest gambling house in Santa Fe, seemed to more than make up for their absence. Apparently, it took four soldiers to carry her in. How many it took to carry her out is not recorded. Not because she was bombed out of her mind, but probably because she caught a glimpse of the paintings of a local artist called D. H. Lawrence – he used to own a 160-acre farm nearby – which were billed as 'banned by Scotland Yard'.

So knowledgeable are the Americans about their continent in general and New Mexico in particular that New Mexicans have to slap USA on their car registration plates to make certain that when they stray outside their borders their fellow Americans don't treat them as a bunch of *pachucos* and bounce them around all over the place as they do with the rest of us.

Wait a minute. It's just occurred to me where the Independence, Missouri connection might come in. I bet you if you link all the pseudo-museums and pseudo-art galleries in Santa Fe together they would stretch all the way to Independence, Missouri. No? Oh well, it was just a thought.

Either way, take it from me, Geronimo, that the real Santa Fe Trail starts not with Rociada, the best restaurant in town, but with the Chapel of San Miguel, the oldest church in the continental States, which is all of 350 years old. And, you've guessed it, this is a semi-pseudo-adobe building as well. Just across the sandy track from the church is La Casa Vieja, the oldest condo in the US, where they sell the oldest T-shirts, oldest baseball caps and oldest stickers in the country and even today are still wishing everyone a Nicey Olde Daye, Amigo.

Now back to the Plaza de Santa Fe, the main square, which is packed with your pseudo this, that and everything else. It is said that after it was completed, the architect, designer and inspiration behind the whole project, the famous J. Robert Oppenheimer, without whom it would not have been possible, said, 'Now I am become death, destroyer of worlds.' Although, of course, I may have been misinformed. New Mexico does funny things to the brain as well as to the body.

Do what I do, *kimo sabe*. Take it steady. Ignore all the lists and directions and instructions you are given. Life is always much more fun if you ignore all the lists and directions and instructions you are given. Start with the Palace of the Governors on the north side of the Plaza. This is famous, not because it is the oldest public building in the USA but because it is where the town's most famous writer, General Lewis Wallace, the famous governor of New Mexico, wrote the famous *Ben Hur* in late 1870. Built in 1610, it has survived six successive governments as well as Bill Clinton, although I don't reckon it's going to survive another six coachloads of Coke-carrying and no doubt coke-sniffing-but-not-inhaling American tourists.

Just by the back door, under a sweaty Navajo vest, is the dead letterbox where Julius and Ethel Rosenberg and friends left nuclear secrets from Los Alamos for the Russians. Damn. I wasn't going to tell you. But now that I have, I'm afraid I'm going to have to kill you. Don't worry. It won't be half as bad as spending a week in Santa Fe.

The Museum of American Indian Arts and Culture, interestingly enough, does not display any American Indian Arts and Culture. Instead there are lots of Native American photographs and things, which was fine by me. I did think of complaining about the slightly misleading title, but I didn't bother. Nobody takes any notice of me at home, so why should they take any notice of me in Santa Fe? Incidentally, I was aware that one or two people have stopped referring to cowboys as cowboys. Instead they call them Anglos. Anglos and Native Americans doesn't sound quite the same, does it? It wouldn't make me get up early on a Saturday morning to catch any films about them, at any rate.

The Museum of International Folk Art sounded interesting, but it was all handmade dolls, dolls' houses and strange-looking guys with long hair and wiry spectacles. The Museum of Fine Arts was fine, but was it art? I don't know. Ask me when I've finished the bottle.

As for the Georgia O'Keefe Museum, ask me after I've finished the next bottle. All I can remember was flower painting after flower painting after flower painting. Another ten minutes in there and I reckon I'd have come out covered in greenfly.

Now, this might come as a shock to you, but because of the genuine authentic nature of Santa Fe, its architecture, its lifestyle, its emphasis on culture, the way they deleted the word 'savage' from the town's war memorial so that today it pays tribute to 'those who died in wars with the — Indians', it has become a mecca for all those who despise reality: artists, painters, poets, writers, hippies, over 200 art-gallery owners and even, I'm told, the occasional lawyer. In the old days it was said that they were drawn by the intensity of the light. But that, of course, got misinterpreted – you know the way things are in the US. So they came up with the reality argument. Either way, you can hardly pick up a genuine Spanish ashtray made in Taiwan without disturbing two or three American artists carrying out some deeply penetrating analysis of something or other underneath it.

Albuquerque is much more the real coyote. The old part is old, the new part is new. The in-between part, well, it's like most American cities, probably because it's the only city in the US to have been bombed by its own military. And not just an ordinary bomb, either, but a hydrogen bomb. The military, of course, say it just rolled out of the plane, the way they do, and landed with a thud on some golf course downtown. There was nothing to worry about. It was just an accident. If it had gone off, it would only have killed a couple of million people. So that's all right, then. But what I want to know is, who flies around Albuquerque with a loose hydrogen bomb rolling around their bomb bay? I'm not stupid. I know what they were up to. They were looking for the Chinese embassy.

Falling hydrogen bombs apart, the trouble with Albuquerque is getting from one side of it to the other. Some clever guy, obviously destined for a long career in the US Forest Service, pushed Route 66 right through the middle of town, splitting it into Albu and Querque. So as well as putting up with the noise, you've got to travel about 65 miles to go and get a bottle of depleted uranium. Not that I would ever dream of getting a bottle of depleted uranium, but you know what I mean.

Out to the east are the Sandia Mountains, so called because as anyone who's been through Valencia, Spain knows, Sandia is Spanish for watermelons, and as we all know, at sunset – don't whatever you do tell anyone in South Dakota, where they go on about their Black Hills – mountains turn as pink as a rich, juicy Spanish watermelon. At least, that's what they say in both Albu and Querque.

The old town square or plaza in Albu is authentic. It's scruffy, it's rundown, it smells. The eighteenth-century San Felipe de Neri Church is badly in need of repair and probably a great deal of redecoration, but at least it's real. So are the bars around town: real beer, real people, real atmosphere.

The Rattlesnake Museum, just south of the plaza, is also real.

Apparently they've got millions of the things. But as my stomping days are over, I decided to give it a miss.

Even more real is the National Atomic Museum out on the Kirtland Air Force Base. I've been to Hiroshima and seen what the bomb did, so I thought it might be interesting to see how it was developed. After all, they say the Americans built it but it was the Europeans who were responsible for the clever bit, the science. I also wanted to see if anyone could tell me why they insisted on dropping the thing in the first place when, on 18 July, a full nineteen days earlier, President Truman was telling his diary: 'Telegram from Jap emperor asking for peace' and on 3 August, three days beforehand, Walter Brown, special assistant to the secretary of state, James F. Byrnes, wrote in his: 'President, Leahy, J. F. B. agreed Japs looking for peace', because it's always puzzled me why anyone should want to drop a bomb on anyone asking for peace. Unless, of course, they just wanted to test the thing, just to see if it worked, regardless of the consequences. But even though the museum is open to the public, they wouldn't let me in. They shot the ground from under me. Which was very odd, as I pointed out to the peace-loving Dr Death on guard duty outside. Surely I had a right to see what they had done in our name. And how come he was letting in everybody but me? But you know what the military mind is like.

First he said he wanted to see my driver's licence. I told him I didn't have a driver's licence with me because I don't like driving in the US. In any case, it's a British driving licence, not an American one. OK, he said. Long pause. Then he told me he wanted to see my car registration, whatever that is. 'But excuse me,' I said, 'I've just told you I don't drive in the US. I don't have a driving licence, so how can I have a car registration, or whatever it is?' OK, he said. Long pause.

Next he asked for my car insurance. I mean, is it me or is it me? And the big argument they put forward for developing the bomb was to preserve and protect our way of life. I ask you. What would he have done if I'd said my name was Klaus

Fuchs, and that I demanded to see the books? Open the gates and let me in? Well, I suppose they did it once, so they might as well do it again.

But of course, I didn't win. He didn't let me in. Nevertheless I came away glowing with pride at the stand I had taken against such pig-headed, stupid bureaucracy. At least, I hope it was pride I was glowing with. Give me a call in twenty years' time, and I'll let you know.

The only good thing about it was that I didn't get a lecture on atomic sentences.

Arizona

Welcome to Arizona, otherwise known as Big Cleavage Country. Or, to one in twenty-five Americans, welcome to Mars. Because, according to the polls, one in twenty-five Americans believes the Americans never landed on Mars but in Arizona instead. Strange people, the Americans or, at least, one in twenty-five of them are. The problem is identifying the one in twenty-five. It's so difficult.

In fact Arizona is nothing like Mars. It's miles from anywhere, it takes hours to get to, and when you get there it's no more than wide, open desert. Aridzona would be a better name for it. As for intelligent life, it's full of nothing but prisons and boob farms.

The prisons are run by people like the weird and wacky Sheriff Joe Arpaio, who believes in chain gangs, tent jails – presumably for people arrested for loitering with intent – and, for some reason, pink underpants. In his book, possessing a single joint warrants a jail sentence. Possessing a gun, however, is OK. Every citizen has the right to bear arms. His whole aim in life is to squeeze a greater and greater mass of humanity into a wholly artificial form of enforced, unnatural constriction.

The boob farms are, of course, completely different although they are run by an equally select band of weird and wacky people who are so deflated they are able to concentrate on only two things at a time. A moment's distraction and they could have a disaster on their hands which, no doubt, they desperately hope the patient will not hold against them.

Those more abreast of the times than me maintain that both kinds of establishment are key indicators of the growth or otherwise of the American economy. The prisons tell you how the poor are doing, the boob farms how the rich are doing. The more poor people there are, the more the prison population rises and the more chains Sheriff Arpaio can afford to buy. The more rich and insecure, as well as not so rich and even more insecure people there are, the more patients will come to be cut to shreds in total privacy and then lie by a pool for six months until the bruises have disappeared. If boobs are going up, so to speak, so is the American economy. In the old days it used to be a second car, a third holiday, a fourth string of diamonds, or whatever. Now it's a quick boob job, a chemical peel or the full body lift. But take care. I heard of one woman who had her breasts lifted so high she couldn't get her wig on. For those who can't afford a facelift, some clinics have come up with another solution. They will arrange to have the body lowered instead. Throughout the 1990s, cosmetic surgery grew almost as fast as the Dow Jones Index. What happens when the bubble bursts, if you'll forgive the expression, nobody knows. Saline breast implants, it is said, will need further surgery – sorry, I meant the economy. Like everything, what goes up must go down. Everything is subject to gravity. Oh, what the hell.

All I know is that Arizona is doing well out of it. First, there's the cost. The average breast op costs around $3,000, a buttock lift a bit more, depending on the size of the lift, the capacity of the forklift truck and how many people are required for the job. Liposuction is charged per location. Per location on the body, stupid, not where the operation is performed. Either way, you're looking at $3,000 to $5,000 a shot. Or, I suppose, a suck. Which, I would have thought, would be enough to make anyone's jaw sag. A fair slice of the cost is, of course, paid in cash. The last thing you want is the bank manager knowing you're a walking implant. It must be bad enough being one.

Then there are the hotel costs. Nobody gets up off the table and catches a flight straight back home to Providence, Rhode Island or wherever. They have to wait for the scars to heal. Say one month, maybe two, depending on the extent of the surgery. Some people eager to test their new products, I'm told, can take anything up to six months, depending on the size of the competition, market forces and the extent of market penetration they are hoping to achieve.

Finally come all the follow-ons: servicing, replacing, updating, new products, new technology and, of course, treatment for diabetes, high blood pressure, high cholesterol, heartburn, gout, arthritis, obesity and everything else your average American suffers from.

The prize for the farm offering the best all-round service is a cup, a 38D. The prize for the farm offering the worst all-round service is another cup, a 38D. I once met a poor guy at Providence Airport who told me that he'd just blown $50,000 on a facelift for his wife. She'd just called to tell him that it had all gone horribly wrong. Now, he said, he didn't know who the hell he was waiting for.

Outside the boob farms, where the distinct smell of silicone came drifting on the evening air, there is, of course, a real, hard, solid world that people have to grapple with every day of their lives. Take Phoenix, for example. Everybody loves Phoenix – Los Angeles without the aggro – even though it's in the middle of the desert and records temperatures way above 100 degrees Fahrenheit in summer, because it was founded by an Englishman, Darrel Duppa, known to his American colleagues as Lord Darrel Duppa. 'From this village will arise a city, Phoenix-like from the ashes of the past,' he declared. It's only in the last few years, with the growth of higher education, that they've stopped calling it Phoenix-Like From the Ashes of the Past in favour of just plain Phoenix.

From then on, its success was, of course, guaranteed. They

threw away the rulebook, as you would expect of your typical English upper-class lord, and decided that anybody could build whatever they wanted wherever they wanted. Rules, after all, were for the common people. They waived all the environmental-impact fees as well. So today Phoenix, which boasts it is the city that offers space to live and plenty of elbow room, is the fastest-growing of all the fastest-growing cities in the US with a population of over 1 million people, 10 million cars, non-stop development, twenty-four-hour traffic jams and Mike Tyson. It must make a pleasant change for him from the upstate New York correctional facilities and Indiana prison, where he probably had more space to roam around. Phoenix is now so crowded and the roads so snarled with traffic that many people who fled Los Angeles in search of peace and quiet have not been able to escape back home because they are still stuck queuing to get out. But who cares? At least they uphold the complete British disregard for any kind of regulation, not to mention all that petty bureaucracy, form-filling, red-tape stuff. And there's nothing to stop the city from expanding still further. At the moment it takes up more than 2,000 square miles, the equivalent of five Manhattans. Being completely surrounded by desert, and with nothing to stop it expanding, it could end up stretching all the way from the Pacific to the Atlantic. So I wouldn't bother to go there if I were you. In another couple of years it will come to you.

Tucson, on the other hand, is worth a visit. The dining rooms are smaller than the hotels, the hotels are smaller than aircraft hangars and the aircraft hangars are for aircraft, not for stockpiling daily supplies of baked lobster, Yukon Gold potatoes, double lamb chops and prime, dry-aged steaks. They also say, after a couple of beers and half a dozen tequilas, that the original US–Mexico border actually flows through the middle of town. Not that it makes any difference to me. As far as I'm concerned, there's nothing better than just sitting slumped in the wonderful, faded old Hotel Congress by the railway line waiting for the good, the bad and the ugly to come stomping into town for some showdown or other. It hasn't happened yet, but it will one day. Yup, it will one day. Get behind me, Tonto. This used to be Geronimo country. This is where, in 1880, the government drafted in thousands of troops to catch him.

The native Americans have had their revenge. Geronimo's guys are now the largest of all the surviving tribes. They control the largest reservation in the US. Because – surprise, surprise – on their reservations, as well as timber, they have discovered not only oil and gas but also uranium and helium, they are growing stronger and more powerful every day. The only people who are against them are the Hopis, which is fortunate for them because the Hopis are a goody-goody Indian tribe who don't believe in war dances, or fighting or scalping or any of that kind of thing. The fact that they've failed at everything they've tried to do since Geronimo was a lad with a single feather in his pigtail is beside the point. This is also John Dillinger country, where America's most famous bank robber, Public Enemy Number One, was arrested in 1933. Bad luck, John.

Greater Tucson is much more boring. It's no different from any other big, or rather, medium-sized American city, like Atlanta, St Louis or Minneapolis, apart from the light and the sunshine it enjoys. The light, they say, is so clear, so sharp, so vivid that if it was in the south of France it would create a big impression among artists. It might even provide the basis for a separate school of painting. As for the sunshine, this is supposed to be the sunniest city in the US, getting, on an annual basis, around 85 per cent of all the sunshine going.

Outside Tucson is what's known as Tumbleweed Country. The clumps of weeds I came across were not so much tumbling as hurling themselves at whatever got in their way: people, cars, trucks. One poor guy I saw had so much tumbleweed over his car that it was itself practically a giant tumbleweed. A sudden gust of wind and the whole thing could have tumbled all the way across to San Fran and the Pacific.

If you can fight your way through the tumbleweed, about 50 miles north of Tucson, in the middle of the desert, you will come across a giant sphere which, given Arizona's reputation, gave me quite a turn when I first saw it looming up at me in the distance. It turned out to be what they call the Biosphere, the world's largest manmade, enclosed eco-system. Covering more than 3 acres, and completely sealed off from our environment, it contains its own artificial rainforests, savannahs, marshes and desert. A bit like the lobby of your typical modern American hotel, except that there are probably fewer pests in the Biosphere than there are in the lobby of your typical modern American hotel.

Now, call me stupid, short-sighted, even a long-lost relative of Lord Darrel Duppa, but how the hell can manmade rainforests, savannahs and what have you tell anybody anything, especially when they're full of electronic monitoring equipment, not to mention fire-extinguishers? Surely the only way to monitor whatever is happening wherever is to go there and do it for real.

Outside the Biosphere, thank God, the real world is still the real world. In the evenings and at weekends people do the ordinary, everyday things. Like panning for gold. So many people are now getting into their pick-ups and heading out to Picket Post Mountain, Mesa or even Apache Junction that Tucson is the only place in the world that offers evening classes in panning for gold. Spend all day swishing through piles of black sand looking for tiny flecks of gold, colours or 'pickers', as they are known to us evening-class graduates, and what do you get? Backache.

Less of a mug's game, and far more satisfying and rewarding, is hunting. Hunting Mexicans. Head out to Mule Mountain on the border and on a good night you can round up fifty or sixty spics, illegals, wetbacks, undocumented aliens or just-in-time labour, as one local tortilla-stuffed businessman-cum-rancher called them. 'They come just in time to start work,' he told me as he chewed his jerky. 'They leave just in time before you have to kick them out. It means if we have the work we can grow fast. It also means if we don't have the work, we can downsize immediately.'

If you're lucky you might even see some Eastern Europeans and Chinese as well. If you're really lucky you might even spot a coyote, one of the mysterious middlemen who bring these illegal immigrants across the border at $1,000 a throw.

'So what do you do when you've rounded them up?' I asked one night-time hunter.

'Hand them over to the Border Patrol,' he grunted.

If he does, he's one of the few. Some hunters, apparently, do hand them over to the Border Patrols, but only after they've 'processed' them. Others keep them and use them virtually as slave labour. I even heard whispers that the local Ku Klux Klan were in on the action. Sometimes, of course, it all goes wrong. The Mexicans get across the border. There is nobody there to meet them, so they wander off into the desert and who knows what happens to them?

Finally, in the land of plastic surgery, it is perhaps not insignificant that Arizona boasts the biggest gash of all time, known to certain members of the community with their own special interests as the Big Crack. Neither, I'm sure, is it insignificant that nobody has ever tried to give it a few tucks and folds if not the full facelift, which is, I guess, due more to the cost of such operations in Arizona than to the lack of any necessary skills. All the same, the Grand Canyon is spectacular. I've flown the length of it once. What I would really like to do is to ride down to the bottom. Not to gaze up in awe at the huge walls of multicoloured limestone, sandstone and shale, nor to meet the Havasupai Indians, one of the smallest surviving tribes, who still live on the canyon floor. But to put to the test the greatest unsolved philosophical problem known to man. If I'm standing on the floor of the Grand Canyon, talking to myself, and there is no woman present, with a boob job or otherwise, to hear what I'm saying, am I still wrong?

One day I'll do it. If, of course, my wife will let me.

The Onion Ones

These are the states I've only got to think about and I burst out crying.

Washington DC – there, I've started already – is an obvious candidate. Whoever it is who is supposed to be running the place, it's a complete nonsense. Kennedy was OK. Apart from the Cuban missile crisis, the Bay of Pigs and everything else. Perhaps we were lucky that he died so young. Johnson was OK. But what about Vietnam? Nixon? You mean he didn't make you weep? Ford? Come on. Carter? That cardigan? That grin? Reagan? Well, love him or hate him, he brought Gorbachev to the table and he had some great one-liners. But was he the ideal president for the greatest power on earth? George Bush? If only you could understand what he was saying. On the other hand, he did throw up on the Chinese. Clinton? Bush? Need I say more?

Then there's what they get up to. They declare their allegiance to the rule of law, yet US presidents quite happily wage war, blanket whole countries with poisonous gases or bomb them back into the Stone Age without even bothering to get approval from Congress as their own legislation dictates.

They trumpet the integrity of international boundaries, but if they want to bomb the capital city of a sovereign independent nation, they bomb it without warning, killing innocent people in the process. If they think a factory is making something they feel it shouldn't be making, they bomb it without warning, killing innocent people in the process. If they want to burst in on a sovereign, independent country, kidnap its head of state, bring him back to the US, try him under their law and lock him up for ever, they go straight ahead and do it.

They go on and on about transparency, but tell me, what would they say if a struggling Third World country elected a president whose father was not only an ex-president but had also run the Secret Service, whose brother was the governor of a key state where they counted the votes again and again until they got the right result and whose cousin was the first to announce his presidency on national radio and television even though they hadn't yet finished counting the votes?

They lecture everyone on the right of self-determination. What did they do about East Timor and Sierra Leone? They turned their backs on them. They urge everyone to support international agreements. Yet they not only refuse to sign the comprehensive test-ban treaty, they're even talking about tearing up the anti-ballistic missile treaty as well. They lay down the law about backing international institutions. Remind me, how long has it been now that they have refused to pay their own fees to the United Nations? Not that that has stopped them for one minute from laying down the law to the UN and telling it what it should and shouldn't do.

If that's not enough to make anyone weep, all the time they say one thing and do the opposite. Third World debt relief. They promised US$600 million aid to twenty-five countries. How much aid have they handed over? Zilch. Even though their GNP has risen by a third in five years and stockmarket values soared by 500 per cent in ten years.

Global warming. They lecture us about the dangers of global warming. Lecture us! They consume 80 per cent of the world's energy. They should lecture themselves. At the environmental summit in Kyoto, Japan, they agreed to cut their emissions by all of 7 per cent by 2010. But what did they do? Nothing. Congress refused to ratify the agreement. And then they proceeded to increase emissions by a further 20 per cent without as much as an apology.

They drone on and on about family values, standards, ideals, peace, harmony; caring for the sick, the elderly, the infirm. Over 40 per cent of their own population has no medical insurance. Welfare has been limited to a maximum of five years. Medicare for the elderly has been cut by $115 billion. On top of that, the USA is the most crime-ridden society on earth. They send more people to jail than the worst military dictatorship – over 5 per cent of the population is behind bars – and with thirty-eight out of fifty states supporting the death penalty, they execute more people than the most crazed military dictator could ever dream of. Then they stand there in their shorts, fancy shirts and back-to-front baseball caps, as their vast spy and satellite networks encircle the earth, the most psycho-analysed nation in the history of the world, and they claim they are being forced to spend billions of dollars on 'a national missile defence system' to protect themselves from a handful of what they call rogue states when they are in fact the biggest rogue state of them all.

And who are these politicians? Take the US Congress. Of the 535 members, three have been arrested for assault, seven for fraud, eight for shoplifting, fourteen on drug charges, nineteen for writing duff cheques. Twenty-nine have been accused of beating up their wife or partner, seventy-one can't get credit, eighty-four have been stopped for drunk driving and 117 for leading at least two companies into bankruptcy. The fact the whole country is built on a swamp can only mean that I'm not the only one weeping buckets. Just think of the number of buckets it must have taken to have created the swamp in the first place.

New Hampshire I feel sorry for, but in a different way. The first state to declare its independence – its motto is 'Live Free or Die' – it is not only now losing that independence to Washington, it is also being overrun by the capital. Practically every politician not worth voting for, not content with insisting on starting his or her election campaign in New Hampshire, now wants to go and live there as well, along with all their advisers. This, as you can imagine, has created all kinds of problems: social, economic and political.

The unfettered land of the Rednecks is, however, coping well. The first thing they've done is to help the newcomers kick their famous drug habit and get back on the straight and narrow by setting up their own unique rehabilitation centres: cheap, tax-free, bulk booze stores all over the state. Is the policy working? You try to get into one on the border with

Boston, Massachusetts any time over a weekend and you'll soon see if it's working or not.

But, of course, there are tears and there are tears, and it's poor, downtrodden West Virginia I really feel sorry for. They weren't exactly dealt a good hand to begin with. They are tucked away in the middle of nowhere; they had a desperate time during the Civil War; they were obviously at the back of the queue when it came to giving out natural resources, too.

Hawaii . . . I'm sorry, I'm crying already. Imagine it. You're living on virtually a desert island. It's one of the most isolated and beautiful places on earth. It's 2,500 miles from everywhere, whichever direction you don't want to head in. It is covered in lush vegetation. The people are the friendliest people on earth. And what happens? You're invaded by Americans. Hundreds of thousands of them. All in their fancy shorts, fancy shirts and, God help us, back-to-front baseball caps. No wonder the volcanos keep threatening to erupt at any minute. As for the Hawaiian rainforest, some say it's not a rainforest at all. It's just God Himself weeping at the plight of the poor, gentle, people-loving Hawaiians.

And finally, of course, there is Oklahoma. Poor, innocent Oklahoma. I defy anyone to read, see or hear anything about the famous Trail of Tears and not shed a tear for the poor Indians and their families. It's just unbelievable. If any other country had treated any of its people like that, we all know what the great United States of America would be saying, what their politicians would be saying, what the protestors would be demanding.

Then Tulsa, scene of the worst race riot in American history: more than 300 dead, over 1,000 buildings destroyed, the whole area called Black Wall Street virtually razed to the ground. It all started one hot, summer's night in 1921 with a rumour that a nineteen-year-old black shoeshiner, Dick Rowland, had assaulted a white lift-operator, Sarah Page, in the Drexel Building on Main Street. 'TO LYNCH NEGRO TONIGHT,' screamed the headlines in the white-owned *Tulsa Tribune*.

Scores of new deputies were promptly sworn in by the police, including many members of the community-conscious Ku Klux Klan. Fourteen hours later, the military were called in to bring it all to an end.

Lastly, of course, nobody will ever forget Timothy McVeigh and the bombing of the Alfred P. Murrah Federal Building, the worst act of domestic terrorism in American history.

Washington DC

If Paris is, as Hemingway said, a movable feast, then for me Washington is a movable Big Mac à la Française.

They've got it all together, but somehow it's not quite as substantial as you expect it to be. Not that I'm blaming the Americans. I blame the French, who designed it in the first place. Who else but the French would think of building a capital city for a rival nation on a swamp – unless, of course, they felt that the capital of the USA would not be the capital of the USA if it wasn't crawling with enormous USA-sized cockroaches. And I can't bring to mind any other country in the world where not only does the Supreme Court look down on the Capitol, or Parliament, but the Capitol or Parliament also looks down on the president. And the whole lot of them, Supreme Court, Capitol and president, who rebelled against poor old King George III under the slogan, 'No taxation without representation', look down on the 500,000 people who live in Washington, so much so they take their taxes but refuse to give them representation in their own seat of government. They've even taken away their only public hospital.

And who in their right mind would put the Library of Congress so close to the Congress itself, where everybody can read for themselves all the wrong votes and wrong decisions they make for the wrong reasons every day of their lives. Provided, of course, that the text is all in different colours, shapes and sizes, is accompanied by extensive charts, pictures, photographs, sketches and cartoons, and doesn't take longer than 3.27 seconds to read.

200

If you need further proof of the French attitude to the Americans, remember that the centre of town is almost completely surrounded by museums, all admittedly established, built and paid for by a British scientist, James Smithson, who for some reason, even though he'd never visited the city, just knew that the Americans were desperately in need of some pretty basic education, not to mention culture.

There is the National Museum of America, which shows you how Thomas Jefferson wrote the Declaration of Independence on his wooden laptop writing table, or computer, as they call them nowadays. You can also see the wooden false teeth George Washington nearly choked on when he first read the document one day while seated beneath a cherry tree.

The National Gallery of Art boasts the works of famous national painters such as Degas, Renoir and Monet, and the Museum of Natural History is stuffed full of exhibits which prove that only birds can fly. The National Air and Space Museum, on the other hand, shows that from the moment Americans could fly, they were desperate to do everything in their power to get as far away from the country as possible.

The trouble is that the Americans are so innocent when it comes to dealing with foreigners, especially the French. Even when the French engineer who drew up the plans for the city told them his name was L'Enfant they didn't suspect anything.

Then there are all the famous Washington monuments. The cherry trees around the White House, which, inexplicably, are still alive and well and blocking the light when every schoolboy knows they should have been chopped down years ago. The Lincoln Memorial. Why on earth is America's greatest president sitting with a live pigeon on each knee in a Roman chair decorated with the sticks and axes of the Roman senate surrounded by Greek pillars? He should at least be wearing a top hat. The Korean War Memorial, which features ten soldiers doing their political masters' bidding. The Vietnam Memorial, a tribute to

Lyndon Johnson's singleminded desire to save his own neck by sending thousands of young Americans from places like Camdenton, Missouri; Attleboro, Massachusetts and Bismarck, North Dakota to Vietnam because he didn't want to be the first-ever US president in history to lose a war. And, of course, the massive thing pointing up in the air which everybody says has something to do with President Clinton.

The last time I was in Washington, I couldn't see the Lincoln Memorial for cherry blossom, Constitution Avenue for coaches, the Senate for men in dark suits waving bags of cash in front of it or the Capitol for hot air. The temperature was way up in the 90s.

As for hotels, there used to be a big white one at the end of Pennsylvania Avenue which nothing on earth could beat, not even the Four Seasons across town. At first it was only available to people with Lebanese Christian parents who were born in China or Taiwan and had interests in pipeline deals in and around the Caspian Sea. Then it was opened up to anybody – anybody, that is, who could stump up the odd $250,000, $500,000 or even $1,000,000 for a night in the very bed in which Abraham Lincoln slept before that trip to the opera, even though, or so I heard, there is gore all over the floor just waiting to be wiped up and thrown out the back door.

When you checked in, apparently they asked you whether your preference was for hard or soft. Whatever you may instinctively think, this was a question about how you were intending to pay. For some reason or other, cheques and credit cards were out. Instead they wanted what they referred to as either hard money or soft money. Hard money, I think, meant coins; soft money, notes. Although I may have got that wrong.

Offer to settle the bill in Taiwanese printed circuit-boards or genuine Chinese video cassettes or counterfeit Omega watches and there was, I was told, a good chance they would also throw in a few words with the big chief, if not the junior manager down in the basement of the East Wing, who actually ran the place.

Either way, it was better than spending a night in the bed Abraham Lincoln slept in the night after he went to the opera. The only drawback, I gathered, was that there was always a lot of banging going on at nights in the manager's office. Then the following morning some guy who was so clever he could munch Big Macs and run at the same time but has yet to learn the right way round to wear a baseball cap insisted on dragging everybody off jogging around town. And to make matters worse, if anybody got back before he did, for some mysterious reason they ended up as a trade attaché in somewhere like Outer Mongolia.

I think it's now some kind of oil company head office, with more autographed baseball bats in the chief executive's office than books: 250 and counting.

If you're just looking for a restaurant, don't worry – the place is full of them, all serving – another tribute to the French – the hautest of haute cuisine. In fact, they're so haute that wherever you go, a glass of chardonnay comes with half a strawberry in it, a slice of lemon and a single lump of sugar. Corton-Charlemagne comes complete with ice bucket and the very best Bordeaux and burgundies are served at room temperature with the aid of a microwave oven.

As for the food, it's out of this world. Menus come with secret codes. D = diabetic, G = gluten-free, L = low-cholesterol, ND = no dairy or egg produce, V = vegetarian. For all their sophistication, people spend more time fussing about the mushrooms and whether the chicken is free-range or from a farm up the road than they do choosing the wine. Then, when they have chosen the wine, they immediately plunge into some exotic salad covered in peppercorns and grapefruit. As for the cost, don't think about it. In Washington, even the waiters believe money grows on trays.

Most of the best restaurants seem to be in hotels. In the Four Seasons, the Willard Inter-Continental, the Hay Adams. It is something to do with it being easier to drift away somewhere quiet to carry on your discussion after dinner. My own favourite is the one on the hill. Anyone who's anyone, or thinks they're anyone, goes there. One thing they eat there all the time is something called 'their words', which I believe is some kind of local speciality, although again, I may have misunderstood. Talking of local specialities, one evening I was taken to a restaurant which I was told was run by local people. It was an Ethiopian restaurant.

Which brings me to the local language. I don't know what they call it, but I have picked up some of the vocabulary, things like 'in my face', 'chronologically gifted', 'benchmarking', 'delayering', 'downsizing', 'geeksploitation', 'blue-sky scenario', '360-degree appraisal', 'Meatspace', 'Umfriend', 'rumorazzi'. And all day long people go around using phrases like 'This is not a garden-variety case', 'It's not on our radar screen', 'Where's the envelope?', 'Are you sure you've got my bank account number?' and 'Thanks a gazillion'.

I once went to a meeting in the State Department, which is now all bright and beautiful, although perhaps a shade too big for its boots, or rather, high heels. It wasn't the Dulles place in town but it was different. The security guard was one of those guys who would think nothing of stubbing his cigar out on your jacket and then go ballistic because you got ash all over his steel-capped, highly polished black boots. I couldn't just go in like I would into any normal building. First, he said, he wanted to know my 'honorific'.

Honorific? What the hell's an honorific? In any case, the attitude he was taking, I was damned if I was going to show him my honorific even if I had one.

In the end, after a great deal of fuss and bother and checking of phrasebooks, I discovered that an honorific is your personal title: Mr, Mrs, Lord, Lady or whatever.

I told him 'Housewife', which seemed to satisfy him. He gave me my security pass and I was in. To get my own back, though, and also to test the effectiveness of their security on the way out, I waved him a big goodbye and kept the security pass. I've still got it. I also, incidentally, still have my security passes to the World Bank and the International Monetary Fund.

If you're lucky, you can avoid all this by getting yourself invited back to dinner or whatever at one of the elegant homes in Georgetown, where all the real decisions are taken. In the 1800s, when the first government officials moved in with all their spin-doctors, they could travel backwards and forwards from Georgetown to the centre of Washington by stagecoach in a single day. Now, of course, it can take anything up to three days.

When I first started going to receptions and parties in Georgetown – No, not the in 1800s, although it often feels like it – you had to stand around all night talking politics to guys with names like Richard and Henry and Robert who were half men and half double vodka martinis. Now it's all changed. You think New York is all zero tolerance? You should try a Washington cocktail party today. Nobody says zero about anything anyone is prepared to tolerate any more.

The last one I went to was given by some guy at Opic – not Opec, but the US Overseas Private Investment Corporation – who was supposed to scour the world looking for opportunities for foreign investors. Trouble was, he refused to set foot outside his office, let alone travel the world, because the outside world wasn't air-conditioned.

I remember I no sooner opened the door of this sprawling mansion than I was hit by this sudden, glorious feeling of well-being. Before I knew what was happening, I was wandering around in some kind of haze, mumbling away to people with names like Ralph and Calvin and Gianni – well, that's what it said on their shirts and blazers – who all seemed to be about thirty-nine and not counting. One kinker I was introduced to, much against my will, told me he was interested in travel and went on to describe in graphic detail how he had worked his passage around the world, although to look at him you would think his prostate was on the blink.

I tried asking him if he had any preferences as far as countries were concerned, but he just wandered off, plunged his finger into this great blob of white blancmange in the centre of the table and crashed out on a pile of Afghan cushions on an Iranian carpet in the corner of the room.

I promptly made my apologies, as they say, and left. But I might as well have stayed. It took me, I think, two weeks to get back to the hotel. No, not the big white one on Pennsylvania Avenue. The traffic was horrendous. The jams must be caused, I think, by the Poles, only because, whenever you talk to anyone in Washington about anything, all they keep saying is, 'Beware of the Poles', or 'What do the Poles say?' With so many Poles all over the place, it's no wonder the traffic is so bad. Except, to be fair, once every four years, when one half of the town seems to move out and another, brand-new half moves in. The rest of the time it doesn't move at all.

One spaghetti snot I met once as I was walking back to the airport – well, it was quicker – told me that Washington was such a mess he wouldn't even go there to consummate his divorce. Clearly something has to be done. Not that, as I say, I'm blaming the Americans. No, sir. It's not their fault if the capital of the greatest and richest nation on earth can't even repair a school roof so badly in need of it that judges have to ban the few children who actually still want to go there from doing so in case the whole thing crashes down on top of them.

So what's the solution? Easy. If the whole place is a move-able Big Mac, then why not move it, lock, stock and pork barrel, somewhere else? Culturally speaking, it would be more at home in the middle of the Sahara desert, though economically speaking, lots of people would be far, far better off if it was stuck halfway up a pipeline anywhere between the Caspian Sea and the Mediterranean. Politically speaking, you could hardly do better than ancient Rome. Let's be honest, the guy with the fiddle couldn't make a worse job of running the place than the present mayor. Not that I would dare come up with such outrageous suggestions. My suggestion is Williamsburg, just down the road in Virginia. It's tailor-made for politics. It was, after all, their first capital.

The historic seventeenth-century centre of the town, the main street with the Capitol at one end and at the other the College of William and Mary, designed, incidentally, by Christopher Wren, is about the same size as the centre of Washington. Added to which they have all the facilities and more for running a country: a market square, a market square tavern, a courthouse, the Williamsburg Inn, which must be one of the best hotels in America, and a very large bank with, no doubt, a very large safe.

The President's House, I'm sure, could be turned into a hotel, although whether it should take hard money or soft money is something to be decided.

Best of all, there is no traffic. Well, apart from the occasional horse. There's no crime. The people are nice and friendly, even though they haven't been able to buy any new clothes for over 200 years, and there's nothing in the coffee apart from coffee.

If it was good enough for the likes of Washington and Jefferson and Patrick Henry and all the others, surely it must be good enough for the present lot? Tell you what. Go and have a look at sleazeball Washington where everyone is a blabbermouth for someone or something, then pop down the road to good, clean-living Williamsburg and see if you feel a moving experience coming on.

West Virginia

Poor old West Virginia. It's the highest and roughest part of the Appalachians. It's nothing but coalmines, or if not coalmines, coal dust. It's small, about 25,000 square miles, more or less the size of your average Indian reservation. It's poverty-stricken. It's also one of the most isolated places in the US. From Washington DC, for example, it's at least four hours by telephone. I should know. I once practically criss-crossed the whole state with a truck-driver who loves the place so much he's spent the last thirty years dumping cement all over it to help him pay for two divorces and to finance his hobby, researching the Civil War, which caused the two divorces in the first place.

'West Virginia. It was created by the Civil War. It's a Civil War state. We refused to go with the rest of Virginia. We seceded from the Union,' he told me as I struggled up into his cab.

We started at the capital, Charleston. See what I mean about being isolated? They don't even know there is another town called Charleston in South Carolina. It was raining, the first time they had had rain in thirty days.

'Heavy precipitation. That's what we need. Heavy precipitation.'

Our first stop was somewhere along Washington Street. Somebody was building a shop or something. All very small-town, all very ordinary. Nothing like the America you see outside *Forrest Gump*.

Job done, we headed out to Harper's Ferry. This is where, back in 1859, John Brown, the ferocious anti-slavery freedom-fighter, thought he could start a war to free all the slaves by attacking the US armoury. All he got for his trouble was imprisonment by Robert E. Lee, the gallows and a mention in a lousy song. We drove along huge, empty highways and tiny lanes, climbing and skidding down one hill after another.

'They say West Virginia has so many hills that if you could lay it flat it would be the same size as Texas.'

The roadside was littered with smashed cars and trucks that had skidded out of control in the rain.

'Not used to the precipitation,' said the truck-driver.

It was also dotted with tiny museums. The Gauley Bridge Historical Society Museum (historical bits and pieces of Gauley Bridge in a society museum), Fayette County Museum (historical bits and pieces of Fayette County in a museum), Hawk's Nest Museum (historical bits and . . . well, you've got the idea).

Harper's Ferry turned out to be not so much a ferry as the meeting place of the Shenandoah and the Potomac, which flows on to Washington DC.

'The most beautiful place in the whole world.'

I wouldn't have gone that far, but it was OK. It wasn't

covered in coal dust or cement. Yet. Although we did smother a bit of it on a site where one of the local hotels was planning to build a garage. While the cement was oozing all over an area large enough to accommodate an aircraft hangar, let alone a garage, I walked down towards the edge of the river. I didn't get far. There was a huge sign blocking the way. 'Foot travel only.'

Across the river was a big metal bridge.

'The longest single-arch-span bridge in the world.'

After that we seemed to visit a string of Civil War sites.

'Eight times, this place changed sides. Eight times. Can you imagine that? The worst one-day battle in the whole of the Civil War. Seventeen September 1862. Two thousand Union troops killed, fifteen hundred Confederates.'

'So who was leading the Confederates?'

'General Robert E. Lee. Yes, sir.'

'Another disaster for General Robert—'

Suddenly, truck brakes. We swerved towards the verge.

'What I meant was a disastrous situation, which I'm sure General Robert E. Lee did his best to . . . but unfortunately . . . circumstances at the time . . .'

My God. You've got to be so careful talking to these, ahem, southerners.

'I'm sure everybody, especially the ordinary people . . .'

We were back in the middle of the road again.

'Soldiers were wounded, exhausted, no shoes. But still they followed . . .' said the driver.

'Of course, of course. Great man.'

We went through Monongahela, the best unpronounceable forest in the world. It's a little bit smaller than it was, thanks to some more cement being dumped on it. We also went to Clifftop Oak Hill and a place called White Sulphur Springs, which is so isolated that it's becoming the number one hide-away for all the mega-bosses of US industry looking for a spot of high-level, secretive chit-chat, not to mention a bit of R&R away from the prying eyes of the rest of us.

On my last night in swinging Charleston – I'm kidding, I'm kidding – I was the big Civil War expert.

'Poor . . . oppressed . . . against all the odds,' I began.

'Determined . . . undaunted,' grunted the guy next to me at the bar, who was, I could tell immediately, from West Virginia. He was so out of touch he was wearing his baseball cap the right way round.

'Brother against brother,' I continued.

'Levelling the place to the ground . . . merciless . . . ruthless,' he responded, slapping his weak beer down on top of the bar.

'Whole families torn apart.'

'Struggle to end all struggles . . . Fight to the finish . . . Determined to win.'

'Unbelievable suffering . . . violence.'

'Pitched battle . . . triumph . . . victory.'

Then it struck me. We were talking about two different civil wars. I was talking about *the* Civil War. He was talking about the civil war currently being waged in West Virginia over the effects of too much coalmining in the state. One half of the population says mountaintop mining is good business, the coal is good coal – it's low in sulphur, burns cleanly, meets all the clean-air regulations, creates jobs, means money for tiny, poor, isolated West Virginia. The other half says it's destroying the environment, wrecking people's lives, ruining their health.

Poor West Virginia. Still fighting. And probably still losing.

New Hampshire

New Hampshire is in the wrong place. It should be in the south. Say between Oklahoma and Texas.

It's slow. It's rural. It's old-fashioned. It's very, very conservative. While the rest of New England pretty solidly votes Democrat, it is strongly Republican. It should be called Old Hampshire instead of New Hampshire, because as far as I can see, there's nothing new about it.

There's nothing supersonic about the capital, Concord. It's more of a De Havilland flying boat. The first time I went there I couldn't believe it was a capital city. For me, capital cities are big, fast-moving places, lots of traffic, millions of people. Now that I understand America even less, I know the difference. It's not even the only Concord. The other one, in Massachusetts, is much more fun, although why Thoreau chose to hide himself away there is something that has always puzzled me. He could have done it much more easily and much more effectively in Concord, New Hampshire. He wouldn't have got as much publicity, of course, because everybody in New Hampshire hides themselves away from everybody else. Not that I'm suggesting for a moment that he only did it for the publicity.

Manchester was also a big surprise. To me Manchester is Manchester, the home of . . . what's the name of that football team? This Manchester was nothing but an airport and a big hotel. This is where practically every American presidential candidate since George Washington has started his campaign, presumably on the basis that the sooner they got it out of the way the better. It was only after many visits in all kinds of weather, ranging from snow and ice to ice and snow, that I discovered there was actually a town surrounding the airport and the hotel.

The further north you go up towards the White Mountains and the Appalachians, the worse it gets. Franklin, which I've been to countless times, is almost my limit. After that it's just hikers and campers and people-carriers and trucks all going round and round in ever-decreasing circles searching for peace and quiet. I tried it once. I think I got as far as Laconia, just south of the White Mountains, before I gave up. It was so crowded I couldn't even open my Appalachian Mountains Club trail map. It wasn't, I assure you, that I believed for one moment that staying in an AMC-approved lean-to, not to mention a tent platform, was my kind of scene, it was just that as these New Age electronic geeks I knew in Franklin kept on at me about the joys of hiking through the forest, staying at designated campsites – coin-operated showers, firewood usually available – I thought I'd better find out why I would hate every second of it. For similar reasons I once tried to get to the Shaker villages around Enfield on Mascoma Lake – that time I suddenly developed my own form of shakes and couldn't make it – and to Mystery Hill, North Salem, which is billed as America's Stonehenge. Apparently, there are all these megalithic rock formations all over the place, and even a huge glacial boulder with a giant split down the middle which lines up with the Equinox sunset on 21 March and 21 September every year. It is supposed to be one of the most important archaeological sites in the western hemisphere. But I didn't make that, either.

They call New Hampshire the Granite State, but I reckon this is more of a comment on its people than on its geography. They not only look like your mother-in-law, they behave like your mother-in-law. Upbeat, cheerful, optimistic, they are not. They're miserable, dour, down-at-heel, and when they are not, they give a good impression of it. They all seem to be hard-working, a touch puritanical, churchgoing; they believe in the family, worry about their children's schooling. Yet at the same time they carry guns. Many's the time I've climbed into a truck to see a couple of rifles strapped to the back of the cab. They hunt, they fish – in fact they do everything southerners do.

The problem is that, precisely because they are all so hard-working, puritanical, churchgoing and believe in the family, all the people who aren't – the take-it-easy, Brie-eating, wine-drinking, secular, quasi-Bohemian New Englanders who are pro-choice, pro-booze, pro-drugs (well, soft drugs, anyway) and pro more or less everything else – want to go and live there because they think it is a better environment in which to bring up their kids than a place where they will be surrounded by people like themselves.

Will they get on? The answer, of course, is no. The old and the new never get on. The old always loses. The gourmet coffee shops, handcrafted wholewheat bread, tiny steel-framed

212

glasses, incense-burning, computer-fluent chinos always win. It's the way of the world.

Hawaii

Aloha. Aloha. Aloha.

Me-fella say. Me-fella no like Hawaii. No like sand. No like sun. No like surf. All that water bad. Specially me with Me-fella allergy. Also me no like plenty big-swank tourists. Specially big-swank Yankee tourists. With crazy big-swank Hawaii shirt and cap of baseball.

Hawaii-fella. He call me Imi Loa. Me-fella tell him, him no good. Me-fella get bad spirit. Bad spirit boil Him-fella in pot.

Him-fella say Imi Loa mean Onrable Big Traveller.

Me-fella say, OK, Him-fella. Him-fella now stand up. Go get me mai-tai size of she-fella with big lighted stick in hand. Me-fella now like Hawaii. Me-fella say, OK, OK, Him-fella. Me-fella no want Him-fella little sister. Just the mai-tai.

Hawaii takes some getting used to. It's nothing like the rest of the States. It's far more sophisticated, far more fluent, far more intelligent. Well, maybe not as intelligent as Texas, but you get my drift.

Honolulu, the capital, is like California in the old days: big, bustling, honky-tonk, but without the way-out craziness. On one side are the Koolau Mountains, on the other the sea, the beach, and, of course, Waikiki, the Benidorm of the South Pacific. In between, there is everything you could possibly want in the shake of a grass skirt. Including hula dancing.

The restaurants serve all types of food – Thai, Filipino, Japanese, Chinese, Cantonese, even, would you believe, hamburgers, though the quality is not so good. The Hawaiians don't like Cooks. They killed Captain Cook, don't forget. Ice creams? They go mad on them. Not only have they every flavour under the sun but they somehow seem to present them in a huge variety of ways. Shops? There are millions where, for millions of handfuls of coloured beads, you can put down a

213

deposit on anything you like in the world. But beware Ala Moana, the biggest open-air shopping mall in the world. Every wife who marches stridently in there ends up by being a moana. Even though it has over 200 shops, she will still complain that none of them have exactly what she's looking for, and if they have it's in the wrong size. Stick with the mai-tais. Shirts? No, don't. I can't stand them. Especially the ones from Hilo Hattie.

Then there are all the extras. Too much traffic, too much noise, too many hustlers, too many thefts. Too many flip-flops.

Away from the bustle of Honolulu is the island of Oahu, so small you can practically jog round it in a morning while sipping your mai-tai. Not that I would, of course. Jog round the island, I mean. Five minutes and you're practically chatting up a tree frog; ten minutes and you're in the middle of a rainforest. Fifteen minutes and you're in a pineapple field. Twenty minutes and there's another damn waterfall and, no thank you, the last thing I want to do is dive into it. What I want is another large mai-tai. As for that hibiscus, make just one move and I'll tell you precisely where you can put it.

Oahu is not, of course, just about tourists enjoying themselves. A lot of people were killed here when the Japanese attacked Pearl Harbor on 7 December 1941 and the great US general Douglas MacArthur did nothing about it. Well, nothing until it was too late.

The famous USS *Arizona* Memorial commemorates the officers and men who died during the raid on Pearl Harbor. One old him-fella, I mean old soldier, told me that the *Arizona* still lies at the bottom of the harbour, oozing oil like 'tears for the people who died'. After that I didn't even feel like a mai-tai.

One afternoon I went native and took a trip to a plantation village, consisting of over thirty different plantation homes and buildings. At first I thought it was going to be another one of those evening folkoriques, but it wasn't. I'll deny it if you quote me, but it was actually great fun. Most of the guides seemed to come from Samoa, and had a crazy, way-out Samoan sense of humour. On the way back to Honolulu somebody told me they were all Mormons, but I'm prejudiced. I still thought they were funny.

Mani, the next largest island, I didn't bother with. This is where everybody goes to see the humpback whales. I've got nothing against humpback whales, it's the people I can't stand. They're like birdwatchers with money, all binoculars and cardigans and going on and on about the greater crested whatever it is.

Me-fella me Imi Loa me say, plenty many big mai-tais left for Me-fella Me Imi Loa to drink with most plenty good luck before all them plenty big swank Yankee tourists come with plenty many glass beads. Me go where Him-fella serve plenty many big mai-tais. Me-fella Me Imi Loa say to Him-fella, Me-fella Me Imi Loa want plenty big mai-tais chop-chop. No. Me-fella Me Imi Loa not want your second-youngest sister, either. Just the mai-tais.

Goodbyeah. Goodbyeah. Goodbyeah.

Oklahoma

Oklahoma City makes a big fuss about being the biggest city in the US. *Biggest city?* That's what I thought. What they mean is biggest city in terms of area which is, of course, something different altogether. The first time I arrived in Oklahoma City from Tulsa, a boring, played-out oil and gas town tucked away in the foothills of the Ozark Mountains exactly halfway between Los Angeles and New York – the only thing I can remember about it is having what was billed as a 'garbage breakfast' at Jimmy's Egg Restaurant – I ended up in some hotel in the middle of nowhere, completely surrounded by fields.

'But I've got a reservation in a hotel downtown,' I protested.

'This is downtown,' said the nice Indian lady on Reception, who turned out to be from Bombay and was for some reason a big fan of Manchester United. What the city fathers had done, she told me, was to stretch the boundaries as far as they could – the city covers 650 square miles, the same area as Los Angeles – so that they could rake in all the oil revenue they could get their hands on. Clever guys, these Oklahomy City fathers.

Eventually, however, I found what I would call downtown. But I admit it took some doing: I kept blinking and missing it. It's only a couple of blocks, a hotel and a newsagent's shop which doesn't stock the local *Daily Oklahoma* because years ago one of their delivery guys beat up the newsagent's old mother. So be warned: stick to the *Wall Street Journal*. It's safer and, if you're in a hurry, quicker because you don't get the lecture.

Apart from the nice Indian lady, who should be signed up by Merchant Ivory immediately and the newsagent, there are three other things I remember about Oklahoma City.

First of all, of course, it is the site of the bombing in 1995 of the Alfred P. Murrah Federal Building, in which 168 people were killed and another 500 injured. They've flattened the whole area now, and are turning it into a vast memorial park. At one end there is going to be a 42ft bronze and concrete gate inlaid with a clockface fixed at 9.01 am. At the other end there will be a similar gate featuring a clockface showing 9.03 am. The bomb went off at 9.02 am. In between will be 168 empty chairs.

Some say it's a bit over the top. I don't think so. This was a small town, away from all the rough stuff. It's not New York, Chicago or Miami America. These guys did nothing to anybody. The impact of such a huge bomb on the local community is on the scale of the impact of the blowing-up of the PanAm jet on Lockerbie, the IRA bomb on Omagh and the mass shooting on Denver, Colorado. Hardly any family in the city was unaffected.

I went there early one morning. Long after the disaster people were still stopping off on their way to work leaving notes and flowers. Children brought teddy bears. And one evening on my way back to my hotel, I saw groups simply standing there, holding hands. Others were reading the notes, rearranging the flowers, just looking.

'We can't forget. We're not going to forget,' one old man told me.

'My dad. I can't forget him,' I heard a young guy explaining to others.

My second, and completely different memory of Oklahoma City is the fact that most of the laundering operations are in the hands of Nigerians, or a good slice of them, at any rate. Nigerians are not among the world's experts at laundering, of course – you've only got to look at the state Nigeria is in today to see that – but in Oklahoma City it's laundering as in laundering they're big in, not laundering as in money-laundering.

Back in the 1960s, Oklahoma City was a big oil town. It had so much of the stuff that it was practically oozing out of the ground. At one time there were so many oil derricks around the State Capitol – the only State Capitol in the US with its own oil well in the grounds busy pumping away, day and night – that they had to build a special wooden walkway to stop the politicians from being splattered. Now, of course, it's unusual to find a politician who isn't stained or splattered.

A series of events changed all that. First, the oil price war, and Jimmy Carter in his cardigan appealing to everyone to turn the heating down. Then many Oklahoma wells running dry. The emergence of Dallas as an oil centre; the advent of new technology. The oil business not only began to shrink, but what was left of it started to abandon Oklahoma City. Many people moved on; others switched to new ways of making a living. A bunch of Yorubas in town, who had been wheeling and dealing in Nigerian oil, either officially or unofficially – it's always difficult to say with Nigerians – were left high and dry. They needed to find something else to do, and for some inexplicable reason chose laundering.

'Well, it's a business. It makes money,' explained one

217

lumbering, 7ft, 30-stone Yoruba from Ibadan after telling me the story. 'And somebody's got to do it,' he added, not too enthusiastically, I must say.

Another thing I learned going around from office to office when I should have been down at the stockyards (the busiest stockyards in the world, where they handle millions of cattle nearly every day) or at a horse show (they run more horse shows and horse events than any other city in the world) was who it was, during the last war, with U-boats sinking practically an oil tanker a day destined for Britain, that saved our bacon. It was the Okies. They sent over a team of forty-two oil men, together with all the latest high-speed drilling equipment and, as the Nazi bombers flew backwards and forwards overhead, they dug over a hundred oil wells, ninety-four of them productive, in Sherwood Forest in Nottingham. So maybe Robin Hood was on to a good thing after all. Production started at 300 barrels a day, and once all ninety-four wells were operating, it soared to over 3,000.

'We saved you. Where would you be without Oklahoma?' one crotchety old J. R. told me.

But the real treat in Oklahoma City was – and I know this is going to sound yucky – the National Cowboy Hall of Fame. OK, I admit it. I went there to sneer, to make fun of a bunch of grown men playing at cowboys and Indians, and to scoff at the state of American art, which I know that to most Americans is short for Arthur. But I couldn't. I was completely captivated. It's a fantastic place, much more fun than the Hermitage, the Louvre or many of these other fuddy-duddy, dusty old museums.

The Hall of Fame building is huge. Maybe not as big as the new Tate Modern, but big all the same. It looks like a cross between a pioneer's tent and a circle of wagons, covers 80,000 square feet and is set in 20 acres of land. Inside it's bright with lots of wide, sweeping corridors and comfortable-sized galleries.

Yes, I know it's all cowboys and Indians and that kind of

stuff but, believe me, some of the paintings and sculptures are superb, a lot better than many of the exhibits you see in provincial art galleries and museums now that they've got so much money to spend and nothing worthwhile to spend it on.

Take Wilson Hurley's five vast, spectacular triptych landscapes of the wild west, each measuring 46ft by 18ft. They're not Turners or Canalettos, or even David Hockneys, and they don't depict terribly chi-chi places like Venice or Penshurst Park or Flatford Mill, but they're fabulous. Maybe it's because of their sheer size that they seem to reach out and grab you. And then the scenes, the colours, almost the magic of them, make you feel as though you're suddenly part of them.

The first, *California Suite*, shows a breathtaking sunset over the Pacific at Point Lobos. *Arizona Suite* is a vista of the Grand Canyon, looking up out of it towards the sky. *New Mexico Suite* has what looks like a huge volcano of light erupting out of the Sandia Mountains near Albuquerque. *Utah Suite* features a typically magnificent cloudless sky over Monument Valley. And finally, *Wyoming Suite* is a view of the lower falls of the Yellowstone, again seen from below, looking up through the pines. Fantastic.

There are also plenty of Old Masters, or at least, what qualify as Old Masters in the US. Charles Russell's paintings of Indians on the plains are full of life, colour and intensity. Each one has character, drama. You can almost feel the events happening. You're almost there.

As for Albert Bierstadt's *Emigrants Crossing the Plains*, I defy anyone not to stand there open-mouthed at the plight of the emigrants herding their cattle and slowly plodding onwards, Indian tents vaguely in the distance, towards the sunset. If Turner had gone to the States instead of to Venice, this is the kind of picture he would probably have painted. Provided, of course, he hadn't forgotten to bring his glasses with him.

I can't understand why the contemporaries are not more famous either. OK, we all know Warhol and his can of Campbell's soup, but these are a thousand times better. They tell stories. They take you into the picture. They're like life. They're exciting. My favourite has got to be *Sharing an Apple* by Tom Ryan. It sounds yukky, but I promise you it isn't. It's the end of a long day. The cattle are munching grass. The cowboy has dismounted, and he and his horse, its reins hanging loose to the ground, are sharing an apple between them.

Then there are the sculptures: Gerald Balciars' 18ft-high slinky, sinuous, marble cougar creeping slowly down the sides of a canyon; the 33ft-high bronze of 'Buffalo Bill' Cody rearing up on his horse, shotgun in the air, by Leonard McMurray; Hollis Williford's *Welcome Sundown*, an exhausted old cowboy on the point of collapse, dragging his saddle behind him, wiping the sweat off his brow, too tired even to ask for a tin of beans; and, of course, the monumental *End of the Trail*, an exhausted Indian, lance still under his arm, on a dead beat, about-to-collapse pony, by James Earle Fraser. Every one of them worth ten years' subscription to the Tate Gallery.

Then there is Frederic Remington. I cannot for the life of me understand why he's not up there with Stubbs. His four cowboys riding hell for leather across the plains, *Coming Through the Rye*, says everything about horses that Stubbs says. Different kinds of horses. Different people. Different period, of course. But just as superb. Then there's *Bronco Buster*, which says even more and, if I had to have a favourite, *The Mountain Man*, horse and rider sliding, slipping, down a terrifyingly steep slope. I've never been down a slope as steep as that on a horse but, believe it, it couldn't be more real.

Maybe the reason nobody takes any notice of Remington and all the others, or gives them the recognition and credit they are entitled to is purely and simply because they're about cowboys and Indians. Anything else and it would be on display in the National Gallery. If Marlboro wasn't so out of favour with the movers and shakers of the art world – they prefer drugs to cigarettes – I'd get them to sponsor a worldwide tour of the best of cowboy and Indian art. It might not appeal to the critics but I've no doubt it would pull in the crowds.

The rest of the exhibition was more showbusiness, but just as much fun. The John Wayne Collection featured many of his personal possessions, including the model 92 Winchester which he had modified when he starred in *Stagecoach* and then used throughout the rest of his career, and, of course, clips from the *Alamo*, *The Man who Shot Liberty Valance* and naturally, *True Grit*. The Western Performers' Hall of Fame had slightly choco-late-boxy portraits of Roy Rogers and Dale Evans, Glenn Ford, Gene Autry, Randolph Scott, James Stewart and many others.

What I didn't see was any reference to the Trail of Tears, which is surprising, especially with the efforts being made to commemorate those who died in the Federal Building bombing. In 1838, President Andrew Jackson, in the face of a ruling by the Supreme Court, ordered all the Cherokee Indians from the four south-eastern states, North Carolina, Tennessee, Georgia and Alabama, to be rounded up with whatever posses-sions they had and marched thousands of miles all the way to the newly designated Oklahoma Indian Territory. By the end of the march, of course, thousands had died of hunger, exhaus-tion and disease. I reckon it should rank alongside many of the other infamous forced marches and relocations in history, but for some reason it doesn't seem to get the attention it deserves.

No sooner had the Indians resettled in Oklahoma than they were once more on the run. Again from the adherents to the Declaration of Independence, which proclaimed to the sound of trumpets that 'we hold these truths to be self-evident that all men are created equal, that they are endowed by their Creator with certain inalienable rights, that among these are life, liberty and the pursuit of happiness'. Except, of course, that at that time, Indians were not considered to be men, let alone equals. The land on which the Indians had been forced to resettle was now being sold by the government from under their feet to whichever white man got there first and staked his claim. No wonder, then, that even today, in towns and villages throughout Oklahoma people re-enact the Trail of Tears.

There are plenty of things to cry about in Oklahoma.

The Tomato, Chilli, Cucumber and Gherkin Ones

These are the bits-and-pieces states, the they're-OK-but-you-could-do-without-them states. That's not my opinion, it's theirs.

Ohio, for example. To me, it's a major manufacturing state. Maybe not as major as it used to be, but still bigger than North Dakota. Yet just as Collinsville, Illinois boasts of being the horseradish capital of the world, Vineland, New Jersey, the aubergine capital, Hope, Arkansas, the birthplace of Bill Clinton, the watermelon capital, so Ohio proclaims itself the tomato capital. The state drink is, would you believe, tomato juice, and the State motto 'If it peels, it's good', words to that effect.

But it wasn't always so. For a long time Ohio regarded tomatoes as not only highly dangerous but inedible, and if not inedible, poisonous as well. Then Wendy's hamburger chain started up in the capital, Columbus, and suddenly tomatoes were in. They were the greatest vegetable, fruit or whatever. Farmers in and around Reynoldsburg who had no more brains than tomato pureé risked their lives to tame and domesticate them. Children were told that tomatoes were good for them which, of course, immediately put them off tomatoes for life.

Tennessee, meanwhile, was the last state to secede from the Union and the first to rejoin. See what I mean about these being you-could-do-without-them states? They're not exactly pace-setters. Maybe that's why Al Whatshisname was so at home in Tennessee. He certainly didn't look as though he was at home anywhere else. Tennessee is, of course, the home of what they call country music, and as far as I'm concerned, that's pretty much a background, side-of-your-plate, take-it-or-leave-it sound. Not that I would want my views to in any way offend Dolly Parton. The last thing I would want is for her to hold them against me.

As for North Dakota, to me it's the gherkin of all the states. It's . . . it's . . . it's, well, North Dakota. Even when President Benjamin Harrison signed the official papers declaring it the thirty-ninth state of the Union on 2 November 1889, he got all confused and thought he was signing the papers for South Dakota. The fact he signed them on 2 November might also be significant, since that's the day when people all over the world remember the dead.

Ohio

I'm sure I'm missing something about Ohio. On paper it should be fine. It has Cincinnati, Cleveland, Columbus, where one night at a quarter past ten the bed fell on James Thurber's father, the Great Lakes, not to mention all those cornfields up in the north. But somehow it's always a big disappointment. Like going out on the town and the following morning waking up at home.

Maybe when the glaciers dumped that fantastic soil over it all those years ago – local farmers say Ohio has some of the best soil in the world – it smothered all signs of life as well. Or maybe it's just that most of the time I'm in Ohio I'm driving up and down Route 1.75, the automobile industry's answer to Silicon Valley, which starts in Detroit, Michigan and goes on to Kentucky, Tennessee, and then all the way down to Orlando, Florida. Along virtually the entire route are manufacturers producing everything you could think of for cars, vans and trucks, from ordinary common-or-garden engine parts to clever, hi-tech, sophisticated ashtrays.

I first discovered Route 1.75 in the early days of just-in-time deliveries, when everybody was cutting their stocks to practically zero and suppliers were being forced to deliver direct to the production lines on time, or else. The last time I was there, almost every company I visited was adjusting to being a '100-per-cent-turnover' business. Competition for staff was so great, the pressure to pay higher and higher wages so intense, that most of them were losing the whole of their workforce every year.

'You'd be surprised,' one hard-pressed gear head told me between large slugs of bloody mary. 'Another 15 cents more an hour down the road, and they're off. The whole plant could be empty by tomorrow morning.' He suggested we continued our chat over lunch at his golf club nearby.

Recruitment was a nightmare, too. The hard-pressed human-resources manager of another company, which made some fancy fuel things for under the bonnet somewhere, told me they could no longer recruit in the old way: advertise, interview, reject half, write to the lucky winners. Instead they used twenty-four-hour telephone-answering machines. The machines asked the questions, people replied and, ostensibly on the basis of their answers, the machines told them whether or not they had got the job.

'What we don't tell them is that everyone who replies gets a job,' he said, swearing me to secrecy. 'If people knew that they wouldn't come. They'd think if there was no competition for jobs we were a bad employer. In any case, everybody likes to think they've got qualifications, whether they have or not.'

We discussed this over a heavily liquid dinner at his golf club. Probably because it was a heavily liquid dinner, we also discussed how the great American free trader is not such a great free trader after all.

Most US firms benefit from enormous levels of government subsidy. The reason they get away with it is that they deny all knowledge of it.

Another bottle of French wine.

What they do is establish an offshore company through which they channel huge chunks of their overseas profits. Not only do they keep these profits outside the US – subsidy number one – they then use them, as credits against their domestic US tax obligations. Subsidy number two. Clever guys, these American free traders.

Another bottle of French wine.

Instead of directly supporting companies financially, the US government commissions too many research and development contracts in the full knowledge that most of the money will be going elsewhere. Subsidy number three.

Another bottle of French wine.

The US government doesn't ban imports. Instead it finds a health reason for not letting them in. The most blatant example was Italian pork products, excluded from the States because of an outbreak of African swine fever in 1967. The ban was not lifted until thirty years later. If they can't find a health reason for keeping out an import, they play games with words. Mexican corn syrup is OK, so that's allowed in, Mexican sugar is not. So let's call Mexican corn syrup Mexican sugar. That way we can ban it. If they can't find a health reason and they can't play games with words, they just go ahead and ban things anyway, just as they've banned over eighty major Brazilian products including sugar, shoes, steel and orange juice, not to mention Australian and New Zealand lamb and European wheat gluten.

Another bottle of French wine.

So are they trying to keep American markets American? No way, say the great free traders. So if the great free-trade America is open to foreign competition, how come the telecommunications market remains totally American?

Another bottle of French wine.

Subsidies, import restrictions, market protection: they might sound boring, but let me tell you, compared to anything else you can do in Ohio, they are a bundle of laughs. Take Cincinnati. I thought it was going to be full of riverboats and casinos and hinks in black suits, big, frilly white shirts, dazzling rhinestone waistcoats, long, gold chains and thick, chunky rings with six-shooters tucked neatly under each armpit. Instead it's whiter than white and purer than pure, which probably should not have come as any great surprise seeing as it is dominated by Proctor and Gamble's worldwide headquarters. Not that anyone had to tell me Cincinnati was Proctor and Gamble's home town. The local buses run on cooking oil. The whole place smells like a fish and chip shop.

In the old days Cincinnati was to pigs what Chicago was to

cattle. In fact it was known as Porkopolis. Today, stuck between the Great Plains, the South and the Great Lakes and overlooked by the Dolly Partons, the local name for the twin towers of Proctor and Gamble's head office, it's more Boringopolis. About the most exciting thing that's ever happened there was the publication of *Uncle Tom's Cabin* by Harriet Beecher Stowe in 1852.

On my first visit, everybody told me to make for Fountain Square and have a three-way, some local speciality involving a bowl of chillis covered in spaghetti, covered in sauce, covered in cheese. The square would blow my mind, they said. It was the centre of the universe. It's nothing. It's about the size of a polo field and surrounded by office blocks. Except, of course, at Christmastime. Then Fountain Square comes into its own. More often than not, prominently on display for the festive season is the local Ku Klux Klan cross, which gives a whole new meaning to the phrase 'I'm dreaming of a white Christmas'.

I was then taken to Bicentennial Common at Sawyer Point. This, I was assured by all and sundry, was like St Mark's Square. St Mark's Square? It's like St Mark's Square insofar as it's not a square. Apart from that, they've got to be joking. All I can remember is pigs: four pigs stuck on top of a steamboat funnel, symbolising the long cultural heritage of steamboats and pork-packing; a pig in the shape of Noah's Ark on a red column showing the highest-ever flood levels to hit the city (79.9 pigs high) and a statue of the pig of a Roman farmer and general responsible for the whole thing, Cincinnatus.

Probably because I didn't display the required degree of enthusiasm, I was next taken to Clifton and Mount Adams, a bit of a hill just east of downtown. From there, everybody said, I could look down on the wonder and splendour of what Mark Twain apparently called the Queen City of the west. As far as I was concerned, the only good thing about it was that I was further away from it.

Maybe it's because Cincinnati is not only named after a pig farmer, Roman, but was also founded by pig farmers, German;

maybe it's because one of its most illustrious sons was an itinerant fruit-picker called Leonard Slye, or Roy Rogers, to you. Or maybe it's that at one time the mayor was Jerry Springer. After all, just one of these connections would be a hell of a burden to carry, let alone all three. But Cin City it is not. Neither is Cleveland. Everybody calls it the rock 'n' roll capital of the States because a local Cleveland DJ, Alan Freed, was not only the first to coin the phrase, but did so on a local Cleveland radio station, to a Cleveland audience on a Cleveland Saturday night. It's also, of course, the home of the famous Rock 'n' Roll Hall of Fame, which I have avoided at all costs. Just across the park, Cleveland's Museum of Art has probably the best collection of Picasso's blue rock 'n' roll period in the world, but nobody talks about that.

When I first went to Cleveland I used to go to Shaker Heights, which is about as far away from rock 'n' roll as an airport x-ray machine is from a proper security check. It was a very prim and proper area which seemed to be full of executive suites. At the time Cleveland, which I always thought of as a teenage Pittsburgh, was coming out of the dark ages. For a long time it had been going downhill fast. Industry was shutting up shop and leaving, people were running away in all directions. The Cuyahoga River was so polluted that one day it just spontaneously burst into flames. The city even had to file for bankruptcy.

Then, like many cities across the States, they girded their loans and started to fight back. They cleaned up the city centre, refurbished all the run-down parts of town, did up all the old buildings and warehouses along by the river and built two new stadiums. The once-fashionable University Circle district once again became fashionable. Today it's a bit like Jane Austen on heat. It's still very much an elderly aunt, and wouldn't dream of blaspheming during Thanksgiving supper, but it's desperately trying to enjoy itself.

Columbus I haven't been to. I nearly did once. I was across the lake in Erie, Pennsylvania, and had a couple of days to spare. I thought, is it to be Columbus, Ohio or Louisville, Kentucky? I went to Louisville. Ohio has that kind of effect on me.

Tennessee

I'm worried about Tennessee. I think it must be the cured-oak water. First there is a ducking stupid hotel, the Peabody, the best in Memphis, which is decorated from floor to ceiling with ducks. There are duck doorstops, duck bars of soap and duck designs all over the place. And at eleven o'clock every morning, you've got it, five ducks waddle into the lobby and up the red carpet and clamber into the fountain, where they splash around until five o'clock, when they up and waddle out again. The Americans, of course, go quackers over them, but it was all too much for me. I dragged myself into the bar – called, inevitably, the Mallard – sank a couple of bloody marys, staggered into the restaurant and, to get my own back, ordered duck à l'orange which, of course, they didn't serve.

'Oh, how could we do that to our friends?' Elmer who, moments earlier, had promised to give me the most exciting evening of my life, shrieked and fluffed up his tail feathers.

Which struck me as odd, seeing as normally Americans will kill and eat anything. Tennessee is the only place I know in the world where it's legal to take home and eat roadkill, in other words any animal you knock down and kill on the road. Deer, skunks, racoons, squirrels, opossums, rabbits, anything.

'Grease that li'l ole skillet, Ma. I'm just agoin' for a run in the ole Chevy. I'll bring you back a couple of skunks so we can have skunk pie like we used to in the ole days.'

Apparently, at authentic Tennessee dinner parties, the trick is for the hosts to wait until the end of the meal before announcing to their guests that one of the two meats they have just eaten was skunk. Even bulimics have been trampled to death in the rush to the bathroom. Serves them right.

The locals have a lot of these crazy delusions which, because Tennessee is known as the Volunteer State, they all voluntarily believe. For example, for some reason or other they think Nashville is Greece. The State Capitol, which has more columns than the daily *Nashville Tennessean*, is Greek. President Jackson's home is Greek. The Hermitage, the most crowded hermitage I've ever come across, is Greek. The Belle Meade Mansion, a museum of horseracing trophies, is Greek. The day-glo taramasalata, the Great Smoky Mountains of moussaka and the half-empty bottles of ouzo you see on the General Jackson showboat that paddles up and down the Cumberland River are Greek, not to mention the full-scale replica of the Parthenon in Centennial Park.

It's a minor detail, I know, but the original Parthenon, as I recall, doesn't have a roof or any walls, let alone a full set of the Elgin Marbles and a towering 45ft-high statue of the goddess Athena inside it. But it does have a huge advertise-ment for Coca-Cola plastered all over it; at least, it did the last time I saw it in the city that has become known throughout the world as the Nashville of the south. But, as always, I bow to American expertise in these cultural matters. It could, after all, have been that third bottle of retsina.

Some days I've been in Nashville I swear I've been so confused I didn't know whether to put on my usual button-down Brooks Brothers suit, a pair of Levi's or a toga.

What I don't understand at all is why Nashville is so Greek. After all, most children nowadays grow up in a carefree envi-ronment of declining moral standards, sexual abuse, violence and death. I speak, of course, as someone who was brought up according to the strict moral codes of Euripides's *Medea*, Sophocles's *Oedipus* and Homer's – Homer Sweet Homer – untruths from abroad, *The Iliad*. To me, it was normal to have long, leisurely discussions about everything under the sun, to encourage old men to commit suicide and to believe that if you didn't hate your father and love your mother, there was some-thing wrong with you. Everybody outside the gates who wasn't Greek or studying Greek was a barbarian. Or if not a barbarian, a shadow on the wall.

While every other kid in the street was studying the *Beano* and Desperate Dan, I was marching with Xenophon and the 10,000 all the way through Persia to the southern shores of the Black Sea. While they were all at the Saturday-morning pictures screaming at Superman not to save the world – I came from that kind of area – I was agonising with good old Sophocles on the relationship between man and the state and whether or not it was worth saving.

Nashville is also, of course, famous as one of the best breeding-grounds for thoroughbred horses in the States. Yet the only horses they could breed in Greece were half man and half horse, something I remember our Greek master could never bring himself to properly explain, although we had our own theories.

The locals try to pretend they're not Greek. They go on about Nashville being the home town of Sam Davis, the boy hero of the Confederacy who preferred to die rather than betray his superiors to the enemy, and the site of many famous Civil War battles including, of course, the Battle of Nashville in 1864, the last battle of the war.

They say it's virtually the Baptist and Methodist publishing capital of America. Pick up any hymnbook anywhere in the States, and I bet you my tattered copy of Xenophon's *Anabasis* that it will have been printed in Nashville. They also gleefully point out that it's a smokers' paradise, boasting a terrible non-PC Museum of Tobacco Art which contains snuff boxes (shame), famous cigarette advertisements (shame, shame) and cigar boxes (shame, shame, shame). And they've got so many cigarettes stashed away in huge piles to the east of town, away from the prying eyes of the PC brigade, that, in typically down-beat American style, they've labelled them the Great Smokies.

They don't fool me. I can't think why they didn't stick with the traditional Greek rebétika songs, bouzouki music and three bottles of retsina. You must admit they would go better with the Parthenon, with or without a roof and four walls, than the mezz they are in today due to the worst kind of male narcissistic personality disorder. In other words, country music.

I freely admit that there are only three things I don't understand in this world: country music, country music and country music. Why grown people would want to spend their lives singing songs like 'I Can't Get Over You, So You'll Have to Get Up and Answer the Phone Yourself', I cannot imagine. It's not that I haven't tried. Many's the time I've dragged myself along their famous Music Row and forced myself to visit their endless country music museums. I've even attempted to listen to the Dixie Chicks belting out 'Sin Wagon'. All I could hear, between the fiddles and banjos, was 'mattress dancing, mattress dancing, mattress dancing'. It's just all beyond me.

Also beyond me is the way they will say and do anything. True, this isn't confined to Tennessee. President Kennedy always maintained that he was 100 per cent fit when all the time he was suffering from Addison's disease. President Johnson used to boast that his great-great-grandfather had been killed at the Alamo when in fact he died peacefully in bed, and also that he had himself won the Silver Star, the third-highest US combat medal for valour under fire, during a 1942 fact-finding mission over the Pacific, when all the time he was at home in Texas. President Reagan swore that he was one of the first photographers to take pictures of emaciated prisoners in Nazi concentration camps when he never even left the US during the second World War. And President Clinton was, of course, President Clinton.

But in Tennessee it's worse than anywhere else. There are apparently sane, sensible people who claim to be able to transcend our ordinary mortal existence, leap across time barriers and be in more than one place at the same time. They might say, for example, that they were inspecting fire and flood damage in Texas with the director of the Federal Emergency Management Agency when they were somewhere else at the time. That they attended fundraising breakfasts when they didn't or hadn't attended them when they had, or that they went to fundraisers at Buddhist Temples when there weren't

231

any fundraisers. If being in two places at the same time is not enough excitement to be going on with, in the more extreme cases they can also suffer from delusions of adequacy. They might claim they invented the Internet, created the US Strategic Petroleum Review, discovered the massive pollution at Love Canal, New York State. They might say they were lulled to sleep as a child by a popular labour union song, 'Look for the Union Label' even though they were twenty-seven years old when the tune was written; that they drafted the Earned Income Tax Credit legislation two years before they even entered Congress and that they co-sponsored campaign finance-reform legislation even though they left the Senate three years before it was introduced. And, of course, the most pathetic claim of all, the last thing on earth anyone would want to shout about even if it were true: that, with their wife, they were the inspiration for that stomach-churning movie *Love Story*.

In extreme cases, the disease then develops a momentum of its own, known as an algorism. It is so prevalent in Tennessee, that this being America, they have commercialised it and every year at Jonesborough, the oldest town in the state, they hold what they call the greatest storytelling festival in the world. Over 9,000 people turn up in a town with a population of just 3,500 to hear the likes of Ray Hicks, a legendary mountain storyteller from North Carolina, regale them with one tale after another.

Each year the biggest storyteller of them all, Al Gore, is invited to present the prize to the person telling the most improbable tale. Each year he turns them down. Or that's what I'm told. But it could be just another story.

The other famous Tennessee experience in a country which must be desperate for heroes involves a bloated, 30-stone, mega-colonic, nappy-wearing, cheeseburger-stuffing recluse, up to his eyeballs on barbiturates, who died fast asleep on the khasi at the age of forty-two. Why anyone would want to worship such an icon I don't even want to try to imagine, but they do.

His house in Memphis is a shrine far more sacred to Americans than St Peter's, Mecca, Jerusalem and Abbey Road combined. There, every day, in an upstairs room, a table is set for twelve, as it used to be when he was alive, except that then one person always ate all twelve huge double cheeseburgers himself. Each year, on the anniversary of his death, 30,000 mourners from all over the world gather outside to pay tribute to their hero's unique skills and abilities.

Even though he died on 15 August 1977, hardly a day goes by when those sideburns, that glittering, skintight 'Cisco Kid jumpsuit and those sunglasses are not recognised somewhere, not only important places such as shops, stores and supermarkets throughout the world, but also in far more unassuming locations such as Wales where, in the Presili Hills, they claim that his grandmother Doll Mansell, came from the Mansells of Oxwich on the Gower Peninsula, his mother was Gladys and his father St Elvis of Munster.

Even more amazing, the Great Cheeseburger in the sky actually still talks to his followers. Try it for yourself. You just dial up *http://elvis.alicebot.com*

'Who is your favourite singer?'

'I don't have a favourite singer. My favourite group is the Beatles.'

'Do you like the Spice Girls?'

'Yes, I love the Spice Girls.'

'How many cheeseburgers do you eat a day?'

'Around 1,000.'

It's no wonder they've named a whole worldwide chain of hamburger restaurants after him. Although how anyone has the courage to go in a Burger King, I shudder to think. Maybe the cured-oak bourbon is to blame.

North Dakota

They were done. Under the terms of the Louisiana Purchase, the early Americans bought all the land west of the Mississippi for an unbelievable 4 cents an acre. It was far, far too much, at least as far as North Dakota is concerned. They should demand their money back if, of course, they've actually handed it over yet. Knowing how slow the Americans are in making their payments to the United Nations, it's quite likely that they haven't.

I'm not saying that North Dakota is the dullest, most boring place on earth, it's just that, given the choice between a trip there and an uncontrollable nosebleed, I'd take the nosebleed. Dinosaurs used to hang around here 65 million years ago, but they got so bored out of their ever-so-tiny minds that they just lay down and died. It's so bad that even North Dakota doesn't want to be North Dakota any more. They want to merge with South Dakota and call themselves simply Dakota. But, of course, South Dakota doesn't want to have anything to do with them, and who can blame them?

Arriving for the first time in Bismarck, the state capital, I thought, with a name like that, it would be a smart, well-organised, well-run city where everything worked efficiently and promptly and trains, if there were any, would run on time. There were no cabs at the airport, so I had to hitch a lift into town. The hotel didn't know how to send faxes, and had to call their phone company to find out. I ordered a cab from my room, and by the time I got down to the front door of the hotel it had gone. Apparently the driver didn't think I was coming and couldn't wait thirty seconds. What the hell he was going to do with that extra half a minute in Bismarck, God only knows.

I made for the North Dakota Heritage Center in a desperate attempt to find something of interest. I'm glad I did. There was never a dull moment. It was dull from the second I arrived to the second I left. The prize exhibits were – I kid you not – a 1991 Junior High School T-shirt, a twenty-year-old police bullet-proof vest and a pair of jungle boots worn by a certain Daniel R. Koper of the 134th Helicopter Assault when he was stationed at Tuy Hao in Vietnam from January 1968 to August 1969.

By now I was beginning to lose it. The phone in the Heritage Center was not working so I couldn't get a cab back. I walked the length of N 7th Street. Everybody I saw, and I didn't see more than three people, looked like either child-frighteners or seat-sniffers or worse. They all looked as though they had married their Teutonic grandmother as well. I staggered into the Peacock Alley Bar and Grill on E Main Street. There was a big promotion for Warsteiner, a new microbeer. It sounded German. On the basis that it must, therefore, be good, I ordered one. They'd run out. The barman, who had the face of someone on his way to his own funeral, didn't think to ask me if I might want something else. He just went on and on about Princess Di, Prince Charles, Fergie, the Queen and the whole catastrophe.

'Dunno. Dunno. Dunno,' I kept repeating.

But it didn't make any difference. Still he was going on and on and on. In the end he was talking in my sleep. To wake myself up I picked up the local North Dakota newspaper lying on the bar. With the American elections looming, the stock-market hitting higher and higher highs, Europe struggling to boost the euro, Russia beginning to flex its muscles under Putin and Africa descending even further into anarchy, what is the main story on their front page? Some kid who'd never missed a day's school. Wowee.

In the far corner, by the door, the cream of North Dakota society, two T-shirts and a baseball cap, were droning on about a teacher at a local school who had been fired for growing a long, ginger beard. But in the end they had to give her her job back.

Steam coming out of my ears, I staggered along E. Broadway Avenue back towards the hotel. I passed the offices of what I'd been told was the best law firm in town, McPhail's.

Back in the hotel, dinner was a pleasant surprise. First because I didn't have to ask for a menu. I could tell what was on offer by looking at the stains on the waiter's apron. Second, because it was the first time I think I've ever had a meal where the chef obviously didn't have to use a timer. Instead, it looked as though he'd used a smoke detector.

Compared to Bismarck, Colma, just south of San Francisco, is the liveliest town in the country. It's a cemetery town where the dead outnumber the living by more than 1,000 to one. It even has a pet cemetery, whose most famous resident is Tina Turner's dog.

Outside Bismarck, people told me, North Dakota was another one of those states where east met west. The east was all grass and hay and sunflowers and trees down to the edge of the river. The west was the badlands, all brown grass, buzzards and bare rock. No way. First of all, it's so flat that you can drive practically the whole length of it in a straight line, and there's nothing to see but weeds. No grass. There's so much weed that every year the state gives away over 50 million weed-eating bugs to try to keep it under control. But it still keeps growing, like some rampant triffid, smothering everything in sight. Local entrepreneurs have tried to tackle the problem their way. So while Indianapolis is cars, big, flashy, high-speed cars, North Dakota is lawnmowers. They organise lawnmower races all over the place, but all in vain. The weed just keeps growing, and growing, and growing.

If you manage to catch a glimpse through the weeds about all you'll see are farms – empty farms. Over the last five years, more than 2,000 farmers have shut up shop, closed down and moved on. Those who are left survive only by harvesting government hand-outs.

I was on the first plane out of there the following morning. At 6.30 am. To make certain I didn't miss it, I was at the airport by 5.30. It was just as well, because not only was the flight over-booked, but even at that ungodly hour there was a waiting list as long as East Broadway Avenue. One woman was so desperate to get out I swear she was faking labour pains just to get a seat. Not that I got involved. I just carried on flicking through a three-week-old copy of the *Bismarck Tribune* I'd taken out of the litter bin, desperately trying to find something interesting to read.

North Dakota, they say, is the least visited of all US states. I'm not surprised. I shan't be going there again if I can help it. I'd rather go home and bite the dog.

The French-Fry States

What other states could they be but Idaho and Texas? Idaho because it supplies the potatoes, well, most of the ones that end up as fries, anyway, and Texas because there they fry everything in sight, whether it's strapped into a chair or not.

Idaho, the Spud State, is no small potato. It produces around 25 per cent of the whole of the US potato crop. Which is a lot of potatoes when you think that each man, woman and fat kid in America wolfs down no less than 28lb of the things a year. Even more important, it was not only the first but remains the world's biggest supplier of potato fries to McDonald's. It's something to do with the type of potato, its size and its ability to hold firm under all kinds of frying conditions. To ensure they get the best possible quality, they're even working on a super-intelligent potato which will glow green when it needs watering. Then there are all the big issues. As with everything in America, size counts. Thin, fat, large, small, straight, crinkly, circular, semi-circular, spirally – you'd never believe the number of different shapes and sizes of chips you come across. But as everyone in the business admits, the most vital factor of all is that the fatter a chip is, the less fat it contains.

And it's not just the quality of the potatoes, it's cooking the damn things. It's not just a matter of throwing them in the pan and hoping for the best, it's a case of fry, fry and fry again. First, there's what you fry them in. The best cooking oil seems to be (please, for the sake of peace and quiet, don't tell the vegetarians, or the Hindus, come to that) 93 per cent beef tallow and 7 per cent cottonseed. Then there's the way you fry them. Fry them like one burger chain, whose name I forget, tried to do and you end up with a Burger King of disasters. Their so-called new, hi-tech stealth fry, a potato stick coated with a layer of starch, which was supposed to make the fries crisper and keep them warmer for longer, ended up as a mash-and-grab that cost them millions. I'm not surprised. I once had a potato stick. It tasted like a half-chewed ear swab. Fry them another way, thinner, saltier and faster, and you've got a winner. Which is why nobody would believe the amount of time, money and technology the Americans devote not just to frying a simple microchip but frying it faster and faster and better and better. At present, a batch of fries take 210 seconds to make. Soon it will be down to 65 seconds, a breakthrough in US technology far more momentous than a mere landing on the moon. I must admit I still can't forget the neutron fries I once had in a diner in Des Moines, Iowa. They glowed inside me for weeks.

Not that Americans know or care about the raw material, the humble potato. Goodness me, even highly intelligent people such as vice-presidential candidates can't spell the damn word correctly. But me, I'm an expert. I come from a long line of Irish farmers, so there's nothing you can tell me about potatoes, let alone chips. I had mine years ago. I've got one uncle or cousin or something, the richest man in County Clare, who treats potatoes the way the great wine connoisseurs treat different vintages. Take him into the best restaurant in town and he'll pay more attention to the potatoes than he will to anything else on his plate.

As for Texas, well excuse me, I can smell something burning. I only hope it's a microchip, but I doubt it. Being Texas, everything is big. The hats, the ranches, the fortunes, the steaks, the prostate glands which, some say, are almost as big as their egos. And, of course, the electric chairs. In fact, being Texas, where 'crisp that chick' has a whole different meaning from the one it has in, say, Kentucky or even Nashville, Tennessee, they probably have the biggest electricity bill as well.

Why they have this obsession with frying people is beyond me. First of all, because it's wrong. If it's wrong for one man to take another's life, it's wrong for the state, in all our names, to take a life. Secondly, it's not a deterrent. History says so. The American Bar Association says so. Current research says so. In states that practise capital punishment, the murder rate is 6.2 per 100,000 people. In states where they don't, the average murder rate is practically half that, 3.2. In Texas and, for some reason, Florida, the two states with the highest number of executions, they also have the highest rate of murders. Thirdly, there's the whole sordid execution process itself: the length of time condemned people are kept on death row, the methods and, of course, that final lingering doubt as to their guilt.

But still, while preaching compassionate conservativism, Texas goes on not only sending the sane and insane alike off to what they obviously believe is hamburger heaven, but also beating one US execution record after another. Not that it seems to worry them. They clearly love it. They even sell toy electric chairs. Switch on the current, and the figure in the chair jerks sharply backwards and forwards, his eyes glow red and he screams, 'That the best you can do, you pansies?'

But then, in Texas they even hang their pictures, so what can you expect?

Idaho

To look at the capital, Boise, you'd think it was just another small, pleasant, quiet, almost dozy upmarket town in a tree-lined valley around 35 miles long by 10 miles wide, warm and pleasant most of the year – even when it's hot, it's a dry heat, no humidity. Ideal, you would assume, for 'retirees', as they call them. Or even couch potatoes.

But no. Probably not for the first time in your life, if you're anything like me, you'd be wrong. Boise is one of the top five or six fastest-growing King Edward's in the whole of the US sack of cities. *Money Magazine* rates it the fourth-best place to live in America; *USA Today* hailed it as one of the six cities of the 1990s. *Kiplinger's Personal Finance* magazine puts it among the top fifteen US supercities. *Newsweek* says it's one of the hottest of the hottest tech cities and the *Washington Post* calls it one of America's safest. *Parenting* magazine, which will not, of course, smack you if you disagree, feels that if the family could talk it through and ever reach a consensus, it would say it was one of the ten best places for raising children in the whole history of the world.

But forget all that. I've got an even greater honour I would like to bestow upon the goody-two-shoes town of Boise: the world's greatest fibbers. Because they claim that, move over John Logie, television was invented in Idaho by that world-famous inventor Philo Farnsworth. Funny, I always thought he had something to do with designing big, complicated Philo diaries for the Bridget Joneses of this world who have nothing better to do than scribble down the telephone numbers of blokes they are never ever going to hear from again. They also say that the first successful television broadcast in the world was made from Idaho, and not from Crystal Palace in England, as the rest of the world foolishly believes.

All of which is, of course, total nonsense. It's like crediting some crusty old Irish boatbuilder who lived in New Orleans with being 'the man who won World War II'. Which, incidentally, is what they do in New Orleans. What's more, they've built a $25 million museum to back up their claim. Goodness only knows what will happen when the man who was really responsible for winning World War II, as well as for developing every major technological advance since the invention of that round thing and being the famous hero of *Love Story*, eventually finds out.

But who am I to argue about such ephemeral matters as the truth? All I know is that, based on the recognised native technological prowess of Boise, all the big international electronics giants are now falling over themselves to move in and open plants employing anything up to 9,000 Philo Farnsworths at a time. It's even – take a bow – the Hewlett Packard printer capital of the world. Boise is no boys' town. To cope with the rush, they've refurbished, as they say, the whole of the centre. You can now stroll around looking at modernised old shops, as opposed to old old shops, wondering what the hell to do before you hit that first bloody mary of the morning.

Gated communities – no, they've got nothing to do with Bill Gates, although most of the residents do look like Microsoft shareholders – are also opening up wherever you look. First there are the gated communities which virtually lock people in. These used to be called something else. The one in Boise is full of the people behind the people who make Boise such a success: Mexicans and, surprisingly, a bunch of Basques. For some reason there are more Basques in Boise than anywhere else in the US. They even have their own Basque museum and cultural centre. So, be warned, don't crack any of those old jokes about too many Basques in one exit. *Mañana* may never come.

The others are communities which virtually lock people out, although nobody would ever dream of putting it as crudely as that. Everybody is welcome so long as they have at least $350,000 to blow on a designer house, $700,000 for legal fees and are prepared to abide by some simple rules. Such as not being over fifty-five years old and not having any kids. Others are more relaxed: everybody is welcome, but no kids under fifty-five.

'We're only looking for smiley faces to live here,' one sourpuss of a prisoner, I mean resident, told me.

'When I bought my house,' said another, 'the sales document was two pages and the rules and regulations forty-two pages. Isn't that wonderful?'

Well, er, yes, if you're that kind of person, although personally, I think I'd prefer a self-contained apartment on death row. At least you'd know you were not going to be there for long.

But Boise is not alone. It's the same story more or less all over the States. Because, they say, of the threat of violence, the need for security and for some control over where and how you live in a country whose planning regulations are practically non-existent – one day you might be surrounded by fields, the next engulfed by a twenty-four-hour shopping mall – more and more Americans are circling their wagons and moving into upmarket open prisons.

One of the worst – I mean, the best – is Celebration, Florida. Designed and built by Walt Disney, it's an instant, designer new town, all designer houses, designer golf courses and a genuine, instant, designer community spirit. All the paediatricians there regularly play miniature golf together on Wednesdays.

For this kind of living arrangement, Houston, Texas is, if anything, better. Or do I mean worse? It's not only almost nothing but gated communities, but they are gated communities Texas-style. Break one of their rules and it's the electric chair. One resident of a lush Houston gated community told me, on condition I would never reveal his name to the local Covenant Administration, the goose-stepping police force that runs the place, that a neighbour of his in a $500,000 house was being threatened with death by stoning because he put his kids' play area by the side of his house to stop them from falling in the swimming pool. It has produced a near-revolution. Don't worry, Mike Mittagovich. I won't say a word.

Rules and regulations don't apply only to gated communities. They are just as strict at the other end of the housing market. In Trentham, New Jersey, not, I admit, one of my favourite US cities, I came across a leaflet produced by the US Department of Housing and Urban Development on residents' rights and responsibilities, written for what they called Caribbeans in what they called Caribbean.

'Yuh as a rezedent,' it began, 'ave de rights ahn de rispansabilities to elp mek yuh HUD-assisted owzing ah behta owme fi yuh ahn yuh fambily. Dis brochure briefly liss some ahf yuh muos impowtant rights ahn rispansabilities fi elp yuh get de muos owt ah yuh owme.'

The bit I liked best was 'Yuh Rispansabilities':

- Payin de carrek amount a rent pan a timely basis everi muhnt.
- Conduktin yuhself in a mannah dat wuhduhn disturb yuh neighbahs.
- Nat engagin in criminal aktivity inna de unit, common areas, aur grouns. Fi kyp yuh unit clean ahn nat littaryn di grouns aur common areas.
- Fi comply wid local kwodes dat affek de ehlt aur safety ahf de rezedence.

But my prize for fortress architecture, if it hasn't yet been stolen, goes to the gated community about 25 miles south of Colorado Springs, Colorado, which offers the maximum possible in security. It is so security-conscious that they have named the whole place Security, the main drag is Security Boulevard and, if that isn't enough to convince the world of the importance of security, the developers behind the project call themselves the Security Development Corporation. Here, in addition to the security-protected homes, the security-protected shopping centre with its security-protected post office, the security-protected medical centre, security-protected library, security-protected fire station and seven security-protected churches, every house has its own vegetable garden so that residents have the security of growing their own security-protected food, free of dangerous chemicals, dangerous insecticides, dangerous germs in the air, dangerous bacteria carried by birds and . . . my God, did you see the size of that worm in the ground?

To lure people into these super-safe, super-prestigious, super-respectable jails, the developers use one of the lowest, meanest, most crooked tricks in the book. Not only do they hire the most luxurious furniture and fittings you can imagine, but they also use actors to pose as a happy and contented ma and pa who are about to slash their wrists because they're being forced to sell up and move back to New York, Boston or, heaven help them, Bismarck, North Dakota.

One developer, well into his fifth bloody mary before lunch, told me he even paid the actors a commission if they helped him offload not just the house but the contents as well. So much for being protected from crooks.

Outside the high standards and principles of Boise, to the north are pine forests, lakes and Washington and Seattle, the biggest gated community of them all. To the east and south is potato country, rich, volcanic valleys and, on the Idaho–Montana border, Ketchum, tucked away in the foothills of the Sawtooth Mountains, where Papa Hemingway, who so loved the world and everything in it he could drink, blew his brains out and, watch out Davos, Sun Valley ski resort. This is an up-and-coming favourite spot for business hideaways where, if you're not careful, you're likely to bump into the likes of the Murdochs wandering around stabbing each other in the back, or Bill Gates – him again – struggling with his laptop, not to mention half the Fortune 500 desperately trying not to attract the attention of the other half in case it gives them any ideas. The only good thing about it is that, all being egotists, they never talk about other people.

But the big Idaho, or should it be Idahoe, potato/potatoe is still the biggest thing in town. Boise was once home to the largest construction company in the world, the largest food company in the world and to more millionaires than any other US city. They are not far behind, either, when it comes to sugar. There are two enormous sugarbeet plants in town, one of them the biggest in the world. So whichever way you go, you can bet your life Idaho will have had a hand in it.

I'm always surprised, however, that, for all the accolades, Boise is not more swinging and far, far richer than it is. Because, for those who know what little American history there is, just up the road was Fort Boise, founded by British fur-traders in 1834 and owned by the Hudson Bay Company; the Oregon Trail and, of course, Grimes Creek, the largest gold-mine in the US and the scene in 1862 of the greatest gold rush in American history, which was bigger than the California gold rush and the Alaska gold rush combined.

'But who's goin' to make a film about Grimes Creek, Boise

when they can make a film about California?' as one old fur-trader commented to me while we were window-shopping in an attempt not to hit the bars too early.

Although one goldmine is still going strong after all these years, which is more than you can say for the California ones, the real gold, I discovered, in Boise is in driving cabs. It seems to be an unwritten rule that unless you've got at least an MBA from John Moores Liverpool University, you shouldn't even think of hiring a cab, especially in the evenings and at weekends. On various trips in and around Boise I met doctors, lawyers, accountants driving cabs – one of the accountants told me he had just finished laundering $50 million for a client for 5 per cent commission – and, of course, Internet managers. You name it, if they're top management, they're driving cabs in Boise.

You can tell they are top management, first of all because they all look like nudniks. Secondly, they are not as well dressed as the full-time cab-drivers. Thirdly, wherever you go you always get completely lost or, as one klutz put it, 'We're not lost. I'm checking out an alternative route.'

I even met the top microchip brain gymnast at Micron Technology, one of the big electronics companies in town, who told me he earned a regular salary of over $250,000 a year.

To all of them, of course, I had to ask the obvious question. 'So what are you doing driving cabs?'

To which they all replied: 'Can't stand the wife and kids. I hate them. I only do this to get away from them. It's either this or drugs.'

As for the money they make – oh bliss – they spend it all on themselves. Not a penny do they give to their wives and families.

'I tell her I'm working late, or I'm in a bar. She doesn't care so long as I give her the regular money every week,' Mr Microchip Designer explained as we took yet another wrong turning.

How much money do they make on the cabs?

They all said they cleared over $1,000 a shift.

If I'm ever successful enough to become a cab-driver, I know where I'm going. Boise, after all, will be Boise.

Texas

Texas is not just big, *big*, BIG, it has the biggest everything in the world. The biggest buildings. The biggest highways. The biggest energy hogs. The biggest hats. The biggest boots. The biggest steaks. The biggest tortilla soups and soft-shell crab entrées. The biggest horseshoe-tossing competitions. The biggest cow chip-throwing contests. The biggest tobacco-spitters. It's touch and go whether it's bigger than the whole universe itself. You think I'm joking? If you thought the Big Bang was big, you haven't seen a Friday night at the B-B-Q Hot Pit in Fort Worth. Now that's something Stephen Hawking could get his teeth into.

So I hay-ave a big admission to make. Because of its sheer size – Texas is bigger than every country in Europe apart from Russia – I still feel I've had no more than a beef encounter with the place which, as they say, in 1836 threw out the Mexicans and in 1845 decided to merge with the United States. As a result, I'm afraid I'm even more hesitant than usual when it comes to passing judgement.

The people, I invariably find, are shy, quiet, modest, restrained. If they holler at you across a discreet restaurant like the Mansion on Turtle Creek in Dallas, they can only just be heard ten blocks away. They struggle to survive in tiny family homes whose front gates are barely 10 miles from the front door. For breakfast they have a meagre pile of eggs, range sausages, steaks, sourdough biscuits, gravy and all the bloody marys they can force down their throats. For lunch, all they can afford is a tiny 72oz steak. For dinner, if they have any money left, they might just manage a light mixture of brisket, turkey, ham, chicken, pulled pork, sausages and pork ribs washed down with several thousand cans of beer. For the main course they'll go Texas Trendy: huge piles of tiny portions of food drowned in a sea of creamy gravy and decorated with mountains of chicken gizzards.

246

They dress in understated clothes. Hats about the size of Wembley Stadium, ties as long and stringy as a mother-in-law's tongue and boots as high as the B-B-Q Hot Pit in Fort Worth on a Friday night. Whatever people say about big hair, I swear I've never seen any women in Texas whose hair was more than 5ft tall, but then, the only women I think I've ever seen in Texas always seemed to be called Leesa, wore frilly white blouses and sat glued to television sets day and night watching true-life murder confessions screened direct from death row. Some of them were so huge it took only six of them to make a dozen.

Because they live in such straitened circumstances, for Christmas and birthdays it is difficult for them to scrape together as much as they would like to buy each other presents. Usually they rely on a little mail-order catalogue produced by a local shop, Neiman Marckus, which offers trinkets such as $100,000, 18-carat gold, diamond-encrusted train sets with 41ft of track, or fully equipped $20 million submarines with a cruising range of 3,500 miles. Mothers-in-law are invariably given a comfortable, high-backed chair, although most of them refuse to plug it in.

Texans, I've noticed, not to beat about the bush, have a talking way of funny called Dubya-speak. Some say it's foot-in-mouth-speak, but I reckon it's more boot-Texas-boot-in-cheek-speak. They mix up words like ascribe and subscribe, enthralling and inebriating, perseverance, and preservation, presumptions and presumptive, tariffs, terriers, tenets and tenants and viable and vile. They come up with funny contra-dictory phrases like honest politician, clean fight, fair election, accurate count, just result and, of course, the biggest laugh of all, compassionate conservative.

Then there's the mumbo-jumbo. Because they live in a state which prides itself on education suckling kids through, where reading is the basics of all learning and budgets have lots of numbers in them, they honestly believe that if you say you're going to do something and you don't do it, it is giving mala-props a good name, if only knew they meant what it.

247

Duh.

But it doesn't seem to stop them. They have amazingly liberal views on everything.

On families: 'Families is where the nation finds hope, where wings take dream. Because parents rarely ask the question: is our children learning then don't realise how bright their children is until they get an objective analysis.'

On pollution: 'It isn't pollution that's harming the environment. It's the impurities in our air and water that are doing it.'

On imports: 'More and more of our imports come from overseas.'

On capital punishment: 'States should have the right to enact reasonable laws and restrictions particularly to end the inhumane practice of ending a life that otherwise could live. They have never put a guilty . . . I mean, innocent person to death in Texas.'

On the future: 'In a world where the most important thing of all is for the human being and the fish to co-exist peacefully, highways on the Internet to become more few and toll booths to the middle class to be eliminated, the time has come for the human race to enter the solar system.'

I don't know about you, but I find that as long as you keep leaping up, punching the air and yelling at the top of your voice, 'Wow-*eeee*!', they seem friendly enough, so friendly and hospitable, in fact, that wherever I went, whoever I met, within minutes they'd be leaping up and offering me a chair. A comfortable, high-backed chair. But if leaping up, punching the air and yelling wow-*eeee* all the time at a bunch of beefheads doesn't work, not to worry. If you don't agree, they don't have to be subliminal about it. After all, you can't take the high horse and then claim the low road.

Why, in the bad old days in Virginia, if you committed a serious crime you faced three possible sentences, imprisonment, death or exile to Texas, I have no idea.

Ask them, however, if they've ever been arrested by the police and they'll get all confused. Interviewed by the *Dallas Morning News* they'll say a blunt no. Invited to fill out a jury questionnaire, they'll leave the box blank. When standing for federal office, they'll talk about the weather. Or, at least, try to talk about it.

If understanding the people is a problem, what hope is there of understanding the place itself? After all as they say, it's your money, you paid for it. The cities are all Stetsons, shoelaces, eelskin boots and big talk about git offa mah lawen, cawse my deddy useta and how many head of cattle are you running, even if parts of it look more like suburban Virginia than cactus-and-prairie dog Texas. The hotels are so tall that whenever I get in the lift to go to my room my nose bleeds. As for the bars, there are more bars in Texas than anywhere else in the world. The trouble is, most of them are in the wrong place. Those that are not are full of Tequila Texans (One tequila, two tequila, three tequila, floor). The restaurants, almost without exception, are low-calorie with towering plates of beef thrown in. But a word of caution: in Texas you can't get into any kind of restaurant without a ressy. That's a reservation to you, me and the rest of the civilised world.

Then there are the buildings around all the hotels and bars and restaurants. Austin, the state capital, is a giant Tex-Mex Silicon Valley smothered in sweet, tangy barbecue sauce and decorated with shrubs, cacti and mesquite trees, the second-fastest-growing city in the US after Las Vegas. One half, the western half, is rich and teeming with what they call Dellionaires: Dell, the world's largest direct seller of computers, is based in Austen. The other half, the eastern half, is poor. They're the people who used to be Dellionaires but couldn't get to their broker in time.

Dallas is odd. It's all hat and no cattle. It makes out it is a great oil capital full of fuel-hardy petrolheads, yet there's more oil washed up on the beach of Knights Island, Alaska than there is wallowing around in the ground in Texas. Whenever I go there the freeways seem to be jam-packed, but downtown is almost empty, even around Turtle Creek, with its ritzy restaurants and antique shops. One evening I went to one of Dallas's oldest and most respectable institutions, Sonny Bryan's Smokehouse Barbecue on North Market Street, founded in 1958. There was nobody queuing up for their famous sampler platter. It was odd.

I'll tell you another thing that's peculiar about Dallas. How come, on the morning of Friday 22 November 1963, Nixon flew out as JFK flew in? I'm not suggesting anything underhand. It's just that it's always struck me as, well, interesting.

The other thing that's interesting is if you look at all the other major assassinations and assassination attempts in history, they were all carried out by lone, crazy nutcases, like François Ravaillac, Henry III; Jacques Clement, Henry IV; Richard Lawrence, Andrew Jackson; Garrilo Princip, Archduke Franz Ferdinand; James Earl Ray, Martin Luther King Jnr; Sirhan B. Sirhan, Bobby Kennedy; Lynette Fromme, Gerald Ford; Sara Jane Moore, Gerald Ford (again. Poor man. What did he do to deserve two assassination attempts? And both within eighteen days); John Hinckley, Ronald Reagan. So how come the Kennedy assassination was a huge conspiracy between the CIA, the FBI, the Mafia, Jimmy Hoffa, Castro and James Ellroy?

Talking of presidents, the other thing that strikes me as odd is how come a Texan, of all people, is the most overlooked president of all time? Eisenhower gets the credit for the inter-state system that shuffled missiles around from site to site in case the Russkis were on to them, but it was Lyndon B. Johnson who built them. Kennedy gets the glory for all the civil rights legislation, but it was Johnson who made it happen. Nixon gets the glory for ending the Vietnam War, but it was Johnson who made it possible.

Fifteen minutes from Dallas, although once it took me about two hours, is Grand Prairie. It is so impressive and so imposing that every time I have driven through it I have failed to realise I was in it. Even the local video store where I kept stopping for directions didn't know it was in Grand Prairie.

Thirty minutes away by fast truck or, if you prefer, cattle stampede, is Fort Worth-its-weight-in-cowboy-stories, where men are rangers, ranchers or roughnecks, women are all called Boicike and music runs the full range from diddly-diddly to diddly-diddly-diddly. Everybody told me I should kick over the barstool, get out my string tie, my fire-iron-branded boots, all the chunky rings I could find and hit their Chisholm Trail Roundup. Which, of course, I did, but quite honestly, it's not Fort Worth it.

The stockyards are not what I thought they would be. I thought it was where everybody in rich, booming Texas went to dump the stock they bought in all those dot-com companies just before they crashed. But it's not, it's the wild west, or at least a goody-goody version of the wild west, about sixteen blocks of look-alike Cowboyville. The bars might have saddles as barstools, but it's about as wild west as Robert Redford. Everywhere there's nothing but rules, rules, rules. In the bars: 'Disrespectful conduct strictly prohibited', 'Loud and/or abusive language not tolerated', 'We will not serve anyone who is obviously intoxicated'. In the restaurants: 'No soiled work clothes', 'Caps must be worn forward', 'No torn or ripped clothing', 'No tank tops or cut-offs. All shirts must have sleeves and be tucked in', 'Clean, neat and untattered clothing required'. And if you try to go out on the town, be warned that the big Wild West Stockyards Hotel locks its doors at eleven o'clock. I ask you, how wild west is that?

The cowboys are more toots in boots, and what's more they're pointy boots. Every morning at eleven o'clock, like the changing of the guard, there is the stampede. Stampede? It's just a couple of grown men in jeans, cowboy hats and pointy boots shuffling one or two lame cattle through the streets.

The historic district was no better. All around the so-called famous Sundance Square, which is basically a bunch of stores and shops, there are yet more rules and regulations. I escaped into the Sid Richardson Collection of Western Art to catch up on two of my western favourites, Frederic Remington and Charles M. Russell. The first thing I saw was a 'Guide to Museum Etiquette'.

'As a courtesy to our other guests, we ask that you use your "Museum Voice", speaking softly to avoid disturbing others.

'Because small hands can cause mischief, children should not be carried on visitors' backs or shoulders and we ask parents to keep a close eye on little ones to prevent any damage.

'Weapons are never permitted in the museum.

'All museum visitors are required to wear shirts and shoes.'

As for the cultural district, I gave up. I couldn't face any more regulations. But they were impossible to avoid. Feeling completely enchiladaed out, I made for some fancy steak restaurant. The place was packed with cowboy boots and ten-gallon hats all busy tearing into their 72oz steaks. I opened the menu, and what was the first thing I saw? 'Don't cut the bread with a knife.'

Maybe I'm just prejudiced. Try as I might, I can never forget the first time I went to Fort Worth. I had plenty of time to spare, so instead of taking a cab from the airport, I got the shuttle. The bus pulled into the depot at Fort Worth and this happy, smiling lady got on to collect our money and issue our tickets. I handed her the money for a return trip; she flashed me a wonderful smile and very genuinely wished me a nice day. Then I looked at the ticket. The miserable, fat, old bag had given me a Senior Citizen ticket, the first Senior Citizen ticket anyone had ever given me in my life.

As for Houston, the fourth-largest city in the US, everybody says it's nothing but oil, West Texas Intermediate; barbecued pork ribs; the first words ever uttered on the moon – 'Houston, Tranquillity Base here. The Eagle has landed' – and guys with a pneumatic blonde on each arm. I wouldn't know. I've been there enough times, but I've never actually seen it. Either it's been covered in a thick blanket of smog or submerged in several feet of water.

As far as the pollution is concerned, the big debate is – cough, cough – whether it is – cough, cough – worse than in Los Angeles, California. Some say Los – cough, cough –

Angeles beats Houston because it failed to measure up to three out of six pollution standards backed by – splutter – the Environmental Protection Agency. Others, especially those in Houston, say, 'Where the hell is the list of pollution standards? I can't see it for the pollution around here.'

As for the water, once I got there just after 3ft of rain had been dumped on the city in a matter of hours, and only two days after twenty-one of their twenty-two streams and rivers had already been swollen by up to 12in of rain. Talk about oil on troubled waters: this was water on troubled oil. Roads and highways were flooded. The Interstate 10 between Washington and the West Loop came apart. Houses were washed away, hotels and offices drenched. Hospitals were floating in water up to their prefrontal leucotomies. Cars, the most important commodity of all, were swept away, damaged, destroyed. The power lines were down, the phones were cut. Jones Hall, home to the Houston Symphony Orchestra, was deep in Handel's Water Music and Wortham Theatre Center, home of the city's ballet and opera companies, were hastily switching from *Cleopatra* to *Swan Lake*. The Hyatt in the centre of town was hanging its carpets out of the windows to dry. There were giant blowers all over the place. Everything was covered in a thick coating of mud. The stench was overpowering.

But, true Americans that they are, the people of Houston were all paying tribute to 'volunteerism' as well as to someone called Al Truism for the rescue work. Total damage they estimated at around $1 billion, which is about how much money they leave on bars and restaurant tables as tips every lunchtime.

Everybody blamed the tropical storm, Alison. I'm not so sure. It just seemed somehow significant that the flood occurred within days of President Bush reneging on the Kyoto agreement. Maybe it was the environment getting its own back on him.

The result is I haven't seen any of their famous historic landmarks. I haven't seen the Beer Can House, for example, which is made up of 50,000 cans. Partly, I will admit, because if I'm going to spend my time looking at beer cans, I'd rather look at full, waiting-to-be-opened ones than a load of dried-out, used-up ones. Neither have I seen any of their millions of museums. Not that, for one moment, I want to see all of them. In fact the only one I was even remotely interested in was the American Funeral Service Museum, which apparently contains all the funeral bits and pieces for every famous American from President Lincoln to Elvis Presley.

San Antonio, meanwhile, is beautiful. It's pure America. The centre of town is, of course, the Alamo, a tiny Spanish mission named after a not particularly good car-hire company. I've no idea why. Hailed as the shrine of Texas liberty, it is almost as important to Americans as Graceland. Every year millions of them pour into San Antonio to visit the Alamo, bend the knee and pay tribute to the mighty Texan heroes who fought and died that they may live.

As the Alamo's own official literature says: 'Undaunted, the Texians and Tejanos prepared to defend . . . the Alamo was the key to the defence of Texas . . . the Alamo remains hallowed ground and the Shrine of Texas Liberty.'

Except . . . except, didn't the Texans turn their backs on the Alamo? Thirteen days before the battle, didn't our Lieutenant-Colonel Travis write his famous letter 'to the people of Texas and all Americans in the world' pleading with them to come to his aid? But none of them turned up. Note for next time: mention Tibet. At least then Richard Gere will turn up.

And then, excuse me, I'm not too hot on my American history, but as far as I can recall, wasn't the Alamo not a victory to be glorified but a huge defeat? The Mexicans won.

Finally, the crunch question: of the 189 so-called mighty heroes of the Alamo, how many were freedom-loving Texans? Eleven. How many were British (yes, British)? Twenty-six. So there were more than twice the number of Brits there than there were Texans. But is there any tribute, any mention anywhere – in the Alamo itself, in the shrine, in the Long Barrack Museum, in the DRT Library, in the literature, in the visuals, in all the promotional material – of the Brits who came to the aid of these mighty freedom-loving Texans when their own people turned their backs on them? What do you think?

I tried to discuss this serious historical matter with a battleaxe of a Daughter of the Republic of Texas who was running the show. It was like trying to talk to your wife. As far as I can work out, the only reason why the Americans go bananas about the Alamo must be because, deep down, they know it was the last time they went into battle and actually killed more of the enemy than they did of their friends and allies.

After San Antonio, Fredricksburg was *mein Gott*, unbelievable. It's Germany comes to Texas. There's no highway or interstate. There's a *hauptstrasse*. Along which there is a Das Peach Haus, Der Lindenbaum, eine Auslander Biergarten Restaurant, eine Rathskeller, eine Edelweiss Markt and eine Der Kuchen Laden with a sign outside reading: 'For the little chef in all of us', which may or may not be what they meant.

It was like going back to nineteenth-century Germany. All the shop signs were gothic with heavy German accents. At the far end of the *hauptstrasse* was the Admiral Nimitz National Museum of the Pacific War. All around were Gastenhauses and Lutheran churches and wineries.

Well, as they say in Texas, Nigeria is an important continent where wings take dreams that cannot be held hostile even though the undecideds could go one way or another and if not that's just the way it goes, which is not insubstantial. It's in English.

The Relish States

There's nothing on-the-side-of-the-plate about the relish states, Louisiana, Nevada and Arkansas. They are all central to the meal, full of flavour, spicy states with the ability to overpower anything that comes within their orbit. Especially Arkansas, which, in recent years, has probably generated as much spice as the whole of the States can handle.

They are also the states that have given us all more than enough to relish. From Louisiana's Mardi Gras, to, well, there's no need to go into detail, but you can bet your life all the dry-cleaners in Arkansas stay open twenty-four hours a day.

Stick them on a spice rack. Louisiana would be hot, *hot*, HOT. It's French. It's Spanish. It's Creole. It's unique. Go to New Orleans Mardi Gras time and it's a glorious, hot, throbbing, sugar mélange.

Nevada is more sweet and sour. Sweet because of all those lucky people pouring into Reno to get back their freedom to go out and start all over again. Sour because that's probably what they'll do. They'll get their freedom back, then they'll start all over again. But maybe I've got that the wrong way round. Either way, it's famous for having the biggest mining industry in the whole of the US: mine's the house, mine's the contents, mine's the car.

Mention Arkansas, and everyone all over the world immediately thinks of the one man who's provided more people with spice than anyone in history: Sam Walton, founder of Wal-Mart. Every day of the year his stores provide tons of the stuff to shoppers, or Wal-Martians, as they are known, all over the USA and increasingly all over Europe as well. What? Who did you think I meant?

Louisiana

Wherever you turned, there they were. In broad daylight. In early evening. At the dead of night. Naked and near-naked bodies swirling along the pavements, weaving in and out of the traffic. Dancing. Prancing. Writhing to all that foot-stomping, be-bopping, heart-stopping twenty-four-hours-a-day jazz. And that was just the fellas.

Go to New Orleans, or N'Awlins, the Birthplace of Jazz, the City that Care Forgot, the Bayou or even the Big Easy, and I promise you, however old and tailored you are, you won't come away untouched. Especially if you go during Mardi Gras.

You'll be touched by the atmosphere. It's electric. Everything is buzzing and crackling and flashing. Especially flashing. And I don't mean 110 volts, I mean 110,000 volts. It's literally non-stop carnival, non-stop jazz, non-stop dancing, non-stop drinking, non-stop eating, non-stop partying. And practically non-stop everything else as well.

The carnival floats are not your ordinary carnival floats. They are wild, gorgeous, extravagant creations the size of the Sistine Chapel. Many have over a million lights apiece. And they keep coming, and coming, and coming. Hour after hour after hour after hour. And on every float you see the krewes – don't blame me, that's what they call them – throw out thousands upon thousands of beads and necklaces – small, large and how the hell am I going to get that round my neck? – to the crowds, to each other, to anything that moves. If somebody told you this was the last party in the world before the whole thing cracked up you'd believe them.

You'll be touched by the noise. The brass bands, the drums, the tubas, the saxophones. The roar as yet another quiet, intro-verted, inhibited, sober member of the crowd goes uninhibited, wild, extrovert and completely bombed out of her mind and everything else.

Unless you've got Van Gogh's ear for music, you'll be touched by the Cajun, Zydeco, gospel, rhythm and blues and something called gutbucket, as well, of course, as the non-stop jazz. Along Rampart Street, down Canal Street and throughout the French Quarter. Under every flickering gaslamp, on every wrought-iron balcony, in every antebellum house, in every neo-Georgian building. In every arcade, in every shaded, magnolia-draped courtyard. Everywhere. Just ten minutes and you'll be telling everyone you remember Miles Davis when he was Kilometre Davis.

I warn you, New Orleans may be subtropical – my temperature never dropped below 120 degrees the whole time I was there, especially along Bourbon Street where, I have to say, it was particularly hot and sweaty – but it won't be the sweat you feel running down your back, it'll be your eardrums. If it's gracious southern living, white-colonnaded mansions and leisurely Pimm's No. 1s you're looking for, New Orleans is not for you.

So uninhibited are they that they will even dance at your funeral. 'We weep at births and rejoice at death,' one dead ringer for Louis Armstong spluttered all over me.

You'll also, of course, be touched by the people. And I don't just mean along Bourbon Street.

From the moment you take your first slug of absinthe for breakfast it's, as they say in that wonderful French of theirs that even Americans can speak and understand, '*Laissez les bon temps rouler*.' You'll be picked up and swept along by the sheer wild exuberance of the place. In Jackson Square, the unofficial centre of the French Quarter. In all the bars up and down every street you come across. And especially in the old Absinthe House at the corner of Bourbon and Bienville. Or was it the Old Bourbon House at the corner of Absinthe and Bienville? Whatever – it doesn't matter. 'If it moves, clap it,' one old local growled at me once, although to be honest most of the things

I could see seemed to have been severely clapped already.

Get an invitation to one of the 150 official balls organised during carnival time and you'll be well and truly touched, especially if you're summonsed to groove it with a krewe member who gives you what is known in carnival-speak as a ball favour. Exactly what it is I have no idea, but I've seen the bruises.

In theory, of course, I'm the last person who'd want to go to New Orleans, let alone Mardi Gras. I don't like carnivals. I don't like noise. I don't like music. I don't like jazz. I don't like dragging myself all over town from bar to bar. In fact, in many ways I'm a second Ol' Man River. I just like to go rollin' along. But in spite of all that, I must admit that New Orleans does something to me.

Maybe it's the buzz. Not even New York can rival New Orleans at party time – and New York knows how to party. Whatever it is, somehow it just gets to you. I've seen serious, sober conference delegates turn into raving maniacs within minutes of arriving in town, doing things with their clipboards I would never have thought possible.

Maybe it's the booze. New Orleans is the only city in the States, apart from Las Vegas, where the bars are allowed to serve drinks twenty-four hours a day, 365 days a year. Bourbon Street is also one of the few streets in the country where you can drink out in the open. On top of that, it's about the only place in the world that knows how to mix a decent absinthe frappé for breakfast. A Hurricane for lunch, and it won't make the slightest difference what you have for dinner. Whatever you drink, you'll feel as though you're somehow floating. Don't worry. You are. Not only is New Orleans 5ft below sea-level, but because it's built on a mix, or rather a lethal cocktail of sand, silt and clay, it is also sinking further into the sea all the time. But what the hell. It's only dropping at a rate of 3ft every hundred years, so you've got time to finish your thenth absinthe frappé. Just.

Maybe it's all those naked bodies. I'm always amazed that

nobody is arrested for parading around the streets like that. Perhaps, Americans being Americans, it's because of the shortage of evidence. Or maybe it's because the city was founded by a man who wore no trousers: John Law, your typical, honest, upright, Godfearing Scotsman, an estate agent and property-developer. He went on to lose his shirt as well – he went bust. The place was then passed on from one owner to another: the French, the Spanish, the French, the Americans, the Confederates, the Federal Union. And, finally of course, the people who seem to run most American cities nowadays, the gangs and drug-dealers.

Maybe it's the voodoo. The dolls, the pins, the potions. The instructions for all kinds of things, including one that has something to do with a 10ft Burmese boa constrictor, but which I didn't quite understand.

One voodoo expert I stumbled over one evening, hanging around the bright, white tomb of the voodoo queen Marie Laveau in St Louis Cemetery Number Two, told me he could make me the happiest man in the world. To keep me fit, young and healthy, he recommended shredding the heart of a live humming-bird and sprinkling it over my partner's head. To ensure that my partner remained faithful, I should write her name on a piece of paper and stick it up the chimney at home. And as for my wife, he recommended a one-way ticket to Florida.

Now, of course, I'm an expert, but at my first Mardi Gras I didn't know what hit me. I had been in Houston, Texas and was on my way to Australia and New Zealand via Hawaii when for no reason at all I decided to stop over in New Orleans. When I checked into my hotel in the French Quarter I couldn't believe what was going on all around me. It was like having planned to go to Moscow and ending up in Bangkok. The whole place was a riot. A laughing, singing, dancing, drinking riot. Carnival. Carne val. Farewell to the flesh. Carnivals in Wickford, Essex are not the same carnivals in New Orleans. This was completely unlike anything I'd ever seen before.

Café au lait and *beignets* in the Café du Monde first thing in the morning. Oyster Rockefellers in Antoine's, the oldest restaurant in the US, which is still run by the same family and where they speak my kind of French. Steaks in Smith and Wollensky's on Poydras Street. Szechuan alligator jambalayas the size of a small dog. Garlic the size of grapefruit. Not to mention the exquisite French cuisine, *poulet frit* Kentucky, *poulet* popcorn and, of course, Le Roi du Hamburger. The plumber's van parked outside Gumbo Ya Ya proclaiming, 'A straight flush is better than a full house.' Mint juleps in the Court of Two Sisters. Peach daiquiris at the Napoleon House, the little one's hideaway, except that he chickened out before Jean Lafitte could lift him from St Helena. Bloody marys at the Columns. The Killer Hurricane cocktails at Pat O'Brien's.

Then there was Rex, the King of the Carnival, who led the parade. After him King Zulu and then the million different carnival floats.

I still can't believe I was there. That I made it, that I survived. Although no doubt things can get better.

As for the rest of Louisiana, I have tried it, but it's trays ennooah. What am I saying? After Mardi Gras in New Orleans, the whole world is trays ennooah.

First, it's nowhere near as Français as they make out. I thought it was going to be small-town France: lots of tray pity villages covered in bougainvillaea, peasants on bicycles, berets, bottles of calvados, thick clouds of Gauloises and local politicians plotting how to break the United Nations embargos and sell guns to the rebels in Angola. But padootoo. There is the occasional sign in French: 'Chez it with Flowers', for example. Now and again you hear what you think sounds like French: toot suite, mercyboocoo and girl-toy du jour, which was how one horndog I met referred to his young travelling companion, although she looked more girl-toy de la nuit to me. In fact their knowledge of Français is so bad that when you get up to go to la toylette in a bar or a restaurant it's a mad scramble, with everybody going in and out of the

Monsieurs and the Mesdames because they don't know which is which.

Secondly, it doesn't look bayou country. I was expecting thick, tropical rainforests, swamps, mosquitos, alligators and deer darting around all over the place, miles and miles of washboard track, the occasional clearing, elegant, gleaming white mansions with horses standing by the door and that slight whiff of *je ne sais quoi*. No way. It's an American sprawl. If there are any bayous left you'd better be quick or you'll miss them.

Lafayette, however, does live up to its name. It's dirty, it's seedy, it's rundown. It's small-town America with a French accent. Grave. Except on Friday nights, when it becomes acute: that's when everybody pours out on the streets, the booze and the bands come out and it's party time. But it's still nothing to write home about. With a name like Lafayette and as much oil as they have in Houston, I'd have thought it was going to be New Orleans meets Texas: a huge, new, gleaming city with bars and oil rigs on every corner.

The town centre is neat, new-looking, touristy, but it's tiny. Only about two or three streets. The further away you get from the centre, the rougher it gets. I got there once after a big storm and everybody was expecting to see alligators walking down the middle of the street. They didn't, which was just as well for them, because they'd have been scared out of their wits, poor things.

The early French inhabitants called the place Petit Manchac, or Rear Entrance, which the locals seem to take as a compliment. 'This popular concept of "coming in through the rear entrance" has endured in south Louisiana culture to this day,' says a local history book. Well, that's the enduring appeal of French culture for you.

New Iberia, the heart of French Louisiana, the Queen City of the Teche, or plain Berry, as it is inevitably known locally, was no better. All sprawl apart from a couple of streets. They made a big fuss about Shadows-on-the-Teche, a manor house built by an old sugarcane-planter, David Weeks, in 1831 on the banks of the Bayou Teche. But it was no big deal. It's like every other house in Sussex, except not as old.

About the only town I came across with any *joie de vivre* was St Martinville, although maybe that was because I went there after lunch. It was small, civilised, polite, almost Français.

In Louisiana they keep on and on *continuellement* about their hot, spicy Cajun cooking and their hot, spicy Cajun music. The cooking, they say, is a unique mix of African creole and French Acadian. If that's the case, they're too heavy on the French and too light on the African. A Louisiana gumbo is either all or a combination of chicken, crab, seafood, sausages, oysters, redfish, rabbit, duck and a pair of old *chaussettes*, all mixed together with onions, peppers, garlic and rice. And *voilà*, you have your gumbo. French Acadian gumbo. African gumbo, now that is something different. It's stronger, richer, punchier and far more exciting. Nobody, for example, ever forgets the thrill of discovering their first alligator tooth, encrusted with the finest bacteria, buried deep inside a choice lump of green rabbit's head trapped in the sludge at the bottom of the dish. That's a real gumbo.

The trouble with all the other Cajun dishes – jambalaya, *sauce piquants*, *etouffées*, *courtbouillons*, *croquettes* and chicken fricassées, even their giant Po-Boy French bread sandwiches – is that they're too hot and much, much too spicy for my tender, delicate palate. This is obviously because, since Tabasco sauce is produced just down the road on Avery Island, they feel obliged to use as much of it as possible. You can visit the Tabasco plant and have a fun-packed time touring the factory, watching forklift trucks running backwards and forwards, looking at things in bottles and studying bottles being put into boxes.

Of the people who pick the peppers not a word. Of the problems they have getting the burning pepper dust out of their eyes not a word. Of the time it takes to wash it out of their skin . . . well, you get the picture. To show they didn't mind me asking them questions about this, one of the guides gave me a handful of Tabasco sweets. Zonk. They practically blew the top of my head off. I'm still drinking iced bloody marys to try to cool down.

Cajun music has a much more distinctive French flavour. Instead of going diddly-diddly, like Irish music, it goes *diddlé-diddlé-diddlé*.

Whether I'm in New Orleans, Lafayette, New Iberia or anywhere else in Louisiana, believe me nothing, but nothing beats a real genuine, authentic Southern Shag: Southern Comfort, orange juice, cranberry juice, ice and a dash of lime.

Out of this monde, as they say in Français.

Nevada

The Statue of Liberty, the Eiffel Tower, the Bridge of Sighs, St Mark's Square, the Doge's Palace, the Grand Canal, complete with gondolas. The famous Chrysler Building in New York. The Louvre, the Arc de Triomphe, the Great Pyramid, the holiest Buddhist shrine in Thailand. The Appian Way. Art galleries bursting with more paintings by Cézanne, Degas, Gauguin, Miró, Matisse, and, of course, Picasso than they ever painted.

You want to see them all? No problem. Go to Las Vegas, Sin City, the home of the mob. They'll welcome you with open palms. Las Vegas, the Spanish for Lost Wages, as Frank used to say, is everything and nothing. Although I must warn you that the last time I saw him, Michelangelo's David looked more than ever as if he had come to Vegas promising every deity in the next world that if he hit the jackpot he would forget the woman living next door and lead a clean and wholesome life and was now bitterly regretting it. He also seemed to have lost practically everything he stood up in.

If, however, you're looking for a touch of English restraint and elegance, head for the St James's Room in the appropriately named Aladdin Hotel. But be quick: knowing the effect Las Vegas has on people, they're likely to stick a life-sized Big Ben with a Tower of London thrown in for good measure in the middle of the green baize any day, with leggy

Beefeaterettes draped all over it. I tell you, there's nothing they wouldn't or can't do in Las Vegas. Not only is the whole city completely off the wall, it's round the bend, up three blocks and straight back down the other side again.

When I first visited Vegas luck was a lady and Bugsy Segal, the friendly local, neighbourhood godfather behind the whole crazy idea, was still on probation. Hotels like the El Rancho, the Riviera, the Flamingo and the Tropicano were still hotels. Swimming pools were out in the open, buffets cost $3.90 a head, drinks $1.99, and the biggest thing in town was Sammy Davis Jnr. Frank used to say it was Chicago in the desert. It was where the mobsters and their molls went not to get a tan. They stayed locked inside the entire time playing Liars' Poker or, no doubt, variations of it.

Then it became Disneyland. Casinos began to look like Treasure Island, King Arthur's Palace or Tutankhamen's burial chamber. Today it's all changing again. It's not merely going upmarket, it's heading for the stratosphere. With gambling in one form or another now legal in fifty states – ten years ago or so only two of them had any form of casino-style gambling – Las Vegas is even more determined to remain the centre of the gaming universe. So it is busy turning itself into what they call a 'resort destination' or, as they say with customary under-statement, a 'total resort destination that cannot be matched anywhere in the known universe, including Atlantic City, New Jersey'.

And however many times they transform Vegas, nothing is ever too gimmicky or too gross for them. Or for the crowds, who keep on rolling in in increasing numbers. Today it's the fastest-growing region in the country. As a result, it has everything for the man who has everything, but not for long. The one-mile Strip, that glorious tribute to American culture, is still there, with its non-stop hot-slots, grind joints, boxy bingo halls, discount prime ribs and everything else you can imagine, but it's bigger and brassier than ever. It's now mile after mile of stucco-encased homes, pools, security guards, gated communities, traffic, smog and diminishing water supplies. Hotels are no longer the size of your average hotel, they're the size of airports. They're so big that by the time you get to your room you owe three days' rent. Suites, complete with your own swimming pool and jacuzzi as wide as the Gulf of Mexico are $3,000 a night. Pick up the phone to order another case of Dom Perignon and you'll be greeted, 'Hail, noble guest.' Even the outside is air-conditioned. Around the gardens, around the pools, around everywhere they spray mists of cool water.

Las Vegas now has more hotel rooms than New York or Paris. They have also built giant 12,000-seater sports and entertainment complexes and huge theatres, not to mention innumerable gourmet restaurants with wine cellars that are not wine cellars. They are four-storey, stainless-steel, glass and plexiglass towers soaring 42ft over the bar and displaying over 9,000 bottles.

'A bottle of Cheval Blanc '47? No problem, sir.'

The wine waiter climbs into his harness, presses a button and before you can say 'Are you sure its going to be—?' he's zooming up to the top of the tower, grabbing the bottle and zooming back down to earth.

What the wine tastes like is, of course, another matter. All I know is last time I had some wine from a wine tower, the wine waiter got vertigo the number of times we had him sky-rocketing up and down his four-storey, stainless-steel, glass and plexi-glass tower.

But, of course, today, apart from $10,000 bottles of Cheval Blanc '47 kept four storeys up in a tower, Las Vegas is still what it always was: gambling, gambling, gambling.

'It's not a town, it's a stage set,' one of the local shoulder-holsters remarked to me. 'It's the world on a stage set.'

Another padded jacket was more to the point. 'This place,' he drawled through his cowboy boots, 'has had more face lifts than Cher.'

In the casinos, clocks and any other form of contact with the outside world is banned and the booze is free. To keep you relaxed, to keep you happy, to keep you huddled round the baize. To keep you losing your hard-laundered money. To stop you falling asleep from the booze, they pump in extra oxygen. These guys have thought of everything. Bugsy would have been proud of them.

So here night becomes day and day becomes the time you realise you've even blown that big white £5 note your mother stitched into your jacket lining all those years ago on your first school visit to France so you still had some money to get home if you happened to be attacked and robbed.

The amount of money they take is terrifying. Ma and Pa gamblers, they reckon, spend around $2,000 a year playing and losing the slots. Each. Income from the high-rollers, as they are known in the business, the Armenians from Burbank, the Chinese from the San Gabriel Valley, who play $20,000 a chip, is a thousand times greater, maybe more. Then there are the Kerry Packers, the whales, who play in tens of millions of dollars.

Did they take my money? No way. Even though I was brought up playing cards – by the time I was three I could count from one to King – I don't gamble. I've only gambled once in my life, and never again. I'm so unlucky that even when I play the stamp machines I lose.

Talking of losing, Las Vegas is also the world capital of the greatest form of gambling ever invented. There are wedding chapels round every corner, up every dead end. And if one of those doesn't suit you, you can get married wherever you like. In a car, in a stretch limo, in a drive-in chapel. Diving out of a plane. At the bottom of the Grand Canyon. If you want you can have a so-called Elvis Presley look-alike officiating. You can even get married in your own suit, if you haven't had to sell it to pay your debts. As for the wedding ring, you can even rent one if you need to. But wherever they get married, whether it's in their own suit or not, and whether the ring is rented or not, more and more people, I noticed, are getting married in the morning so that if it doesn't work out they haven't wasted the whole day.

But if Las Vegas is everything, the rest of Nevada, which is bigger than Britain, is nothing. Take Reno. It's no gamble. It's a straight loss. Many people maintain that the dice are more loaded against them there than they are back in Vegas. There is also talk of the injustice of having to carry on paying instalments on a car after it has been written off. 'There's only one thing more expensive than a car,' one poor, distressed, ex-millionaire complained to me, 'and that's an ex-car.'

The Reno women have nothing but praise for their faithful husbands, which, in their case, is one whose alimony cheques arrive on time. But Reno is not all twisted and cynical. In spite of everything they've been through, lots of women, I was told, remain soppy and sentimental and insist on getting divorced in the same dress as their mother got divorced in.

Arkansas

State troopers throwing girls at you the whole time. Women walking unannounced into your hotel bedroom all hours of the day or night. Wherever you turn, real-estate agents offering you fantastic land deals. Brokers guaranteeing you unbelievable commodity trades that will turn $5,000 into $73,000 overnight, if not more. Complete strangers thrusting so many cheques at you with your name on them that thanks ta t'good Lord and an even better attorney, you completely forget who they are.

The atmosphere in Little Rock is unlike the atmosphere I've experienced in any other part of the States. But I promise you, I didn't inhale.

The town itself is on the banks of the Arkansas River, which I always think should be pronounced Ar-kan-sas as in ah-Kansas, that crazy place which still doesn't believe in evolution. It isn't, of course, but then they do lots of things in Arkansaw that I don't necessarily agree with.

Away in the distance are lots of forests, the Ozarks, wild turkeys, striped bass and several thousand trailer parks. The population has risen since Bill Clinton, 'The dope from Hope', as the bumper stickers proclaim, arrived on the scene and created the whole bimbroglio. Which tells you a lot about Clinton. In Washington DC, where the bumpers are bigger and longer – probably everything in Washington is bigger and longer – the bumper stickers say, 'The Dope from Hope, known as the Gentleman Rapist, a serial sex offender who talked and fondled hundreds of women in and around Little Rock between 1976 and 1992'.

Main business activities? There's no doubt about that. Everybody says – well, half the population says – that not only did Clinton more than leave his mark, he ruined the market for them all. What was costing $20 before he arrived 'could now cost $200,000, for all I can afford. Gee, it's so expensive now, you'd think they'd got a Cadillac in there,' as one of the more sophisticated Arkansas state senators put it to me, if that's the right phrase, in the somewhat colourful way they have in the deep south.

'We put it to Clinton,' he went on. 'All he did was promise not to hold it against us.'

But whatever they say, it's obvious that Clinton has had a big influence on the town. There's a farmer's market, a river market, a museum of discovery, high heels all over the place and, I couldn't help but notice, about a million dry-cleaners. The best bar in town is Slick Willy's. Whichever restaurant you go to nobody, but nobody, is ever smoking a cigar. And whatever you want is available and rentable by the hour. Or half-hour, if you've got another cheque not to collect from your broker.

Unless Clinton, who brought a whole new meaning to the phrase an Act of Congress, is in your intimate circle, which may or may not be what you intended, I can imagine that life in Little Rock must be nothing but spicy alligator sausages and a can of Arkansas moonshine in the back of a trailer. I could hardly go into a bar and order a glass of white water without people coming up to me and offering me loans for property deals or various commodity trades. They seemed happy when I told them I would follow the local custom by immediately

269

throwing away any cheques I received made out in my name and pretending I had never had them.

As for the hotels, I could hardly get in them for all the state troopers. My favourite, the Capital, is not typical of Little Rock. It looks as though it hasn't been touched for over a hundred years. It still has its original wooden floors with their own built-in 250-year-old creaks. There, in the bar one lunchtime, I met the only Democrat left in Little Rock now that the Clintons have moved out. Over our bottles of white water, he told me he was a Yellow Dog Democrat.

'Goddarn it, a Yellow Dog is so stubborn he'd rather vote for a yellow dog than anybody else,' he hollered at me louder'n a turkeycock sat on a rattler.

He also told me that he used to be Clinton's next-door neighbour. 'When he was governor I used to lean across the fence and steal his tomatoes.' His voice ricocheted around the room. 'His were always much bigger than anyone else's.'

But he was not without praise for his former neighbour. He said that somehow or other, during the sixteen years Clinton lived in Little Rock, he managed to get under the skin of the people of Arkansas. Or under the skin of most of them, anyway. 'Slick Billy,' he grinned. 'He comes here all the time because he knows we won't tell on him. We're used to him. We know he's a hard dog to keep on the porch.'

I asked him what else Clinton had done for Arkansas.

'Positive things?'

'Positive things,' I said.

He thought for a while.

'He cleaned up six Superfund waste sites.'

Clinton had also, he said, recently been the chief guest of honour at a big state Democratic fundraising dinner at, appropriately enough, the Congress Center. He had stayed on afterwards until way past midnight to shake hands with every single one of the 2,000 people present and promise them all a presidential pardon. Which, like him or hate him, proves that not only was he the only recent US president who could speak in sentences, he was also a consummate politician. But then, there's never been anything unconsummated about him.

As Clinton's old next-door neighbour was obviously clued up on local history, I asked him what was worth seeing in town before I threw my tail over the dashboard, as they say.

'Little Rock Central High School,' he grinned. 'That's where Bill learned everything that was to prove useful in life: honesty, integrity, the supremacy of the rule of law, duty to one's country . . .'

And, of course, he added, the actual little rock that Little Rock is named after.

Apparently, in the old days the rock was a marker for boats coming into land. So who knows, but for a quirk of fate, the place could have been called Rusty Bucket, Pile of Dead Fish or Mrs Clinton's Dirty Laundry. Not that anybody makes any fuss about it. The rock, I mean – they're used to the dirty washing. It is almost buried in the river embankment by the Excelsior Hotel. If you can't find it, go into the hotel and ask them. Preferably during check-out time in the morning. They like nothing better than traipsing along the river, where the odd fisherman sits dangling his apparatus in the water, with people who are never going to stay in their hotel to point out a lump of rock sticking out of the mud.

The real excitement was the courthouse where, I was told, in ninety-nine divorce cases out of a hundred, the biggest dispute between the two sides is over who gets custody of the trailer. Everybody seemed to be there. I know you're going to find this hard to believe, but I actually met one or two people who had not been indicted, let alone convicted, of anything whatsoever not to do with the Clintons.

A word of advice, however. If you spot the courthouse in time, resist temptation, cross the road and walk by on the other side. As I was passing it one morning one of those eager young lawyers came bouncing down the steps, pushed past the herd of photographers perpetually camped outside, grabbed my jacket and asked me for a character reference for Clinton. I knew then he was in trouble.

The Governor's Mansion, which is tucked away in a side street, is much smaller than I thought it was going to be. But it's clearly feeling the reverberations of Clinton living there for twelve years. It has a string of enormous white pillars holding it in place. On the edge of the lawn by the gate is a bust of the great man. Alongside it, apparently, they are planning to display the bust of Monica Lewinsky. But a bit lower down. However, I didn't notice any signs saying, 'Keep off the grass'.

The State Capitol, which, contrary to rumours, does not have a cigar on top of it, is a mini Washington State Capitol built in the 1900s for far less than it cost to spend a night in the White House when Clinton was around. That includes the six 4in-thick Tiffany-designed brass doors. Even then Little Rock was beset with scandal. With the exterior nearly completed and the dome waiting to go on, the local construction company was accused of bribery and corruption. A New York architect had to be brought in to fix the dome and finish the job. How do I know? They brag about it in all their promotional literature. Funny people, the Americans.

Outside, in the far corner of the lawn, is the Arkansas Vietnam Veterans' Memorial. I was told Clinton did not have much to do with this, either, which is probably not surprising, bearing in mind the 1960s anti-draft movement slogan, 'Girls say yes to boys who say no.'

One day, on my way to the local Democratic Party head-quarters, which, incidentally, is located in a bungalow because, as the locals say, 'Our Billy, he ain't got nothing on top. He got it all down below,' I noticed that the capitol was full of schoolchildren being taken on a guided tour. Goodness only knows what they were telling them.

In the bookshop on Markham Street, without any prompting from me – honest – the manager told me that Clinton was going to write his memoirs. They were going to be called, *Arms and the Man*. He also showed me his bestseller: a cardboard cut-out comic book of the Clinton family, Bill, Hillary and Chelsea, who you could undress and dress up again in all kinds of outrageous clothes. He said he'd sold millions.

At the far end of the street, on the other side of the road bridge, on what looks like a derelict patch of ground – in other words, between Little Rock and a hard place – is where they are going to build the $125 million Presidential Library, which everybody in town felt should be like a trailer park. The first trailer would feature the 1968 aqua blue Mustang our Bill used to drive around Little Rock, one hand deep in a bag of chips and the other controlling the action. Playing in the background would be a tape of his well-known speech, 'I feel your pain. Do you mind if I keep on feeling . . . ?'

The next would be a tribute to Hillary's obsession with cooking nothing but chicken and rice deluxe from *The Evening Shade Cookbook*: a pile of hamburgers. Another, called the *Humility of Power*, would recall the famous haircut on the tarmac which brought practically every aircraft in the States to a standstill for three hours.

There would be a trailer devoted to the one feature that proved to be Bill's Achilles' heel. Except it wasn't his Achilles' heel. Scattered on the table would be copies of the magazine *Cigar Aficionada* featuring their Woman of the Decade. In the closet would be a pair of his gravitationally challenged trousers and the famous dress he denied ever splashing out on. In the background, President Bill would be saying: 'I did not have sexual relations with that woman. Now, those over there . . .'

One trailer would be completely empty. This would symbolise Clinton's success as president. How he was responsible for no major legislation apart from the Family Leave Act. How no children in public schools were better educated when he left office than when he was appointed. How no sick people and none of the elderly were better looked after when he left office than when he was appointed. How there were no fewer drugs and no less violence on the streets when he left office than when he was appointed. How he had no major foreign-affairs successes apart from a pile of half-eaten hamburgers at

273

Camp David when he was wooing the Arabs and the Israelis, the glorious successes in Haiti and Somalia and arm-twisting all those massive party donations from guys with funny-sounding names. And how, in the end, six out of ten Americans were ashamed of him. Even in Little Rock, the *Arkansas Democrat-Gazette* relegated his presidential swansong to the bottom of page 1 under a story about the death of 5.5 million chickens in a storm.

Alongside the empty trailer would be an empty trailer with holes in it, symbolising the integrity, honour and truthfulness of the First Lady. How, in between misplacing the billings record of a local law firm, 'she was once chosen as one of the hundred top lawyers in the country'. How she was one of the luckiest amateur futures-traders ever. How, with the aid of an Arkansas lawyer and a regular White House Lincoln bedroom guest called Blair, she was able to turn $1,000 into $100,000 over ten months. How, because of her, for eight years the post of attorney-general was filled by an incompetent woman. How she wasn't responsible for firing seven long-serving travel experts so that the business could be handled by a cousin and a bunch of her friends. And, of course, there would have to be a whole display devoted to her belief that 'it takes a village to raise children'. A village? I always used to think it took a mother and a father, but then, what do I know?

The man with the – what's the word? – challenging job of raising the money for the Presidential Library is a certain Dale Bumper who, apart from being a former Arkansas Democratic senator, was also apparently the slowest runner in town the day they were looking for a volunteer.

What are his chances? Pretty good, I would have thought, aside from the fact that the city wanted to purchase the land by raising taxes on hotels and restaurants and the hotels and restaurants were against it. They said it would be a stain on the neighbourhood. The city then decided it would raise the money by issuing bonds. A lot of people were against that as well. They said it was a waste of money building a presidential library which could only be open to twenty-one-year-olds and over. The city then said it wanted to rename the street Clinton Street. A lot of people were against that as well. They said if it was going to be renamed Clinton Street, traffic would have to go both ways up and down the street, whereas Bill only knew one way. The last I heard, they were going to name it Kneepad Gate.

Outside Little Rock, Arkansas is full of charming little places like Smackover, Prattsville, Forrest City – named after Nathan Bedford Forrest, the father of the Ku Klux Klan – Harrison, the site of their national headquarters, and Bentonville, which saw the opening of Sam Walton's original store. Today, Sam Walton's is the world's biggest private-sector employer – it has 1.2 million staff – and also the world's biggest company in terms of sales. Then, of course, there's Bill's home town, Hope, full name Hope to Hell Nobody Finds Out, which, if memory serves me correctly, is halfway between somewhere I think is called Toad Suck, on the big bend in the Arkansas River near Conway, and Delight, which is on Route 26 near Arkadelphia. Go down the Arkansas River and you come to a small tributary called the Purgatoire River, which may or may not be significant. Finally, there's Hot Springs, which used to be called Hot Water. This was where young Bill developed his interest in sax in nightclubs with names like the Vapors.

How was Arkansas for me? It was a great ride while it lasted, but then, I suppose it always was for Bill as well.

The Ketchup States

Ketchup does, of course, mean different things to different people. It means that yukky red stuff that Americans insist on smearing over everything in sight and call catsup, which, I would have thought, like ratatouille, would be enough to put anybody off anything. It means those states that have been smeared in horrible red stuff in their time, whether it was during the Civil War or during the civil rights campaign. According to President Reagan, it was a vegetable found in school lunches. It's also a technical term I'm sure I've heard Americans use when referring to a favourite baseball team, football team or even something as unimportant as a city or a whole state that has fallen down on its luck and has a long way to go to draw level with everybody else. And then it is South Carolina.

Alabama, the Yellowhammer State, certainly has some ketching up to do. Admittedly, it has come a long way since the days of Governor Wallace, Martin Luther King, the 1960s and all that violence. Huntsville is now about as hi-tech as you can get. Think of any company in the space, defence or electronics business, and they are there. In Tuscaloosa it's the same story, but with the automobile industry. But throughout the 1960s, when the race was on across the south to modernise, update and industrialise, they missed out. Governor George Wallace was more interested in fighting for segregation than for new investment and new industries. When their two 'big mules', steel and cotton, crashed, they had nothing. Except, of course, huge unemployment.

Under new leaders, they fought back, but they aren't there yet. Because they have relatively little industry, they've got a low tax base. And they have no state lottery and no casinos. They've even banned the local Poarch Creek Indians from having their own casino. As a result, spending on state services is desperate. Take education. Alabama ranks low in practically everything from spending to the numbers of students completing high school and graduating. And if you're behind in education, you're behind in everything.

Michigan and Mississippi are ketchup states for different reasons. Michigan, especially Detroit, because once it was there but it lost it, and now it's got to get it back. Mississippi because it was never there – well, apart maybe from Vicksburg pre-Civil War – but deserves to be, if for no other reason than to kill off once and for all the old joke:

What's the difference between the State of Mississippi and the Mississippi River?

At least the river knows where it's going.

South Dakota and South Carolina are different again. Presumably both are called 'South' because everything about them is heading south. They're certainly not trying to ketchup with the north.

The main city of South Dakota might be called Rapid City, but that's about all that is rapid about the state. Work on Mount Rushmore is running over fifty years late. It stopped in 1941 and has never been resumed. As for the partly finished carving of Crazy Horse, it's, well, crazy. Either they're going to commemorate him or they're not, but at the moment it looks as though they're still trying to make up their minds.

As for South Carolina, it's so far behind it is not even interested in trying to ketchup. Their state senator, Strom Thurmond, is so old he *is* the past. By the time they've lit the last candle on his birthday cake, the first one has gone out. At ninety-eight, he is the oldest man in the Senate. Not that he doesn't have the right credentials. He believes in flogging and hanging, that there should be more executions, not fewer. A

277

Democrat, a neo-Confederate 'State's Rights' candidate and now a Republican, he is still considered a liberal by many for declaring, 'We believe there are not enough troops in the army to force southern people to admit the negroes into our theatres, swimming pools and homes.'

If that's not enough to make you throw up, the pro-slavery Confederate flag, the Stars and Bars, is still practically everywhere. I once even saw a giant Confederate flag flying outside a Piggie Park restaurant. To make matters worse, they were also distributing leaflets giving what they claimed were the 'Biblical views of slavery'. Africans brought to America as slaves were lucky, it said, because 'what they had over here was far better than what they had over there'.

The flag is printed on both covers of the state's legislative manual; it also, until very recently, flew above the State Capitol in Columbia. They only took it down when they were faced with a massive tourism boycott that was costing them over $30 million a year. But, fair-minded liberals that they are, they then promptly raised it again on a flagpole directly facing the Capitol, still on state property. Which is a complete nonsense. If flying the Confederate flag on top of the state legislative building is wrong, it must surely also be wrong to fly it on a flagpole opposite. And if flying it on a flagpole on state land is wrong, it must also be wrong to continue glorifying anything to do with what the flag represents. You don't find any flags or statues to the Nazis on any official buildings in Europe. Or on any flagpoles on public land facing public buildings.

In Mississippi and Georgia, however, the Confederate flag is part of the state flag. In Richmond, Virginia, you will find a statue of Robert E. Lee outside the state house. In Alabama, there are slogans praising the 'Heart of Dixie' all over the place. In Opelousas, Louisiana, there are not one but two Confederate flags flying over the parish courthouse.

Anywhere in the south you're still likely to see rebel marches and parades. Some states still have 'Confederate History Months', which revel in everything Confederate under the sun.

But there is never a word about the evils of you-know-what.

In other wars there are winners and losers. The winners win; the losers lose. Not in the American Civil War. The south have never accepted that they lost. Instead they say, with that wonderful American ability to twist all meaning out of the English language, that they were 'cast unwillingly into the role of the defeated'. It is absurd. Surely it's time for them to ketchup with the times, acknowledge that they lost and ban everything that has anything to do with racism, discrimination or slavery and everybody who advocates anything to do with racism, discrimination and slavery. All those Ku Klux Klan meetings still going on on Saturday mornings in towns and cities across the south; the KKK banners you see decorating Fountain Square in Cincinnati, Ohio at Christmas; memorial plaques to the veterans who died in the world wars that divide them into whites and 'coloureds' like the one in Orange City, Florida. And, of course, Confederate flags flying on state terri-tory. While they are at it, how about renaming Forrest City, Arkansas? Who on earth wants to live in a town named after the father of the Ku Klux Klan? It must be like living in a place called Hitler or Stalin. But I doubt they ever will. They've spent so long living in the past, they'll never ketchup now.

I once met a decrepit old southern hopplehead, a man who was to the civil rights movement what King Herod was to play-groups. The world's greatest triumph, he told me, was 'Swannee River', the famous song of which everybody knows at least two lines. Originally it was going to be called after the Pee Dee River, which runs through the eastern end of South Carolina, but at the last moment the writer, Stephen Foster, changed his mind.

'Thanks be to God,' King Herod mopped his brow. 'If he hadn't done that, we'd've been known for ever as a black slave state.'

Now, how does that song go?

Alabama

Alabama I like. No, that's not true. Alabama, I love, honour, respect and admire. The most southern of all the southern states, it might not be beautiful like, say, West Virginia, and it certainly doesn't have the buzz of a New York or a Massachusetts or Montepelier, Vermont, but this is where modern America was born. It's still far from perfect, but can you imagine what the US would be like today if Rosa Parks hadn't refused to give up her seat to a white passenger on that Cleveland Avenue bus in Montgomery on 1 December 1955, as the driver, James F. Blake, demanded? It certainly wouldn't be the fair, liberal, open-minded, civilised, tolerant society it is today.

What amazes me most about the whole civil rights move-ment – and everything about the civil rights movement is amazing – is that, in spite of generations of being treated like dirt, denied any form of education, the right to vote or even any basic, human respect, people like Rosa Parks suddenly found the ability and, above all, the strategy not just to become heroes but to become superheroes. One day they were your ordinary, run-of-the-mill, downtrodden dinks, the next they were heroes. They were protesting and marching and being beaten up, and some of them were even dying for their beliefs.

Rosa Parks wasn't the first person in Montgomery to refuse to give up her seat to a white passenger. The first was a certain Homer Plessey, way back in 1892. The matter went to the Supreme Court, which ruled against him. Public transport, the judge said, should be separate but equal, which was why the city's buses had thirty-six seats: ten at the front for whites, ten at the back for black and sixteen in the middle for blacks and whites. However, if a white person was standing, a black person, to show that he was both separate and equal, had to stand up and give the white person his seat. Not only that, but blacks and whites were not allowed even to sit on adjacent seats in the same row. If a white chose to sit on an empty seat next to a black, the black had to stand.

The bus boycott wasn't the first bus boycott, either. That was in 1900, and it forced the bus company to desegregate. Until 1920, that is, when the local Ku Klux Klan forced them to resegregate again.

The remarkable thing about the Rosa Parks bus incident that triggered the civil rights movement was the way it was masterminded not by a highly paid professional political strategist with sleeping rights at the White House, but by a Pullman train porter, E. D. Nixon, who was president of the Montgomery branch of the National Association for the Advancement of Coloured People. They needed an issue, and the buses were an issue that affected everybody. Secondly, they needed the right person. The previous month, another woman had refused to give up her seat but a bunch of local black activists had rallied round and paid her fine. As a pregnant unmarried mother, she was not the sort of person, they felt, around whom to build a nationwide bid for equality. On the other hand, Rosa Parks, quiet, well-spoken, respectable, churchgoing, married and the secretary of the local branch of the NAACP, was just the ticket, if not a gift from heaven.

It was not the first time she had been thrown off a bus, either. It had first happened to her in 1943, at the hands of the very same driver. This had spurred her to join the Alabama branch of the NAACP. Three times she had also tried to register to vote, and three times she had been refused. When her brother had come back from the Second World War still in his military uniform, and she saw how he was treated by whites for whom risking their lives for their country amounted to no more than sitting up all night drinking beer, she began monitoring attacks on black soldiers and other veterans. She also worked with the NAACP's Youth Council on civil disobedience campaigns.

The bus-driver, James F. Blake, was already a hate figure among the black community. Not only did he make the blacks pay at the front of the bus and then get off again and walk to the back to get back in again, more often than not he would pull away before they even reached the back, leaving them standing there in a cloud of exhaust. This had happened so many times to Rosa Parks that in the end she refused to get on any bus he was driving. Until, that is, that fateful evening of 1 December 1955, when she was returning home from work at the Montgomery Fair Department Store.

Nixon now had everything: the issue, the ideal symbol of injustice, the hate figure. The bonus, though he didn't know it at the time, would be the town's new twenty-six-year-old Baptist minister, the Rev. Dr Martin Luther King Jnr.

To me, the completely unsung and overlooked heroine behind the whole business was Jo Ann Robinson, another member of the NAACP. As soon as she heard what had happened to Rosa Parks, on her own initiative she started typing, printing and distributing over 5,000 leaflets calling for a bus boycott the following Monday. Come Sunday, of course, every preacher in Montgomery was on his hind legs backing the idea and urging everybody to support it. It was the perfect response at the perfect time. Sheer genius.

But for some reason in Montgomery today, Jo Ann Robinson hardly rates a mention. No special solo displays in the Rosa Parks Museum, no special plaques, no tributes, no nothing, which seems odd. Not that I'm suggesting there is too much emphasis on Rosa Parks, although others may disagree. When I went to the museum, built on the very spot where she was taken off the bus, I was hounded by a southern battleaxe who kept screeching, 'Ah didn't come down heah to heah about nothin' but Mizz Rozza Parks. Rozza Parks? Rozza Parks? Anyone would think this was a northern state. I'm gonna write to the governor about it.'

That was embarrassing enough, but I was even more embarrassed by the Civil Rights Memorial. It was no bigger than a trailer. It should be the size of the Statue of Liberty. The Statue of Liberty offered freedom and justice to outsiders; the Civil Rights Memorial offers the same to the country's own people.

Selma, the town where the civil-rights protesters began their famous marches, is still a pretty miserable-looking, rundown sort of place. Bits of it have, of course, been fixed up, repainted, even rebuilt. The St James Hotel, for example. That's now very smart, very attractive, very there's-no-way-I-was-ever-involved. Brown Chapel, from which the marchers set out, is still very much the same. The Edmund Pettus Bridge, where they were savagely beaten, attacked by dogs and choked with gas, is completely different. And they've washed the blood away.

One day I'd like to go on one of the re-creations they do of the Selma–Montgomery march, which follows the route taken by the protesters, led by Martin Luther King, campaigning for the right to vote. Hopefully before Jesse Jackson devalues the whole thing out of existence. He goes to Connecticut, where unemployment is creeping up, and compares it to the Selma march. He goes to join the pickets at a meat-packers' strike in Minnesota and compares it to the Selma march. He protests against budget cuts in New York State and turns up in Palm Beach, Florida during the votes fiasco and he compares them both to the Selma march as well. He goes to see the film *Chocolat*, the story of a woman who sells goodies, among other things, to the mayor of a small French provincial town and, God help us, tells us that it's about 'us going to Birmingham to get the right to vote'.

When I do the march, I'd like to try to find out why, in spite of everything, they kept re-electing Wallace as governor; why it took Selma thirty-five years to elect a black mayor, and in the meantime they kept voting back the same segregationist mayor who had been in office when the state troopers attacked the black protesters; why today Alabama not only has the highest number of death-row inmates per 100,000 head of population in the USA but is one of only two states that doesn't even guarantee the prisoners a lawyer to ensure that they can take advantage of the full range of appeals allowed by the legal system. I'd also like to find out whether or not the ribs in Lannie's Bar-B-Q Spot, the favourite meeting place of both protesters and police during the battle for voting rights, are the best in the south. If they are, I might recategorise Alabama as a burger state. A King Burger state, of course.

When I first quietly mentioned, in my usual diffident way, that I had to go to Birmingham, Alabama, I remember everyone, without exception – well, the two people who care about me more than anybody else in the whole world, my driver and my travel agent – telling me not to. It was dangerous, they said. I was going to get beaten up. There was nothing there. The place was a mess. Couldn't I make some excuse and get out of it? Otherwise it was highly likely that I wouldn't be able to give them any more business.

But in the end, like most people who peddle good advice, they were completely wrong. Birmingham is a fantastic little town. In fact, one of the biggest, most expensive and most luxurious hotels I think I've ever seen anywhere in the world is in Birmingham: the Winfrey. The first time I staggered in there I thought I was in one of the world's hotspots, Vegas, New York or Suzou, China. But, of course, I wasn't. I was in Birmingham, Alabama. I had a couple of drinks in the bar – well, that's my story – and then, instead of turning left and heading for the sunshine, I turned right and ended up at the back of the hotel in a vast, deluxe shopping mall just bursting with spending power.

The problem is that to most people Birmingham is still Bombingham, the Birmingham of the old black-and-white television days, of Governor Wallace, of police dogs, fire hoses, riots, churches being bombed and, of course, of Rosa Parks and Martin Luther King. Don't you believe it. Today it's a totally different world altogether. Skyscrapers, flyovers, enormous hotels, huge gallerias, big, expensive homes off Route 495. What's more, it's neat, clean, tidy and safe.

Like the original British Birmingham, it used to be big in coal and steel. But, as happened with the British Birmingham, that's all long gone, although they still have a huge statue of Vulcan, the Roman god of iron – the second-largest cast-iron statue in the world – atop a 125ft column looking down on where the action used to be.

They also have all the usual head offices and electronics companies and art galleries and museums and festivals and jazz clubs and halls of fame and IMAX domes and state parks (no relation to Rosa) and everything else you can think of. Forget the Alabama Theater with its mighty Wurlitzer. Forget the Alabama Sports Hall of Fame, or even the F. Scott and Zelda Fitzgerald Museum, which not only displays all the couple's dirty linen in public but also highlights their individually mono-grammed bath towels as well: hers and hers. For me Birmingham is the Civil Rights Institute.

I don't care who you are or what you believe in, I defy anyone to go there and not be moved by the images and the story of Rosa Parks and the unbelievable struggle that gave birth to the modern civil rights movement, transformed Martin Luther King into a world figure and was responsible for the greatest social revolution in American history. There I listen again and again to Martin Luther King's 'I have a dream' speech. I'm not ashamed to admit that no matter how many times I hear it, I still dissolve into almost as many tears as I do if my brother-in-law ever offers to buy me a drink. It's the situ-ation, the drama, the tension, that rasping voice. I just crumple on to the ground. Martin Luther King's speech is very moving as well. It has to be one of the greatest orations in history. I've just got to listen to it again and again. It's unbelievable.

I was listening to it once when a shrivelled-up old hamfather shuffled up to me. We kibitzed about the old days. How his grandfather always slept in a rocking chair with a double-barrelled shotgun on his lap because he was terrified of being attacked in the middle of the night by the Ku Klux Klan. How, in the middle of the bus boycott, he and other protesters faced down the deputies and state troopers on the Edmund Pettus Bridge and how they celebrated when they finally brought about the Voting Rights Act. They all went to church.

Then he told me that after all the fighting was over and the

Supreme Court had ordered the integration of all transport facilities in Montgomery, a team from *Look* magazine turned up to interview Rosa Parks. Afterwards they wanted to photograph her standing alongside one of the newly integrated buses. They stopped the first bus that came along and asked if they could take their photograph. The bus was being driven by James F. Blake.

Another old podunk joined in with the reminiscences. The congressional gold medal Clinton presented to Rosa Parks as 'a living icon for freedom in America' wasn't a gold medal at all, he said. Even though America was the richest power in the world, even though the presentation was being made in Washington before all the great and the good, not to mention the world's press, and even though they had had over forty-five years to prepare for the occasion, the bunch of crooks only gave her an artist's impression of the medal. If I were her, not only would I have given it back, I would have refused to get up off my seat to receive it in the first place.

If you come out of the institute and turn left, you'll see the 16th Street Baptist Church where four little black girls died when it was bombed by white segregationists, where Martin Luther King was imprisoned and from which the infamous white police chief, Bull Connor, unleashed police dogs and water cannon on protesters. Immediately opposite the institute is the Kelly–Ingram Park, where protest after protest took place after the bombing. Today, in the centre, is a bronze statue of Martin Luther King together with others symbolising the brutality the civil rights movement faced and the hope of its members.

There is to be another memorial to Martin Luther King, in Washington DC, on the shore of the Tidal Basin between the memorials to Abraham Lincoln and Thomas Jefferson. For the first time, a private citizen will be honoured in an area up until now reserved exclusively for presidents. The least they should do for Rosa Parks, I reckon, is to tear down that statue of Vulcan and put her up there as the mother of the civil rights movement and one of the key figures of the twentieth century.

After all, as Nelson Mandela said, 'Before King there was Rosa Parks. She is who inspired us, who taught us to sit down for our rights, to be fearless when facing our oppressors.' The inscription should be her simple reason for refusing to give up her seat on the bus: 'I just wanted to be free like everybody else. I did not want to be continually humiliated over something I had no control over: the colour of my skin.' And alongside it there must be a small column and a small statue of Jo Ann Robinson.

However – the question I shouldn't ask – are the blacks more free today because of Rosa Parks? Obviously, yes. But are they as free as they could be? The honest answer is that I don't know. My impression is yes, but. Yes, all the crudest, most blatant forms of bigotry seem to have disappeared, but maybe there is still a sense of wariness or distrust on both sides. In offices, factories, stores, there's no problem. But in bars, clubs and even restaurants there still seems to be a split. In housing, there is even more of a split. And the more downmarket you go, the wider it is.

Now the crunch question: what of the future? However you hedge it, however you dress it up, the odds, you have to say, are still far and away on the whites. Education in the States is bad in general, but black education is worse. Opportunities are limitless, but they're still more limitless for whites. Having the right is one thing, but having the right and the education and the opportunity is the package.

Colour prejudice is not of course the only form of discrimination in the States. They discriminate and anti-discriminate and anti-anti-discriminate against everything. Mothers' Day is banned because it discriminates against fathers. Fathers' Day is banned because it discriminates against mothers. Bibles are banned because Christ's words 'I love you, Mark' are said to be sexually suggestive and discriminate against those who do not believe in being sexually suggestive. Backpacks are banned in schools because they discriminate against those who cannot afford them. And apart from that, in the security-obsessed world in which we live there's no way of knowing what might be inside them. Golf carts have even been banned because they discriminate against people who don't need them.

Then there's anti-discrimination discrimination. Hardly a day goes by without some feminist group suing an art gallery or a museum for not displaying enough paintings or sculptures by women, or a ballet school for not accepting 20-stone monsters, or a theme restaurant for not hiring women as waiters in these restaurants when there wouldn't have been any women waiters, or even a restaurant for not hiring men to be busty, sexy, female waitresses. As if that's not bad enough, having abolished Miss and Mrs, the anti-discrimination feminists are now moving towards the ultimate. They want to replace 'he' and 'she' with 'ze', 'his' and 'her' with 'zer' and 'him' and 'her' with 'zim'.

I wonder if Rosa Parks could ever have guessed, the day she refused to give up her seat on that bus, that this is where we would end up. Or Mr Nixon. Or poor, old, overlooked, neglected Jo Ann Robinson.

Michigan

Not just one derelict office building; not just one street of derelict office buildings, banks and stores, but whole blocks of derelict office buildings, banks, stores, hotels and theatres. Welcome to Detroit, originally named by its founder, Antoine de la Mothé Cadillac, as far back as 1701 as Ville d'Etroit, or City in a Right Mess. Which at least proves one thing: the French are not always wrong.

But that's not all that sets it apart. Rare among the cities of the world, it witnessed an invention that changed mankind for all time: the ice-cream soda. Less important, certainly in American eyes, or rather stomachs, although it didn't invent the wheel itself, it invented, as every schoolboy used to know, the next best or worst thing, depending on whether you eat genetically modified food or not: the motorised wheel. In fairness, it's wrong to also blame Detroit for traffic jams, speed cops, road rage, increased pollution and the destruction of the countryside. I blame the city's founders, the French. After all, if the French had never developed vanadium steel, which was not only lighter but stronger than ordinary US steel, Henry Ford would never have been able to build his Model T in the first place and we would never have had to cope with all these problems. On the other hand, I'm sure we have to be grateful to the French that the original Model T was far better at retreating than advancing. The only way a Model T could climb even the slightest incline, never mind a hill, was by turning round and reversing up it. To the French, of course, the 'T' stands for *triomphe*. To the rest of us, it simply means *typique, n'est-ce pas*? I hate to think what the models A to S looked like.

Originally inhabited by Indian tribes such as the Hurons, the Ottawa, the Ojibwa, the Pontiacs, the Cadillacs and lately the Granadas and the Escorts – the famous 'T' in Model T in fact stood for the Tecumseh – at one time Detroit was not only the motor capital of the world, and one of the richest cities in the United States, it was synonymous with industry and everything industry stands for: graft, organised labour, trades unions, strikes, harassment, corruption and 'Oooh Baby Love', that song by Diana whatshername, the one who shrieked going through security at Heathrow and brought every policeman in the south of England rushing to her assistance.

Today, however, it's more like the Third World, but without the aid organisations. The first time I went to Detroit I couldn't believe I was in the States. I've been to plenty of rough areas in the US: the Bronx, New York; South Side, Chicago; Coral Gables, Miami. I've also seen more than my fair share of poverty, in Chelsea in Boston, Massachusetts; Trentham, New Jersey; Palm Beach, Florida. I've even seen the occasional small town or city rotting away, such as Camden, New Jersey, where the sewers are full to overflowing and there are great pools of yuck all over the streets, piles of rubbish everywhere and the whole place stinks to high heaven. But nothing prepared me for Detroit, America's ninth-largest city.

The centre appears to have been designed by Saddam Hussein. Street after street after street is just deserted, reduced to rubble. Pavements, where there are pavements, are thick with weeds, broken bottles, jigs, winos and bundles of rags who look as though they'd enjoy nothing more than rolling a couple of jigs and winos before breakfast and goodness knows what else. Even the stray dogs have mange.

Buildings are collapsing. Some, such as the former Hudson Building, are in such a bad state that they actually end up imploding. At one time the Book–Cadillac Hotel and the Statler Hilton were as famous as the Waldorf in New York or the Fontainebleau in Miami. Today they're empty and abandoned. Baby Face Nelson's favourite, the Royal Palms Hotel, has gone for ever; so, too, have the once-famous Wurlitzer, the David Broderick Tower, Miley and Miley, famous the world over for their shrimps, Kales, United Artists, Fine Arts, Park Avenue, the Adams Theatre. All decomposing slowly into the ground. The Grand Michigan Theater – at one time Detroit had more theatres than New York – is now a not very grand car park.

The Michigan Central Railroad station, a huge, sixteen-storey Chicago gothic block supported by massive Corinthian columns built in 1913 to last to the end of time, is now in such an advanced stage of decay that it has been completely cordoned off. Cough, sneeze or wave a railway timetable at it and the whole thing will come tumbling down.

Those buildings that are not collapsing of their own accord have been smashed to pieces, as if some invading army led by Arnold Schwarzenegger has been told to take everything out and make it uninhabitable. Those that have not been smashed to pieces are boarded up. Even the most famous building of all, Oooh Baby Love, the home of Motown, which admittedly sports some rather fetching purple boarding. It stands in the middle of this wide-open, derelict no-man's-land that everybody calls the Badlands. But to get to it is no problem: all you need is an army tank, a fully equipped platoon and all the luck in the world.

Hospitals have been closed down because of lack of funds – and this, don't forget, was Helen Keller territory. McDonald's and Burger King have shut up shop. Even Chinese restaurants have gone, and they're usually the last to leave anywhere.

As in all good war zones, everything is up for grabs. Candy from kids, mail sticking out of mailboxes, cheques, credit cards, bank account numbers. Anything from any shop anywhere. Cars, guns, huge 300 to 500lb bronze statues. Even the bank managers are at it. One spent thirty years siphoning off millions of dollars from elderly customers' accounts before he was rumbled. Suspicions were aroused when he turned up at the office one day wearing a clean shirt. Then there's all the grown-up stuff: carjackings, arson, drugs, murder. Not only is it not safe not to leave your home any more, it's the kind of town where it's not safe not to take your wallet into the shower with you. It's no wonder Detroit doesn't have any towns with which to twin. It has suicide pacts instead.

The reason it is in such a mess is simple. In the 1960s it was the riot capital of the US, in the 1970s it was the murder capital of the US and in the 1980s it was the arson capital of the US. So it's hardly surprising that in the 1990s it became the war zone capital of the US.

From the 1960s, people just began to move out, and the exodus rapidly gained momentum in the 1970s and 1980s. At one time the city had a population of over 2 million. Now it's down to less than 1 million. Some went to the older suburbs such as Wyandotte, Ferndale and Royal Oak. Most left Detroit altogether. Industry followed. Inevitably, as inhabitants and industry moved out – a lot of them through the Detroit/Windsor Tunnel to Ontario, Canada – people desperate for a roof over their head, any kind of roof, moved in.

The result is that today Detroit is one vast mish-mash of the hopelessly poor, the poor and the not-quite-so-poor from the four corners of the earth, everywhere, in fact, except America. The Italians, Greeks, Irish and Mexicans are all over the place. The Palestinians are in Farmington, the Christian Lebanese in

Bloomfield Hills. Poles are big south of Hamtramck. In what is naturally known as Poletown, they have their own stores along Chene Street, their own Polish Yacht Club tucked away in the Ivanhoe Café and their own church, St Hyacinth. Brush Park, out towards Highland Park, the site of Henry Ford's first plant, where the Model T was built, was once one of the wealthiest parts of town. Nowadays it's known simply as the ghetto.

The Model T plant, opposite what used to be the Sears store, is a wreck. Which explains why I've been waiting so long for those spare parts. Although I have to say I've never quite understood why it was called a car. There were no illuminated glove compartments, no CD-players, no crisp packets all over the floor, no chewing-gum on the seats, no dog hairs in the back. No mother-in-law moaning because you're taking her home the short way.

Yet it is because of the Model T that there are now more highways than there is America. Not because everybody loves the idea of 400-ton trucks hurtling down the roads on seventy-three wheels, chock-full of more hamburgers. But because – the Americans' reason for doing everything – they needed them to defend themselves. If you were going to build intergalactic global missiles that didn't work, you had to be able to shift them around to as many different sites as possible as quickly as you could so that the enemy wouldn't know where not to fire their missiles that probably didn't work either. The man behind the idea was Eisenhower who, it is said, could never forget the army's first transcontinental truck convoy, which he took part in. It left Washington DC on the Lincoln Highway for San Francisco in 1919. Most of the trucks arrived just after Pearl Harbor, although some are said to be still negotiating the traffic on the Beltway. Afterwards, and after a word with his lady chauffeur – Ike never did anything without checking with his lady chauffeur – he gave the go-ahead to a plan to build 41,000 miles of highway linking 90 per cent of the 209 towns containing over 50,000 people. The cost was an estimated $27.5 billion, give or take the cost of a missile defence shield one way or the other. The legacy of this fantastic highway system is that it now takes longer to drive from Washington DC to San Francisco than it did in 1919.

To ensure that nobody complained about it they built the roads along the old Indian trails and named them 'I' for Indians followed by a number. The I-15, for example, is on the old Indian trail through the Wasatch Range in Utah, with the desert to one side and the forest to the other. The I-25 runs along the edge of the Rockies. The I-70 tracks Necomalin's Path and the Cumberland Road between Pennsylvania and Missouri. The I-80 follows in the footsteps of the Mormon Pioneer Trail between Nebraska and Missouri, going on to Nevada and San Francisco. The I-84 runs from Portland along the old Oregon Trail to Twin Falls, Idaho. The I-81 is, of course, the famous Shenandoah Trail. And so on.

Walking along the streets around the Model T plant today, with all their Arab bakeries and restaurants, Arab doctors and dentists, an Islamic Institute and of course, a mosque, it's difficult to remember that you're still in the States. Not that the Ford family have abandoned all their connections. They still send all their old cast-offs to St Martha's, the family church for the poor and needy of the parish of Dearborn. Get there early, and on a good day you can pick up a decent suit for next to nothing. Whether there's any money left in the pockets is another matter.

Some of the old-time Ford family magic is beginning to rub off on to their new neighbours. Over a coffee and the promise of a hubble-bubble round the corner in Warren, one very smart-looking Somali in what may have been a Ford family suit told me that the local Muslims had developed the perfect way of raising money. Whenever a Christian church comes up for sale in the area, they immediately put in a bid for it. Every time, the city authorities mysteriously discover some ancient clause in the lease which says that if the church ever has to be sold it should first be offered to the city as a community centre for all the people in the area.

'At first, we were mad.' He switched to Ford boardroom mode. 'We knew they were making it up. But what could we do? We made a fuss, accused them of all kinds of things. Then, to buy us off, they offered us $500,000 to cover our costs. So now we are putting in bids for every Christian church we can find, just to be bought off.' Henry would have been proud of them.

He would also have been proud of another group of Muslims I came across, in Palos Heights, Illinois. They wanted to buy the old Palos Heights Reformed church and turn it into a mosque. Here, too, the city council suddenly decided, after the church had been up for sale for two years, that they had plans to turn it into a recreation centre. Here, too, they apologised for their mistake and offered the Muslims $200,000 to walk away from the deal. Funny, that.

Just outside Dearborn, the man who, thanks to the French, condemned us to sitting in tin boxes, jammed up our roads and destroyed the countryside, lovingly rebuilt a typical Cotswold village which he had shipped over from England, complete with a flock of traditional Cotswold sheep. Hopefully, disease-free. The only car allowed in the village was the very first car he ever built, and even this was confined to a barn and not allowed on the village streets.

Today, the fightback has begun in Detroit. And they're doing it American-style. First they built two new state prisons north of East McNichols, between Ryan and Mound. Next came a brand new flashy baseball stadium. The only problem is they can't afford a decent team to play in it. I'm not saying they're desperate, but the church next door has a huge sign hanging up outside saying, 'Pray for the Tigers.'

Then it was a casino, built on the edge of the Detroit River in, appropriately enough, what was once the city's Internal Revenue office. 'It's rumbucktious,' one old gambler who looked as though he had graduated in bootjacking and gone on to get an honours degree in persuasion remarked to me as he lost another fortune.

Finally, they began to tackle the city centre. To symbolise the city's regeneration, smack in the centre of town, between Jefferson Avenue and the river, right opposite the casino, Henry Ford II built the Renaissance Center, composed of five circular glass towers incorporating the seventy-two-storey Marriott Hotel, which has a circular restaurant on top. It was, he said, hand on heart, tears in his voice, his vision of the new Detroit. He then promptly sold it to his arch-rivals, General Motors, as their worldwide headquarters. Now that they've got it, the best thing General Motors can do, if they're serious about regenerating the city, is to close down that circular restaurant because from seventy-two storeys above the city you can see far better than you can from the ground just how bad Detroit is and how much regenerating they've still got to do. Long, deserted streets. Huge, empty eight-lane highways. Vast wastelands. It's like a set for a movie with a name like *The Day After They Dropped the Bomb* and subtitled: 'We are building the nuclear missile shield for peace not war.' Even the newfangled monorail, or people-mover, as they call it, built to bring people back into the city, is, you can see, on the skids. Fewer and fewer people are using it, and, of course, the fewer people use it, the fewer people want to use it.

Yet in spite of all this, the mayor, Dennis Archer – named by his father after his two heroes, Denis Thatcher and Jeffrey Archer – when he's not walking on water remains optimistic. The trouble is, not many people know what he's on about. He's like a cross between George Bush Snr and George Bush Jnr trained by John Prescott.

I heard him once giving some kind of mass press conference underneath the Spirit of Despair, sorry, I mean the Spirit of Detroit statue outside City Hall. He kept on about what sorts of judges Bush would appoint as president and how the media nationally, all across America, had looked under every eyelid, every orifice that Vice-President Al Gore has, and how 'if you're going to be a national president representing all of America, as we've come to learn watching these past administrations –

President Reagan, President Bush and almost eight years now of Clinton and Gore – you know there are demands placed on the United States to be very helpful to other nations in terms of setting tones for trying to eradicate poverty, trying to feed the hungry and the like and yet there are some issues that have not been addressed in the state of Texas.'

But all praise to him – he only had one official car. The other one had been stolen.

The other reason so few people know what's going on is that the city's two daily newspapers, the *Detroit Free Press* and the *Detroit News*, have been crippled by a five-year strike. They've continued publishing with the aid of replacement workers and many returning strikers, but the papers are a fraction of the size they should be and circulation has plummeted eight times faster than in the industry as a whole.

One day, I suppose, Detroit will make it. I sincerely hope so. In the meantime, for tourists – I say tourists: I mean the odd one or two people a year who come to Detroit because they have to – the attractions are few and far between. Of the 'top ten things to do around town' recommended by those optimists of all optimists, the hugely underworked local tourist board, only four are actually in Detroit, one of which is the underused and therefore, highly dangerous 2.9-mile monorail system. Two are way outside the city and the remaining four are actually through the Detroit/Windsor tunnel in Canada.

As for the rest of Michigan, I now know why Hemingway spent most of his time in Europe. The upper peninsula is all nature, beautiful landscape, very few people. The lower peninsula is industry, factories, people, power, money and politics. If you live in the upper peninsula with all the Finns, you're known as a Yooper. If you live in the lower peninsula, especially in the south-west, with the Dutch, on a good day the Yoopers will call you a Troll, if they refer to you at all. On a bad day it could be anything under the sun.

On the other hand, you have to admit that Michigan helped Hemingway to hone and perfect his writing style. As there were so few people in the upper peninsula when he was young, and those there were couldn't speak much English, the only way he could make himself understood was by using short, simple sentences. So much. For all the high-flown. Theories. About how the great man. Honed and perfected. His writing. Style.

Mississippi

Mississippi is like a riverboat gambler. On an off-day. It has a fantastic deck of cards, but it doesn't know how to play them. It's got history. Pre-Civil War, Civil War, post-Civil War, cotton, the civil rights movement. It's got the Mississippi, that ole man river known to the Algonquin Indians as Michi-sipi, the Big Water, which flows 1,000 miles from Cairo, Illinois through to the Gulf of Mexico. It's got riverboats, gambling, bars, clubs, high livin', singing, dancing – the works.

It's got the blues. Bessie Smith, W. C. Handy, B. B. King. And at Rupelo is one of the holiest of all America's holy shrines, the birthplace of Elvis Presley where, for $1.50, you can see where the great man used to . . . No, it's too disgusting to even think about. But every year thousands and thousands do, and hand over their money as well.

It's got a full stack of writers: William Faulkner, Tennessee Williams and, of course, Samuel Clemens, who I blame for the mess Mississippi is in now. As soon as he started on about the 'great Mississippi, the majestic, the magnificent Mississippi rolling its mile-wide tide along, shining in the sun', and making out it was the centre of the world, everybody turned and ran. The same applies to Dickens in England. I'm convinced that if he hadn't gone on and on about Chatham, today it would be a world-class city. Well, that's my opinion. Clemens has his, I have mine, and I'm sure never the Twain shall meet.

And to cap it all, it's got the second-oldest continuously occupied governor's residence in the country.

In theory, then, it should be New Orleans, San Francisco and Williamsburg combined. Instead it's a nice, quiet, sedate little backwater. Jackson, the capital, in the very heart of the deep south, is . . . well, the capital. Well planned, well laid out, small, clean, antiseptic. A bit like Atlanta's little brother, but without the billboards. But don't get me wrong: I love the place.

Occupied no fewer than four times by Union troops during the Civil War, Jackson was finally more or less reduced to dust and ashes. But the locals reconstructed their lives, their fortunes, their town. The Old State Capitol, where they decided to secede from the Union, is still standing, though now it's the Old Capitol Museum. The New State Capitol, built in 1903, is still known as the New State Capitol, which can only mean that so little work has been done inside it that it is still in brand-new, sparkling condition.

I went to my first state fair in Jackson. It was like a cross between a summer fête and an agricultural show. There were all the usual stalls selling all the usual junk, all the usual games and competitions. The difference seemed to be the noise, the booze and the people. The noise was unbelievable. There were boom-boxes everywhere. The booze was apparently unlimited. I've never seen so much of the stuff disappear so quickly, although judging by the reaction it was creating, I think it must have been mixed with something else. As for the people, most of them looked as though they could start a fight in an empty room. The worst were what they called the 'gangbangers', who are like piranhas with attitude. A whole swarm of them would suddenly appear from nowhere, completely surround a stall or a group of people and pick everything clean. Some of them will even take the clothes off your back.

Most of all I like Jackson because they serve the best Guinness I've ever had in the States. It's better there, would you believe, than in Boston. Not chilled to death like you normally get, but room temperature, beautifully poured, with a nice, rich, thick head on it. I landed there once, as we Irish say, on St Patrick's Day. The restaurant was practically deserted, and service was non-existent, but the Guinness! Gee, I'm beginning to feel thirsty already.

Outside Jackson, the place seems to be full of what they call antebellum houses, although from my little knowledge of Latin I'd have thought they ought to be called prebellum houses. But obviously the Americans not only speak better English than me but better Latin as well. Along the roadsides, almost everywhere you look, there are gangs of prisoners – those wearing green stripes are non-violent; black stripes means violent – hacking away at the grass, tearing up trees and generally clearing the place up. Keeping an eye on them are mounted warders armed to the teeth.

'So would they shoot if . . .' I asked one old hash, who looked like Buffalo Bill on a bad-hair day.

'You bet your goddamned,' he said. Etc. etc. etc. 'Some of 'em are probably just prayin' that one of those guys is goin' try it one day.'

If Mississippi is a riverboat gambler on an off-day, Vicksburg has thrown all its cards out of the window and stomped off for a sarsaparilla and a dash of cherry. Here's a town that should be the centre of everything. It has more to offer than Gettysburg, Mount Rushmore and Graceland, Tennessee combined.

At one time, admittedly because it was living off the back of the slave trade, it was the richest city in the country. Come the Civil War, it was the prize both sides wanted. President Lincoln, when he wasn't busy knocking back the mercury, called it the key. The Civil War, he said, could never be won until he had the key in his pocket.

To collect the key, federal forces fought their way southwards from Illinois and northwards from the Gulf of Mexico, capturing town after town after town. Once they had control of the Mississippi, Union troops and supplies would be able to pour into the south. This would also isolate Texas, Arkansas and most of Louisiana, which between them made up around half the Confederacy and provided it with most of its troops and supplies.

During the winter of 1862, the battle for Vicksburg began.

On one side were the Union troops, led by Ulysses S. Grant, the great failure. A failed farmer, a failed estate agent, even a failed West Point cadet. But a great soldier. He won the first major Union victory of the Civil War at Fort Donelson, Tennessee, and then the Battle of Shiloh Church, also in Tennessee. On the other side were the Confederate troops, led by Lt Gen John C. Pemberton, a Pennsylvanian and West Point graduate.

First Grant tried to attack across the river. But failed. In desperation he marched south and crossed the river at Bruinsburg, well south of Vicksburg. He then struck way out east to Jackson, fighting off southern attempts to stop him at Port Gibson and then Raymond. On 14 May he took Jackson. He then swung west and headed towards Vicksburg along the old southern railroad track. Again he met Confederate attacks, at Champion Hill and Big Black River Bridge, but he fought them off. On 19 May he reached Vicksburg. He attacked immediately. But failed. On 22 May he attacked again. Again he had to pull back. But he had the Confederates cornered. There was no way they could escape. He decided the only answer was to hammer them into the ground. He began blasting the city from the land and, using iron-clad gunboats, from the Mississippi.

Forty-seven days and 16,700 casualties later, on 3 July, it was all over. Grant demanded unconditional surrender. Pemberton refused. The meeting broke up. The following morning Grant gave in and agreed to let the Confederates off if they signed good-behaviour paroles not to fight again. He also allowed the officers to keep their sidearms and their horses.

The Mississippi was now in federal hands or, as President Lincoln put it in that catchy, homespun manic-depressive way of his, 'The Father of Waters again goes unvexed to the sea.' Which makes you wonder what on earth it would be like trying to have a conversation with him over breakfast. But it took a long time for the wounds to heal. The Mississippi might have been unvexed, but for years afterwards Vicksburg refused to celebrate the Fourth of July.

Then there was all the fuss about the state flag. For nearly a century the state flag featured in the top left-hand corner of the Confederate cross. For years black residents bitterly complained. Most white members tended to shrug their shoulders and say, 'So what?' But they would, wouldn't they? Then, suddenly, in 2000, the Mississippi Supreme Court ruled – surprise, surprise – that actually the state flag had not been the state flag since 1906, when the legislature forgot to include it in a codification of state laws. Whether the mistake was made by a black member or a white member, they didn't say. Now it's back to the drawing board. They need to come up with a brand-new design. With or without their Confederate symbol.

Now, what could be more exciting than commemorating the Battle of Vicksburg? OK, OK, I know in the end it was a defeat, but that's not the point. I'm talking the United States of America. It's history. It's action. It's excitement. Vicksburg should be the centre of the world. Gettysburg was important, but the capture of Vicksburg was a thousand, well, all right, a hundred times more crucial. Apart from putting the key into Lincoln's unvexed pocket, it opened up the whole North American waterway system, enabling ships to sail all the way from the Ohio River Valley to the Gulf of Mexico.

So there should be bars all over the place, casinos on every street corner and every kind of restaurant you can imagine. But there isn't. The town is nothing but shacks, lean-tos and mobile homes. Practically everything looks as though it is collapsing, even the best hotel in town, and there's hardly a bar in sight.

About all they've got are riverboat casinos, and there are so many of them along the length of the Mississippi, from northern Minnesota to the Gulf of Mexico, that I wonder if the only reason they dug the river was so that they had somewhere in the centre of the country to put them. Not that they are what you and I would call riverboat casinos, first of all because they're not exactly riverboats. They're more boats on stilts on the edge of what might be a river. What happened was – such

301

innocence – that a law was passed saying that riverboat casinos were OK on the river. In other words, on the Mississippi River and its navigable tributaries. So of course, the big boys just moved in, dug huge ponds and stuck a casino in the middle of each of them on stilts. Then they built mini-canals and trenches connecting the ponds to the Mississippi, and hey presto, they were not only in business, but it was legal, too.

Neither are the casinos exactly the traditional casinos that Clemens kept on about, 'long and sharp and trim and pretty' with tall, fancy-topped chimneys and pilot houses that were 'all glass and gingerbread'. They're more low and thick and squat and scruffy; the kind of place where you actually expect to get nothing for something. I went on one that was actually on the river proper which was so dirty it should have been closed down. Or sunk. Not that it seemed to make any difference to the punters. They sat glued to the slot machines, huge mountains of food in one hand, buckets of quarters in the other, feeding the coins into the machines non-stop for hour after hour after hour. One guy I noticed had on his Italian-style suit. There was spaghetti all down the front. The woman he was with – it must have been his wife – was so old about the only thing that wasn't wrinkled was her teeth. They gambled all day and every day, they told me.

Did they win?

'Naahh,' they whined, like a pair of demented rhinos.

So why did they do it?

They both shrugged and turned back to the machines.

The Vicksburg National Military Park in town is supposed to give you a tour of the battlefield. But it's run by the old women at the National Park Service, and by the time I'd finished reading all their granny notices – federal law prohibits relic-hunting; federal law prohibits the use of metal detectors; federal law prohibits weapons of any kind; picnicking is only allowed at the USS *Cairo* Museum and at Tour Stop 12; fires and camping are not allowed; pets must be leashed or physically restrained at all times; do not climb on cannons or monuments; do not disturb plants or animals; whether driving, hiking, jogging or bicycling, be alert to potential hazards; avoid running on steep slopes; watch for fire ants and poison ivy; severe thunderstorms can develop quickly at any time of the year – be prepared to seek shelter; report all accidents to park rangers, who are here to help you – I'd forgotten who the hell Lt Col Grant was, which side Pemberton was on and why everybody was fighting over the manufacture of something you rubbed on your chest or, better still, somebody else's.

Instead I headed for the nearest bar, where miraculously I stumbled across that rare thing, a happy man. Not only that, he had just hit the jackpot as well. But he wasn't a gambler. He was the local, friendly, neighbourhood bail-bond officer.

A suspected drug-dealer had been arrested at Jackson Airport. He'd been taken to court and bailed for $1 million. Within minutes of the case being over, the local, friendly, neighbourhood bail-bond officer told me, he was approached by a mysterious lawyer offering him a suitcase containing $2 million, enough to cover the bond, court expenses, tax and a donation to charity for causing so much trouble to the court. He took the suitcase, paid the money into court and secured the release of the young prisoner. Bail-bond officers work on commission, and his cut for ten minutes' work $50,000.

'Gee,' I said, in my best Mississippi drawl. 'The guy was lucky getting out so quick.'

'No way,' he drawled back, taking another gulp from the 5-gallon tank of Dr Pepper's strapped to his belt and spittin' it out on the floor – I told you the bars in Vicksburg were rough. 'He was probably dead within the hour. They don't like their people being caught. They also don't like paying out even one dollar, never mind two million.'

'You mean . . . ?'

'Yup.' Another gulp. Another spit. 'Unless, of course, he was family. Then the guys who were supposed to look after him would have got it.'

Before becoming a bail-bond officer, he told me, after another spit, he had been a bounty-hunter.

In the States, prisoners can be remanded on bail by obtaining a bail bond. The person guaranteeing the bond puts down 10 per cent of the total bond. If the guy does a runner they have to pay the remaining 90 per cent into the court. Which is where the bounty-hunter comes in. For anything between 10 and 25 per cent of the bond, they find the runaway for the guarantor and bring him home.

'So which do you prefer?' I asked.

'Bail-bonding.' He shot another gallon of Dr Pepper's all over the floor. 'It's more respectable.'

With Dr Pepper's best friend, I spent a couple of days visiting the bail-bond officer's Mississippi. We went to beautifully furnished antebellum houses full of everything that credit could buy. To the back door. We went to apartments. The downstairs entrance. We also visited the real down-and-outs in ramshackle shacks and trailer parks. There, where there was a front door, we went to the front door.

Like everyone else, I know that in the US poor is not poor. More than 40 per cent of Americans defined as poor have an average family income of $13,200 a year and own their own homes. Ninety-two per cent have colour television sets, 72 per cent have one or more cars, 72 per cent have washing machines and 60 per cent have microwaves. And that's the way they want to live anyhow.

But this was not the statistics, this was reality. The poor people we saw were the other 60 per cent. They were living in filthy conditions. Most were desperate. Most were destitute. Most were black. Some even talked about share-cropping and pickin' cotton. We went to one shack in the heart of the delta, where I expected to see great bales of cotton all over the place. Instead there were nothing but smashed-up old wrecks. And there were lots of broken-down old cars as well.

There we found an old man, black face, white hair, greasy overalls, straight out of a Faulkner novel. He seemed just about ready to lie down and die. He owed over $500. He didn't look as though he had $5. Was he worried?

He shook his head slowly from side to side. No, he said. He was due his slavery cheque.

Slavery cheque?

He showed me a letter he'd received telling him he was eligible for $5,000 in slavery reparations. All he had to do was to send his Social Security number in the enclosed envelope, together with $100 to cover administration expenses, and he would receive his $5,000 cheque by return.

'Identify theft,' spat Dr Pepper's best bail-bond officer.

With the subject of slavery reparations more and more in the news – a group of high-profile blacks, led by Johnnie Cochraine, the lawyer who walks on water, I mean the lawyer who defended O. J. Simpson, are planning to sue the government for trillions – the crooks have moved in. The old man was lucky, said the bail-bond officer. Usually the letters say you are entitled to $500,000 and ask for $500 to cover administration expenses.

Talking of dodgy scams, one morning towards the end of my trip I ended up in some two-bit town called Clinton, on the edge of which a super-rich local woman had promised to build a racetrack that would transform their fortunes. Plans were drawn up for a string of hotels. Shopkeepers were planning to expand. Big promotion deals were being lined up. Then, suddenly, she changed her mind and everything collapsed.

Clinton, they told me, would never get over being let down by a woman.

South Dakota

I made only a rapid visit to Rapid City and a rush tour of Mount Rushmore, which is presumably why they are not called Slow Town and Ambling Hill. I also saw the big Crazy Horse memorial, which was, er, very interesting. But I enjoyed it. I'd like to go back there again some time and really explore the area; try to understand the local culture. I'll take a Greyhound bus tour.

I went there only because I was in Denver, Colorado and suddenly found myself with some time to spare. The choice was stay in Denver, not my favourite city, or to take a look at either Rapid City or Omaha, Nebraska, neither of which I'd been to before. As it happened, the first flight I was able to get was to Rapid City.

There was nothing rapid about the flight. It was typical American Airlines. We were late boarding and extra late taking off. And then, just as we were about to get airborne, the pilot slammed on the brakes. There was, he said, an awful smell on the plane. Being an old British Airways hand, I'd smelled it as soon as I got on, and naturally assumed it was the food. But it turned out that one of the air-conditioning systems had burned through. With the cockpit lit up by warning lights like a Christmas tree, there was no option but to turn back. The result was that by the time I got to Rapid City, my trip had to be even more rapid than I planned.

I grabbed the first limo I saw. Actually, it was a truck, but the guy driving it insisted on calling it a limo. I didn't want to waste any more time so I agreed. At least there wasn't an awful smell inside.

'Why are they called the Black Hills?' I asked.

'Because they look black at night,' he said.

'Don't all hills look black at . . .'

Careful, I thought. I'm already late and I've already been thrown off one plane today. Don't risk being thrown off a truck/limo as well.

'Sure,' I said. 'Of course. Of course.'

We swung along high roads and took a twenty-three-lane highway into some trees.

'So these are the . . .'

'Yup.'

Well this might have been the land of Wild Bill Hickok, Deadwood Dick and Calamity Jane, but to be honest, there was nothing spectacular about it. The Black Hills certainly looked far more exciting and spectacular from a distance than close up. But I suppose that applies to many things.

We swung and juddered along more highway.

'I suppose this gets packed in summer with all the tourists,' I tried again.

'Yup.'

'Bet you can't move for . . .'

'Yup.'

Then, suddenly, there it was. Mount Rushmore, America's shrine of democracy. Although why they go on about it being their shrine of democracy puzzles me. Does it mean that it's under only four presidents that they have had democracy? Do they mean that democracy in America ended with Theodore Roosevelt? Although I suppose when you think about the civil rights movement, Rodney King, all those illegal killings, the CIA and all those wars they've got involved in without ratification from Congress, that's probably about right.

But standing there, looking up at it, it's difficult to say what I thought, not being one for words. It certainly is spectacular. In fact, it's so spectacular, it's crazy. Can you imagine the scene when that all-American sculptor Gutzon Borglum first suggested the idea?

'Now let me see, Mr Gutsy Borgly, if I've got this straight. You want to make a sculpture of four of our greatest presidents.'

'Yup.'

Goodness me, it's catching.

'But, Mr Gusgly Borsy, you don't want to make it down here on the ground.'

'Yup. I mean, nope.'

'You want to make it, as I understand it, Mr Butsy Gorgly, up there on the mountain.'

'Yup.'

'Actually out of the mountain.'

'Yup.'

'Well, let me see now, Gutsy Baby, if I can call you that. It's much easier. I've never been able to handle anything longer than two silly-labels, or whatever you call those things. First I'll have to discuss it with the chairman. Then, no doubt, the mayor will want to have his say. There's an election coming up next year, and you can't be too careful, you know. Then we must consult the local people – surveys, that kind of thing. They might not like the idea of four presidents peering down into their backyards. Then there's the environmental-impact study, the safety assessment and the US Forest Service will have their views. Yes, I reckon it shouldn't take too long. Come back in 2025, by which time I'll probably be able to get your name right. As for your statue idea, you're crazy.'

The other thing that struck me, of course, was how on earth they actually built the thing. How could they work on that scale? How did they get the likenesses? How did they make certain nobody made a wrong move and half the mountain fell away?

Down on the ground there is a big presentation centre, two 125-seat theatres, a museum, an avenue of flags representing all the US states, commonwealths and territories and all that jazz. But I didn't have time for that. I was on a rapid visit. Another reason not to go back there one day.

A lasso-throw away is Keystone which, as far as I'm concerned, is the perfect little American town for four American presidents to look down on, although, not being surrounded by trailer parks, in Clinton's case, it's more the kind of town he would look up to.

At first I thought that with a name like Keystone it was going to be a cop-out. But it's for real. Imagine a mass of shops thrown together by a bunch of Disney World rejects and you have Keystone. Everything is not only fake western but throw-up fake western. There's a throw-up fake restaurant, Ruby's House. If this is her house, I hate to think what her garden shed is like. There's a throw-up fake Dakota gold shop, a throw-up fake goldmine shop, a yucky, sticky, really throw-up old-fashioned fudge shop. Then there are all the things Washington, Lincoln, Jefferson and Roosevelt stood for: the

World's Greatest Bargains Store, a Discount City USA store and a Bargain Store store.

If you can't stand too much excitement, be warned. In order to give Keystone the flavour of a typical American town, at any moment of the day or night, two gunmen will leap out into the middle of the main street and shoot each other dead. But this is such a common occurrence nowadays, whichever part of the States you come from, that nobody takes any notice.

Another thirty or forty yups down the road was the Crazy Horse Memorial Carving, which, as I understand it, is a massive tribute to American honesty, truthfulness and integrity because didn't they promise Crazy Horse the earth, agree a truce, wave white flags in the air and then literally stab him in the back? On the other hand, I suppose, less controversially, it could just be a tribute to the wide range of injustices to which the Indians were subjected and the mountainous holocaust on which America was built, not to mention the slaughter, persecution, land-grabs, slavery, racism and corruption.

If you look at the leaflets, read the brochures, study the books you'll think the Crazy Horse Memorial is like Mount Rushmore only bigger, better and more impressive. All I can say is, it isn't. They've only just started it. Well, I say, only just started: that stern, strong, unyielding face was actually carved over fifty years ago. Apart from that they've pencilled in, as it were, the outline of his horse's face, and that's about it.

'So how come . . . I thought . . .'

'Yup.'

'But the leaflets and books don't actually say . . .'

'Yup.'

'So when will it be . . . ?'

'Yup.'

For all that, you can see that once it is completed, it will be one of the wonders of the world. Crazy Horse's face is nine storeys high; the head of the horse alone another twenty. storeys high. So when will it be completed? First, they've got to raise the money. Mount Rushmore was government-funded. Crazy Horse relies on support from, I suppose, the descendants of many of the people he killed and butchered. The sheer scale of the thing is mind-boggling. Even with all the latest technology, all the state-of-the-art drilling, specially developed explosives, engineering and rock removal needed just to carve the horse's head will, they reckon, take decades. So, knowing how history relegates its heroes to the dustbin, it should, with a bit of luck, be finished just about by the time everyone's forgotten who Crazy Horse was. But not, let's hope, who stabbed him in the back.

If it wasn't for that I'd have thought the money would have been better spent looking after the live, or rather almost live, Indians holed up on the casino-free Oglala Sioux reservation at Pine Ridge, North Dakota. Or maybe even on finishing the National World War II Memorial in Washington DC which, amazingly, still hasn't been completed, in spite of the number of Vietnam memorials the Americans have managed to finish in every town and village throughout the country.

After Crazy Horse, it was crazy decision time. The Flintstones' Theme Park which, I was told, was awash with brontosaurus burgers, Yogi's Jellystone Park or Custer State Park? I took a stand and went for Custer State Park, one of the biggest state parks in the US and home to 1,500 bison. In the old days, when US presidents were the size of mountains, bison were everything to the Sioux. They ate them – buffalo meat was a million times better than beans; they dressed in them – buffalo skins provided everything from cloaks to moccasins. They also used the skins for boats, buckets, shelters, even saucepans for boiling water. From the bones they made knives, spears, spikes, axes.

'Hey. You cook?' the driver suddenly asked me.

'Nope,' I said.

Then he was off.

'Can you make a Montana Medley?'

'Nope.'

'Tagines, lamb. Rus el hanout spice mix. Slug of bourbon. Great. Real great.'

'Yup.'

'What about a Chicken Yamoon?'

'Nope.'

'Chicken grilled with summac berries. Onions . . .'

'Wait a minute. Isn't this where Custer—'

'. . . pine nuts . . .'

'Where Custer started exploring the—'

'. . . ground mountain thyme laced with . . .'

'Black Hills?'

'. . . and all covered in . . .'

'And they found gold around here—'

'. . . olive oil.'

'—somewhere.'

Then it was restaurants. Which were my favourite restaurants? Who were the chefs? How many awards had they won? Did they have any secret ingredients? He'd read that you could mix chilli with everything: coffee, chocolate, even Coke. Had I tried?

The trip back to the airport wasn't rapid enough, I can tell you. But I will return. And next time I'll take a cookery book.

South Carolina

Scarlett O'Hara is alive and well and, yo, flouncing it around all over the place. Except, hell, look at her, she's no longer in Georgia, she's living in South Carolina.

I don't think I've been anywhere in the States which not only feels Civil War but, y'hear, still in it. At first, I used to think it was just showbusiness, the good ole boys doing the dandy thing jest for my benefit. But yore onna, suh, the more I go back there and rattle my chains, the more convinced I am it's for real. They don't regret the last 150 years. They don't even consider themselves to be resting between engagements. They believe they are still living the Civil War. It's in their blood.

If the poor colonials were invited to such a low-class thing

311

as a ball, the house would be 'garlanded in roses', with 'vases on every mantel and brackets filled with fragrant flowers'. The women would be in 'gorgeous costumes of real lace'. The gentlemen would be sampling 'Scotch or Irish whiskey'. About midnight, supper would be announced and the hostess would lead the way to the dining room. On the table there would be the meagrest selection of 'cold meats, salads, salamis, galantines quaking in jellied seclusion and an infinite variety of à las'. Side tables with flowers 'trailing from the tall silver épergne in the centre to the corsage bouquet at each place' would be groaning with 'fruits, cakes in pyramids or layers or only solid deliciousness, iced and ornamented; custards, pies, jellies, creams, Charlottes Russes or home-concocted sponge cake spread with raspberry jam encircling a veritable Mont Blanc of whipped cream dotted with red cherry stars; towers of nougat or caramel, sherbets and ice creams served in little baskets woven in candied orange peel and topped with sugared rose leaves or violets'. On the drink front there would be 'various wines in cut-glass decanters, each with its name carved in the silver grapeleaf suspended from its neck; iced champagne deftly poured by the waiters into gold-traced or Bohemian glasses'. Illuminating the scene would be 'wax candles in crystal chandeliers, and on the table, in silver candelabra'. After dinner it would be back to the floor for more dancing, and when it was time to leave 'a plate of hot gumbo, a cup of strong black coffee and enchanting memories to sustain them on the long drive to their abodes'. The poor dears.

Most of them, I swear, are convinced they were on the sea wall the day in 1861 when General Pierre Beauregard ordered the bombing of Fort Sumter out in the middle of the harbour, which started the whole thing off. In the elegant eighteenth-century houses with their Georgian porticos and Adam fireplaces and Hepplewhite chairs and, of course, immaculate gardens, the talk is not of Civil War but of the War of Northern Aggression, the War between the States or even the Great Period of Unpleasantness.

Accept an invitation to an antebellum house, a real one not a tourist one, and you will find that the whole atmosphere is Civil War, or rather, the War of Northern Aggression between the States during the Great Period of Unpleasantness. And remember, these are not houses, they are plantations. A house is about the size of a bus shelter. Everything else is a plantation.

The old Civil War families, the Middletons, the Montagus, the Pinckneys, the Ravenets and the Rutledges, who all look and dress like Colonel Sanders' younger brother, are still the old families, and as snobbish and as degenerate as ever their English ancestors were. Except that you can bet your life their English ancestors did not have an Australian accent.

One family of hoots I met not only had a house, sorry, plantation full of antiques which, to me, at least, did not look all they were cracked up to be, they even had their ancestors' name, Earl Grey, embroidered on their teabags. But fair's fair, they made me feel at home. Whenever I went to speak to any of them they immediately gave me a pair of kneepads. That's southern hospitality for you.

The talk is still Civil War talk. Lincoln, they tell you, is a disgrace. Note the present tense. General William Tecumseh Sherman is 'that horrible man' and, Lord a' mercy me, is it only three weeks to the Debutante Ball at the Hibernia Hall? The food is Civil War food, especially those damned grits. Which not only look like dollops of sloppy cement they taste like dollops of sloppy cement.

Look at the menu for a typical day.

Breakfast: Pan-seared chicken livers in a crisp crust, buttermilk mashed potatoes, spicy tomato chutney. And grits.

Lunch: Seafood gumbo, currant bread pudding, rum sauce, home-made vanilla ice cream. And grits.

Dinner: Barbecued shrimps, porterhouse of pork; duck doused in a mixture of honey and pepper, salty country ham. And grits.

Heaven help us, they even hold a World Grits Festival, which runs from April through to October. The festival itself is actually in April, it's just that it takes until October to chisel all the grits off the plates.

By the end of the day I can't face even the thought of another bucket of grits. If only they had dumped the lot in the harbour, there wouldn't have been any Fort Sumter, any General Beauregard, any shooting or any Civil, I mean, War of Northern States Unpleasantness.

About the only thing not civil about the people of South Carolina is the way they serve their drinks. By the gallon. At first I thought this was just another example of traditional southern hospitality. Then I realised it was a reaction to traditional southern bar hospitality. Go into a bar in South Carolina and all you'll be offered is one of those silly little miniatures. Full-size bottles have been banned in the state since 1976. And since any change in the law requires not only two thirds of the votes in both houses of the state legislature but the majority in a state-wide referendum as well, they're likely to remain banned. What's more, the whole process can only be attempted in even-numbered years. Who said big bottles were invented by northerners?

Charleston in particular is more Civil War than the Civil War. Because it was neither wholly destroyed during the hostilities – General Sherman spared it rather than face the wrath of the Daughters of the Revolution – nor affected by the economic boom afterwards, it stayed the way it was. There was no money to renovate or rebuild. The result is that today there are no skyscrapers – no new building can be taller than the steeple on top of St Philip's Church – and no shopping malls. Or at least, not in the centre of town. All the columns and cupolas, you see, are real. So are the windows and the fanlights, the hardwood floors, the oak panelling, the brickwork, the fireplaces, the plasterwork. Even the cobblestone lanes are real. Dig up one stone and it has to be replaced by another of the same size, shape and colour. And it has to be put back in exactly the same place, position, angle and level of deference to the shoes on General Robert E. Lee's horse. In fact,

Charleston is about the only place in the States where if something looks very old, well 150 years old, you can bet Abraham Lincoln's stovepipe hat that it is 150 years old, not a pale, plastic imitation of something dreamed up by Walt Disney.

Not surprisingly, everybody raves about Charleston. So much so that – the greatest honour that can be bestowed on any American city – it is featured in any number of historically accurate and authentic films. *The Patriot*, for example, whose principal character was an English-hating landowner with an Australian accent, and which featured hordes of marauding British soldiers going around terrorising and burning towns, committing one atrocity after another and cold-bloodedly murdering innocent children.

They say Charleston is the most beautiful American city. Nonsense. It's the most beautiful English city in America. It was designed and built and civilised by the English, though admittedly bits of it look as though they could have been lifted from plates by Palladio and Inigo Jones. But it is still an English city, not an American one. You can tell just by looking at it. It's not like New York, which was built by the Dutch, all square and angular and everything at 90-degree angles. It's not like Boston, built by the Irish, which is all bars and clubs and balaclava helmets. No, Charleston is Jane Austen comes to America. All pride and prejudice but without the pewter.

The pride is everywhere. In the fact they have more Civil War and pre-Civil War buildings than anybody else; in all the narrow streets and alleyways and back passages with their pretty 'single houses' and yellow jasmine and wistaria and roses and azaleas all over the place. Pride in all the narrow, shuttered townhouses in Rainbow Row, once home to most of Charleston's big trading families, many of whom came from the English colony in Barbados. Go inside one and within five minutes you'll be expecting the whole tribe of Bennet girls to come bouncing through the door with Mr Darcy in hot pursuit.

They also take great pride in the Old Exchange, one of the most historic buildings in America, which looks like a Greek temple after the Romans dropped by; in Dock Street Theater, the oldest theatre in the whole of the States; in all the churches especially St Michael's and St Philip's of steeple fame, both of which are positively Christopher Wren. The only American one is the Circular Congregational Church, which is pure American fundamentalist. It's round to stop the devil from hiding in any of the corners. The original, designed by Robert Mills, a Charleston architect who also designed the Washington Monument, was destroyed in 1861, not by the devil but by a fire. And, gee whizz, are they proud of their antebellum mansions, especially Drayton Hall, with its great white columns, the antebellum mansion to end all antebellum mansions, not to mention Middleton Place, whose gardens were designed by André Michaux, the man who designed the gardens at Versailles. This is home to the famous Middletons: Henry, president of the First Continental Congress; his son Arthur, who signed the Declaration of Independence; grandson Henry, who was minister to Russia and governor of South Carolina. Well, they think they're famous anyway.

They're even proud of the fact that the only time Oscar Wilde was ever lost for words was in Charleston. Apparently, during one of his swings across the States, our Oscar landed in South Carolina. After dinner, no doubt feeling very boozy, he stepped out onto the porch of some famous antebellum mansion.

'Isn't the moon beautiful?' he sighed in that Stephen Fry accent of his.

'Ah yes,' said another guest. 'But you should have seen it before the war.'

All poor Oscar could do was chew his green carnation to bits.

What they don't talk about, of course, is their prejudice. And there's plenty of that around. All those pro-slavery Confederate flags, for a start, which they'll tell you are an innocent reminder of historic times past. Rubbish. Then there's their interpretation of the Civil War. You practically have to wrestle them to the ground before they'll admit that they wouldn't be where they are today if it wasn't for the slaves; that Sullivan's Island in the harbour was where slaves were kept for two weeks to be deloused before they were brought ashore; that the port handled over a third of all the slaves shipped from Africa and destined for the States; that of the 15 million who were shipped only 4 million survived; that all those pretty little townhouses were originally owned by people who, directly or indirectly, lived off the slave trade; that the Old Exchange was not some kind of nineteenth-century boot sale but a slave market; that all the servants or field workers on all those grand plantations were slaves; that still standing on a pedestal in Marion Square is a statue of John C. Calhoun, an arch-advocate of slavery, and finally, to reduce it to terms Americans will understand, that Porgy and Bess were both from Charleston.

I mentioned this to one ancient Daughter of the Revolution who had warned me in no uncertain terms that she was brought up to always tell the truth. 'Oh piffle,' she said in that tone of voice that took pity on me for not knowing that slavery was invented to add to rather than subtract from the sum of human happiness.

Colonel Sanders' younger brothers are not much better. Last time I was in Charleston I got into a discussion with a wet brain of a would-be senator. I asked him about President Bush's plans for a missile defence shield.

'I ain't pullin' my trousers down in front of nobody,' he twanged. And that was it. End of sophisticated political discussion about a project which could, I suppose, decide the fate of the world.

Yet plate-warmers, porcelain door knobs, petticoat mirrors, baccarat crystal chandeliers and all the other dang things that make up what they call the aristocratic splendour of the old south, they'll go on and on about. I was at a dinner once when another one of Colonel Sanders' younger brothers leaned across the table and confided that he was a great admirer of Red China. To this day I don't know whether he meant Red China or red china, if you see what I mean.

But nobody will tell you anything about the big slave revolt in 1823, led by a freed slave, Denmark Vesey, who had bought his freedom in 1800 with winnings from a local lottery. The slaves planned to take over the armoury, burn Charleston to the ground, slaughter anyone who got in their way, seize a string of ships and escape to Haiti. At the last minute they were betrayed by a fellow slave, and Vesey was tried, convicted and then hanged, on 2 July 1822.

What I don't understand is why a country that is always claiming to be a guardian of liberty, and which boasts a Holocaust Museum in Washington that commemorates the suffering and death of so many people who were not American in a country that was not America, has done nothing to commemorate the suffering and death of so many of its own citizens. If I had my way, I'd build a National Museum of Slavery on the site of the Old Exchange. The old flag-wavers wouldn't like it, but frankly, my dear, I don't give a damn.

The Salt State

Spill it or not, throw it over your shoulder or not, the salt state has just got to be Utah.

First there's the Great Salt Lake itself, which makes the Dead Sea look fit and well and healthy. It is so full of salt that not only is it impossible for anyone to drown in it, but the only organisms that can survive in it are blue-green algae and the occasional brine shrimp. For about thirty seconds.

Then, as far as I'm concerned, everything you hear about Utah has to be taken with not a pinch but probably a handful of salt.

Take the story of Joseph Smith, the man who founded the Mormons. While I'm quite prepared to accept that God is perfectly entitled to appear to whoever He likes wherever He likes, I'm afraid I have to take with a handful of salt any story about Him appearing to an eighteen-year-old crook, well known to the police, in New York, of all places. Let alone that he should bring with Him, presumably for His protection, New York being New York, even in those days, two angels called Urim and Thummin. Urim and Thummin? They sound more like Old Testament spelling mistakes than even the lowliest celestial beings.

From then on, I'm afraid the handful of salt grows to a block, and from a block to a whole Great Salt Lake covering over 1,000 square miles. Especially when I discovered that Joseph Smith relied heavily on his wife, Emma, and shared with her the daunting responsibilities involved in building up the church. It was she, for example, who compiled their first hymn-book. If that is not enough to hold against him, he also believed that the Red Indians were the Lost Ten Tribes of Israel. Really? And the Chosen Land is Nauvoo, Illinois. Oh yes, one day we will all reunite along the 'sacred' Rocky Mountains. All I can say is that if we do, it will be a miracle. I couldn't even get a car from Salt Lake City to the Salt Lakes, so how we're all going to get to the Rockies, heaven only knows. Maybe Urim and Thummin are still working on it.

Brigham Young, however, is not to be sneezed at, if that's the right phrase. Whether you agree with him or not – and I don't – he was obviously an organiser, a fixer and a superb leader. He was also, incidentally, a good carpenter, but maybe that goes with the job.

After Joseph Smith was murdered in 1844, Young reorganised the whole business and, like a modern-day Moses, threw out the troublemakers and led his flock into the desert. He then marched them, with far less fuss and bother than Moses marched the Israelites, over 1,000 miles to Salt Lake, where he built a whole new city. He ruled the city and the church for thirty years without, as far as I can gather, any help or advice from any burning never mind second-generation Bush.

While I can understand some of his teachings – baptism by immersion, nobody to be baptised until they're eight years old and so on – I cannot for the life of me see how on earth, being the man he was and given his beliefs, he could justify the practice of bribery and corruption. When the Mormons were fighting to have Utah recognised as a state, this pillar of honour and integrity grandly told his church elders to go forth and 'grease the wheels' in order to serve a 'higher cause'. Were they a bunch of one-eyed sleazeballs, or were they a group of highly religious, highly principled individuals? In any event, they succeeded, and Utah became a state in its own right. Which, of course, puts the row about bribery and corruption and Salt Lake City and the Winter Olympics of 2002 into perspective. If you can 'grease the wheels' for something as unimportant as establishing yourself as one of the fifty states of America, it stands to reason that you will do the same for something as grand as the Winter Olympics.

Then, of course, there's their special joy of sects: the whole polygamy business, which you have to take with another huge lump or maybe pillar of salt. Souls exist before birth, said our Brig. Therefore, the more wives a man has, the more children he has, the more souls will find a living home. That I find difficult to believe, too.

Now, had he come out and said that marriage was invented to ensure that men spent as little time as possible in purgatory, and that the more young, innocent, teenage brides he could lay his hands on, the more wives he had, not to mention mothers-in-law, the quicker he would go to heaven, that I could accept. Just as, being a typical reasonable, sensible, civilised man, I see the sense in the Mormon argument that if you ever happen to come across a wife you really like, you should keep her on for at least a second week.

I've got nothing against women, after all. I married one, didn't I? In fact, having been to Utah, I'm wondering whether, if I took a second wife, it would be bigamy. Or would people still think as little of me as they do now?

Utah

Well, what a letdown.

I thought Salt Lake City was going to be all frock coats, stovepipe hats, lots of 1950s Chevies, Bibles, choirs and pompous old buffers with muttonchop moustaches not spaking unto their eighteen young wives, who would all look as though they came out of someone's rib, not to mention their families of fifty-three children. And counting. A bit like the Amish communities you come across around Holmes County, Ohio, but without the horses. But, by the word of the prophet Moroni – no, it doesn't mean what you think it means – it was not. Salt Lake City was as modern, as wide-awake, as lively and as dynamic as a thousand other American cities.

What's more, they even have bars. Well, they're kind of bars. It costs you a $20 membership fee just to get in, and as soon as you do they give you a leaflet that reads: 'We train our beverage-servers to be alert for intoxication. They will advise our guests when switching to non-alcoholic refreshments has become necessary.' Obviously not written by any of the evangelists present at the marriage feast at Cana, this is to stop people having too much to drink and then getting up and going round the bar asking people how many mothers they have. As for switching to non-alcoholic drinks, forget it. You could live in either of the Salt Lake City bars for a month and not get intoxicated. The strongest drinks I came across were beers, none more than 3.2 per cent proof. Way out in the Wasatch Mountains, however, they brew their own special, homemade Valley Tan, so called because if they catch you drinking it these good, honest, Godfearing Christian Mormon gentlemen will tan the hide off you.

Nobody, though, was taking any notice of the local cinema, which was showing, believe it or not, a film called *Organzmo* about a Mormon missionary who gets caught up in the porn business. As for nightlife, apart from the girl in the lobby of the Hilton, who made out she was there solely to save souls, there didn't seem to be any.

But then, SLC, I mean Salt Lake City, was built by the Mormons. I mean the Church of Jesus Christ of Latter-day Saints. They don't like you shortening their name. Not to the Mormons, not to the Latter-day Saints Church, and especially not to the LDS Church. Brigham Young arrived here in 1847, when it was still part of Mexico. With him were 143 men, three women and two children. It was one of the most infertile places on earth. The ground was rock-solid. The lake was nothing but salt. It was surrounded by mountains. But they should worry – they brought their fertility with them. In addition, they also unloaded all the bare necessities of life they had brought with them to help them survive the harsh, unforgiving environment: pianos, sofas, rocking chairs and, of course, every survivor's number-one necessity, a rolltop desk. You don't believe me? Go and look at the Pioneer Museum. Between them they then laid out the city as it is today: 10 square-acre blocks surrounded by streets 132ft wide – 'wide enough for a team of four oxen and a covered wagon to turn around'.

Today the Mormons make up around 40 per cent of the city population and 75 per cent of the state population – the rest they call Gentiles – which is why it's the healthiest, hardest-working, longest-living and fastest-growing population in the US.

They are also not only the biggest doorknockers in town, they also seem to own most of the doors they knock on. They own a whole slice of the town centre, including the huge buildings from which their three-member First Presidency and their Council of the Twelve Apostles run what is now the world's fastest-growing church with 11 million members in 123 different countries. They organise convention after convention after convention and are in the process of building another massive 22,000-seater convention centre at a cost of $25 million, which they have paid for in cash. The Hotel Utah, recently refurbished for the use of church officials, has enough gold leaf to keep the prodigal son whooping it up for the rest of his life. Which is not bad when you remember that they claim to be a non-prophet organisation. Well, apart from Moroni, of course. Sticking to the Ten Commandments, or rather their version of them, is obviously good for business.

They also have city art galleries and museums and what looks like a particularly dodgy state ballet company whose various *pas-de-deux* would, without any shadow of a doubt, have steam coming out of the ears of our Brig, I mean Brigham Young, even though he was himself a pa-de-goodness knows how many. As for the different productions put on by the Utah Shakespeare Festival, I'm positive that many of them would not have been As He Liked It.

But the biggest surprise of all is that in Salt Lake City there's none of the in-your-face let alone in-your-wallet Sunday-morning knock-on-the-door Mormonism that we all know and

323

love. In fact, I reckon the average tourist could visit the place and not even realise the Mormons were around. Me? I can always tell a Mormon, but I cannot tell him much.

So if you can stand the idea of seeing out the rest of your days surrounded by earnest, dedicated, well-dressed, well-educated, soft-spoken, hardworking people who don't smoke or drink (no alcohol, no coffee, no tea, no Coke, no Pepsi – it's the caffeine), and queuing up for thirty minutes to pay your $20 to get a weak beer, SLC is a great place to retire. There's no real crime, doubtless because *Playboy* and other sex magazines are banned in the state prisons, and no real violence, well, no street violence, anyway. Utah also has more high-school graduates than anywhere else in the States.

They use the same modern technology as everybody else, except that the spell-checkers on Mormon-style computers automatically change all your 'yous' to 'thous'. They also ban access to any Internet sites other than Snow White. It's all good, clean, old-fashioned entertainment. Even the videos you rent from the local video store have the sex scenes cut out. The married women, I was told, spend their time watching doubles tennis because, like marriage, it's a game that enables one partner to glory in the mistakes of the other. Emphasis is on the family and family life. One night a week is family night. Then there's the weather. Nobody ever gets cold in Salt Lake City, but whether this has anything to do with polygamy I don't know.

One interesting, fun guy I met explained that he was a Jack Mormon, the non-practising Mormon term for a non-practising Mormon. The Mormons, of course, call them damned. His great-grandfather, he told me, arrived in Salt Lake with Brigham. Even at fifty-three, he said, the old boy was still taking teenage brides to add to his ever-growing collection.

We also discussed the more important things of life: the bars. Until recently, apparently, there weren't any. And if you went to a restaurant you had to take your own booze. You weren't even allowed to take full-sized bottles, only those little ones like the ones they used to give you on planes before they started getting mean and cutting back. Even today they still only serve mini measures: 1oz of alcohol compared with the 2oz you get everywhere else in the States.

'So what happened to all the Indians, the Navajos, the Anasazi and, of course, the Utes who used to live here before old Brig and his peaceful, Godfearing pilgrims arrived?' I wondered.

'Jesus Hubbard Christ!' he shrieked 'You sure know how to ask the questions. Look, I'll drop you off at the Catholic Cathedral. Not many people know there's a Catholic Cathedral in town, but the Catholics arrived here soon after Brigham Young and they still form the backbone of the old money. They seem to provide all the mayors. The Mormons just let them think they run the place.'

Another thing the Mormons don't tell you is that their first sheriff, James Ferguson, was an Irishman. Born in Belfast, he made a fortune in the California gold rush and then headed north. In 1848 he arrived in Salt Lake. Brig himself appointed Ferguson as their first sheriff. He also put him in charge of his own hand-picked, élite group of bodyguards. Much the same, I suppose, as Christ had his own élite team of bodyguards. From then on, for Ferguson, true to his heritage, it was a roisterous life of posses, arrests and hangings, often all in the same day, then afterwards writing, acting, qualifying as a lawyer, starting a newspaper and dying of the drink at the grand old age of thirty-five.

So much for the beverage-server advising him when to hit the non-alcoholic stuff.

As for the Mormon holy of holies, Temple Square, it might be big, around 10 acres, and right in the middle of town, but it's no Vatican City. Neither is it a Bible theme park like the 15-acre Holy Land Experience in Orlando, Florida which, as you would expect, sells Goliath burgers. It's more of a large parish garden populated almost entirely by smart young women who sidle up to you when you're not looking and ask you whether you would like to be transported to heaven. But I had my answer ready, honed on many a Sunday-morning doorstep.

'Tell me,' I gazed earnestly into the eyes of each heavenly body who stopped me in my tracks. 'Do you believe in the hereafter?'

'Oh yes, yes, yes,' they would sigh, hands clasped, gazing up to the clouds.

'Well, in that case,' I grunted, 'hereafter will you leave me alone.'

It didn't work, of course. It never does with the Mormons.

The Tabernacle, home of – what do they call that world-famous choir? – is spectacular. The acoustics are absolutely unbelievable. If somebody drops a pin at one end of the building, at the other end, precisely 175 feet away, the optimum distance to run whenever you hear that knock on the front door on a Sunday morning, you can hear it as clearly if you had dropped it yourself. Unless, of course, another 50 million visitors are tramping through the door ooh-ing and ah-ing, complaining about their feet and begging for the rest-rooms.

The Salt Lake Temple, with its six spires, is not so hot. It's what a Presbyterian cathedral would look like if they ever got round to building one, let alone even mentioning the word. The Assembly Hall is an assembly hall; the two visitors' centres are the Vatican designed by Walt Disney. All deep carpets, enormous Michelangelo-meets-socialist-realism-with-a-dash-of-Norman-Rockwell-style paintings, circular ramps, a huge statue of Christ and deep, rich, booming, all-American accents. If these doorknockers ever heard Christ speaking in his own voice, I swear it would blow their minds, and if I ever heard Christ speaking with a Mormon accent, it would blow mine.

But, of course, far more important than all this, and the place that draws the crowds, is the Mormons' Family History Library, where they reckon they have details on everybody who has ever lived. I was tempted to check out the Biddlecombes. But in the end I didn't. I mean, can you imagine the shame if, after all these years, I discovered we were not related to Henry VIII, that Marie Antoinette was not a great-aunt, that Lily Langtry was nowhere in the family tree and that the Biddlecombes were genuinely respectable. But there are plenty of people I know who must be related to people like King Herod, Judas, Shylock, Hitler and George Bush. It would be fun to check them out. Maybe next time.

Yet wandering around SLC, visiting the various Mormon sites, try as I might, and oh Moroni, I've tried, I can tell you, I still can't for the life of me understand what it is they believe in. OK, they are Christians, because they believe in Christ. But not necessarily in everything He said or did. They believe in the Old and New Testament, although not necessarily in all of them, either. Then there is this guy Moroni. Who the whatever is he, and where does he come from? And if they're not allowed to drink tea or coffee or Pepsi or Coke, why aren't there so many rules and regulations in Salt Lake City about drinking them as there are about alcohol? And what's all this business about Mormons taking an oath of resentment against the United States for not capturing and punishing the man who murdered their founder, Joseph Smith? If that ever got out, I could see every Frenchman the world over queuing up to take the oath for him, too. In French, of course.

But at the same time you've got to admire the Mormons. There are plenty of other similar, well, vaguely similar religious groups that are nowhere near as big or as rich or as dominant. There's one led by Owen Allred somewhere or other in Montana called something or other. There are the Strangites, the Original Church of Jesus Christ, founded by Joseph Strang in Wisconsin. There's the Bountiful Commune up in the north of Idaho, on the Canadian border, run by Winston Blackmore, who has over thirty wives, one, presumably, for every day of the month. And then there's the odd bunch of Messianic Jews wandering around.

Perhaps the reason why the Mormons survived is that they really believe in whatever it is they believe in. They give 10 per cent, sometimes much more, of their gross income to the church. They help the poor. All I did was turn up in Salt Lake with my old suit on and they were falling over themselves to help me. Admittedly, they were helping me to leave town as soon as possible, but at least the thought was there. And, dedicated, hardworking, muscular Christians that they are, they also do everything they can to get everyone to smarten up, pull themselves together and get out there and get themselves a job, a family and start paying their 10 per cent dues to the church like everyone else.

Many Mormons also spend a great deal of time overseas, building churches, helping the poor, standing on empty street corners preaching to nobody in sight and, of course, signing up as many converts as they possibly can. So successful are they that they reckon that if they maintain their present rate of 250,000 conversions a year, in fifty years' time they'll have a worldwide membership of 250 million, which will put them up there with the big ones. In fact, it's probably just as well I admire them so much, because I will undoubtedly be a Mormon myself one day. You see, another of their beliefs is to go around baptising the dead to ensure that, whether they want to or not, they too will have to spend all eternity in a drinkless paradise with Brig and all his followers watching porno films about Mormon missionaries. So be warned. Slamming the door on them on Sunday mornings will do you no good. You might as well invite them in for a glass of lemonade, because they'll get you in the end, dead or alive. I know they've already got my name on the list.

Coming back to life in Salt Lake City can pose some problems for the dedicated missionary. While I was there, for example, a group of Brigham Young University student punchies were banned from watching the family-rated Brad Pitt movie *Fight Club*. They got together and formed their own Fight Club where, surrounded by hordes of screaming, near-hysterical men and women – mostly women, I gather – a bunch of punchies left-hooked to the breadbasket, right-crossed, left-jabbed, landed any number of jarring little uppercuts and duked for fresh air.

'So how come,' I asked one smart suit, collar-and-tie Mormon I met in one of the visitors' centres, 'you can't see the movie but you can watch the real-life action?'

'Easy.' He gave me the Sunday-morning smile seen on a thousand doorsteps. 'The movie is shown early in the evening, and that violates our family-evening regulations. The real fight takes place after the family evening is over, so it's OK.'

Next question: how many Brad Pitts are there skewered on the head of a pin?

Many of the Gentiles, locals to you and me, criticise the Mormons. Over a glass of orange juice – I know, I know, but I couldn't spare the time to queue up outside a bar, become a member and hand over $20 all for one small, weak, practically non-alcoholic beer – a happy-clappy charismatic went on about the Mormons turning the place into a magnet for the poor and destitute from all over the States.

'If you come here, not only do you get money from the Mormons but also from the state social benefits system. Because that is run by guys who are Mormons as well, it is fast, efficient and generous. What more could they want?'

While he no doubt had a point – the only poor man I saw the whole time I was there was the one staring at me out of the shaving mirror every morning – I felt he could hardly complain. After all, the Mormons were here before him, and if he didn't like it he could hitch his wagon like Brigham Young did and go off somewhere else. With or without a couple of dozen teenage brides.

The fact is, however, that it's not just the poor who are heading for Salt Lake City but the well-off, too, in spite of those bars and their damn-fool notices. Salt Lake City is a great place for companies. Thanks to good old Brig and his eight-wives policy, it has the youngest population of any city in the US. And these young people are well educated – all their tattoos are spelled correctly – well mannered, hardworking, dedicated, loyal and have a greater interest in life than money. What more could any cynical, hard-bitten human-resources manager want?

There is, though, as there always is in the States, a drawback. Drugs. Salt Lake City has a big undercover drugs scene. It is said to have more meths (that's short for methamphetamine) labs than anywhere else in the world, each equipped with a small hand-operated machine capable of turning out over 10,000 pills an hour at a cost of next to nothing. It seems one of the well-educated, well-mannered, hardworking, dedicated, loyal Mormon missionaries with a greater interest in life than money went off the rails and switched sides. And, as I'm sure Brig would agree, converts always have far more enthusiasm than a group's original members. So for all its uptight, buttondown image, it cannot be long before Salt Lake City becomes known as Salt Angeles, and instead of being Mormons its citizens will be Shakers. Which is not to be sneezed at.

The reason for the drug problem is obvious: the lack of booze. In the old days it took half a bottle of Scotch before you had the courage to hit the tranquillisers. Now, because you can't get a drink, it's straight into them.

Sorry, Brig. You made a mistake there.

The Fruity States

Can you think of any fruitier place on earth than California? It's like a lush fruitbowl full of lush fruits, especially around the Bay area of San Francisco. I don't think I've ever come across anywhere in the world that has not only more fruit, but more exotic varieties. California seems to cater for all flavours, all tastes and all diets. You've only got to listen to people talk to realise that fruit is embedded in their psyche. They hurl fruit, they juice their lights out, they hit the office juiced up to the eyeballs. Everyone is a fruitfly. Not only that, but their appetite seems to know no bounds. Five times a day they have to have their fruit: for breakfast, at lunch, after lunch, before dinner, at dinner.

Trouble is, not every fruit-hustler let alone fruit-juicer is a greengrocer, and not every fruit bar serves fruit drinks. My God, is it any wonder I'm confused? They even think brussels sprouts are a fruit. The clue, of course, is their state nickname, Golden State. After Golden Delicious.

Florida comes a close second. In fact, it runs California so close that it's difficult to tell where one ends and the other begins. Fruit is Florida's biggest industry. The reason why that well-known fruit Ponce de Leon discovered it in 1513 was that he'd heard about their Florida fruit diets, the Keys to the Fountain of Youth, which he wanted to take back to the ladies of Spain along with all the other little souvenirs he'd picked up in the New World. The problem was, as anyone could have told him, the Florida Keys have little to do with youth. The sea

331

is only as blue as it is because of all the blue rinse leaking into it every day of the year. At the other end of the scale, as well as of the state, the millions going through Orlando are too young even to be counted as youths. And that includes the grown-ups.

As for Vermont, it's not just fruity, it's sticky as well. Tacky sticky. Throw-up sicky sticky. To try to give themselves a bit of class, the locals called their state after the French name of the Green Mountains that cover practically the whole of it. But because they're not the international sophisticates you would find in, say, North Dakota, instead of settling on Mont Vert they twisted it round and called themselves Vertmont. Likewise, the tree state is the maple sugar; the insect state is the beehoney and the place whole covered in is syrup maple.

Ask for eggs and bacon for breakfast, and they drown it in syrup maple. Order a hamburger for lunch and they drown it in syrup maple. If you have an ice cream afterwards and it's made by Ben & Jerry, window out of throw it. When they launched their worldwide empire from a converted petrol station just north of Waterbury, they kept on and on about being New Age entrepreneurs. They weren't doing it for the money, they were doing it for fun. Employees were not employees, they were friends. What was more, they were only going to pay themselves what they paid other people.

So what happened? As the business grew and grew they very quickly stuck a cornet up the level-salary deal. Then, when the time came to cash in their chocolate chips, having spent years running down the evil multinationals and promising and promising and promising that they would never ever sell out their integrity, compromise their freedom or surrender to big business, instead of going for a plain vanilla they went for the full tutti-frutti with nuts on and sold out to – a multinational.

For that they deserve to be frozen alive in a tub of syrup maple cream ice. Without nuts on. Theirs.

California

Suddenly, the traffic lights went dead. Shops turned black. Factories came to a standstill. The hotels started handing out torches. In Silicon Valley, the world's greatest concentration of hi-tech companies, they were even reduced to using paper and . . . what's that thing called with a black lead running through the middle of it?

The most economically powerful and most densely populated US state – its economy, the sixth-largest in the world, is almost as big as the US drug rehab industry – transformed in an instant into a Third World country. Except that everything was *très* lavender and they made sure they reserved enough electricity to keep the chair going.

'So what are you going to do about it?' I once asked a minor eco-pinhead politician who was complaining that he had what he called an overhand, which I did not dare ask him to explain.

'Shucks,' he groaned, or some such word. 'We're going to pass a law getting people to turn off their windscreen-wipers whenever they go under a bridge.'

Everything about California is unbelievable. It's not just a different world, it's a different planet. In a different galaxy, in a different solar system. All covered in peach paint.

Ask an energy-hog businessman the time, and he'll press his Mickey Mouse watch. Mickey's voice will announce, 'Hey, the time is thirty-seven minutes after twelve. Wow.' He'll also tell the businessman it's time for him to go to the gym.

Listen to a group of women with fantasy hair and on Paxil up to their newly sliced cheekbones doing lunch. They'll be talking about the joys of giving birth – dolphin-assisted birth – and about how important it is that children are taught to communicate with their psychiatrist at as early an age as possible.

At the theatre, Gertrude does not accuse Hamlet of being 'fat and scant of breath' and Falstaff is not a 'roasted Manningtree ox with the pudding in his belly', because that's sizeism, and sizeism is against the law in California. On the other hand, Mark

Antony will beseech the crowd: 'Friends, Romans, countrymen, lend me your earrings.' As for the opera, nobody but nobody wants the Prince to marry the Princess at the end of the show. When, of course, he does, the whole audience rises as one, squeals in horror and throws their handbags at the stage. They then give everybody the slow handclap.

California is like one of its big, horrible, healthy bowls of muesli: nothing but fruits and nuts. And if you take away the fruits and nuts – especially the nuts who keep la-la-ing to themselves 'Search for the Hero Inside Yourself' – all you're left with are the flakes. So much for Californication. The people are just plain crazy. So much so that even if you don't have your own personal, private psychiatrist, people still think you're crazy. Not that they're identifiable people anyway. They're wannabes – the wildest, most outrageous wannabes in the world. They all wannabe somebody else: a model, an actress, a sportsman, a singer. Anyone up to their nose in selective serotonin re-uptake inhibitors. The most pathetic case I think I ever heard about was the poor, stressed-out businessman who desperately wanted to be a father – to prove to his psychiatrist that he wasn't impotent. And not only do they all want to be somebody else, they want to look like somebody else as well. They even play games over lunch and dinner . . . What am I saying? They even play games over the single slice of red pepper they call lunch and the three delicate strands of angel-hair pasta they call dinner, begging people to guess who they look like. One old bag who seemed to have been overdosing on the testosterone to jump-start her libido once asked me which famous film star I thought she resembled. I took one look at the beautifully styled hair, the bright, sparkling eyes and long, thin, delicately manicured nails and said, 'Lassie.' That did it. The old dink she was with wanted to take me outside, give me a good thrashing and sue me for a million dollars, but he got himself so worked up that his wig kept skewering all over the place and he couldn't see where he was going.

Not that I blame them. Half of them look as though they've

just been rescued from a disused tank of permatan. The only thing that saves them is the reflection in their lip gloss of Da Vinci's *The Last Supper* tattooed on the tips of their tongues. And that's just the men. Well, I say men. It was only when I went to California that I realised that homophobia had nothing to do with being frightened of going home. The other half do nothing but trawl the streets and bars with their Beverly Hills Triple AAA teeth and more zinc in their sunblock than was used to galvanise the Golden Gate bridge, desperately looking for their fantasy gynaecologist.

Everybody says they're an enviro-extremist health fanatic, but that's not my impression. They're so laid-back that the only exercise they seem to get is valet-jogging. Whereas I'm no fitness fanatic, but many's the time I'm out four nights running. If I get the chance.

The reason they're the way they are, I used to think, was drugs. I mean herbal narcotics. But it isn't that. Then I wondered whether it might be because they still haven't got over the fact that Nixon, of all people, was born in Yorba Linda, just east of Los Angeles, where his upbringing was to prepare him for the life ahead of him. His father was a failure at Yorba Linda: their orange farm there gave him the pip and very little else. So they moved to the suburbs proper, where Mr Nixon Snr ran a petrol station and grocery store. From then on it was downhill all the way. Nixon became a lawyer, a failed businessman – he couldn't even sell orange juice to the Californians – an assistant attorney-general, a Republican, a member of Congress, vice-president, owner of Checkers, the dog, defeated governor, president, and then I forget what happened to him. For a time I also thought that perhaps it was because they still hadn't got over it being Nixon, again, who established the Environmental Protection Agency, public-service broadcasting, affirmative action and the biggest leap ever made in the US towards a welfare state.

But in the end I decided that it's neither of those things. It's just that they're naturally a bunch of athletically correct body

Nazis given to bike-rage; a group of androgynous, slack-faced, platinum-haired, android, silicon tank-top jocks with $200 haircuts who are obsessed with their southern polar passage and can't wait to shed their surfer duds to get in touch with their inner natures by absorbing Buddhist chants and dangling a pendulum over their scrotums for six hours at a stretch.

Not that there's any point in trying to talk to them when they're in their gym shorts and sneakers and green shirts, because you can never understand a word they say.

'Good morning. How are you? Nice day,' I always begin politely whenever I step over a treehugger.

Then they're off. They're riding so goofy. They were in the middle of a vegetable shuffle. They were lucky enough not to get amped. All around them were half-pipes, shifties, stiffies, indies, pokes, bonks and jibs. They felt badical. They went postal. Any minute now they're going to go whoopass and hit it in both directions.

'Yes, of course, but it makes a nice change to see the sun,' I go on.

Do I want a chin check? they invariably respond.

'Well that's very kind of—'

And then they're off again. Am I some form of fitshaced, friendasaurus looking for a sesh? If so, they know a hyper-tweaked chopsocky who would be only too pleased to give it to me.

I'm sorry, but although I lean over backwards to try to accommodate them, I can't. Whether you understand what they are saying or not, they talk nonsense.

If it's not the shock of living in the same state as Nixon used to, maybe it's the food. California has one of the wildest attitudes to food it is possible to imagine. I say food, but they've got so many rules and regulations you're scared even to look at the stuff in case you drop down dead on the spot.

Meat? If you so much as glance at it you'll not only die of cancer, but your reproductive system will seize up and your whole body will be covered in sodium-nitrate sores. Fish.

Smoked, shell, with dips. My God, I can see the magnesium coming out of your ears already. Eggs? Global salmonella. Touch one and you and your descendants will suffer from microbial contamination for ever. Your descendants will probably all end up as one-armed waiters as well.

Pizza. With up to twenty slices of pepperoni on it, it's a dairy product. So you'll be dead from cholesterol by tomorrow morning. With over twenty slices of pepperoni on it, it's a meat product. So you'll be dead from cholesterol by tomorrow afternoon. Bread gums up your intestines. Butter. Hello? Can you hear me? Can you hear me? Cream. In a plastic sachet: plastic-sachet poisoning. Not in a plastic sachet: there's no such thing in California. Sugar. All your teeth will drop out, your heart will stop. You're practically dead already. Ice cream will make your hair drop out. What little you've got left. The dioxins will block your tubes and you won't be able to tell whether it's strawberry ice cream you've been eating or something else.

Even mineral water and vitamins are bad for you. Just one half cup a day and you'll end up looking as though someone opened the sluice gates at both ends.

Now, don't get me wrong. I believe in a balanced diet as much as the next man: a large bloody mary in each hand. But it's not just the regulations that stick in my throat, it's the whole surrounding lacto-ovo vegetarianism, fruitarianism, virtual kitchen spirituality they dress it up in. The result is that thirty minutes after arriving in California I'm already beginning to feel guilty about going into a passing restaurant and ordering a quick, simple meal of genetically modified dollops of foie gras decorated with hummingbird tongues, followed by a huge slab of psychedelically marbled Kobe beef from pedigree Wagyu steers massaged daily with the finest sake.

In this climate of fear, lunches and especially dinners become the weirdest occasions in the world. Instead of the usual drink-as-much-as-you-can and tell-as-many-silly-stories-as-you-can and to hell with what the wife says when she decides it's time to leave early because of some daft promise she made to a babysitter who doesn't exist, everybody goes on and on and on about what they can eat, what they can't eat, what they are allergic to, what they are not allergic to. At one dinner party I went to, as well as all the usual grumbles from the veggies, somebody didn't like the buckwheat in the bread, somebody was allergic to pistachios, somebody wanted to know how close the pasta had been produced to some power station or other, three people were on about power lines, one woman moaned about the mustard, another took out a dirty plastic spoon and measured her own sugar into the coffee and everybody complained about the amount of lead in the glaze on the plate.

In the end, of course, it gets to you, and like everybody else, you end up going into restaurants and ordering a typical Californian meal: veg and two veg. Raw, not cooked. The real food comes later: a couple of handfuls of Lipitor and Zocor cholesterol tablets. Sometimes, I admit, it is boring, but in one restaurant it came with the most delicate aromas: a combination of peppermint foot lotion from the earnest, New Age, muesli-scoffing drop-out sitting at the table to the left of me and an overdose of vitamin C moisturiser from the totally tubular eye candy to my right. I tell you, it took all my determination not only to shovel it down, but to keep it down as well.

Not the rest of them. They were all doing their level best to bring theirs up. They say there are no anorexics or bulimics in California, but you try getting into a toilet, or rather a bathroom, in a restaurant anywhere between San Diego and the Oregon border at lunchtime, let alone the evening. It's impossible. Then, the following morning you can't get anywhere because the highways are jammed tight with people rushing off to their psychiatrists to confess their sins.

As if that wasn't bad enough, when I got back to my hotel they were going bananas about their annual tofu festival. There was nothing for it but to hit the bar. They were serving green cocktails. Would I like a sweet, refreshing, nutritious organic apple martini with 7Up; an organic apple Manhattan, puréed

338

organic apples with Calvados; or organic apple juice, organic honey and a shot of vegetarian vodka? It was no good protesting. I was hungry, I was thirsty, I was in the advanced stages of orthorexia nervosa. I had one of each. If I'd known what the rest of the state was going to be like, I would probably have had six or seven.

The apple-cider martini towns – 1oz vodka, ½oz cinnamon vodka, 1oz calvados and 2oz apple cider – such as St Helena, Rutherford, Oakville, Yountville, Sonoma and the whole of the Napa Valley not only lift my spirits but I also lift quite a bit of theirs as well. The problem is it's completely unlike any other wine-growing area I've ever been to. The vineyards are not vineyards, they're estates. The vineyard-owners are not vineyard-owners, they're alcohol-farmers. The grapes are not grapes, they're fruit. The wine is not wine, it's a meritage blend. The last thing anyone should think of doing with it is drinking it. Life, they used to say, is a cabernet, old chum. Not any more it isn't. There are so many warnings plastered up all over the place that you daren't risk even looking at bottles of the stuff.

But soon it might all be over. Not the restrictions, the vineyards themselves. They are being attacked by a glassy-winged insect which could literally wipe them all out unless – irony of ironies – they start using all the kinds of chemicals called carbaryl this and chlorpyrifos the other that they have up until now insisted on slapping on California's bad pesticide list. Who says God isn't a jealous, old-fashioned, traditional French vigneron?

In spite of everything, while they are still there the vineyards are worth visiting. Some people sneer at the big wineries like Christian Brothers, Domaine Chandon and, of course, Mondavi's. Not me. I'm not prejudiced. I take them all in, as well as the so-called boutique vineyards such as Screaming Eagle, Stagi Leap and the Hess Collection, although maybe it's just the names that appeal to me.

Some of the restaurants are also among the best restaurants I've ever eaten in. But be warned: the talk is all technical wine talk. Vineyard land is selling at $100,000 an acre. A 5-acre stretch in St Helena with an ordinary house recently went for over $4 million. A château no bigger than a garden shed in Sonoma is on the market for around $10 million. And, gee didyahear, there's a corkhead in Napa Country wants to build a house the size of St Peter's, Rome with a wine cellar at floor level as big as the Sistine Chapel, completely made of glass so he can sip his cheap plonk looking down on his very own valleyful of vines being eaten by the glassy-winged insects.

Malibu, which has the J. Paul Getty Museum, built with the money he made charging people for the use of his telephone at his home, Guildford Place in Surrey, is also apple-cider martini country. Of course, it's pure California. Who else would even think of building a museum in the style of an authentic first-century AD Roman villa, complete with air-conditioning, but an American? It works, though.

The green-apple martini towns – 1oz vodka, 1oz calvados, 1oz frozen green apple purée and a cup of crushed ice – such as San Diego and Palo Alto, the heart of Silicon Valley, are where it's @, or at least where it was @ until all the recent dot-commotion puréed the whole area, plunging most of the local tech-heads into what they call sudden loss of wealth syndrome.

San Diego, famous as the birthplace of the Egg McMuffin is, they say, the ultimate urban success story. In American terms, that is. It has the best marine display in the USA, two superb art galleries, a string of fantastic museums and a reproduction of London's famous historic Globe Theatre where, according to the guidebook, 'You can even buy an authentic English tart while enjoying the performance.' For years it was either somewhere you passed through on the way to Mexico or a dead end. Many people even thought it was an island somewhere in the Caribbean. Not any more. Now it's a rip-roaring, bustling, action-packed fun city in its own right. This is partly because the National Weather Service of America promotes it as being 'the most ideal in all America' with sunshine, sea breezes and a balmy constant temperature between the late 60s and 70s practically the whole year round, partly because, as Los Angeles has continued to expand and develop, people have moved out and on to San Diego, and partly because of the growth pushing up from Mexico. But most of all it is due to the efforts and the strides San Diego itself has made towards putting itself well and truly on the map. Not just as another city, but as a city for the family.

Within minutes of the centre of town is Balboa Park, which must rate as one of the finest city-centre parks in the world. Well, apart from all the others. Then there is Mission Bay, nearly 5,000 acres of beautifully reclaimed land with play areas, marinas, hotels and restaurants which have well and truly reclaimed San Diego's reputation. Further out of town is Coronacho, the island that shook a nation and toppled a king. For this is where, it is said, King Edward VIII when Prince of Wales, met Mrs Simpson. Even further south is Baja, which most people recognise for its shopping and Mexican food, but which to animal-lovers, or rather mammal-lovers, is one of the five-star spots in the world for dolphin-watching.

What San Diego is really famous for is, of course, its zoo, although I sometimes wonder whether the animals, or rather the 'endangereds', are behind bars for our protection or for theirs. A zoo of a different kind, where a wide range of exotic creatures are continually at each other's throats, is Silicon Valley: silly because people were silly to invest all their hard-earned money in dot-coms which had no track record, no practical technology, no management and virtually not the slightest idea of what they were doing and where they were going, and con because that's what all the hi-tech companies and their advisers persuaded them to do. Believe me, IPO does not stand for initial public offering. It stands for it's probably overpriced. I thought everybody knew that.

When I first went to Silicon Valley – I had this great hi-tech idea – nobody had heard of Stanford University, now probably the highest hi-tech university in the world, which started the whole thing off. It was because of Stanford's outstanding reputation in electronics that Bill Clinton, like all politicians everywhere a fierce advocate of public education, insisted on sending his own daughter there for her private education – in history. In those days Palo Alto didn't even have a taxi stand. All it was famous for was fruit. Now the only fruit it has is Apples. But its core operations have generated more money than any other patch of dust in the history of the planet, although I wouldn't mind betting there are a couple of back streets in India where they can strip down a giant, organic, light-emitting, ultra-thin, stereo, web tablet, Windows-powered jet black, complete with 13in diagonal OLED colour display, that goes all fuzzy when you switch it on and reassemble it again blindfold in about three-and-a-half minutes that would give them a run for their money.

Stretching 40 miles along Highway 101, with its giant bill-boards yelling: 'Forget French – teach your children to read ticker', the valley runs through Redwood City, Menlo Park and Palo Alto, Mountain View, Los Altos, Sunnyvale and Santa Clara to San José, where once, I remember, they welcomed a high-powered delegation of Filipino businessmen with the stirring slogan, 'Tuloy po kayo'. Unfortunately, *tuloy po kayo* doesn't mean welcome Filipinos, it means circumcise all Filipinos. It is the richest area in the world: at one time over sixty new techno-yuppy millionaires were being created there every day because, being in California they got paid three hours earlier than they would have been in New York. By the time the New Yorkers got into the office, they'd already milked all the technology stocks for all they were worth, taken their money and gone off to the pool.

Not surprisingly, the whole area was suffering from a severe dose of the affluenza. It had the second-highest property prices in the US after Manhattan. A single family home, for example, would set you back around $750,000. If prices went any higher, they said, not even the rich would be able to afford to live there. With 40 per cent more men in town than women, Highway 101 was continually blocked with eye candy pouring in from all over the States. MbRSD? HHOJ. GAL.

Then came the dot-com crash and it was a case of dot-come what may. Affluenza turned into double pneumonia. As the entire dot-com boom dot-com bombed, over US$3 trillion disappeared off the face of the earth, let alone the screens, 20 per cent of the industry went bust and 40,000 jobs went up in smoke. Every ticker in town came almost to a complete stop. Suddenly, Silicon Valley was full of tech-wrecks and what they called MOPs, millionaires on paper, and Highway 101 was not so busy any more.

But shed not a tear for them. The alpha males may all look a touch omega, but they've still got the garage made of clicks and mortar where William Hewlett built his first typewriter and television set combined. Nola's Bar still serves warm Anchor Steam pale ale, and if you're looking for something to do at the weekends, it still costs around $100 million, depending on who you know, to buy a secondhand F16 supersonic combat aircraft from the Defence Department. The 2 square miles along Sandhill Road, venture-capital country, are still responsible for investing nearly $7 billion in the dot-com business, more than one third of the total venture capital invested in the whole of US industry.

And everybody still goes on about how hard they work; how 100 hours a week is the norm; how they haven't got time to breathe. I'm not surprised. Not only do they take their dogs, their lap cats or their parrots to work with them, they take their children as well, and spend half their time in the office running around taking the damned kid outside every ten minutes, playing Teletubbies with the dog and shouting at their lap cat. I'm surprised they get away with 100 hours.

I remember visiting one company, in Irvine, that was counterfeit Nintendo game meets car-crash television. The place was like a kid's playground. There were toys and games everywhere, and the noise was worse than at a football match. And if that wasn't bad enough, one of the senior executives, a woman, turned up to lunch with her baby. I didn't go back there again, I can tell you. Two minutes out of the door and it was splitsville.

I was, incidentally, surprised at the size of their offices. I always thought that people working in microcomputers would have micro offices, but rather than downsizing they were supersizing.

Fast catching up Silicon Valley is Telecom Alley, out to the east in the Sierra Nevada foothills around Nevada City. Gone are the days when you could sit in Moore's Café all morning with a black coffee wondering why on earth, if the worldwide web was invented at CERN, the big high-energy physics laboratory outside Geneva, Switzerland, it was the Americans who exploited it. Surely European scientists could have done what American chip-heads did (although admittedly around 25 per cent of the companies in and around Silicon Valley are run by ethnic Chinese and Indian immigrants). Surely European universities could have done what Stanford did? Surely a European Silicon Valley could now be stretching all along the Franco–Swiss border? Or wondering where it was all going to end. Some people, nano-technology theorists, believe that the speed of technology today is so fast that it won't be long before molecular-level assemblers begin generating everything from low-cost solar power through cures for cancer to the rebirth of the dinosaurs. In other words, robots can beget robots. Who's going to control them? Who's going to make certain the technology doesn't fall into the wrong hands? What happens if it does fall into the wrong hands? What the hell? Who cares, so long as I know where the next bloody mary is coming from. Now Starbucks are moving in. They're already in Green Valley; soon they'll be in Nevada City and the old days will be over.

The super, fantastic idea I took to Silicon Valley? Well, between you and me, everybody is talking about transferring the printed page to the screen. What I want to do is transfer the technology of the screen to the printed page. In other words I want to build a mass-market version of what we geeks call a 20-qubit quantum computer which, apart from running the entire universe, would bring the printed word to life in a way no other technology in the world has yet done. For example, you're now reading about Silicon Valley. To see a picture of Silicon Valley, all you would have to do is stand in front of any screen – a PC, television, anything – point this very book at the centre of the screen and then double-click on this page. In other words, tap your finger twice anywhere on it. Do it properly and you would not only have access to the whole world of new screen technology, but it wouldn't cost you a penny in access fees, usage fees, anything. The name of the service: Biddle.com.

To become a shareholder in this exciting new company, all you have do to is send just US$1 million direct to my lawyers, S. Windlers, Krooks and Thievis, Cayman Islands.

Well, why not? If all the others could raise so much money for their hare-brained ideas, why can't I?

The two grown-up sour-apple martini towns – six buckets of apples, a tanker of apple schnapps, a DeKuyper sour-apple pucker and an Olympic-sized swimming pool of vodka – are, of course, San Francisco and Los Angeles. San Francisco, or rather San Fran, is, like it or not, one of the world's great cities, along with New York, Paris, Hong Kong, Cape Town or Luan Prabang. That fabulous setting. The Golden Gate bridge. The ships. Alcatraz. The cable cars. The fog. I mean the haze created by all the drugs. The streets littered with drunks and dopeheads who have every right to be there. Because, according to the impeccable logic of Sue Berman, a member of the San Francisco Board of Supervisors, the streets are the home of the drunks and drug-addicts. So, just as the ordinary American has the right to get bombed out of his mind in the privacy of his own home, so the drunks and drug-addicts who live on the streets of San Fran have the right to get bombed out of their minds in their home, the streets of the city by the bay. Or Junkiedom.

Fisherman's Wharf is the world-famous Fisherman's Wharf,

a collection of tatty souvenir shops, fast-food joints and some pretty indifferent restaurants. But because it's San Fran, it's not Fisherman's Wharf but, wowee, *F-i-s-h-e-r-m-a-n's Wharf*! It's the same with Ghirardelli Square. Ghirardelli Square is just a pedestrian precinct, full of what you find in every pedestrian precinct in the world. Tatty souvenir shops, fast-food outlets, ice-cream parlours, a fountain, restaurants, a hundred buskers. One I saw had so many hooks and eyes and 6in nails sticking out all over him that he reminded me of the people I always get stuck behind queuing up for security checks at airports.

Chinatown is CHINATOWN. It's bigger than China. Well, maybe not bigger than China itself, but it certainly has more Chinese living in it than in the whole of China. The Cannery and Jackson Square with the Transamerica Pyramid are just as famous because they're not Fisherman's Wharf or Ghirardelli Square.

North Beach is North Beach, birthplace of the Beat Generation, the greatest literary movement in the history of the world, hang-out of Allen Ginsberg, Lawrence Ferlinghetti and, of course, the legendary Jack Kerouac, who was such a wild, way-out rebel and drop-out that he used a 120ft-long roll of toilet paper to explain in 125,000 words of barely punctuated near-prose why he drove all the way across America thinking of his friend, Dean Moriarty, meeting people who kept saying, 'What t'hail' and continually being accused of talking absolute bullshit to get to California, which had air, he said, 'you can kiss'. Which shows you how much he knew about California. Try kissing the air there today, sunshine, and you'll be dead by the time the fog clears. *On the Road*? It should have been called *In the Gutter*.

I can't remember much about the Beat Generation – I was more into the question of Schrödinger's Cat and whether or not the whole thing is a *reductio ad absurdum* of orthodox quantum-mechanics theory – but I cannot imagine that they were literate and well-read with a love of the classics. I reckon the only reason they ended up in North Beach was that they got Coit Tower, a well-known landmark, mixed up with something else. But by the time they had chilled out it was too late, although their presence has obviously had a lasting effect on the area.

And while we're on the subject, will somebody please tell me why, if North Beach is in California, South Beach is 3,000 miles away in Florida? Maybe if Kerouac had had another 120ft-long toilet roll and more of the readies, he could have told us.

Then there's everything else that makes San Fran San Fran or, if you prefer, Frisco Frisco. Whispering-pine muzak, pagan drumming circles, Ethel Merman memorial choirs and management conferences. San Fran management conferences. I was once summoned halfway round the world to attend a management conference in San Fran, the main feature of which was what they called a function check. I discovered just in time that this involved the delegates gathering together somewhere in the woods outside town, sweating off their inhibitions in a steam room, smearing each other with crushed herbs, banging away on drums for hours on end, chanting their heads off and then, finally, hugging each other to Kingdom Come. I can't remember exactly why now, but for some reason I didn't make it. I think I missed my connection somewhere between Fukuoka and the Transamerica Pyramid.

Los Angeles, Raymond Chandler's 'big, hard-boiled city with no more personality than a paper cup', the world centre of muscle-drug sales, is exactly the same, but different. It's wilder, crazier, more extreme. Of the forty-four biggest cities in the US it is rated bottom of the heap for fire, police and ambulance services. It also has less industry. All the big companies are pulling out, and 95 per cent of those left employ fewer than fifty people. This is where Kerouac and the Beats should have ended up.

They speak the same kind of highly specialised language: 'spiel' means to talk. 'Chirp' means to sing. 'Legit' means legitimate theatre. 'Zitcom' means a television series aimed at teenagers. A fax, though, is a facsimile transmittal. They have the same regard for literature. On one trip I was invited to what I was told was going to be a literary evening. It was called 'Big Love – an evening of plus-sized poetry. Snacks available.' I quickly discovered a feasibility study I hadn't written.

There is enough material in LA to fill as many caffeine-addled books as it would take, if you placed them side by side, to cover the entire length of Kerouac's trip across the States. There's the mix of people. Gone are the days when Alexis de Tocqueville, some kind of French Alastair le Chef, reckoned there were only three races in America: Anglo-Americans, native Americans and African slaves. The Franco-Americans he obviously considered more than a mere race – more gods in their own Champs Elysées overseeing the antics and activities of this disparate bunch of strange humans below which was le totalement tosh. Guess who's coming to dinner? is no longer a question you can answer in black-and-white terms. Ask the question today and you'd get over 125 different answers. Poor, rich, super-rich, black, white, yellow, brown and every colour of the rainbow. LA is made up of the blacks in South Central, the Mexicans in Broadway, the Japanese in Little Tokyo, the Vietnamese in Little Saigon, the Koreans in Koreatown. There are more Koreans in Koreatown than anywhere else in the world outside Korea. Then there are the Thais in Thai Town, the Indians in Arcadia, the Scientologists around, appropriately enough, Ron L. Hubbard Way. The gays are in West Hollywood, where it's against the law to call anyone a pet-owner, on the basis that any form of ownership is wrong. Instead they have to be called pet guardians. Wait till my dogs hear about that. Finally, the Iranians. There are more Iranians in LA than anywhere else outside Iran.

There's every activity you can think of: lying, cheating, scheming, double-crossing, beating up innocent people in front of live closed-circuit television cameras. It's violent, but surveys regularly show that nearly 70 per cent of middle America fights over whether LA is more frightening and even more lawless than Miami or New York. Some even rate it the danger capital of the US. They're the ones without guns.

The people are also very weird, even by Californian standards. Los Angeles is the seven ages of tan. Everybody wears a tank-top. Everybody pushes their bare midriff between your eyes. Everybody also probably has a facelift, a tummy-tuck, gastric long-limb laparoscopic bypass surgery, a duodenal switch, half a million collagen injections, a failed liposuction operation and a throbbing souvenir melanoma to their name.

They're also, if such a thing is possible, even more health-conscious than the most health-conscious types you could possibly imagine. Talk about surfing and skateboarding and egg-white omelettes and whatever they call that ice-skating on land (I'm told Disneyland can always be relied upon for providing a good ride). It makes you wonder what on earth they would do if they had to go out and work for a living like the rest of us.

Then, of course, there's the whole Hollywood, Sunset Boulevard, Beverly Hills thing. Here, they say, all the girls are looking for husbands and all the husbands are looking for girls with a couple of showreels tucked inside their sweaters. It is so unreal it could only be in America. Everything is valet-parking – hotels, restaurants, stores. Even valet parks have valet-parking.

The hotels pile luxury upon luxury, I suppose to help adults enjoy adultery as much as they enjoyed infancy. I'm still reeling from the Beverly Wilshire, the Biltmore and, of course, the Bel-Air. They used to say that when good girls die they don't want to go to heaven, they want to go to the Bel Air, the long-time favourite of such famous, fun-loving, gregarious, serious, sensible types as Howard Hughes and Greta Garbo. But they don't say that any more because there are no good girls left in Los Angeles. All the same, if there's anything to be said against the likes of the pink stucco Beverly Hills Hotel, with its notorious Bungalow 8, the Peninsula or even the Four Seasons on Doheny Drive, discretion is the better part of valets.

The restaurants are all full of overtanned sleazeballs who

have clearly overdone the reverse-crunch sit-ups and women who look as though they've all been mislaid so many times they don't know which way to turn. Even the waitpersons – there is no such thing as waitresses or waiters any more in the States – seem so laid-back it's difficult to think of them in a vertical position. In the unlikely event that they found themselves in a vertical position, I'm sure they would pull themselves through.

I think they've yet to discover what restaurants are for. I went to one fantastic restaurant once. Everybody else ordered bananas and sat there munching them the whole time. I felt almost embarrassed eating my run-of-the-mill Hollywood pizza topped with smoked sturgeon, genuine handmade horseradish cream and smeared with golden caviar; then my rack of lamb, asparagus, roast artichokes, Niçoise olives, cured lemon, black olives and chips, followed by a sweet something that appeared to be the result of a road accident in Tennessee.

I was promised that, to make up for my embarrassment, the following evening I would be taken to the best restaurant in the whole of Los Angeles. I ended up in the Ginza Sushi-ko, a tiny Japanese hang-out in a Beverly Hills office block which had two tables and nine chairs. We gorged ourselves on about 2½ cubic inches of something that looked like mashed whales' eyeballs.

Finally, of course, the one thing I know nothing about: shops. All I can say is, there are so many of them in LA that it's no wonder they are not only all maladjusted but

Damn. The power has gone off again. I can't possibly do any work without the air-conditioning. I'm going to go and have one of those organic apple mint vodka smashes, or whatever they call them. If, of course, there's enough ice. That's how California gets to you.

Florida

When I first went to Miami it was Alzheimer's Little Acre, full of fossilised old fruitcakes who had all destroyed their better halves. Millions of world-weary, crumbling little old ladies in the full Miami: white shorts, white shirts, white shoes and dripping with blue rinse. In spite of all the agony and unhappiness they probably caused in their lives, even I will concede that most of them didn't deserve to be as old as they looked. A few of them even made you wonder whether death was going to make much difference to them.

God's Waiting Room, everybody called it. *Time* magazine, in its usual clipped, succinct, punchy style, intoned deeply that the 7-mile-long island had degenerated so rapidly that it could 'fairly be described as a seedy backwater of dust-ridden hotels, gaudy condominiums and decaying apartments – lifeguards spend more time assisting heart-attack visitors on the sand than pulling foundering swimmers out of the surf'.

Today it's a totally different enchilada altogether. The state that invented the McFlurry, a gungy mix of ice cream and candy, is a fast-moving, fast-growing, high-octane, hip-hopping, slick, twenty-four-hour-a-day city. Big flashy hotels, fancy restaurants, some of the most fashionable and most expensive shopping in the whole of the States. What am I saying? In the whole of the world. The trouble is, it's no longer American, it's Hispanic. You've practically got to be able to speak Spanish just to order an ordinary chilli con carne, not to mention a couple of bottles of Rioja to go with it.

Landing at Miami Airport, you haven't got a hope in *infierno* of ever finding your castanets, let alone negotiating your way through the Control de Pasaportes without getting them crushed, unless you can speak Español. Fight your way into a limosino, and you're unlikely to end up at the address you want unless you can tell the matador where you want to go. In Spanish. Order a guacamole at a small, *tradicional* Yankee restaurant and you'll probably get a mucho huge dollopo of mashed avocado on top of a cornmeal pancake unless you

351

chatto up the señora behind the bar. In Spanish. Forget the señoritas. They get so many offers they can't remember you from one gaucho to the next.

You read in the *périodicos*, I mean newspapers, about how the Hispanics are taking over the States; how in 1492 there was only one, Chris the Colon, but today there are more American Hispanics than there are American blacks – 35.3 million compared with 34.7 million – and how, in five years' time, they'll not only have got back everything they lost, but they'll be running the whole place. Actually, they're already running the place. In five years' time they'll also be running the people who are running the place.

In Miami I've already seen it happen. Well, maybe not literally seen it happen, but I've seen the results of it happening.

In the old days, if you had a gardener or a maid, they probably came from Alabama or Mississippi. Today, 15 per cent are likely to come from Central or South America, 15 per cent from the Caribbean, 65 per cent from Mexico and they're all 180 per cent likely to be illegal immigrants. In the old days, if there was any muzak in the stores and offices, it would be Liberace plays Bach. Now you can hardly go anywhere without being blasted by a son, a danzon, a bolero or a guajira.

In the old days it was practically impossible to get a cab, so clogged up were the roads with wheelchairs and funeral cars. If you failed to stop one, the driver was probably on the run from New York. If you did stop one, it was odds-on that the driver would be from Jamaica, Barbados or one of the other Caribbean islands and in his first week in Miami. If you couldn't understand a word he said, the chances were he was from Kansas or Nebraska. If he was polite, civilised and spoke perfect English, then likely as not he would be from Haiti. Get a cab nowadays and you get a tour of Latin America.

The increase in the number of Hispanics in the States has been so dramatic that they are talking about translating those stirring lines on the Statue of Liberty, 'Give me your tired, your poor, your huddled masses yearning to breathe free, the wretched refuse of your teeming shore . . .' into Spanish: '*Aqui está mi pasaporte. Ho venido por pasar las vacaciones.* I'll get a job as an odd-job man/gardener/babysitter for a leading politician who makes fine speeches about equality but keeps me out of sight, refuses to give me any papers and pays me less than the minimum wage.'

In many ways, however, Miami's transformation into the enormous booming, non-stop, runaway, capitalist success it is today is all down to one man: Fidel Castro. Without him it would still be God's Little Alzheimer's Waiting Room. Why on earth he continues to protest that he is a socialist, goodness only knows. Donald Trump would be even more insufferable if he had achieved one tenth of what El Grande Barbe has achieved in Miami. Can you imagine the number of books he'd be churning out telling us what an even greater guy he is, how he did it and how he only loves them for their brains?

Cubans and, of course, what they call hyphenated Cubans, Cuban-Americans, make up one third of Miami's population. Even the mayor, Joe Carollo, is a Cuban-American. And, of course, there are as many different Miamis as there are Cuban-Americans with opinions as to what should or should not have been done with little Elian. All of them equally unreal and equally implausible.

First, there's the original Miami, Miami Beach which, somehow or other, even after all these years still manages to live down to its image. Ibiza with a baseball cap and rollerblades it is not. You're not even allowed to drink on the streets. If you even look as though you might, you'll be behind bars for the rest of your life. I wish.

All the same, it's a must. If you only have time to go to one place in the whole of Miami, go to the famous Fontainebleau Hotel, which is pronounced the correct Miami way: Fountain Blue. It's the kind of hotel that gives luxury a bad name. It's . . . it's . . . it's just so Miami, you'll never believe it. Lots of colour, lots of curves, lots of deep, deep pile carpet. Lots of crazy statues. It's also so big that it's best to reserve your place by the pool before you reserve your room. Even the architect, Morris Lapidus, boasted that it was 'the world's most pretentious hotel'. Which immediately stopped everyone in their tracks. It was the first time anyone had heard an architect speak the truth. Asked whether he really meant 'pretentious' he said, no, what he had meant to say was that he wanted people to walk inside it and immediately drop dead. Nobody had the strength to ask him any more questions after that.

Next, if you're not still playing with the wrong team, try Coconut Grove. It used to be the hotspot, then slipped way down the charts, but is now on its way back up. To me, it's still a bit unreal, maybe because I went there once to a Comedy Club which had about as many laughs as Aristotle's *Theatre of Comedy*. And the only funny thing about that is that he spent so much time agonising over it and then, having finally finished it, promptly lost it.

Not only could I not understand what everybody was laughing at, I couldn't even understand what they were saying. The biggest joke of the evening, I was told later, was a guy howling down the microphone, 'Have you noticed how when you fart you can't stop laughing?' There followed a full five minutes of uncontrolled, hysterical laughter. 'Have you noticed when you laugh,' he continued, 'you can't stop farting?' Another five minutes of uncontrolled, hysterical laughter. Funny place, Coconut Grove.

South Beach is a kind of guilty pleasure. It's the hot, *hot*, HOT, ultra-swinging art-deco, fashionable end of town. I often wonder whether the whole art-deco thing wasn't just some clever American entrepreneurial dodge to avoid pulling down some pretty ropey buildings. 'Gee, Elmer,' you can hear them saying. 'A slap of paint. Just think of the money we'll save.'

Shops apart, and it's as difficult to avoid shops in South Beach as it is to avoid rollerblading hardbodies, Washington Avenue is like the Strip in Las Vegas, but without the gambling. The restaurants are fabulous. I once had a 26oz steak in one of them, Torino, that was fantastic. After months of non-stop spinach roulard, washed down with a quorn yoghurt, my little white corpuscles couldn't believe what had hit them. Not that I'm criticising my wife's cooking in any way at all, you understand. When I ordered it I thought it was going to come as one solid lump of meat, but instead they sliced it up and spread it out around the edge of the plate.

I guess they just didn't want to embarrass me. Because everybody else, they told me later as I staggered out, orders the 52oz steak. So considerate, these guys.

The club scene or rather, the new boutique club scene, is typical South Beach, Miami. You can easily blow $550 on a bottle of Dom Perignon for a complete stranger, let alone on someone you've just met. If you want to shake your bonbon, as they say, you can go slutty clubbing. The best place is in BED, which stands for beverage entertainment dining – there, that fooled you; Crobar, which is what you need in order to get in, and Club Chaos, which just about sums it up. Not that I've ever been to any of them. I don't fancy the idea of going round slapping high-fives, grinding my hips like a repartero and booty-dancing it with all and sundry. I'm always too busy trying to digest my tiny, 26oz steak. In any case, apparently most of the women who go there wear so few clothes so tight that you can hardly breathe.

Little Havana is Cuba without Castro. Busy, clean, organised, hardworking. But at the same time, it's so much like the rest of Miami that it's difficult to know where Little Havana ends and Miami begins. Not that these days it's that easy to know where Miami ends and Cuba begins. One is home to more Cubans than the other, believes it is entitled to invade innocent, defenceless countries purely because of their internal politics, that it is legitimate government policy to as good as starve children to death and makes a habit of executing people with a mental age of seven.

Little Haiti is more fun. All the white, middle-class, martini-drinking Americans I know warned me against it. 'You'll be robbed,' they said. 'You'll be killed. Even worse things than that will happen to you.' Perhaps they meant that I might meet the guy from the Comedy Store in Coconut Grove. In the event, it was *très amusant*, as they say, pleasant, well laid-out, *un peu* scruffy, but certainly nothing like the back streets of Marseilles or even round the back of the Sacré Coeur in Paris.

So there I was, on my first visit, all alone, my life in their hands, ambling casually down *la rue*. I turned the corner and, *mon Dieu*, what did I see in front of me? A pub! And not just a pub but an English pub, called, would you credit it, the Winston Churchill. In I went. It is run by a couple of black guys from Stoke Newington in north London. They've been over there for years and they do a roaring trade. They even have their own fleet of London buses and taxis which they hire out for tours of Miami. Did all the white, middle-class martini-drinking Americans believe me when I told them about it? What do you think?

My favourite spot in Miami is Hialeah Racetrack. It has a non-stop supply of mint juleps – heaven. It's down to the parade ring, all the horses looking immaculate, every one a winner. As they go out on to the course I make a quick dash up the stairs to the top of the stands for the race. Fabulous. Gamble? Not at all. I told you before that I gambled only once in my life, and never again.

My favourite hideaway? OK, promise not to tell anyone. It's Jimmy's, a collection of scruffy shacks behind the Virginia Island Sewage Plant on Key Biscayne. It used to be a hang-out for bikers, but now it's a hang-out for whoever knows about it. Ravers, drop-outs, college kids, middle-aged millionaire rappers. Their personal trainers. Their personal trainers' personal trainers. It is what Key West must have been like in the old days. It's got the atmosphere, the booze and it's also got the smokes. The best smoked fish in Miami. What they smoke it with is, of course, another matter.

As for the rest of the state, I reckon I've seen more than enough of it, thank you. From Pensacola, your typical sunbelt boomtown way out on the westernmost tip of the Panhandle, or the Redneck Riviera, as they call it, to Jacksonville on the Atlantic. Then from Jacksonville all the way down to Sloppy Joe's, the capital of Key West, where the smoked fish is nothing like it is at Jimmy's.

Pensacola is great on paper. It claims to be the oldest settlement in the US. First, because it was shuffled backwards and forwards so many times between the French, the Spanish and the British – obviously because nobody wanted it – before it was finally handed over to the Americans in 1821. Secondly, its architectural wealth, they say, makes for a grand day of head-craning. A grand day of head-craning? It's got about three small blocks of old buildings. The rest is sluburbia. Even the Palafox area around North Hill was an effort. I had more fun along Car Showroom Alley, and that's nothing but car showrooms. Miles and miles of them. First the real things and then the secondhand ones. I preferred the secondhand ones. Always have done.

Panama City, further along the Panhandle, bills itself as the wet-T-shirt capital of the world. The only wet T-shirts I saw were mopping up the overflow from the ice machines overheating in the hotels and motels I stayed in. Just outside of town there is supposed to be a collection of Victorian cottages preserved in all their immaculate Prince Albert splendour and Teutonic detail. But as Prince Albert never wore a wet T-shirt, I didn't bother to check them out. And I'm still waiting for them to mop up the overflow.

Follow the Panhandle and you come to the nut in the centre of this fruit state: the capital, Tallahassee, which would get my vote any day, provided they could be relied upon to count it. It's nice, it's calm, it's innocent. On the other hand, I don't think any town in the States has made such a fool of itself as Tallahassee has. Ask anyone anywhere in the world about free and fair elections and the primacy of the ballot box and they're off into a long, involved rigmarole about democracy – democracy is the freedom to make mistakes; democracy is rejecting half the votes; democracy is where people can say what they think. But the trouble with the US is that people invariably say what they think without thinking. Then they've got to press the right button, the right button has to make the right mark on the ballot paper and the ballot paper has to come up with the right chads. Once you have the right chads, the election officials have then got to be able to count.

One, two, three. Duh. Three, three, three . . .

And not just to count, but to count accurately.

One, two, three, five, six. Duh.

Time after time after time.

One, six. Duh. Five, two. Duh.

I was in Tallahassee shortly after the presidential election. At Florida State University I was told that – though not for a moment were they suspicious – a few months before the count all the Democrat counters they knew, many of whom had been official Democrat counters for twenty or in some cases thirty years, had been contacted by election county officials and informed that their services would not be required for the presidential count. It was, they said, an attempt to Floridate an election.

Eight, seven, four, two. Duh. Five.

On the other hand, are we really surprised anyone in the States would want to Floridate an election?

Before I went to Tallahassee I was in St Louis, Missouri. There hundreds of registered voters turned up to vote but were turned away because, officials said, they were not listed. If that happened to you or me we'd shrug it off and go and have a drink. Not the Americans. One elector immediately reached for his lawyers. They demanded that the officials double-checked their information and insisted that their client had the right to vote. The judge ordered the polls to stay open until 10 pm to allow all those who wanted to vote to do so. Within two minutes of his decision, other Americans reached for their lawyers and got the ruling overturned. They discovered the registered voter the original lawyers were acting for had died the previous year. After all the fuss and bother, the laugh was that most people then voted for a dead man.

But nothing about American elections surprises me since a black Buddhist Republican I met in Tallahassee – and there can't be many of those in the States – told me what goes on on presidential campaign press flights. Apparently, the big thing is not continual earnest discussion of policies and how they will affect the ordinary voter, but organising skateboard races on teatrays down the aisle as the plane takes off and begins to climb into the clouds. Doesn't it make you proud? Not to be an American, that is.

North Florida is nothing like south Florida. It's more Montgomery, Alabama than Miami. Jacksonville, way up near the border with Georgia, I know quite well. Some people rave about it. The airport, they say, is one of the best in the world. The town is one of the nicest in the world and the beaches ditto. If this is true, they must be talking about a different Jacksonville from the one I know. But my opinion of it might be coloured by the fact that I once spent the night at the sheriff's office. In other words, the local Holiday Inn. The sheriff's office is located right in the middle of Reception. I can only assume that the best parties in the United States take place in the Holiday Inn, Jacksonville, otherwise why would they have a sheriff's office on the premises?

The Jacksonville I know is OK: pleasant and full of near-empty factories that have seen better days. Some of them look as if they should have been condemned about fifty years ago. If they were in South Beach, with a can of paint slapped over them they would be worth millions by now. I visited the last few remaining survivors in one of these. I found everybody was poring over the latest edition of *Playboy*. There were copies of it everywhere: on desks, on tables, on workbenches. Managers, technicians, even the secretaries were all agog at the photographs. Some of them were even scrutinising the pictures through enormous magnifying glasses and high-intensity microscopes. Apparently they had just developed a special yellow pigment that went into the printing inks used to reproduce the fleshtones and they were checking to see how well it was working. Well, that's what they told me, anyway.

Daytona, the Harley–Davidson capital of the world, I couldn't find. Or Nightona, where, I was told, they have stock-car racing at night.

I have yet to see Disney World, which is about the size of Manhattan, though I have spent years of my life changing planes at Orlando International Airport, which is about the size of New York. One day, between planes, I did manage to grab a cab and visit the Holy Land Experience theme park. It calls itself a living biblical museum. As you pass through its remodelled Jerusalem City Gate, it claims, you are transported back 2,000 years in time and 7,000 miles away to an ancient and mystical land. Nonsense. You're transported only as far as Hollywood.

The Jerusalem Street Market has the Old Scroll Shop, Methuselah's Mosaics, soft drinks, T-shirts and Holy Land Experience baseball caps. The authentic Oasis Palms Café, with its jugs and urns from Turkey and its chandeliers from Morocco, does a nice line in Bedouin beef wraps from God knows where, not to mention Hebrew national hot dog pitta wraps. But there is no sign of water being changed into wine. In fact, wine and other alcoholic beverages are banned from the Holy Land Experience altogether, which seems odd. Correct me if I'm wrong, but I thought the founder of Christianity was pretty hot on wine.

As for the exhibits – the Wilderness Tabernacle, the Temple of the Great King, Calvary, with the tomb conveniently tucked underneath the Cross – they are enough to put even the most Christian Christian off Christianity for ever, or at least to make him think seriously about joining the Church of England, which amounts to the same thing.

The other thing that's odd about the authentic Holy Land Experience is that not only is a strict dress code enforced, but a strict behaviour code as well. There must be no 'inappropriate behaviour', no 'drunken behaviour' and no 'lewd and lascivious conduct'. So there's no way Barabbas would ever be allowed in, and where would be the Holy Land Experience be without him?

What's more, nobody knows anything. When I got to the entrance and asked some Mary Magdalene look-alike in a B-movie Old Testament costume how many pieces of silver it would cost me to go in, she just stared at me. Not for the first time, I felt as though the end of the world could not come a moment too soon and we would all find out who was right and who was wrong.

Talking of the end of the world, I did once, in the line of duty, as they say, take a Disney Cruise out of Cape Canaveral. Not that I know anything about life on the ocean wave. All I know about cruising is that if you cross the Atlantic on the *Titanic* you get about halfway.

I went, I admit, not only to do launch, but to take the Mickey Mouse, not to mention the Donald Duck, out of all those grown-ups who seem to see nothing strange in worshipping a rodent. I hate myself for saying this, but I thoroughly enjoyed myself. The style, the fittings and the service were all fabulous. No sooner had I boarded, for example, than one of those sun-drenched, pert little Disneyettes smooched up to me, the way they are trained to do, took her lipstick out of her top pocket, pouted, ran it round and round her mouth like the blue-rinsed Miami monsters do, putting on layer after layer after layer, and asked me if I would like my own personal navigator. After the customary hesitation I promptly agreed. It turned out to be a copy of their daily newsletter.

The bars were great, the size of the drinks enormous; the restaurants were fantastic, the food superb. Although it must be said that they were not charging Minnie prices. As for the clubs, all I can say is I had a Donald Ducking good time.

There wasn't too much Mickey Mouse, either. I thought wherever I turned there'd be Mickey Mice everywhere, but there weren't. He appeared only two or three times a day, which was not enough to rodent my enthusiasm.

It wasn't all plain sailing, however. The first problem I had was with Housekeeping or, I suppose, Shipkeeping. I'm more than prepared to concede that, dragging myself around the world the way I do to scrape a living, I may not exactly be the best-groomed person on planet earth, but I do think the Filipino guy in charge of my room overreacted. No sooner had I embarked, checked in, dumped all my gear in my cabin, with its sweeping 450-degree view of nothing but water, and wandered off to splice the mainbrace than he had sent all my clothes – yes, all of them – off to the laundry or dry-cleaner's. So for twenty-four hours I was obliged to live in the same shirt, jacket and everything else. It was probably just as well we'd set sail, otherwise I might have been condemned as a derelict and sent back to Jacksonville.

Then one evening I was invited, along with all the other lucky girls and boys on board, to a reception in the main cabin to meet the people responsible for what they described as our magical experience. In other words, the crew. I asked one of them why they kept referring to shore excursions. Were there any excursions they weren't sure about? I think he appreciated the point I was making because he told me that if I stepped outside he'd give me a complimentary punch.

Another thing I didn't understand was the number of times we had lifeboat drill. I didn't realise there were that many icebergs in the Caribbean.

I'm not exactly over the moon about space travel, but seeing as our magical experience delivered us back to Cape Canaveral, I just couldn't miss the opportunity to pay homage to that marvel of hi-tech electronics, super-sophisticated engineering and man's enduring ability to do the impossible, the Kennedy Space Centre, which once built one half of a spaceship in inches and the other half in millimetres. They're not just gravity-challenged, I can tell you, they're something else-challenged as well. On one occasion the US and Russian astronauts aboard the International Space Station had to remove four plates blocking access to a floor panel, which should have been secured with screws. Instead they found these had been secured with rivets. The planet's top space engineers had the solution to the problem: a hammer and chisel. Never stand under the moon at night – you never know what might hit you.

On the other hand, they do go to extraordinary lengths to ensure that even the simplest tasks are performed to the letter. Take the operating procedure for the Chemical Urine Volume Measuring System (CUVMS) Condom Receiver. The great brains at Canaveral have come up with no fewer than twenty instructions to be followed.

1. Uncoil collection/mixing bag from around selector valve.
2. Place penis against receiver inlet check valve and roll latex receiver on to penis.
3. Rotate selector valve knob (clockwise) to the 'Urinate' position.
4. Urinate.
5. When urination is complete, turn selector valve knob to 'Sample'.
6. Roll off latex receiver and remove penis.
7. Obtain urine sample bag from stowage location.
8. Mark sample bag tag with required identification.
9. Place sample bag collar over selector valve sampler flange and turn collar 1/6 turn to stop position.
10. Knead collection/mixing bag to thoroughly mix urine and tracer chemical.
11. Rotate sample injector lever 90 degrees so that sample needle pierces sample bag rubber stopper.
12. Squeeze collection/mixing bag to transfer approximately 75cc of tracered urine into the sample bag.
13. Rotate the sample injector lever 90 degrees so as to retract the sample needle.
14. Remove filled urine sample bag from selector valve.
15. Stow filled urine sample bag.
16. Attach the CUVMS to the spacecraft overboard dump line by means of the quick disconnect.
17. Rotate selector valve knob to 'Blow-Down' position.

18. Operate spacecraft overboard dump system.
19. Disconnect CUVMS from spacecraft overboard dump line at the quick disconnect.
20. Wrap collection/mixing bag around selector valve and stow CUVMS.

Now, how can you pay such minute attention to some matters yet mix up your inches and millimetres and screws and rivets in others?

All the same, the Kennedy Centre is not exactly a waste of space. It's a bit Epcot Centre comes to the Science Museum, but it's not your full Walt Disney. The Saturn V space rocket is impressive; so, too, is the International Space Station. When one of these takes off, they say, the earth shakes for up to 50 miles around.

I often wonder, though, what happens at the other end when the guys up there in the outer reaches of nowhere unpack one of these things and find that, not only is the spacecraft itself built half in inches and half in millimetres, but that we've spent all this time and money on sending them a long-playing gold-plated record of Chuck Berry's 'Johnny B. Goode', an aria from Mozart's *Magic Flute* and a Navajo night chant, Navajo being a language that doesn't have a single swear-word, which, incidentally, surprises me after the way they've been treated down the years. Maybe it's why no extra-terrestrial beings have ever bothered to contact us. I know if I was one of them, I wouldn't bother.

Watch this space.

After Cape Canaveral it's practically a straight road all the way to Key West. With one or two diversions.

Okeechobee is the middle of nowhere, but even in the middle of nowhere it's still America. The Greyhound bus pulls up alongside a Wendy's. I get off. I cross a dusty, sandy track to a huddle of wooden shacks that obviously makes up the local shopping mall. At the far end, outside one shop, is a scruffy sign. 'Wanted,' it reads. 'Experienced customers.'

Gainesville is smart, upmarket, about a million students;

Cocoa Beach is the poor millionaire's Palm Beach. The real Palm Beach is unreal, even more unreal than the rest of the place.

It's supposed to be the richest 14-mile strip of élite meat anywhere in the world. It's got everything twenty times over and at fifty times the price. It's where multibillionaires look down on your ordinary, everyday billionaire. But the amazing thing is it's so mean. Everybody hustles everybody else. Everybody wants a discount. Nobody will spend a penny unless they have to. Go into any store, and it's like downtown Tel Aviv. My God, they even boast they built the smallest synagogue in the world. Their favourite meal is wilted spinach; their favourite spectator sport – I swear you're not going to believe this – greyhound racing. But for all that, and their glorious Spanish–Moorish–Romanesque–Gothic–Renaissance–to-hell-with-the-cost style of architecture, I forgive them everything, if only because Sprinklers Ice Cream and Sandwich Shop on Royal Poinciana Way serves what they call a Mike Tyscream: chocolate ice-cream sprinkled with ear-shaped gums.

Tampa and St Petersburg, out on the gulf coast, are an odd couple. When I first went to Tampa I didn't know where I was. I arrived late, checked into some hotel downtown and when I looked out of the window the following morning, I thought I was somewhere in Detroit or on the southside of Chicago. All I could see were broken-down factories, disused car parks, streets lined with smashed-up trucks. I was astonished, because, of course, Tampa is one of the most important towns in the whole history of the States: it was here that, in 1938, on the eighteenth hole of the campus golf course of the Florida Bible Institute, Billy Graham received the call. Unlike poor old St Paul, who had to make do with a scrap of desert on the outskirts of Damascus. Not that it's in any way unusual to hear Americans promising the Almighty all kinds of things on the eighteenth hole of any golf course. What is unusual is that on this occasion He spoke first.

Having had his call, St Paul had to clamber into a basket to be lowered down the city wall. Not our Billy. For him it was back to the golf course, this time as a caddy. But in the time it took poor old St Paul to descend the city wall in that basket all the members clubbed together to send him off to Wheaton Theological College, Illinois. They say it was to study the Bible. I reckon it was to get him off the golf course so that they could enjoy a decent round of golf, swear and retell all those old stories about Jack Nicklaus playing golf with God and you-know-who losing without having to listen to Billy going on all the time.

Today, Tampa has totally changed. Spanish, Italians, Cubans and the Anheuser-Busch family have taken over. The Spanish, Italians and Cubans have completely renovated whole swathes of the city. The downtown Ybor area I remember as a mess. Now it's full of bars and clubs and restaurants, with live bands all over the place. A couple of tequila slammers and you could be in the Zona Rosa in Mexico City, or Guatemala City, or anywhere, actually. Old Hyde Park Village is now a trendy shopping area. Busch Gardens started off as a 300-acre bird sanctuary where, as an old man, August A. Busch Jnr, president of Anheuser-Busch Inc., used to hand out sweets to the kids, J. D. Rockefeller style. It is still owned by the Busch family, but now it is a theme park, world-class zoo and funfair combined. I didn't pay it a visit. I decided I could help the family more by having another beer. Not that they would have noticed. They are already far and away the world's biggest brewer in terms of sales.

I don't know how, but St Pete's, as they call it, always keeps itself up to date. That includes the Renaissance Vinoy, a grand old 1920s marble-and-pink extravaganza on Fifth Avenue. The Salvador Dali Museum houses the largest collection of his works anywhere in the world. Nobody is ever able to explain to me why it is in St Pete's and not in, say, the Prado or even Barcelona. A prophet in his own land and all that, I suppose. Or money. Or both. I also like Haslam's Bookstore, one of the biggest family-owned bookstores in the States.

Everybody keeps on about the Florida Everglades. Why? To

366

me Highway 75, the Everglades Parkway, is more like Alligator Alley meets every potentially fatal bacterial infection known to man. Including leptospirosis. In the Everglades you can forget about Gumb Limbo, Snake Bight Trail Pay-hay-okee, let alone groupers, flounders, blowfish, swordfish, guitar fish. All you ever see are alligators, big alligators, even bigger alligators and hey, where's-my-other-leg? alligators. About the only other wildlife is mosquitos. Millions of them. Most of them the size of alligators.

Florida Keys, I thought, was also disappointing. It's more or less just one long highway with downmarket hotels, peeling, white wooden motels and beach resorts stuffed with a million plastic pink flamingos. OK, maybe not Islamadora in the Upper Keys, which had some smart houses for rent, but the beach there was practically non-existent.

Key West is, of course, Oak Park, Illinois; Piggott, Arkansas; Paris; Seville; La Ronda; Cuba and any bar in between. In other words, impure Hemingway. Impure because it's not the Key West that Hemingway knew when he was around, or at least the Key West that he knew before lunch. Then it was the Caribbean comes to the States, the poor man's St Tropez – a place where people could go to watch the sun go down without making a lot of fuss and bother about it.

Nowadays it's tourist Hemingway. Number 907 Whitehead Street is as important a place of pilgrimage as St Peter's in Rome, if not more so. The coral-stone Spanish colonial-style one-storey house – the Americans, of course, call it a mansion – has eight rooms, which puzzled me. You would have thought that Hemingway, of all people, would have insisted on nine, or one over the eight. Inside it seems more Scott Fitzgerald than Hemingway. There are fancy antiques, an eighteenth-century travelling desk, a cardinal's chair, Italian porcelain, Moorish statues, a hand-blown Venetian glass chandelier. But not one empty bottle.

The pool out the back, the first one ever built in Key West, was built by Hemingway's wife at a cost of $20,000 as a surprise for him when he got back from the Spanish Civil War. And a surprise it was, too. To pay for it he had to write *A Farewell to Arms, For Whom the Bell Tolls, Death in the Afternoon, Green Hills of Africa, To Have and Have Not* and *The Snows of Kilimanjaro*. To achieve this he set himself a killing routine. Every morning he'd start at six, agonise over anything between 300 and 700 words and then, at noon, hit the town. Usually Sloppy Joe's. Although if the kind of people you find in Sloppy Joe's today are anything to go by, I think I'd have carried on agonising until late in the evening. When he finished a book, however, it was party time. For one week, two weeks, as long as he needed to try to forget the people he'd met in Sloppy Joe's. As a result he never had any time to use the pool he'd drunk so hard to pay for.

Down the road is a tiny, one-storey wooden cottage where somebody called Robert Frost used to stay every winter from 1944 until 1960. But he can't be that important, because they have no boozing in his memory, no T-shirts, no look-alike competitions, no fishing tournaments. Not even a baseball cap.

Hemingway apart, Key West is the Costa del Sol run by Americans. You arrive a Republican and within a day you're a Democrat. By the end of the week you're high on Hog's Snort, wondering who the hell Ralph Nader is and referring to the wife as your favourite holiday snap. If you leave the wife at home and go on what they call a guilt-free vacation, within half an hour you'll be stopping people in the street and asking them where you can find Crabby Dick's. The answer is about halfway down Duval Street, near Angela Street. Great seafood. Tell them Hemingway sent you.

Vermont

Vermont should be rough and tough. The men should be mountain men, the women mountain women – after all, the entire state is practically one single mountain – but it's gone soft. Smothered in maple syrup, with sugar added in spring. It's Norman Rockwell, Forrest Gump, covered bridges and threequarter-horse towns – they're not big enough to qualify for a whole horse. It's an old-time, 1950s Hollywood America you thought no longer existed.

It's also, God help us – I've hardly the courage to say it – o-ho, lay-dee o-di-lee-o, the *Sound of Mucus*. There. That's done it. I'm going to throw up.

But it hasn't always been so, so, so syrupy. In its own way, it's been quite rough and tough and hard-nosed in its time. During the revolution, the people of Vermont were the first to kill British soldiers. At the Battle of Lexington, on 19 April 1775. And for fourteen years after the Declaration of Independence, the state remained a totally independent, sovereign republic. It had its own mint and post office. While other states were dillying and dallying, Vermont was the first to abolish slavery and the first to volunteer its troops in the Civil War.

It was after that that it seemed to go all soft and goody-goody Julie Andrews two-shoes. With sugar on top in spring. Ask the locals what they are famous for and they'll ignore all the rough, tough, fighting and killing stuff. The Indian wars, the war with the French, the war between the colonial governments of Massachusetts and New Hampshire, which was fought out on Vermont soil. The war against New York. The war they are currently waging with all the yuppies and middle-class hippies invading the place from all over, bringing with them their townie, even more syrupy attitudes. Instead they'll go on, in their environmentally friendly I-love-the-hermit-thrush way, about having the oldest log cabin in the country; over a hundred wooden covered bridges, including the only railroad-covered wooden bridge in the US; the first canal ever built in the States and how they were responsible for the invention of the electric motor, the USA's first globe, the printing of the first American postage stamp and the invention of Ben & Jerry's ice cream.

Ask them about their famous sons, and nobody mentions Solomon Brown, who killed the British soldier at Lexington, or Admiral George Dewey, who was responsible for the deaths of goodness knows how many people during the Spanish–American War. Or the Burlington doctor who was the first person to drive across the country, initiating the Americans' love affair with the car by introducing them to the joys of long-distance driving and the rest of us to road accidents and the perils of global warming. Instead they'll go on about Stephen Douglas, who debated with Abraham Lincoln during the 1860 presidential campaign, Chester A. Arthur, the twenty-first president of the US and Thomas Davenport, the editor of the first electrical magazine.

Montpelier, pronounced the Mont Vert way, the state capital, is pure motherhood, apple pie and everything that you thought no longer existed in the USA. With around 8,800 people, it has the smallest population of any state capital in the country. And even though for some reason it has more lawyers per head of population than any other city in the country, it's still very friendly. Total strangers come up to you in the street and wish you good morning – and mean it. People ask if they can help you. Given half a chance, even old ladies insist on helping you across the road. I once went into the barber's shop on State Street. I only had a haircut: I didn't have time to listen to a shave as well. So a word of advice: if you're on the lam and want to disappear, don't go to Montpelier. Within twenty minutes the whole town will know you're there.

It seems to have suffered a nasty outbreak of clapboard-building. Most of the houses are built of wood, as are most of the offices. Goodness knows what will happen if they ever hear of steel and aluminium.

On my first trip to Montpelier I was there for three days before I got out of the habit of checking that my gun was still in its shoulder holster, my body armour wasn't showing and that there were no television cameras setting me up for some game show. Now that I'm a regular, I've got the hang of the place. I stay at a tiny hotel a million miles away from your typical chain hotel. It's old – well, in American terms – it's wooden and it creaks. Call Reception and the phone rings for three minutes. You can't get shirts washed after 10.30 am. The restaurant is not open all day. And, goodness me, I actually once had to wait all of 35.7 seconds for a hamburger.

Wander down the main street. Wander down the main street! You don't know what that means to a poor, world-weary traveller. Montpelier not only has a main street, but you can actually wander down it. No bumper-to-bumper traffic, no screaming police cars, no 50-ton trucks trying to carve you up. It's even got a pavement. I forget the number of American towns I've been in where there is no such thing. Not that they would know what to do with it if they saw one. Americans were not born to walk. Just as they were not born to go outside unless there is air-conditioning.

At one end is the State House, which could not be more small town America if it was on a chocolate box. You almost feel it actually has the interests of the local people at heart. The other end there are real bars which make you wait all of thirty seconds before they serve you with rough old drinks like chocolate stout; bookshops that have heard of Shakespeare and Dickens, though not, surprisingly, of Jeffrey Archer, and a hundred fantastic places to go for breakfast. Not only that, but bed and breakfast is still bed and breakfast; antique shops still sell antiques, not 'collectibles'; hardware stores are still hardware stores, even if some of them do brag that they are 'legendary'.

As for the arts, they've not only heard of Oscar Wilde, but the local theatre actually puts on productions of *The Importance of Being Earnest*, the local radio station boasts it is not for the 'repetitively disinclined' and, with a bit of practice, it's possible to park in front of any particular shop you want to go to, which is something else you can't do in most US cities.

Now prepare yourself, because this is going to come as even more of a shock. Not only can you walk the streets at night, you can even leave your car in one all night, unlocked, and it will still be there the following morning. With all its wheels.

The rest of the state is much the same. Small, low-key,

homely. Nothing but 'historic places', maple syrup, apples, Christmas trees and those damned covered bridges. Stowe, about halfway up Mount Mansfield, is pleasant – when there are no skiers in town. During the ski season it goes downhill. During the snowboarding season, it's practically underground. Not content with hurtling down slopes in their attempts to break a leg, for some reason snowboarders insist on taking concrete pipes, picnic tables, tree trunks and the kitchen sink with them.

Just outside Stowe, I discovered a great, old-time, rambling, dusty, secondhand bookshop where I bought so many books I had to have them shipped home. I also tried White River Junction, apparently the place where the White and Connecticut Rivers converge, which everybody said was a must. All I could see were buses.

But just as I was beginning to get the hang of Vermont, something, o-ho, lay-dee o-di-lee-o, had to ruin it and it was Julie flipping Andrews. Whenever I go to Vermont now I feel Von Trapped. Because this is where the Von Trapp family fled to try to shake off not the Nazis, or the nuns, but Julie Andrews. They came to the Champlain Valley because, they said, it reminded them of what home used to be like before all that High on a Hill was a Lonely Goatherd stuff ruined it for them.

All I can say is, they should have climbed another mountain. They have done at least sixteen-going-on-seventeen things to ruin the Champlain Valley. Today, if you want to fit in with the locals, it's best to go dressed in either a nun's habit or in *lederhosen*. No, don't go dressed as a Nazi – they're Austrians, they haven't got a sense of humour. You'll find that the whole place is Von Trapp this, Von Trapp the other. There's a Von Trapp Family Lodge, a Von Trapp Family shop, Von Trapp Family Maple Syrup, a Von Trapp Family Maple Syrup and Cabot Cheese Box, a Von Trapp Family Tea Box and, if you haven't thrown up already, a Von Trapp *Sound of Music* Book featuring in-depth interviews with Julie Andrews and Christopher Plummer. Which is not one of my favourite things,

I can tell you. The one thing they haven't got is any curtains. Presumably they've all been pulled down to make clothes for the kids.

There is even a Von Trapp message from Johannes von Trapp, president of the Von Trapp worldwide Von Trapp enterprises: 'Living here, high in the Green Mountains, provides an extraordinary perspective on nature,' he trills to the sound of kids yelling their heads off. 'This year, the Mountain Kids Club again offers wonderful opportunities for children to explore and learn about nature. It's hard to say who enjoys the experience more – the child as he pets a cow, kayaks or observes a deer in the woods, or the parents who listen with rapt attention to their stories at the end of the day.'

Well, dip me in maple syrup and throw me to the Dr Spocks of this world, I've got news for you, Jack. You should keep your Von Trapp closed. The world has changed since those kids trilled their lay-ee o-di lay-ee-os on that mountain. Kids are no longer flibbertigibbets or will-o-the-wisps, let alone clowns. As for parents listening with rapt attention to the stories of their kids' experiences, they're not even interested when an armed police squad arrives to lift their little Elmer for holding up little old ladies, running the biggest drugs operation in town or blowing half his school to Kingdom Come.

O-ho, lay-dee o-di-lee-o,
O-ho, lay-dee o-di-ay.

The Drinks States

There are as many different drinks in the States as there are zanies. There are weird ones. There are crazy ones. There are way-over-the-top ones. There are lots of strange drinks as well, although I find most of them can be easily divided into three kinds: yucky ones, yucky ones and vodka martinis.

All of them, apart from an overdose of testosterone, have one thing in common: ice. Nothing, but nothing, can be made or served in the USA without ice. Even at christenings, kids are plunged into a font full of ice. I've stayed in strict American monasteries where the monks lead lives of extreme austerity, but their midday glass of water still comes with ice.

The other thing I've noticed in the States is that they don't drink their drinks, they jerk them down.

Georgia is, of course, the biggest drink state of all. Just think where the world would be if Georgia never existed. Scarlett O'Hara I'm sure we could all do without, but Coke? Can you imagine a world without Coke? It's impossible.

The ice states must be Alaska and Colorado. America probably uses up the equivalent of Alaska in ice cubes every day. The fancy ice cubes, the ice sculptures and everything else they do with ice has got to come from Colorado. It's more select, more upmarket and they are able to charge higher prices for it.

After Coke and ice, the other American American drink is coffee. I still automatically assume I must be in the middle of a nasty hangover whenever I'm offered it at all hours of the day and night. I mean, why coffee? What's wrong with vodka martinis? But it's there and we can't fight it. The two coffee states have to be Washington State and next-door, even more boring Oregon. One of them caff, the other decaff.

Most people remain in one state all their life, but there are others who commute regularly from one to another. I knew one guy who spent practically the whole of his life in a perpetual state of drunkenness. Yet however drunk he was, his wife stood by him. For some reason, he suddenly commuted to the Coke state, and a few years after that to the coffee state. His wife then left him. Which just goes to show how unreasonable women can be.

The Coke State

Georgia

Scarlett O'Hara didn't do Rhett Butler any favours. She didn't do Georgia any favours, either. Neither, come to think of it, did that other posturing feminist, President Carter. To look at him, you'd have thought Georgia was a weak, wishy-washy, limp-wristed state where everybody sat at home in their cardigans eating peanut shells, spitting out the peanuts and worrying themselves to death about what their brother was going to do next.

Instead it's big, booming, fast-growing and fast-moving, except when the Olympics are in town, then everything comes to a standstill. It's also still got Hartsfield International Airport, one of the worst airports in the world. It's worse than Detroit, which is dull, gloomy, has hardly anywhere to eat and no flight-departure monitors. Whenever I go there I can guarantee that my flight is going to be either delayed or cancelled. It's worse than Dallas–Fort Worth, which has a people-mover that never moves any people, and is always out of action. It's even worse than JFK, which is practically a building site.

Yet everybody raves about Atlanta. Hot-lanta, they call it, the

375

capital of the south. An economic powerhouse. Home to 400 of the top Fortune 500 companies. I can't imagine why. To me it's a no-tears-before-bedtime town. It's just Peachtree and the Martin Luther King Jnr National Historic Site.

Peachtree was a whole new revolution in building design. Instead of building separate buildings, they decided to put up masses of them all clumped together: hotels, restaurants, shopping malls, offices. Cities within cities, they called them. Well, for better or worse, they're now all over the place, as is inside-out architecture. The Hyatt Regency in Peachtree was the first hotel in which everything was designed to face the huge, central twenty-two-storey-high lobby. The rooms, the balconies, the elevators. Which is great unless you've just got off a twenty-two-hour flight, they can't find your luggage, you're desperate to sleep and the local Elks are in town whooping it up in the bar. You can hear every boring thing they're yelling.

As for the Martin Luther King Jnr National Historic Site, it's not as good as the Civil Rights Institute in Birmingham, Alabama. Maybe because it's not in Alabama. But it's still one of the most moving displays I've ever seen.

The other places I visit when I'm there, unless I'm too ripped out of my mind, are Georgia Tech and, of course, Buckhead. I've been in and around a good few universities and colleges in the state in my time but Georgia Tech really buzzes. Most of the key departments seem to be run by businessmen who have decided they want to put something back into the community. Most of the projects they are working on seem to be either directly business-related or in partnership with business. This means that things happen. There are deadlines. There are targets. There are budgets. And they get results.

After about four o'clock in the afternoon, however, downtown Atlanta is deserted. I once walked all the way from the big flashy Arts Center back to the Peachtree Hotel and didn't see a single person, let alone a taxi. It was eerie. As if President Carter were coming to town and everyone was so eager to get out that nobody had bothered to tell me. Or they'd all gone for their daily visit to the World of Coke. Which, I confess, I still haven't seen. Somehow it feels wrong to pay more attention to the mixer than to the real thing.

But, however bored out of your mind you are in Atlanta, a word of advice. Forget the President Jimmy Carter Memorial Library. Well, if it's not memorial yet, it should be. You'll have more fun looking for alligators in the Okefenokee Swamp. To look at, I grant you, it's impressive. It's set in beautiful parkland. It's low slung, in keeping with the landscape. It oozes quiet, silent authority. On my way there once I met a big, beefy Texan who told me that it reminded him of the shape of Jimmy Carter's brain. I could see what he meant. It was half empty. And not just half empty, but embarrassingly half empty. There were just huge areas of nothing.

You'd go into one exhibit, and there would be a single picture on the wall. Another display contained picture after picture of our Jimmy, obviously because they had to fill the space and had nothing else to use. Not only that, but even these are so low-key and insignificant it's a nonsense. Pictures of Jimmy at work. Pictures of Jimmy and his wife in Washington. Jimmy signs his most important foreign initiative. Jimmy Carter? Foreign initiative? To hand back the Panama Canal, of course. How could I have forgotten such a momentous decision? And the biggest omission of all: no cardigan. I asked one of the guides where the famous cardigan was. She said she'd find out, but she never came back.

I was also going to ask whether there were photographs of Carter enthusiastically doing the extremely politically incorrect 'tomahawk chop' during an Atlantic Braves baseball game, or rushing on to the pitch in 1992 when they got into the World Series, not to mention one of the helicopters that got bogged down in the sand in Iran trying to rescue the American hostages. But in the end I didn't think anyone would know about them either.

Buckhead is completely different. It's alive. It's fun. It's what downtown Atlanta should be. Bars, clubs, restaurants, the regulation quota of drag queens and pillheads you find in any American hang-out. The trouble is, everybody there keeps on and on about Elton John: how he moved to Buckhead because he heard it was the world centre for Coke; how he's got a 1,600-square-metre apartment there in a huge skyscraper with an ill-fitting wig on top and a huge back passage; how the local paper runs an Elton sightings column and how the last time they saw him he was trying to mingle with the crowds by wearing a discreet red velvet Versace suit with matching glasses.

I had a meeting once with a guy in the carpet-textile business who did not stop talking about how Elton John had moved into the same apartment building as him; how he'd bought two apartments and knocked them together; how he kept inviting this guy in to see his collection of Armani shirts. I kept wishing the wind would blow his candle out. As for business, he never got round to it.

Lots of the areas around Atlanta have grown dramatically over the last few years. One place I remember, Alpharetta, was hardly more than a muddy field when I first started going there. Within three years, it became a booming industrial park, and now it's virtually a major city in its own right with six-lane highways, massive car parks and its own expanding sluburbs.

Further away, as that drawl gets even more languorous, the chatter more incessant, the so-called humour even more impossible to understand, the chicken farms dirtier and more numerous and the onions more like baseballs, the more desolate and miserable it becomes. You'd have thought that a Georgia farmer, albeit a peanut farmer, finding himself in the White House, would have done something for his own people, but no. Not that I reckon our Jimmy ever knew what was going on. In fact I'd say he's spent all his life in a world of his own. He sees what's going on, recognises what's going on, but, like a second banana, he doesn't connect. He doesn't realise things are wrong. Worse still, especially for someone who claims to have beliefs and principles, it doesn't seem to occur to him that he should do something about it.

Take the story from his book, *An Hour Before Daylight*, about growing up in rural Georgia. He describes how, as kids, he and his friend Alonzo Davis, a black boy, would occasionally be allowed, when fieldwork was slack, to go off to town together to see a movie. They travelled by train, separately, Jimmy sitting in the seats marked 'white' and Alonzo in those designated 'colored'. In Americus, they would walk together to the Rylander Theater and separate again, Alonzo paying his dime at a back entrance and sitting in the high third level while Jimmy went in by the front door and sat downstairs or in the first balcony. 'Afterward, we would go back home, united in friendship though physically divided on the segregated train. Our only strong feeling was one of gratitude for our wonderful excursion; I don't remember ever questioning the mandatory racial separation, which we accepted like breathing or waking up . . . every morning.'

He never questioned the 'mandatory racial separation'? Good God Almighty. And this man grew up to become president. It's incredible enough that it never troubled him then that something was wrong, and that he should do something about it, but it takes your breath away that even when he got to the White House, it still hadn't dawned on him.

As a result, all over Georgia there are towns like Cabbagetown, just on the edge of Atlanta, which is a mess. The local mill closed in 1970 and since then it's just crumbled into the dust. Further out, I've been through towns – I say towns, but they're more like diesel-choked drag strips – where the poverty level is three times the national average, where four out of ten people are illiterate and unemployment is think of a number, but forget about single figures. Everything is falling to pieces. Stores are boarded up, streets are overgrown and there is rubbish everywhere. It's almost like parts of Africa before they clean it up for tours by visiting American presidents who have come to see the desperate poverty people live in.

Savannah, however, is everything Jimmy Carter is not: interesting. It's like New Orleans without the jazz. It's hot, humid, slow, so old and elegant and graceful that it's like some nineteenth-century backwater. In other words, fantastic, a tribute, naturally, to the Englishman responsible for the whole thing, General James Edward Oglethorpe, whom sailed up the Savannah River in 1733 and claimed it for George II. With military precision, he then laid out the city, which is divided by roads as straight as an arrow. In between, at various intervals, there are spacious city squares for mustering the troops and to provide meeting points for the local populace.

In theory, of course, it shouldn't exist at all. It was burned down once in 1796 and again in 1820, and if it was anything like a typical American city it would have been torn down years ago and a sprawl of huge strip malls and forty-seven-storey chrome-plated office blocks and condos put up in its place. But in stepped the Historic Savannah Foundation. 'Here in Savannah,' an elderly city father drawled all over me, 'city projects go in three phases. First slum-clearance. If slum clearance takes too long, it becomes urban renewal. If urban renewal takes too long, it becomes historical preservation. Here we have historical preservation.'

But some things they couldn't save. The old city market has gone, replaced by a multistorey car park. Four nineteenth-century squares are no more and have been replaced by – well, nothing, actually. They were supposed to have made way for a road, but it still hasn't been built. Obviously urban renewal in the course of becoming historical preservation. But entire chunks are still standing, including every type of building you can imagine: antebellum, Greek revival, mock English regency, clapboard, brick, American gothic, English pub – The Six Pence Pub still serves a decent pint and shepherd's pie – southern Victoriana and my God, I didn't realise Lord Rogers was working over here. And many of the original city squares are still surrounded by massive oaks and huge palm trees.

Blink and you could be back in the days when it wasn't

Savannah but Port Prosperity, when the biggest business here wasn't upmarket tourism but cotton, thanks to a local school-teacher, Eli Whitney, whom locals used to dismiss as a wet blanket until he came up with the cotton-spinning ginny and turned Savannah into one of the richest towns in the county. In fact, so important was Savannah to the south that come the Civil War, the Unionists wanted to burn it to the ground. Eventually, however, they relented and gave it back lock, stock and two dozen smoking ginnies to Abraham Lincoln as a Christmas present. It is said he only accepted it because the one thing it didn't have, in spite of all its nineteenth-century finery, was an opera house.

The Ice Ones

My teeth are chattering already just thinking about how obsessed the Americans are with ice. The whole country is on the rocks. Not just the occasional lump in the occasional weak lemonade shandy, but huge floes of the stuff in everything. In soft drinks, which, I suppose, is OK. In wine, which is unbelievable. In fact it's so unbelievable I wouldn't believe it if I hadn't seen it myself a million times in a million different restaurants. And I'm not just talking about your downmarket airport bistros. I'm talking about your swish, upmarket, thick-white-tablecloth, silver-forks-and-spoons restaurants (there are no knives in American restaurants, not even the expensive ones). And I don't mean only in your ordinary vin de plonk, either. I mean, *mon Dieu*, in your very, very best Bordeaux at $250, even $500, a bottle. *Incroyable.*

Then they also unload it by the ton into their bourbons, into their whiskies and, *mon Dieu* a second time, into the most fabulous cognacs you can imagine, totally oblivious of the centuries of devotion, dedication and love it has taken to produce that fabulous bouquet.

And the fuss they make about it, too. To me, ice is ice. Not to the Americans. They don't only want to know whether it's made from still water or sparkling water but where it comes from. Michigan is just about OK. New Mexico, especially around Albuquerque, is borderline. If you tell them it is from New Hampshire they'll be out of the bar or restaurant so fast that they probably do more damage to their bladders, kidneys, lungs and livers than a lifetime of drinking tapwater could wreak, even tapwater from Montana. Worse, they want to know how many carcinogens it contains, what the arsenic content is – is it fifty parts per billion or ten parts per billion? – and has it been passed by the director of the Environmental Protection Agency?

The even bigger laugh is that while they are consuming all this ice they go on and on about the North Pole melting. I could save the icecap at the North Pole at a stroke. Ban Americans from putting ice in their wine and cognac and there would be more than enough left for them to shovel into their horrible Florida orange juice at breakfast every morning, and for the rest of us as well. It would also help to cut down on medical bills for those of us of a more delicate constitution who have to witness the terrifying desecration of the world's finest wines and cognacs.

On the other hand you have to commend them for spotting, years ago, the coming consumer revolution, the advent of the all-pervasive soft drinks and the non-stop demand for whole glaciers of ice with everything. Instead of just talking about it or setting up a committee of inquiry or simply looking the other way, as the British government would have done, the Americans went out and bought Alaska. Not for all its untold resources, but for the ice.

In fact from the beginning they saw it as nothing but a giant icebox. When their secretary of state, William Henry Seward, bought the place from the Russians in 1867 for just US$7,200,000 and, no doubt, an unspecified sum in a Swiss bank, it was known as Seward's Icebox. And Seward's Icebox it remained for over a hundred years, until they discovered oil there. Only then, when they feared it might lose its value, did the Americans, who preach justice and fairness to governments throughout the world, decide to share out the land in equal proportions. To the native Alaskans they gave the cold shoulder. They got 44 million acres, 11 per cent of the total, and $962 million in compensation. Guess who got the rest?

To further consolidate their relations with the native Alaskans, the Americans then did what they lecture everybody else about not doing. Instead of respecting the thousands of years of indigenous culture, they went around like any other bumbling old colonial power renaming everything in sight with red-raw American names.

Mount Denali, the 20,000ft mountain known to the local Indians for centuries as the Great One, they called Mount McKinley, after, God help us, not a president but a presidential candidate. It hardly bears thinking about. But for a matter of timing it could have been called Mount Quayle. Imagine how sore you'd feel if somebody did that to your favourite mountain. And when the jokes started, as inevitably they would with a name like that, you'd feel doubly sore.

The stretch of coast close to the capital, Juneau, they renamed Tracy Arm, not after whoever you might think, but after President Lincoln's secretary of state for war, Benjamin Franklin Tracy, which must have caused all kinds of problems. What might have happened, for example, if Clinton's secretary of state had been called Tracy? After changing their minds a number of times, the bay near Anchorage they christened Turnagain Bay, which conjures up all kinds of images.

I just thank God that when they got around to naming the cigar-shaped coastal strip down in the south-east Inside Passage, President Clinton wasn't around, otherwise goodness knows what they would have called it.

If Alaska is mass ice, Colorado is designer ice, upmarket ice, rich, rich, rich ice. The people who go to Alaska do not go to Colorado, and I would very much doubt whether the people who go to Colorado would ever in a million years dream of mushing their way from Skagway to the Yukon River. There are just not enough bars serving elegant, expensive French wines which would be improved by a great lump of ice.

Colorado also sees itself as more discreet, quiet, reserved. So I won't embarrass it any further by saying any more about it.

Alaska

Forget the whole idea of baked Alaska. To most people Alaska – the forty-ninth state of the Union, the other forty-eight having melted in 1959 and allowed it to join the gang – is nothing but brrr, brrr, brrr 600,000 square miles of snow, ice and enormous oil spills.

They go on about the beauty of the place: bear pawprints in the snow around the dustbins in every back street in the state, the lumps of ice floating down the Kongakut River calving away to their hearts' content and the enormous oil spills. A place where June is spring, July is summer, August is autumn and the rest of the year is . . . talk about the age of shivery, my God, what on earth did you do with the brandy? But for me it's Africa, because it's the best place in the world for meeting African politicians and businessmen. Certainly far better than Africa itself. Or at least it was when the only way to fly east was via a pitstop in Anchorage.

You'd try to get to talk to a minister in Lomé, Togo. For hours you'd wait to see him, and back would come the message: 'The minister regrets, but because of his commitments to world peace etc. etc . . .' In other words, pushez-vous off. You'd have an urgent appointment to see the mysterious Tunisian businessman who sits in an office next door to the prime minister of one of the poorest countries on the continent. Three days after the meeting should have taken place, you'd read in *Le Monde* that the old Croque Monsieur had been in Paris the whole time, meeting armaments-manufacturers. You'd be summoned halfway across the world for a secret, hush-hush parlez-vous with the president of the Congo. You'd arrive three heart attacks later with a minute to spare, and nobody could remember why it was they wanted you.

Get off the plane in Anchorage, however, and ice and easy does it, there they'd all be. Strolling around the duty-free. Leaning up against the Coke machine. Looking out of the window at the snow and ice and all those enormous oil spills. It was like Shannon Airport with ice. Within two minutes you'd meet everybody you wanted to meet, and better still, you'd meet everybody who didn't want to meet you as well.

The only problem was, because it was in those days the only place in the States not to be air-conditioned inside and out, just to get off a plane in Anchorage you had to pack your long-johns, your polar-fleece vest, your eiderdown jacket, your snow pants, your Russian fur hat, your inner socks, your outer socks, your felt-lined boots, your undermittens, your overmittens, your goggles and an all-over face mask. But it was more than worth it.

Once when I was working with the African Development Bank I spent an entire weekend chasing one particular finance minister from the bank's headquarters in Abidjan, Côte d'Ivoire, to Egypt, to Paris and back to Abidjan again. We needed his signature on a bit of paper, and everybody agreed it was stupid, but it was the only way to get it. Did I get it? Of course not. I met him in Egypt, in Paris and again in Abidjan, but there was always a reason why he couldn't sign it. So I gave up and flew back to London. The following week, on my way to Tokyo, I got off the plane in Anchorage and there he was, buying some odd-looking videos. He signed the piece of paper immediately.

Another time, with skate expectations I tried to get to Alaska from San Francisco on Alaska Air, whose safety record is the reason why everybody travels by dog sledge. I wanted to go and visit Prudhoe Bay and then Kaktovik.

Prudhoe Bay has supplied around 25 per cent of all America's domestic oil since the late 1970s. It is supposed to be a model for technology and environmental development, but when the scheme was first suggested everybody went bananas. Well, frozen bananas. They said it would devastate the countryside, destroy the environment, kill off the wildlife for ever. Instead the opposite happened.

Kaktovik, part of the 19 million-acre Arctic National Wildlife Refuge, has reserves of 16 billion barrels of oil, enough to replace imports from Saudi Arabia for the next thirty years. The pro-oil lobby was saying that if the development went ahead, it would only take about 2,000 acres of flat, treeless countryside to do the job. As had happened with Prudhoe Bay, the developers would leave everything in better condition than it had been when they found it. The antis, who specialise in pouring trouble on oiled waters, naturally felt thaw about it. They were saying that it would see the end of the vast herds of Arctic caribou, which would have nowhere to go.

The trouble with the environment debate in the States is that everything is either Prudhoe Bay or Kaktovik. Nothing is ever Prudtovik. Nobody can seem to agree on anything. Is the earth warming? Some say yes, others say no. Are carbon-dioxide levels rising? Some say yes, some say no. Are ice-core samples vanilla or strawberry? Some say yes, some say no. One day trees are our salvation, the next they're smokestacks, the biggest pollutants of all.

I was hoping that by going to Prudhoe Bay and Kaktovik, and leaving the towels half inside and half outside the bath, using washing powder on one half of my shirts and not on the other and dropping all my newspapers in the bin for recycling, I could try to get both sides of the argument.

But my visit was not to be, which was probably just as well seeing as the flight alone would have generated more than twice as much carbon dioxide as each person alive today should be allowed to produce in a year if we are to avoid serious changes to our climate. Instead we got as far as Anchorage – or was it the capital, Juneau, French for D'you know how much these antis are going to cost us if we can't get this thing off the ground? Anyway, we circled overhead for the length of time it takes a glacier to calf and then turned and headed back to Seattle. That was it. Any airline that does that to me can never be forgiven. I don't mean not landing where we were supposed to, I mean dumping me in Seattle when I don't have to be there. I've since been to Alaska a million times, and I've thawed, but I've never actually set foot on the ground. Not, I suppose, that there is much ground there. Except, of course, for snow, ice and enormous oil spills.

As for the snow, snow I can see anywhere. It's the important things – the countryside, the fields, the forest, the rivers, the mountains, the bars, the clubs, the restaurants – I want to see. Also, I can't see any point in going to any place that only encourages people to tear down more trees in order to clear the ground and put up prefabricated chipboard log cabins flown in from Seattle. To the native Alaskans, this is even more of a violation of the environment because they believe that each tree has its own soul. Whenever they are forced to chop down a tree they hug it, bless it and virtually give it the Last Rites.

The ice you can keep. Alaska may have about 130 times more ice than all the other states combined, but I have no wish to make friends with any glacier, let alone hug it. Blue/grey, white, white with navy blue stripes. None of them can be as good as the ones you see on the labels of vodka bottles.

As for water, and especially whitewater rafting down a river called Nenana, which means icy death, you can forget it. I get enough of the big chill as it is.

Oil? I spend enough money on oil and petrol without wasting more on seeing where it comes from, let alone plodding through it in my wellies.

All in all, I can think of nothing worse than flying halfway round the world to spend a night in Anchorage, continually rated the worst city in the US, even worse than Trenton, New Jersey, especially as a night in Anchorage lasts from October to May. There is nothing that appeals to me less than the idea of playing golf on a frozen lake in subzero temperatures with purple balls. Neither do I want to go to Anchorage on a cruise

387

ship which, for all the money it might add to the local economy, probably contributes more pollution than half a dozen pipelines.

Most Americans, however, go on and on about how much of their life they've devoted to developing their perfect, in-depth, touchy-feely relationship with the place.

'So how long did it take you to develop this perfect, in-depth, touchy-feely relationship?' I once asked a buck-toothed, gangly, wacko-bango of a schoolteacher from Little Rock, Arkansas, who was so obsessed with the environment that she probably used recycled toilet paper. Which, knowing the environment industry, would be more expensive than the normal stuff.

'A weekend,' she gasped.

She had taken the six-hour Tundra Wildlife Tour. 'It was ars'm,' she trilled.

She had seen sheep, black and brown grizzly bears, a wolf, caribou, moose, bald eagles, ptarmigan cheeses from Italy, whole herds of Sitka black-tailed deer and a thousand other binocular-toting tourists and had still got back to the hotel in time to catch the repeats of *Pee Wee's Playhouse* on television. By the time the next load of tourists have returned from seeking their perfect, in-depth, touchy-feely relationship with the Big Place on their six-hour Tundra Wildlife Tour, the poor bears will have been shot for trying to eat the empty polystyrene cups they throw away when they've finished drinking their organic coffee.

The only wildlife I want to see – well, the only wildlife I want to see in Alaska – is the white beluga which, I'm told, I can do propped up against a bar or sitting in a restaurant practically anywhere in Juneau, which must be why it's known as the politicians' paradise. That and the fact that there's no way the ordinary man on a sledge, the voter, can get there and upset their lunch and dinner schedules – I mean serious deliberations of the problems facing the world today. It's completely enclosed by mountains, and the only route in is by air or sea which, you must admit, dramatically limits the number of people likely to turn up to lobby their representatives, let alone organise a mass protest.

Forget the Klondike, 1898, 20,000 prospectors and all that kind of thing. As far as I'm concerned, it's all gone down the pan. Yet Americans still pour into Fairbanks to try their hand at sifting for gold.

The place I would like to wheel into is Barrow, a tiny outpost 300 miles inside the Arctic Circle, which has gone dry. Here, not only will you not get any ice in your $500 Bordeaux, you won't get any Bordeaux either. Or any bourbon. Not even a beer. Try to smuggle some in and it'll cost you two bottles of Bordeaux: $1,000.

The boring old Barrow boys and girls say they voted to ban alcohol because they wanted to keep out their fellow Americans. The goodies don't say a word. They're already totally smashed on homemade whale-blubber juice or whooping it up in Anchorage.

In fact they have such a good time there that the Russian TU–95 Bear bombers spend all their time circling overhead to pick up some ideas for when they get back home to Anadyr in north-eastern Siberia and can celebrate properly. Vodka. No ice.

Colorado

Trouble getting your regular supplies of Mogadon? Take a trip to Denver. Itzzz just azzz . . . azzz . . . exzzziting.

Why Jack Kerouac raved about Denver I have no idea. I can only think that he must have been bombed out of his mind at the time. As far as I'm concerned, it's one long, terribly trendy yawn. It's not much more than one street with buses running up and down the centre of it. And it's so empty that I've never seen any kind of queue outside their Hard Rock Café, which must be some kind of world record.

No wonder they call it the Queen of the Plains. It's staid, matronly and not to put too fine a point on it, a bit old-fashioned. It's certainly no swinging, indiscreet princess. And the people are plain, all right: I can't remember one fun person I've ever met there. The plain truth is something else. Denver is one of the few cities in the States which organises grand Columbus Day Celebrations – but without mentioning Columbus. Not that I see any reason to hold a Columbus Day Parade in the first place. As far as I'm concerned Columbus didn't do the native Americans any favours. Come to think of it, he didn't do the rest of us any favours, either. We'd probably all be better off if he hadn't discovered America in the first place. But the fact that they hold the parade but ignore him gives you an idea of what Denver is like.

Don't get me wrong. I go to Denver whenever I get the chance. Not to throw bricks through the windows of Galileo, the worldwide airline ticket-booking agency that my travel agent always says is responsible when my flights start falling apart and instead of ending up in Paris, France, I end up in Dirty Woman Creek, South Dakota. But I've warned them, one more mix-up and it'll be boulders at dawn. No, I like going there just to have breakfast in the Old Brown Palace Hotel in the gloriously dyslexic Ellyington's Restaurant. It's fantastic: breakfast like it used to be. Thick white tablecloths, silver service, staff all over the place. As much coffee as you want. And their corned-beef hash just about sets me up for the week. They've also got this crazy way of serving the toast, all knotted up together. By the time you manage to unravel it, it's lunchtime. But what the hell – there's nothing else to do in town. Might as well stay for dinner as well.

I was in Old Brown's once having breakfast with a double dollop of corned-beef hash when there was a big fuss about the toast. One of those earnest, dedicated, horn-rimmed American couples at the next table were going on and on about what was in it. I can just about understand people asking for decaff instead of caff, brown bread instead of white, but when they start griping about the type of wheat in the wheat-bread toast then I start to lose it. There's only one kind of toast I'm used to – burned – and if you don't like it, you don't eat it. Goodbye.

Most people, however, don't go to Denver for the breakfasts, the sights or for anything you can see or touch. They go there for what you can't see: its thin air. The sports-mad, competitive Americans just love it. Athletes can run faster, skiers can break their legs quicker and golfers say it's better for their balls. They can hit them further. The trouble is, if they hit them too far they'll either hit an unexploded bomb or, Colorado being the gateway to the old west, where the Great Plains give way to the Rockies, somebody will pull a gun on them.

Last time I was in Denver they seemed to be finding not just unexploded bombs but whole arsenals of unexploded weapons all over the Rockies. Five were found close to an area designated by Congress as a refuge for the local wildlife which is also visited by thousands of coyotes, deer, bald eagles and what have you every year. Even worse, the dumps contained goodness knows how many unexploded sarin bombs – sarin is the lethal gas that was released in a Japanese subway, killing twelve people and injuring 5,000. Which might, of course, explain why Denver is so boring. Perhaps the gas has been slowly seeping out over the years and sending everyone to sleep.

As for guns, they're everywhere. Now, I know all the arguments. Every American sees himself as a natural-born hunter. Everyone, under the terms of the second amendment to the Constitution, has the right to bear arms. Guns are part of American culture. Husbands e-mail their wives, 'Honey, I miss you. But my aim is getting better.' Magazines carry cheesy, apple-pie ads crooning: 'Those sure were the good times. Just you, Dad and his Smith & Wesson.' For birthdays Mom, ex-Mom, the next-to-be-Mom, Dad, ex-Dad, the next-to-be Dad and all this one's, that one's and the other one's kids give each other as presents defensive firearms training courses: 'Shooters walk down a street and as they proceed, electronically controlled targets appear. Each shooter will have to make decisions whether or not to shoot since some of the targets are good-guy targets.' At Christmas families gather round the tree, join hands and sing traditional carols about a cartridge in a pear tree.

Gee whizz, wherever I go in Colorado, everyone I see is asking me if I'm going to go out and shoot the rapids.

Now before you vaporise me, I should warn you I've got a large-calibre rifle in my pocket and besides, I know all the rest of the arguments as well. Because most people are responsible citizens – nearly half of all Americans have a firearm in their home – this means that most handgun owners are responsible citizens. Guns are not freely available. There are strict laws about them. In Massachusetts it's illegal to sell a handgun without a serial number or trigger lock. In Spades, Indiana it's against the law to fire a gun at a tin of dog food. In Maple Ridge, Michigan, it's forbidden to use a gun to stop people from taking your newspaper while you're sitting in your rocking chair on your front porch falling asleep over it. Even more severe are the gun-control laws in Kentucky. There the full majesty of the law will come crashing down on you if you go around firing guns that aren't loaded.

Finally, guns don't kill people, they are for what the Americans call spree-shooting. Oh well, that's all right, then. It's husbands who come home early who kill people. Guns are for self-defence, which is why New Hampshire and Vermont, the states with the highest levels of gun ownership, are also among the states with the lowest murder rates.

All the same, I'm still against them. They're dangerous. They injure people. They kill people. And what's more, one day one might be pointed in my direction and it might go off.

Not that I'm prejudiced. As a result of going to Colorado, I'm also against strapping short planks under your feet and hurling yourself down mountains. I mean skiing. I don't ski. I'm not even a one-legged skier. I learned a long time ago to beware not just the slides of March but those of the rest of the year as well. So, however important skiing is to Colorado, I'm completely objective about it.

It destroys the environment. It's not just the ski-runs, which scar those beautiful, untouched pristine mountain slopes, it's the constant skiing, skiing, bump, another broken leg, skiing that shreds the slopes to pieces, thrashes the undersoil, creates unnecessary extra erosion which will ensure that in years to come there won't be a snow-covered peak anywhere in sight for anyone to schuss down. And that's just the effect of ordinary skis. What about the fatties – the skis, stupid, not the skiers – the ones that are about as wide as a hospital operating table? More and more skiers, fat and thin, are using these for powdery snow. Think of the further damage they will cause.

Then there are all the pistes and facilities – the hotels, the bars, the chalets. However many towels people leave on the bathroom floor, in the kitchen sink or jammed inside yet another badly made lasagne or . . . or . . . or whatever that is, the continual building and construction work is bound to not only destroy those beautiful, unspoiled views but to wreak yet more havoc on the environment. Not to mention what they do with all that uneaten lasagne or . . . or . . . or whatever that is.

Skiing is also dangerous. In spite of all the space-age helmets, the tight, unrelenting one-piece zoot suits, the extra slugs of bourbon for confidence and the dainty pink-and-green streaks of warpaint on their cheeks, more people are injured skiing than boxing, and look at the outcry there always is if a boxer gets a bruise or a cut eye, let alone has to be carried out of the ring.

It ties up the medical services and diverts much-needed resources and highly trained professional staff from caring for the genuinely ill and suffering. Like alcohol-burdened businessmen. And it encourages more mindless hooligan behaviour, judging by everything I hear about *les nouvelles sensations de glise*, and sets a bad example to others prone to mindless hooligan behaviour. Like various US police forces. Yet none of our upper-class, effete, gin-sipping opinion-formers ever breathes a word against skiing. Funny that. They must have something else on their minds.

If it were banned, of course, it would probably mean job losses, mass unemployment, thousands of chalet girls taken out and culled and, of course, the biggest and most convincing argument of all, the closure of places like Aspen. Not that I would shed too many tears over that.

Tucked away deep in the Rockies, there's nothing rocky about Aspen. It's about the smoothest place on earth, full of the smoothest people paying the smoothest prices for the smoothest and biggest rocks this side of Mont Blanc. There is so much money sloshing around there that $100 bills are known as Aspens.

'So how much is that slice of toast?'

'Just give me an Aspen ten.'

'Yeah, but what kind of wheat's in't?'

'No idea.'

'Ahfuggit.'

Aspen is not just Aspen, it's four mountains: Buttermilk, which two-legged skiers reckon is the best mountain in the world for beginners; Aspen, the one where the likes of Kevin Costner, Michael Douglas, Jack Nicholson and all the other celebs I haven't heard of slope off to – some of its slopes, I am told, are steeper than even Michael Jackson's nose – and . . . wait a minute, whose idea was it to put Fanny Hill Mountain right next to Sam's Knob? Either way, it seems there's something to break all legs.

Another reason why I think Aspen has got to go is what they do to Christmas. You think a German Christmas is a bit over the top? You should see an Aspen Christmas. It's almost enough to make you turn Christian. The lights, the lanterns, the red hats, the prices – it's difficult to know which is the telephone number and which is the price. The rows over whose turn it is to sit on top of the tree. Maybe that's where the Queen of the Plains comes in.

Then there is the Little Nell Hotel. It is always packed, which shows you how much Americans know about Charles Dickens. The Little Nell I know hardly had the strength to look after a tiny country cottage, let alone a full-scale hotel. I wouldn't go anywhere near the place. I'd be scared I was going to get pneumonia. As for her cooking, even breakfast, you can kiss my Aspen. I'm sticking with the Old Brown. But please, if you see those awful people in there arguing about the damned wheat in the wheatbread toast, shoot me. Please.

The Coffee Ones

Well, I don't know about you, but as it's the end of the meal, I feel like a coffee.

In the old days it was simple. Coffee was either coffee, or some strangely flavoured slops, or some strangely flavoured slops served in slimy mugs, very slimy mugs or old British Rail mugs. Then things went upmarket, and coffee was either Irish coffee or not Irish coffee.

Now it's so complicated that it's easier and quicker to become a brain surgeon than to understand a coffee-house menu. And I mean an ordinary coffee-house menu, not one of those Dutch coffee-house menus.

The two coffee states have, therefore, got to be Washington State and Oregon. Why else would they both be so proud to stand either side of a river they call Columbia, whose second-largest export is also found in homes, offices and factories throughout the US? This is the region that was the scene of the great Gold Rush, known locally as the Gold Blend Rush, and it is also, of course, the site of the Cascade Mountains, so called because of all the money cascading into Starbucks paper cups.

Today coffee is caff and or decaff. Caff is upright, respectable, hardworking, dedicated. It gets on with it, no fuss and bother, and is maybe a touch boring. Which is Oregon.

Decaff is, well, different. And we all know where that is.

On second thoughts, forget the coffee. I'll have a bourbon instead. Make it a large one. I need it.

Oregon

Oregon was another big disappointment, especially Portland. I expected it to be a mini Boston. Big, but not too big; fast-moving, lots of excitement. A bit like Chicago on a Sunday afternoon.

Everybody told me that Oregon was nothing but trees. One old toot dressed like a lesbian minister droned on to me about Oregon having more trees than a first-grader could count. Which is completely untrue. It has far, far more than whatever it is that comes after seven. Portland, people said, was a strong, impressive, sturdy, granite city on the banks of the Willamette River. It had the most architecturally pleasing and meticulously planned downtown of any major city in the US. It was full of 'view corridors' providing, they said, glorious vistas of the Cascades and Mount Hood. There were many little parks, neat trolleybus lanes, red pavements. Seats everywhere.

So I then imagined something like Minneapolis meets Aberdeen, or Quebec City, or even Xian in northern China, with towering city walls, wide-open city squares and lots of tiny houses and back streets. Not for the first time, I was totally wrong.

What it proved to be was what the locals called 'European'. Small-scale, pleasant. Housing and shopping within walking distance of bus and railway stations. Bus and rail transport have priority over roads. Trains are not allowed to travel faster than 15mph. All shops are at street-level. There are strict parking regulations. One per cent of all building costs have to be devoted to the arts. Surrounding the whole city is their 'urban growth boundary' which rigidly controls where the town ends and the countryside begins. If nothing else it shows you what strange ideas they have of Europe.

It also shows you how little they learned from European experience. Everybody from Cape Roca in Portugal to the Urals knows that as soon as you begin introducing such restrictive planning controls and regulations urban growth just jumps the boundary. Drive out of Portland today and, after you hit their urban growth boundary, you pass through the beautiful, untouched surrounding countryside. And then, within two minutes, you're in another city which couldn't care less about urban growth or what they do or do not do in Europe. As a result, Vancouver, across the state line in Washington State, is getting all the growth and development that should have been Portland's, although there's so much sprawl going on that before long it will be difficult to tell where Portland's non-growth ends and Vancouver's maxi-growth begins.

Another effect of urban growth boundaries has also kicked in. The price of housing inside it is now so high that people are being forced out of Portland. To Vancouver. The city is turning into a rich man's ghetto. Although why anybody would want to go there in the first place puzzles me. Portland doesn't exactly go out of its way to welcome visitors, or blow-ins, as they are affectionately known. Regardless of whether they're Californians from down south, with their big bucks, their big ideas, their big cars, their big 1,000-megawatt smiles and their well-toned, well-honed, well-tanned bodies, or whether they come empty-handed. Except that, to Portland, empty-handed means no return ticket. Which is, of course, how the original Portlanders arrived, having dragged themselves first along the Sante Fe Trail and then, at Fort Leavenworth, along the Oregon Trail. They thought they were heading for the Willamette Valley where, they had been told, the soil was the richest in the world. Instead it turned out to be a real slog. They suffered cold, hunger and disease, not to mention the incessant rain. For tens of thousands of them, it would prove to be the longest grave-yard in the world.

Fly into Portland International Airport nowadays and, I promise you, it's almost as bad. Portland has one of the worst airports in the States. Atlanta, Georgia is bad because they do everything they can to stop your baggage getting in. Portland does everything it can to stop either passengers or baggage getting in. The Immigration and Naturalisation Service, however, deserves a gold medal for treating everybody according to the same unflinching standard of courtesy and respect. They assume that everybody is an illegal immigrant until they can prove otherwise. Even if your passport is worn and greasy from being overthumbed by Portland immigration officials on previous visits, or fraying at the edges from being X-rayed and re-X-rayed, you'll immediately be handcuffed, strip-searched and detained for two days before they bother to start checking whether it's genuine or not.

But whatever you do, whatever the harassment and provocation they subject you to, don't tell them why you've come to Portland. They suspect everything. The first time I flew in I told the immigration officer I was going to Ashland for the big Shakespeare Festival, where *Richard II* and *Richard III* were being staged. You'd have thought I'd said I was going to take tea with the Taliban. He kept calling *Richard II* and *Richard III* the Two Dicks. Why had I come all this way to see Two Dicks? Couldn't I see Two Dicks back home in London? Did that mean I thought Dicks were better than . . . and so on. I was taken outside, put in a special interview room and grilled by two more senior immigration officials.

Now I don't know about you, but whenever I have to fill in any form I always make an accidentally-on-purpose mistake just to test the system. Going into the States, I put a different passport number on the immigration form from the one in my passport. Portland Airport is the only place in America that has ever spotted the difference. For a moment it looked as though I was going to get the rubber glove, but I got away with it. I told them I had three passports, and that I had simply got mixed up and given them the wrong number. Very sorry, sir. Won't do it again. Please don't hit me. If I hadn't had my return ticket with me, I dread to think what might have happened. The Tower, probably, in the room next door to the two princes

Coming into Oregon by road is not much better. The state legislature wants to put up signs at each highway entrance spreading the message: 'You are welcome to visit Oregon. But please don't stay.' Already practically every car you see has a

398

bumper sticker reading: 'Welcome to Oregon. Now leave.' Now I know why Nike was founded by two guys who met at Oregon University. Doubtless they were eager to do everything they could to help people run long distances. Away from Oregon.

When you do finally get in, Portland is hardly open arms, a big fat cigar and as much organic apple juice as you can drink. They don't want you to have your own car. They want you to share one. Oregon was the first US state to launch a car-sharing scheme and it will probably be the last. With everybody sharing everybody else's car there's no peace and quiet – nobody can agree on what time they want to leave.

The first time I was there all the shops and stores and art galleries, as well as the bars and restaurants, were open until midnight. First Thursday, they called it. But they didn't fool me. The next night it was Second Friday, then Third Saturday, and so on. Everybody was talking about a gang of thugs who had just smashed their way through town, beating up anybody who came anywhere within slashing distance of them, including lots of defenceless old people out walking their dogs who, because they were wearing their Walkmen, obviously couldn't hear them coming. That was the police. The demonstrators they were supposed to be protecting, however, were calm and quiet and well-behaved. The fact that most of them were out of their minds on heroin might, of course, have had something to do with it.

Because this undercurrent of violence is never far away from people's minds, everybody tends to be quiet and reserved, almost deferential, for all the world as if they're being nice to you so you won't turn round and hit them. Total strangers say 'Hello' and 'Good morning', and don't even ask for money or beat you up afterwards. I also saw – prepare yourself for another shock – people, again, obviously scared of the police, actually picking litter up off the pavement and putting it in bins. Granted, these were usually the older, more sensible types, but it does happen.

There is, though, a lot of tension, nervousness and pent-up

emotion simmering below the surface. One evening, in order to escape yet another of the famous Oregon urban growth oatmeal extravaganzas, I was in the Heathman Hotel, which is meant to be one of the great restaurants in America, although why they have some guy outside dressed up like a dandified English Beefeater, nobody could tell me.

Some lush at a table across the way from me was having dinner with his young son, who appeared to be at the stage of learning to read and write. I suppose he must have been, I don't know, around nine or ten. He was just about able to eat with a fork. It takes Americans about another fifty years to manage the knife as well. Anyway, halfway through the meal, the guy got up and went out, presumably to recycle the wine. The kid, who was evidently suffering from some attention-deficit disorder, immediately ducked down and hid under the table. When the father came back he went berserk. He started yelling and screaming. He ran up to the restaurant manager and shouted at him. For a moment I thought he was going to thump him. The whole restaurant went quiet. The guy must have thought the kid had been kidnapped or, worse still, had fallen into the hands of the police.

Then, of course, the kid crawled out from under the table.

Later, in the bar, the guy told me he owned a big electrical company and was negotiating with Goldman Sachs to sell out because he wanted to spend more time with his son. That was the reason, he said, he was so stressed out.

The following day I went to his hotel to check he was still with us. Because of their strict security measures, the girl at the front desk said, even though he had invited me over she couldn't give me his room number. Instead I would have to write him a note. She would then arrange for it to be delivered to his room. I wrote the note, put it in an envelope and gave it to the girl. She immediately turned round and put it in the pigeonhole for room 312.

It's not only the threat of violence that terrifies them. They also seem frightened of breaking the strict urban growth

400

environmental regulations. Practically everything you see is printed not only on recycled paper but in soy-based inks. The horses that trot around town are made to wear thick rubber shoes so as not to create any extra noise. And there are anti-smoking signs and posters everywhere. The best was a giant two-storey high Marlboro-style ad showing two cowboys riding out into the sunset. One is turning to the other and saying, 'I miss my lung, Bob.' Fantastic.

People are not only restrained in their behaviour but conservative in their dress as well – for the US, anyway. In every office I visited I swear I saw at least three jackets and two ties. I even met a John D. Rockefeller look-alike. He was tall, thin, slightly stooped, very frail. Wire glasses. He always wore a double-breasted suit – it must have been the only one left in the country – an overcoat and a trilby. But he wore them absolutely all the time. In the office, when we went out, in the car, in restaurants. He probably sat up all night counting his money in them as well.

If all that doesn't make you think twice about Portland, there's the weather. First they try to drown you. If that doesn't work, they bury you in mountains of volcanic ash.

Portland is one of the wettest places in the world, with over 150 days of rain a year. The locals claim to be descended from the famous Indian tribe the Webfeet. Because they have so much rain, this is the only part of the US never to have been captured or conquered or colonised by any Europeans. When Sir Francis Drake arrived with the *Golden Hind* in 1579 (he would have got there sooner, but he was delayed by immigration officials) he thought he was back in Plymouth and immediately turned tail and ran back to fight the Spaniards. At least that guaranteed him some sunshine. So it was left to Chinese traders desperate for otter skins to help the early Americans grab Portland for themselves.

Even then the violence bubbled just below the surface. Asa Lovejoy of Massachusetts and Francis Pettygrove of Maine both owned huge stretches of land along either side of the

Willamette River, and both of them wanted to name the new city after the capital of their respective home states. As the Supreme Court was tied up trying to decide whether Sir Francis Drake and the tobacco companies could be sued for knowingly selling a product that could be dangerous to anyone who voluntarily smoked it, was pregnant or operated heavy machinery, they decided to toss for it. Francis Pettygrove won. The Supreme Court case is, incidentally, still going on.

As for the volcanic ash, there's no shortage of that. Oregon is home to no fewer than four great volcanos: Mount Hood, to the south-east, is named after the second-in-command of the British fleet during the Revolutionary War; Rainier, to the north, the highest volcano in the country, was so called to please Grace Kelly, who used to erupt quite regularly if there wasn't enough gin around. Adams, the second-highest, is named after the second president and St Helens – or as it is known to the local Klickitat Webfeet Indians, Tawonlatkla, or Fire Mountain – commemorates Lord St Helens, an English ambassador to Spain.

The last eruption, in 1980, prompted by the growing number of visitors who were beginning to discover Portland and its urban growth attractions, produced the biggest avalanche in history. Just imagine what it would have been like if it had been in Texas.

'It was crazy,' remembered one retired businessman who looked as though he was used to eating salami sandwiches on Yom Kippur. 'We couldn't hear anything. But we could see thick, black smoke shooting into the air. Then we could see clouds of smoke heading towards us. After that everything went dark. For days we were just covered, literally covered, in ash. It was everywhere. People rushed around and put masks on, put pantyhose on the filters in the cars so that it didn't get sucked in. Then, when all that was done, we looked after our wives and children.'

Oregon is so keen to relive this event and explain it to visitors that the most popular spot for tourists to stop for six seconds and spend three seconds learning about the blast is Silver Lake, which is in Washington State.

But even without the rain and the volcanic ash, you can't just casually wander around the town as the fancy takes you because they've come up with another beautiful incentive for visitors: an ugly combination of booze and barricades. Portland claims to be the microbrew capital of the US, which is not surprising given that everything about the place is small beer. What it means, of course, is that wherever you turn there's a bar. Some people say they always make a point of going into any bar they come across that is named after them. I'm not like that. I make a point of going into every bar I come across that is not named after me. But it doesn't take you long to realise that Portland is not the easiest city in the world to stagger around. Because of their 1 per cent art tax on building, they've got all these statues and pools and troughs and fountains all over the place. There are so many fountains that there's even a Portland Municipal Fountain tour, which, I hasten to add, I have never taken.

I did, however, go to Pioneer Courthouse Square, known as Portland's living room, because inscribed on all the bricks are the names of people who were falsely sentenced to death but then declared innocent and who are still alive today. Then there is the famous Tom McCall Waterfront Park on the north bank of the Willamette. This used to be a four-lane highway, but now that all the people who wanted to leave for Vancouver have left, rather than let the road go to rack and ruin, they have converted it into a giant open-air playpen for grown-ups where locals can go to gloat over how they've very cleverly diverted all those boring people away from their urban growth development area.

Crazy immigration officers, road signs, bumper stickers, even the invention of running shoes – all that I can understand. I don't agree with it, but I can understand it. What I can neither understand nor agree with is what is perhaps Oregon's most extreme policy for keeping visitors out and the numbers down:

euthanasia. They don't just believe in doctor-assisted suicide, as they call it, but they are prepared to practise it: Oregon is the only state in the US where it is legal. In fact, switch on the television and they'll even show you how to take your own life: crush the tablets into a fine powder, stir it into your yoghurt, add a dash of vodka, lie down, and that's it. Goodbye Portland. If you can't get the drugs, get a gas mask. If you can't get a gas mask, get a plastic bag.

Yet I can almost forgive Portland for everything when I think of Powell's, the biggest bookshop in America, which takes up a whole block on W. Burnside and Tenth. It's City Lights, San Francisco; Ruminator Books, St Paul's, Minnesota and the wooden tables on the east side of Central Park, New York all rolled into one. In many ways it's probably better. It's vast, and it's nothing but books, books, books. And apart from during the occasional strike, it's well-stocked, organised, efficient, unlike say, City Lights. OK, so it was founded by Lawrence Read-My-Poems-to-Jazz Ferlinghetti in 1953, and was a hangout for Kerouac, Ginsberg and the other Beats. It was also the first bookshop in the US to sell only paperbacks, stay open after midnight and, as the publicity says, offer corridors 'lined with stools', and for all that it still never seems to have the books I'm looking for. Maybe it's because it's no longer the way-out, reckless, leftist, anarchist place it used to be. Or maybe it's because it's now been officially declared an endangered cultural landmark.

But Powell's is different. Well worth the price of putting up with the abuse at the airport and the car stickers, even the mock kidnap attempts in restaurants. I also like Powell's because it was there that I bought one of the best books I've ever bought in my life: a US road atlas showing me the quickest way out of Oregon.

That evening I was on Route 101, which runs all the way from California through Oregon and on to Washington State. I pulled into the Geiser Grand Hotel, which grandly promotes itself as an historic monument.

'So why is this an historic monument?' I couldn't help but ask the 307-year-old Rumpelstiltskin on Reception who was far too old to be covered in zits.

'All our breakfast selections are a hundred years old,' he told me.

Quick! The tablets, the gas mask, the plastic bag – anything.

Washington State

Rain, coffee, Microsoft, Amazon.com, Boeing, rain, coffee, *Frasier*, seafood, riots, rain, coffee, riots, earthquakes, rain, coffee: Seattle is obviously a special blend.

It's San Francisco in the rain, where surfing and surf-speak have a totally different meaning. It's the most American–Asian city on the Pacific Rim. It has more techno-nerds per square mug of cold latte than anywhere else on earth. They say that if the techno-nerds of the world actually had hearts, you would find the word 'Seattle' engraved on them. It's also, if you're lucky, sleepless.

www.washingtonstate/seattle/rain.com

At first, I must admit, I thought this was a rather weak Starbucks double latte. But it wasn't. It was rain.

I don't care what they say about the amount of rain it gets, although sometimes, it's true, it feels as though the North Pole is melting and the whole lot is being poured on top of Seattle. But I still think it's a brolly good city.

I have to say that I don't think I've ever been there when it hasn't been raining, but I'll say one thing for it: it made me appreciate the African rainforests. Because it doesn't rain there as much as it does in Seattle. In Seattle they say that 38ft of rain a year is not much. Or maybe it's 38in. It's difficult to tell the difference. It always feels as if they get their annual 38 whatever-they-are of rain every day.

So I suppose it's no wonder the place is so full of pale, gaunt, sallow-faced, multimillionaire geeks who spend all their time indoors playing with their computers rather than go out

in the rain. Even if they did, they would only get their disks
floppy, catch pneumonia and have to live out the rest of their
days indoors as pale, gaunt, sallow-faced, multimillionaire
geeks who spend all their time playing with their computers.
With the Windows closed.

In any case, what do you expect? If you went to live in a
city overlooked by Mount Rainier what would you think you
were going to get? Sunshine?

www.washingtonstate/seattle/the city
Seattle I like. Because it's not Silicon Valley. Also because it
was founded by a breakaway group of twelve adults and
twelve children who had had their fill of Portland, Oregon and
decided to upgrade. It's like an e-mail downloading in coffee
on a rainy day inside a Boeing 747.

Everybody says it's the laptop of the pack, one of the richest,
smartest, nicest mainframes in the US, where all the rich, smart
and nice people go to Seattle down and spend the rest of their
lives counting their cybermoney and deciding how much
they're going to donate to environmentally friendly websites.
God knows why. Apart from the Space Needle, and perhaps
Saturday night at Kells, there's not much to e-mail home about.
Seattle is pretty much your ordinary, standard, run-of-the-mill
clicks-and-mortar US city, jammed solid with traffic logging on
and logging off all day long.

And like all cities full of rich, clever, intelligent people, it's
also pretty stupid. The city council once spent no less than two
weeks doing nothing but debating whether or not circus
elephants should be allowed in. They finally voted yes – by a
trunk. If they weren't rich, clever and intelligent, presumably
the debate would have taken five minutes and the elephants
would have lost by a tail.

Some of the non-elephant parts of town are quite pleasant,
such as Kirkland, which everyone says is too picturesque for
its own good, though this is obviously just a play to drive up
the property prices even further. But Bellevue is the place to

go if you're looking for tiny, bijou, deluxe cottages like the one owned by Bill Gates, which cost a mere $50 million. With Windows, of course, it would be more.

Seattle was also home to that strange baby-talk poet Theodore Roethke. I can remember that he was bath-crazy. He had seven or eight baths every day. But I cannot remember a single line of his poetry.

www.washingtonstate/seattle/bars and restaurants.com

On my first trip to Seattle, I felt like Bill Gates on payday. I had a long list of places to go for a byte: the Flying Fish for flying fish, Elliott's Oyster House for oysters and Wild Ginger for whatshername.

The trouble is, in Seattle they believe in what they call 'shareables': meals where everybody shares everybody else's chips, not to mention microchips. Now, there are some things I'm prepared to share, but having someone take a megabyte out of my scallops, white rice, pak-choi and shiitake mushrooms is not one of them, so in the end I didn't bother. I stuck to the bars and, with the help of mailservers, kept my search engine ticking over with pints of Perseus Porter, a not-bad Seattle version of Guinness, and plates of the local grilled king salmon oysters or the occasional Japanese marinated, flash-fried chicken washed down with an ice-cold amber beer.

Seattle is not, though, so hot on bars. They believe in them, but you get the impression that they're a bit Church of England: they don't believe in them with their full heart and soul and mind and strength. Similarly the wine bars. But I did my best. My favourites were Hair of the Dog, Full Sail and Alimony, which, as I understand it, is named in honour of the situation where two people make a mistake but only one of them pays for it. As for local Seattle bar-room jokes, most of them seemed to be variations on the themes of Hugh Grant, Divine Brown and Bill Gates and why he's known as Mr Microsoft. You could always tell the geeks who worked for Microsoft. They never laughed.

www.washingtonstate/seattle/coffee.com

Coffee, of course, is Seattle's religion. I've never known anywhere in the world make such a big deal out of such a simple thing as a decaff triple grandé, skimmed, no whip, wet mocha, Costa Rica La Laguna filter. Or to make so much money out of it, either. Starbucks is well named. They obviously starbucked the trend away from beer, wine-drinking and lower profits. Not that I have anything against them. It's just that I don't think coffee is worth a bean, let alone the millions Starbucks have tucked away in their balance sheets.

What I find even harder to swallow are the people who drink the stuff and the way they cross their still-unused Nike personal trainers and go on and on not just about the coffee, but about where it's grown, how it's made, whether the workers are under- or overexploited and whether Bach wrote his *Coffee Cantata* in Starbucks or Coffee Republic. My own bet is Coffee Republic. Even Bach, with all his royalties, couldn't afford the coffee in Starbucks.

To tell you how obsessed they are with coffee, I once heard one of those magazine-cover American mothers turn to her Goldilocks kid in the middle of a Seattle restaurant and tell her, in that softly-softly, we're-all-equals-really, Dr Spock way, that if she didn't stop yelling and screaming and throwing her food all over the place, the Tooth Fairy wouldn't come and put an espresso under her pillow. If it was me, I'd have given the kid a click in the teeth and left it at that.

Going into a brightly painted coffee bar in Seattle at seven o'clock in the morning would blow my mind. I couldn't cope with all the complications. Whether the stuff is Ethiopian Limu, Sidamo or Yirgarcheffe I couldn't care less. And what the hell is mocha skinny latte, or even mocchiato, anyway?

All this caff/decaff business is just as much of a nonsense. Slurp caff and you're going to end up suffering from dehydration, adenosine poisoning, which affects the brain's alertness, and increased blood hydration. Slurp decaff, and before you can say Starbucks you'll be diuretic, your blood pressure will come out of the top of your head, you'll increase your risk of getting Alzheimer's, arthritis and bladder cancer and, if that's not enough to be going on with, it can also lead to cocaine, nicotine and morphine addiction.

In fact the more you look at it, the more you wonder why, instead of the Prayer of Jabez, there isn't some kind of government health warning on every cup of triple Puerto Rican Limu maxi-filter coffee-zilla they serve. Or maybe that's precisely why the Prayer of Jabez is on every cup of triple Puerto Rican Limu maxi-filter coffee-zilla they serve. The safest thing is to do what I do: order half caff, half decaff. A full-blown, 75-per-cent-proof slug of half caff, half decaff is not only a powerful protection against the worst effects of bronchial asthma, anxiety, bladder cancer, chronic angina, colon cancer, depression, dermatitis, gallstones, hayfever, heart disease, hypertension and Parkinsonism, it's also an invaluable aid to fighting off the hangover, staying awake, getting the job done and making things up as you go along. It also helps that I learned a long time ago that two singles are better than one big one. But then, that applies to many things in life.

The next problem is finding somewhere where you can drink coffee without being completely surrounded by data coolies and wild, cyberdelic technogeeks. The only decent place I've found so far is the Piroshky-Piroshky Café in Pike Place Market. This is where all the old Russian emigrés hang out and feel miserable about the old country. It was here that I once saw an exponent of what I believe she said was laptop-less technology besieged by a bunch of enthusiasts eager to download their portfolios.

Or maybe somebody put something in my coffee.

www.washingtonstate/seattle/coms.com
In Seattle everyone prays that Microsoft will be long to rain over them. Ask anyone if they think the company should be broken up, and suddenly you'll hear language you can easily understand. Even the politicians are united. None of them is

prepared even to consider the idea. Every single one is not only a personal friend of Bill but can also vividly remember him when he was nothing more than a mouse, not to mention his mother, Dot Matrix.

But they're not alone. The place is covered in webs. There are over 2,300 software companies alone in Washington State. How many of them will grow up to be Maxisoft – or is it Maxihard? – I have no idea.

www.washingtonstate/washingtonstate.com

Beyond the damp coffeepot of Seattle, the rest of Washington State is a warm cup of instant granules.

Along the coast it's virtually all trees, apart from the multi-million-dollar luxury yachts. East, beyond the Cascades, it's farming, lots of wheat and apples, and not many multimillion-dollar luxury yachts. More rowing boats with great gaping holes in the bottom.

Along the Columbia and Snake Rivers the debate is electricity or salmon. The various dams along these rivers generate huge double lattes of cheap electricity but stop the salmon from spawning. Leave things as they are, say the black coffee-drinkers. To remove them would mean economic ruin. The salmon will survive. Take them down, say the double-decaff-with-a-splodge-of-cream-and-a-cherry-on-top drinkers. The fish have as much right to spawn as everyone else.

www.washingtonstate/maydaypunchup

E-mail bomb attack planned for 1 May. Everything to be destroyed. Except the coffee bars. Keep your windows closed. Or better still, board them up.